WITCHCRA. MAGIC
AND CULTURE
1736–1951

MANCHESTER
UNIVERSITY PRESS

WITCHCRAFT, MAGIC AND CULTURE 1736–1951

Owen Davies

Manchester University Press

Manchester and New York

Distributed exclusively in the USA by St. Martin's Press

Published by
Manchester University Press,
Oxford Road, Manchester M13 9NR, UK
and Room 400, 175 Fifth Avenue, New York, NY 10010, USA
http://www.man.ac.uk/mup

Distributed exclusively in the USA by
St. Martin's Press, Inc., 175 Fifth Avenue, New York,
NY 10010, USA

Distributed exclusively in Canada by
UBC Press, University of British Columbia, 6344 Memorial Road,
Vancouver, BC, Canada V6T 1Z2

British Library Cataloguing-in-Publication Data
A catalogue record for this book is available from the British Library

Library of Congress Cataloging-in-Publication Data applied for

ISBN   0 7190 5655 1 *hardback*
       0 7190 5656 X *paperback*

First published 1999

06 05 04 03 02 01 00 99   10 9 8 7 6 5 4 3 2 1

Designed and typeset by Lucy Morton & Robin Gable, Grosmont

Printed in Great Britain by Biddles Ltd, Guildford and King's Lynn

CONTENTS

PREFACE

This book is undeniably ambitious, and will inevitably fail to satisfy all those who read it. But to resort to a corny phrase – someone had to do it. For years historians have recognised, and occasionally remarked in print, that there is a great lacuna in our knowledge concerning the nature of witchcraft and magic in England and Wales after the period of the witch-trials. Yet while there has been a steady flow of papers, and, more recently, a wave of fine books on witchcraft in early modern England, no one has sought to extend research beyond that period. This book is an attempt to redress this imbalance. It is only a beginning though, and is far from being a comprehensive survey of all aspects of magical belief in the period concerned. Instead, I have looked at the subject from a variety of different cultural aspects in order to illustrate the diversity of ways that witchcraft and magic in the period can be understood and studied from a historical perspective. As such, it will hopefully serve to demonstrate the potential rewards of researching witchcraft and magic in the modern period, and stimulate others to treat the subject with the academic respect it deserves.

In order to convince the reader of the continued importance of witchcraft and magic I have felt it necessary to provide numerous examples of the beliefs and practices being discussed. As any historian working in the field of witchcraft and magic knows, the material with which we work is often extraordinary and fascinating, and there is always the urge to want to display everything we have found with a suppressed exclamation of 'just look at this!' However, I hope I have struck the right balance between demonstration and explanation, and not deluged the reader with too much extraneous detail.

The demands of modern academic publishing require considerable concision, and much pruning has been required to reduce this book to an acceptable length. I have been forced to refer only fleetingly to some important and interesting areas of discussion, and I have tried as much as possible to avoid repeating what I have already written in previous publications. One omission that requires a brief further comment is the lack of any discussion on the subject of the 'Occult Revival' of the second half of the nineteenth century. The middle-class founders of the Golden Dawn and their successors claimed to be the heirs of a long-held secret tradition of magic and pagan religion handed down through generations of persecuted witches and cunning-folk. Although this is an important topic, much has already been written about the movement itself, and, more significantly, Professor Ronald Hutton has been researching the relationship between the tradition of popular magic discussed here and the ritual magic and organisation of the modern witchcraft movement. His book is set to make an important contribution to the subject, and will bridge the gap between this study and the development of twentieth-century occultism.

Finally, there will be those reading this book who might take exception to my bringing fortune-telling and astrology under the category of magic. Today, as in the past, there are many who believe that there are legitimate and serious principles behind these practices. I do not mean to denigrate those who believe so, but, as will become clear in these pages, in the period concerned, fortune-telling and astrology were inextricably bound up with more overtly magical beliefs and practices.

ACKNOWLEDGEMENTS

The core research for this book was conducted while writing a Ph.D. dissertation, generously funded by the ESRC, which was finished in the spring of 1995. Since then I have had to do a lot more research in order to advance and expand my initial findings. This book, therefore, is a summation of over seven years' work. Unfortunately, over the last four years no university or funding body has taken any further interest in my research, and much of it has had to be conducted while unemployed, with all the obvious obstacles to research this has thrown up. I mention all this only to stress that this book could not have been written without the total support, in every way, of my parents and the rest of my family, and also of Cèline Chantier and her parents. To all of them I give special thanks. I should further mention that my brother, Angus, provided a valuable proof-reading service as well as constant encouragement. I have also received much welcome support over the last few years from several academics, namely Professor Ronald Hutton, Professor Marijke Gijswijt-Hofstra, Professor John Walton, Professor Jim Sharpe, Professor Charles Phythian-Adams, Dr Steven Pumfrey, Dr Bob Bushaway, and Jacqueline Simpson. I thank them all. I would further like to express my appreciation to Professor Hutton, Professor Gijswijt-Hofstra, Professor Roy Porter, Dr Willem de Blécourt, Dr Éva Pócs, and Dr Jonathan Barry for providing me with copies of their unpublished, published and forthcoming work.

One of the difficulties of trying to write an academic book while unemployed is the lack of access to university libraries. It has been a somewhat arduous task to conduct the necessary background reading in order to keep up with new developments in the field. I would like to express my appreciation, therefore, of those libraries, which shall remain

ix

unnamed, that did not conduct library card checks, and so enabled me to undertake surreptitious but crucial reading. Gathering the sources for this book over the years has required visits to many libraries all over the country. Those which I would like to single out for the quality and friendliness of their service are, in no particular order, the staff of the Somerset Local Studies Library; Bath Reference Library; the Norfolk Local History Library; Birmingham Central Library; Mr Wesencraft, curator of the Harry Price Library; the British Library; Colindale Newspaper Library; the Folklore Society Library; and Cambridge University Library.

GLOSSARY

Astrological terms

Astrology can be divided into two forms: natural and judicial. Natural astrology concerns the general effect of lunar phases, planetary positions, eclipses and meteors on natural phenomena and animal and plant behaviour. The state of the heavens can be used to forecast the weather, and to indicate the most propitious times to plant crops, pick herbs, and apply medicines. Judicial astrology, on the other hand, involves mathematical calculations concerning the precise position of the planets at specific moments in order to predict or advise on future personal actions. There are two main types of judicial astrology. Nativities or horoscopes concern the position of the planets at the moment of a person's birth, while horary astrology is based on the position of the planets at the moment a question is asked.

Bible and key

This was a common form of divination, and was usually employed to identify thieves or future husbands and wives. A door key was placed in a Bible, either at Ruth, i, 16, or Song of Solomon, viii, 7. The ring end of the key was left sticking out, and the Bible was bound with a garter. The Bible was then suspended by the end of the key and the names of potential suspects or possible partners were pronounced. The Bible would turn at the mention of the person who was being sought. Numerous minor variations on this ritual have been recorded from all over England and Wales.

Dragon's blood

Dragon's blood was the name for a reddish brown resin obtained from several tropical trees, most notably *Dracaena draco*. It was used as a colouring, but herbalists sold large quantities of the substance for use in popular magic. Its main use was in rituals for procuring love.

Hag-riding

Hag-riding was a term used in parts of southern and western England to describe a nocturnal sleep disturbance phenomenon attributed to witchcraft. In northern counties the term 'witch-riding' was used instead. Victims would wake up at night with the feeling of a heavy pressure on their chests, and would find themselves paralysed and unable to speak. This frightening experience was often accompanied by visual hallucinations of someone sitting upon them trying to strangle or suffocate them. These symptoms can be identified with a medically recognised condition known as sleep paralysis. The terms 'hag-ridden' and 'witch-ridden' were also used to describe the state of horses which were found excited, sweating, and with tangled manes in the morning. It was thought that they had been ridden at night by witches or fairies.

Maleficium

This technical Latin word was used to denote the various inexplicable misfortunes attributed to witchcraft. The term was usually applied to illness and injury caused by witches.

Rough music

Rough music was a shaming ritual performed to ostracise people like adulterers who had offended communal norms. In its simplest form, people would gather together around the transgressor's house at night and make a cacophonous noise with pots and pans to show their disapprobation. This could continue over several successive nights, and was sometimes accompanied by the parading or burning of effigies. The term can also be used in a generic sense to describe a variety of other similar regional shaming rituals such as 'stang-riding' in northern England, the 'skimmington' in the south, and the 'ceffyl pren' in Wales.

Scratching

Drawing blood was considered one of the most potent methods of breaking a witch's power. This was usually achieved by scratching the bewitcher with a pin. There was a tradition of 'drawing blood above the breath', which basically meant scratching the witch's forehead. However, in practice it was easier to draw blood from the suspected witch's arm, and there was less chance of causing serious wounds which might lead to a heavy prison sentence if the scratcher was prosecuted for assault.

Swimming

Trial by immersion in water has a very long history, but in England it was only used to try witches from the early seventeenth century onwards. Suspected witches had their right thumbs tied to their left toes, and their left thumbs to their right toes. A rope was then tied around their waists, and they were thrown into a pond or river while two men held either end of the rope. If suspected witches floated, then this was interpreted as a sign that the 'sacred water of baptism' had rejected them because of their crimes. If, however, they sank, then God's water had obviously embraced them, thus signifying their innocence.

Weighing

The weighing of witches was another trial that came into use during the seventeenth century, though its origins remain obscure. The suspected witch would be placed on one side of a set of scales or a seesaw, and a large church Bible placed on the other. If the suspected witch proved lighter than the Bible then this was a sure sign of his or her guilt.

Witch bottle

The witch bottle was a widespread and commonly employed method of sympathetic magic for countering witchcraft. A bottle was filled with the urine of the bewitched person, and some of his or her hair or nail-clippings were also put in, along with some sharp objects like thorns, pins or nails. The bottle was then either buried or heated in a fire. The bottle represented the witch's bladder, and the sharp objects were meant to cause the witch excruciating pain. This would force the witch to break the spell. There were numerous subtle variations on the practice.

CHAPTER I

EDUCATED ATTITUDES
TOWARDS THE POPULAR
BELIEF IN WITCHCRAFT
AND MAGIC

In 1736 Parliament decided in the name of justice and reason that witchcraft was no longer to be considered a criminal act, but rather an offence against the country's newly enlightened state. The law effectively prevented any member of the legislature, judiciary or Anglican Church from formally expressing a belief in the continued existence of witches. The responsibility of all men of authority was reversed. Instead of instigating the scratching or swimming of a witch, the justice of the peace now turned to censuring those who took it upon themselves to perform such actions. Instead of overseeing the weighing of witches against the church Bible, Anglican clergymen now preached that the mother of all witches, the Witch of Endor, was nothing but a mere impostor. The fight was not now against the evil of witchcraft, but, instead, against the evil influence which such 'ignorant' and 'superstitious delusions' had on the minds of the uneducated masses.

This simple depiction of the changing position of secular and ecclesiastic authority, as embodied in the Act of 1736, is not necessarily inaccurate, but is far from being representative of educated attitudes towards witchcraft and magic in general. Over the next two centuries educated discourse concerning witchcraft and magic never entirely declined. The nature of that discourse certainly changed over time, and new kinds of debate emerged, but similar themes can be found running through the centuries. The aim of this chapter, therefore, is to look at these patterns of educated responses to the continued belief in witchcraft and magic, and examine how new ideas and changing interpretations of the supernatural amongst the middle and upper classes influenced and impinged upon the continued popular belief in witchcraft and magic.

The denial of witchcraft and the defence of property

The Witchcraft Statute of 1736 (9 Geo. II., c. 5) was presented to the House of Commons on 27 January by John Conduitt, John Crosse and Alderman George Heathcote. It not only repealed James I's witchcraft statute of 1604 but also introduced a new fourth clause, 'for the more effectual preventing and punishing any pretenses to such arts or powers as are before mentioned, whereby ignorant persons are frequently deluded and defrauded'. From the twenty-fourth day of June 1736 all those who pretended 'to exercise or use any kind of witchcraft, sorcery, enchantment, or conjuration, or undertake to tell fortunes' were liable to face a year in prison without bail, and four quarterly visits to the pillory. Henceforward no person could be prosecuted for the crime of witchcraft in any civil or ecclesiastical court.

Although there is a paucity of parliamentary archival material for the period, and newspapers were forbidden to report parliamentary debates until 1772, one still gets the sense that the Act generated only a modicum of debate. The *Journals* of the House of Commons and of the House of Lords indicate that a number of amendments were suggested, but the only significant voice of opposition to the bill was that of Lord James Erskine. His objection to the Witchcraft Act has, perhaps unfairly, marked him out as an isolated eccentric verging on the insane. Walpole apparently commented that after hearing Erskine's opposition he considered he need fear him no more as a political threat. However, as Ian Bostridge has discussed, Erskine's opposition was not simply inspired by an avowed belief in witchcraft, but was rooted more deeply in Scottish political and religious considerations that were undoubtedly shared by other silent sympathisers.[1] Erskine also had a fervid dislike of Walpole and took any opportunity to be obstructive. Outside the governing institutions debate was also muted. The only manifestation of passionate feelings generated by the passing of the Act was embodied in two polemical pamphlets printed in direct response to it, one in support and the other against. Although one is not a reply to the other, the two pamphlets represent, albeit in a rather hackneyed form, the last gasp of the rather vitriolic debate between the supporters of the new 'mechanical philosophy' and their detractors concerning the existence of witchcraft, as epitomised by the published exchanges between Meric Casaubon and John Wagstaffe, Joseph Glanvill and John Webster.[2]

The Witch of Endor: or, A Plea for the Divine Administration By the Agency of Good and Evil Spirits (1736) was, as its full title states, written years before the passing of the Witchcraft Act.[3] Its reprinting seems to have served merely as a vehicle for the views of the anonymous, anti-papist and probably Tory author of the 'Prefatory Discourse'. The author set out to affirm the existence of witchcraft, and criticise Conduitt, Crosse and Heathcote for their '*Zealous Principle*, that now animates and displays itself in so *signal* a Manner, for preserving the many *Lives* of His Majesty's good subjects, which might otherwise perish by a weak Judge, and an ignorant Jury; as also for *rescuing* all of us in general, (such as pass under the Denomination of *Protestant*) from the grievous Oppression of such *Relicts* (as I suppose you take *Witchcraft* to be) of *Popery* and *Superstition*'.[4] The author went on to address the proposers of the Witchcraft Bill in the following manner: 'GENTLEMEN, It would be highly obliging, and much for the satisfaction, not only of your *Electors*, but of *Thousands* besides: If you would please (some way or other) to communicate your *Reasons*, for bringing in your Bill; by answering the following short *Queries*'. The queries which followed referred to the oft-quoted Biblical passages condemning the crime of witchcraft; for example, 'whether *Witchcraft*, and *dealing with Familiar Spirits*, was not, by the *Judicial* Law of Moses, an *Offence* immediately against the Divine Majesty?' Also, 'whether there be any *Reason* to be assign'd, why the *Judicial* Law against *Witchcraft*, &c. Should not still be in *Force*, as well as *that* against *Buggery*, Exod. xxii. 19.'[5] A running argument throughout the 'Discourse' was that if Queen Elizabeth, 'of glorious Memory', considered witchcraft to be a punishable crime, then who dared gainsay otherwise?

While the author of the above 'Prefatory Discourse' rebuked the House of Commons for passing the Witchcraft Act, the anonymous author of *A Discourse on Witchcraft* praised the same institution for its wisdom and humanity. The author began by stating his 'great Satisfaction, that every Man of good Understanding, must hear of the BILL now depending in Parliament ... which, as it before stood, was a Blot in the Statute Book, and ought to be expunged. Had this been done sooner, it had prevented many poor Wretches from Suffering great Torments and Miseries, at the Hands of the Superstitious and ignorant Vulgar.'[6] Just as John Wagstaffe had done nearly seventy years before, the author went on to attack at great length the translators of the Bible for mistranslating and misinterpreting those passages relating to witchcraft, and so making out, for example, that the alleged powers of the Witch of Endor was something more than mere pretence and imposture. Echoing John Webster's view that it was 'impossible for either the Devil or witches to change or alter the course that God hath set in nature', the author of *A Discourse* also argued that to believe that witches held power over natural forces was to deny the Almighty's own supreme omnipotence, and therefore 'the Affirmers of *Witchcraft*, may more be accounted *Heathens* than the Deniers of it *Atheists*.'[7] Based on this premiss, the case against witchcraft was also presented from the logical point of view that if the power of the Devil's minions were so great why did they not use it to their best advantage? 'I argue from the miserable Poverty of our vulgar reputed *Witches*, that they are wrongfully accused: For I am not willing to believe, that they have such a Power with the Devil, as to make him do wonderful Things at their command, when they never command him to fetch them money, and to fetch them Bread'.[8] The conclusion to *A Discourse* was actually based on an unacknowledged passage from Wagstaffe's *The Question of Witchcraft Debated*:

> the Blood of Men ought not to be so cheap, nor so easily to be shed, by such who under the Name of God, gratify exorbitant Passions and selfish Ends; for without Question, under this side Heaven, there is nothing so sacred as the Life of Man, for the Preservation whereof all Policies or Forms of Government, all Laws and Magistrates, are most especially ordained; and herein is the Goodness and Wisdom of our present Legislature shewn.[9]

If the author of *A Discourse* considered the Witchcraft Act to be a step towards a new enlightened society in which the preservation and protection of human life was to be the foundation of the state, he was sorely mistaken. In legislative terms, human life was to become cheaper than ever before: it was to be the preservation of the property of 'Man', rather than 'His' preservation from Satanic chaotic forces, which the policies of government would concern itself with.

'Government', wrote John Locke in 1690, 'has no other end but the preservation of property'[10] – certainly a fitting motto for eighteenth-century government. Between 1688 and 1820 the number of capital statutes grew from about fifty to over two hundred; the great majority of these concerned offences against property. As the eighteenth century progressed, more and more offences were added to the list of capital crimes: sheep-stealing, pick-pocketing goods valued more than one shilling, cutting hop-bindings, illegal cutting down of trees, and sending threatening letters were some of the more inoffensive crimes which became punishable by death. The notorious Waltham Black Act (1723) enshrined fifty new capital offences in one piece of legislation. Commenting on the passing of the measure, E. P. Thompson wryly remarked that, 'a House prepared to debate for hours a disputed election could find unanimity at creating at a blow some fifty new capital offences.'[11] Paradoxically, though, there was no concomitant rise in the number of executions over the same period. As J. M. Beattie concluded from his analysis of the Surrey assize and quarter sessions records for 1736–53, 'neither juries, nor judges nor the King thought that these laws needed actually to be put into effect very often'.[12] Comparing this comparative judicial leniency with the harshness of the legislature, we find an obvious discrepancy between promised threat and actual punishment; however, as will become apparent, what is of significance here are the reasons for the increase in legislative severity rather than those for the apparent judicial circumspection.

For Brian Easlea, the ten-year period between the introduction of the death penalty for framebreaking in 1726 and the abolition of the crime of witchcraft in 1736 is a marker enabling historians to locate the end of one era and the beginning of a new one. Easlea sees the period as being one in which the ruling elite turned from persecuting 'old women who cursed and railed against an oppressive rural and patriarchal system of control', and who used diabolical means to contribute to its malfunctioning, to suppressing the real actions of 'those who opposed the new, oppressive system of incipient industrial capitalism'.[13] Although I doubt that accused witches railed against the 'patriarchal system of control' any more than their accusers did, Easlea is correct in regarding the two acts as reflective of a fundamental shift in the nature of the ruling elite's insecurities as to their own privileged position. The ruling elite's confidence in its own supreme power received a massive boost from its rejection of the Devil. They no longer needed to fear the continual imminent threat to their earthly power from the forces of supernatural chaos, but in their new found security they divested themselves of their legal defences against witchcraft, and sought, instead, to strengthen the legislative bulwarks against the temporal threat from below. The chaotic forces that those in power saw as the supreme threat to their stability were no longer embodied in the shape of the Devil and his disciples, but in the guise of a labouring population which was perceived as being increasingly lawless, and which in Lord Chancellor Hardwick's view, writing in the 1730s, was a worrying sign of the 'degeneracy of human nature'.

According to Douglas Hay, this distinctive period of legislative history saw nothing less than a 'ruling-class conspiracy' whereby the judiciary and gentry manipulated the statute and common law in defence of their own authority.[14] As Hay himself makes clear, the legal definition of 'conspiracy' does not require explicit agreement between those concerned provided they are working together for the same ends. The massive increase in capital offences was thus a consequence of a shared, unquestioned idealisation of the law as a selective instrument of class justice. Hay accounts for the perplexing discrepancy between the increase in capital statues and the relative decline in executions by suggesting that it was actually akin to a stick-and-carrot policy. The increased threat of death on the one hand, and the comparative show of discretionary leniency on the other, instilled a sense of lower-class deference: 'It was an important self-justification of the ruling class that once the poor had been chastised sufficiently to protect property, it was the duty of a gentleman to protect "his" people.'[15]

Hay's thesis has been subjected to detailed dissection by John Langbein and found wanting.[16] One of the major flaws that Langbein identifies in Hay's argument is the latter's playing down of the fact that, although the criminals against whom the statutes were usually invoked were overwhelmingly of the lower classes, so were their victims. In Langbein's view the criminal law and its procedures were not bulwarks of elite protectionism and repression, but 'existed to serve and protect the interests of the people who suffered as victims of crime, people who were overwhelmingly non-elite'.[17] In addition, those who exercised the powers of discretion could not be fairly described as the ruling class, and Langbein accuses Hay of exaggerating the extent of prosecutorial discretion, and of negligently underemphasising the importance of jury discretion. Where I think Hay's argument remains intact, however, is in his depiction of the ruling elite's perception of the threat to property, rather than his interpretation of the actions of the elite in response to that perception. Patterns of legislation can reflect not only patterns of crime but also patterns of elite anxieties.

In the days of witch prosecution the ruling elites and the 'people' had 'conspired' together (in the legal sense), rather than against each other, in a sustained attempt to rid the country of witches, though each stratum had acted upon rather different fears. The poor and labouring masses, ever fearful of the witch's threat to their own goods, chattels and health, were little concerned by the Devil's threat to the established order as represented by state and Church; they saw witchcraft in purely personal terms – one less witch was seen as one less threat to their own meagre property. The elite, however, were little concerned or personally affected by the often petty malicious acts of the witch, and were far more preoccupied with the supernatural threat to their own authority over their fellow men and women. By 1736 though, with the omnipotence of the Devil and his minions having been successfully fought off with 'reason', the governing elite now turned towards ensuring the security of their own property from the depredations of the poverty-stricken masses around them, who, despite elite scepticism, continued to consider themselves subject to the continual malicious attacks of witches. The partnership against witchcraft was split up, but, as we shall see in a subsequent chapter, the witch-believing majority were slow to realise that their fellow conspirators no longer considered them to be the prey, but rather the predators.

Witchcraft: an anachronism in the 'Age of Enlightenment'

Although by 1736 many among the ruling class considered witchcraft to be a vulgar notion bred of ignorance and credulity, for long afterwards a significant number of highly educated and respected people continued to express a certain ambivalence towards the wholesale rejection of a supernatural evil which the Bible so plainly stated existed. No less a person than William Blackstone, the foremost eighteenth-century writer on legal and constitutional matters, gave it as his opinion that,

> To deny the possibility, nay, actual existence, of witchcraft and sorcery is at once flatly to contradict the revealed word of God, in various passages both of the old and new testament: and the thing itself is a truth to which every nation in the world hath in its turn borne testimony ... indeed the ridiculous stories that are generally told, and the many impostures and delusions that have been discovered in all ages, are enough to demolish all faith in such dubious crime; if the contrary evidence were not also extremely strong.[18]

Blackstone's point was not so much that witchcraft still existed, but that it had existed, and therefore the reality of witchcraft could not be denied. He concluded by stating his concurrence with Joseph Addison's belief 'that there is, and has been such a thing as Witchcraft', even though at the same time he could 'give no Credit to any Particular Instance of it'.[19] A similar view was expressed by Dr Johnson in reply to an advocate called Mr Crosbie, who thought it 'not credible, that witches should have effected what they are said in stories to have done':

> 'Sir, you have all mankind, rude and civilised, agreeing in the belief of the agency of preternatural powers. You must take evidence: you must consider, that wise and great men have condemned witches to die.' – Crosbie. 'But an act of parliament put an end to witchcraft.' – Johnson. 'No, sir! witchcraft had ceased; and therefore an act of parliament was passed to prevent persecution for what was not witchcraft. Why it ceased, we cannot tell, as we cannot tell the reason of many things.'[20]

There was certainly a conflict between the perceived absurdity and irrationality of witchcraft and the evident ubiquity of the belief in every known culture going back to antiquity, together with the irrefutable word of the Bible on the subject. This was still presenting educated minds with a casuistic dilemma nearly a century later. In 1830 the author of a series of essays on the 'Progress and Decline of Witchcraft' in the *Gentleman's Magazine* concluded, 'That witchcraft may be, and that it hath been until a late period practised, seems to be abundantly capable of proof, were any collateral evidence necessary to confirm the truth of the divine testimony'.[21] Several decades later a more unsure contributor to the periodical *Notes and Queries* enquired, 'Is there, or has there ever been, such things as witchcraft, demonology, charms, astrology, foretelling events to happen, ghosts, and such like? Or are they simply the delusions of the Devil? Yet I ask, how comes it to pass that they have credence in all ages?'[22]

It is often stated that by the early eighteenth century the elite ceased to believe in witchcraft, but, as the opinions of the above gentlemen show, this is a misleading generalisation. There was a definite shift in elite attitudes towards witchcraft by the eighteenth century, but it was more subtle than is usually suggested. Many educated men and women continued to believe that witchcraft had existed and could exist, but ceased to believe that it continued to exist in their own times. Men such as Addison balked at rejecting witchcraft outright even though he had never come across a convincing case to prove its existence. Writing in the mid-eighteenth century the learned rector of Llangamarch, Theophilus Evans, could look back on the previous century and condemn the excesses of the prosecution and execution of innocent people as witches, but still confessed that he did 'not deny there may be real Witches in the common Acceptation of the Word, i.e. such as have communication with evil spirits and deserve to be capitally punished'.[23]

There was an undoubted political undercurrent to these expressions of belief in witchcraft. The likes of Blackstone, Johnson and Evans were all Tories, and their conservative political beliefs often went hand-in-hand with conservative religious tendencies, expressed in terms of holding to the literal truth of the Bible. For some Tories the denial of witchcraft was associated with noxious, free-thinking, sceptical Whiggery. Whigs, in turn, could make political capital out of the opposition's 'credulity' in such matters. Thus in 1726 the sensational case of the Godalming woman, Mary Toft, who claimed to have given birth to rabbits, was used to score political points.[24] There is also a sense here in which Whig parliamentary opinion concerning witchcraft was far ahead of the more generally conservative public opinion, including some elements of the elite, such as the clergy and squirearchy, who in their role as justices had to implement the laws on the ground. Addison's fictional country justice, Sir Roger de Coverley, was probably representative of some members of the Tory squire-archy at the time. In the story of Roger's visit to a local witch, Addison wrote that he

> could not forbear smiling to hear Sir Roger, who is a little puzzled about the old woman, advising her, as a justice of the peace, to avoid all communication with the devil, and never to hurt any of her neighbours' cattle ... I have since found, upon inquiry, that Sir Roger was several times staggered with the re-ports that had been brought him concerning this old woman, and would fre-quently have bound her over to the county sessions, had not his chaplain with much ado persuaded him to the contrary.[25]

With the belief in witchcraft tangled up with conflicting political and religious interests for much of the eighteenth century, it is not surprising that, with the exception of crusading evangelists such as John Wesley, there was so little vociferous public debate concerning witchcraft. In this context Jonathan Barry has made the useful point that where witchcraft was concerned, in the eighteenth century 'public discourse may be only an approximate guide to private belief, dependent on the rules of public debate'.[26] Henry Durbin's account of the Lamb Inn witchcraft case of 1761–62 was only published posthumously on his own instructions, be-cause he 'was abused in the public Papers' for what was termed his 'cre-dulity': 'Should I publish the Narrative, the same abuse would be revived, and I wish to live and die in peace with all men.'[27] We can assume that amongst friends, and in the privacy of homes, the subject of witchcraft continued to be earnestly debated by gentlemen and women. In 1762, for example, a contributor to the *Gentleman's Magazine* wrote about a recent visit he had made to a tavern where he 'met many gentlemen discoursing about several matters, and turning from one to another, as usual, at last disputing about the existence and nature of conjuring and witchcraft, which some did affirm, and others deny'.[28]

Among those who viewed witchcraft as a pernicious and foolish belief, there would seem to have been a general air of confidence that the passing of the law would, in itself, effect a passing of the old notions of witchcraft without any need for interference. Even after only two years the *St James's Evening Post*, reporting on a case of supposed witchcraft, could confidently remark on the 'Incongruity of such Sorcery being yet surviving in Great Britain'.[29] Writing with hindsight, Walter Scott believed that once the people were denied legal redress against witches in 1736, popular belief in witchcraft declined dramatically: 'Since that period witchcraft has been little heard of in England, and although the belief in its existence has in remote

places survived the law that recognised the evidence of the crime, and
assigned its punishment – yet such faith is gradually becoming forgotten
since the rabble have been deprived of all pretext to awaken it by their own
riotous proceedings.'[30] As the years passed, though, and the belief in witchcraft remained pervasive, occasional voices could be heard reminding the
reading public that the popular belief in witchcraft had not died with the
Witchcraft Act, and that the rapid progress of human knowledge in their
'enlightened age' was not necessarily an antidote to such beliefs. Thus John
Dove, the author of several works on moral philosophy, wrote in 1771:
'what stupid ignorance must possess the minds of men to give credit to the
idle tales concerning wizards, witches, &c. propagated amongst us to this
day, and held in dread by them? We live in an enlightened age no doubt!'[31]
In the following decade Samuel Norman, the surgeon of Yatton, Somerset,
observed, 'If we for a moment consider the rapid, the daily improvements
that have lately been made in the Arts and Sciences; how must we wonder
at that darkness and superstition which prevail at this time!'[32]

The two most sensational eighteenth-century cases of popular 'superstitious credulity', the Tring witch-ducking of 1751 and the Cock Lane ghost
of 1762, both gave rise to condemnatory literature. An anonymous pam-
phleteer was driven by his disgust of the latter case to write a 64-page
work entitled *Anti-canidia: or, Superstition Detected and Exposed*. The author
described his work as a 'sally of indignation at the contemptible *wonder* in
Cock-lane', and hoped it would help combat the 'mighty Colossus' of
popular superstition.[33] The author was well aware of the lack of effort that
had otherwise been made to eradicate the belief in witchcraft and magic,
which he considered injurious to pure religion: 'It is, I am conscious, a
feeble hand, that here aims a blow, and it will be no wonder if one of the
first attempts of this kind makes but little impression, but at least it may
perhaps encourage some abler arm to push the tottering monster with
great force; and fetch it to the ground.'[34] How this was to be achieved was
quite a different matter, however, and the author rather contradicted his
own good intentions by refusing to circulate his 'sally' among those he
considered in most need of it: 'it is only the *reasonable* part of the world,
to whose candid perusal the author is induced to recommend these sheets.
The credulous herd, who are blindly prepared to swallow every thing with
an implicit faith, he leaves to their own ignorance and weakness.'[35] In fact,
the author had little new to say to the 'reasonable' world. His first two
chapters, which concerned the scriptural evidence for witchcraft and magic
and the nature of the witch of Endor, merely ploughed over old ground,
arguing, for example, that 'the sacred writings frequently adopt the use of

vulgar language, and fall in with the ordinary prevailing notions of the times; without any intention to teach, support, or confirm such notions; or to give them the authority of divine revelation.'[36]

Despite such calls, neither the state nor the Anglican Church had the taste for a campaign against the continued popular belief in witchcraft and magic. It was considered by most educated people that witchcraft either no longer existed, or, at least, no longer posed a social and economic threat, and therefore was a matter of little concern. The shift in opinion was not so much a change from a position of belief to one of disbelief, as one from a perception of relevance to irrelevance. This lack of interest, combined, perhaps, with an element of Tory intransigence on the ground, may help explain why there was no reform movement at the time. The authorities very occasionally prosecuted people for attacking suspected witches, but usually only when there were a sufficient number of assailants to constitute a riot, and therefore a potential threat to social order. Generally it was up to determined individuals to instigate prosecutions. Not long after the passing of the Witchcraft Act, for example, Margaret Goldsborough of Baildon, Yorkshire, requested the justices to restrain some of her neighbours who accused her of witchcraft, and in another instance Mary Hudd of Thornbury, Gloucestershire, lodged an official complaint after she was stabbed in the arm by a cheese-monger's wife who claimed Hudd had bewitched her.[37] Certainly, little effort was made to enforce the fourth clause of the 1736 Statute 'for the more effectual preventing and punishing any pretenses to such arts or powers'. There were hundreds of cunning-folk and fortune-tellers practising at the time, but few were prosecuted. Among the unfortunates who were arrested was Elizabeth Fowl, a 'pretended Fortune-teller', who, in 1739, was sentenced at the Exeter assizes to the statutory year in prison and four visits to the pillory in Topsham. Another case was that of Daniel Jones, a cunning-man of Llanafan Fawr, Breconshire, who was sentenced at the Brecon assizes in 1789 after having been consulted by Thomas Daniel of Ystrad Fellte to cure his bewitched cows. Lastly, in 1815, Benjamin Evans, who lived near Minchinhampton, Gloucestershire, was pilloried in Stroud after being found guilty at the Gloucester assizes of defrauding a young man who had asked him to locate some stolen money.[38]

Continuing religious interest in witchcraft

While some of the most respected minds of the day might have accepted that witchcraft had existed at one time or another, few of the intelligentsia would admit that witchcraft still existed in the enlightened kingdom of the Georges. Those who did, and who were ready to say so publicly, were usually Nonconformists who held by the literal truth of the Bible, and who considered the Witchcraft Act to be in direct contravention to the law of God. Thus in 1743 the Presbytery of the Secession Church in Edinburgh severely censured the passing of the Witchcraft Act. In a published acknowledgement of national sins it specified the 'Repeal of the Penal Statutes against Witchcraft, contrary to the express laws of God', and a year later John Bisset preached a similar message in the New Church of Aberdeen.[39] Edmund Jones, a Welsh Independent minister and millenarian, of Pontypool, writing thirty-six years later, also opined that,

> had his Majesty King George II read the History of Witchcraft, and known as much as we do in some parts of Wales, he would not have called upon his Parliament to determine that there are no such things as witches, and his Parliament would hardly have complimented him therein. If they say there never was such things as witches in the world, the Scripture is against them.

Probably the most influential critic of the repeal of the laws against witchcraft was the founding father of Methodism, John Wesley (1703–1791), who was, at one time, on friendly terms with the opposer of the Witchcraft Act, James Erskine. It was Wesley who famously wrote:

> the English in general, and indeed most of the men of learning in Europe, have given up all account of witches and apparitions as mere old wives' fables. I am sorry for it, and I willing take this opportunity of entering my solemn protest against this violent compliment which so many that believe in the Bible pay to those who do not believe it … the giving up of witchcraft is in effect giving up the Bible. With my latest breath I will bear testimony against giving up to infidels one great proof of the invisible world; I mean that of witchcraft and apparitions, confirmed by the testimony of all ages.[40]

Wesley's formative years were heavily influenced by the experience of the noisy haunting of the family home in Epworth, Lincolnshire, during the winter of 1716–17. John was actually away at school at the time, but the events seem to have engaged his thoughts considerably in later life. The story of the haunting can be pieced together from the letters written by Wesley's mother and other family members to John's brother, Samuel (1690–1739), depositions collected later from family members by John, and also a written account of the visitation by John's father, the Rev. Samuel Wesley (1662–1735).[41] Towards the end of his life John Wesley also published his own succinct account of events in the Methodist journal, the *Arminian Magazine*.[42] The disturbances began on 1 December when the Wesley children and the parsonage servants began hearing strange noises, groans and knockings all over the house. Footsteps were heard going up and down the stairs at night, and, on one occasion, Molly Wesley, then aged about twenty, heard the rustling of someone wearing a silk dress or night-gown. One day another daughter and the mother heard noises from under a bed and saw something akin to a headless badger run off. The Rev. Samuel Wesley seemed to have considered the ghostly intruder as an evil spirit, and when several gentlemen and clergymen advised him to leave the house, he answered, 'No, let the devil flee from me: I will never flee from the devil'. Towards the end of January the disturbances ceased and did not return.

While Samuel seems to have interpreted events from a theological perspective, as manifestation of the Devil come to test them, one of the daughters, Emily, had her own views on the matter. In a letter to her brother, Samuel, she confided:

> If you would know my opinion of the reason of this, I shall briefly tell you. I believe it to be witchcraft, for these reasons. About a year since, there was a disturbance at a town near us, that was undoubtedly witches; and if so near, why may they not reach us? Then my father had for several Sundays before its coming, preached warmly against consulting those that are called cunning men, which our people are given to; and it had a particular spite at my Father.

In Emily's opinion the strange badger-like creature was the witch in animal form: 'The last time he [a servant] saw it in the kitchen, like a white rabbit, which seems likely to be some witch; and I do so really believe it to be one, that I would venture to fire a pistol at it, if I saw it long enough.' As will become apparent in a later chapter, Emily's beliefs were very much those of folk tradition rather than the theological tradition of her father. This may suggest that she had been listening as much to the stories of witches told by the family servants as to her father's religious teachings. John's views were, perhaps, somewhere in between. He accepted the stories common people told him about their trials and tribulations with witchcraft, but reinterpreted them from his own perspective: for Wesley, the root cause of such afflictions was not the old women accused of being witches, but the omnipresent Devil.

Considering Wesley's outspoken opinions on witchcraft, it is not surprising, perhaps, that both he and the Church he founded were frequently accused of inflaming the popular belief in witchcraft and magic. Such 'pernicious' beliefs were thought by Anglicans to be the relics of the country's Catholic past. According to the author of *A Discourse on*

Witchcraft, for example, 'after the founding of the *Dominican* and *Franciscan* Fryars, and the setting up of an Office of *Inquisition*, the World grew so full of Devils and *Witches*.'[43] While Catholicism was on the decline, Methodism was on the rise, and the noxious reputation of the old Church was transferred to the new. Methodism became almost synonymous with credulity concerning the supernatural. In the opinion of M. J. Naylor, lecturer at the parish church of Wakefield, writing of the belief in witch-craft in 1795,

> The belief of these extravagancies was indeed gradually yielding to the powerful progress of science, but of late it has again been nourished and revivified, in no inconsiderable degree, by the many extraordinary relations, which the late ven-erable MR. WESLEY inserted in his Arminian Magazine … Their conviction has insensibly spread amongst the multitudes connected with them by the common intercourse of society, and once more reilluminated the fading flame of vulgar superstition.[44]

Yet, were such accusations justified, or, indeed, fair?[45] Certainly, many Methodists continued to believe that witchcraft was alive, and a real threat to the fabric of Christian society in eighteenth- and early-nineteenth-century Britain. Methodist literature was noticeable for its sensational supernatural content. One nineteenth-century Welsh commentator observed how Methodist books 'swarmed with marvels, supernatural appearances, warnings, singing in the air, sudden judgements on rulers and persecutors; God's miracles and the Devil's miracles abounded everywhere.'[46] Methodists were also more likely than Anglican clergymen to intervene in cases of witchcraft. The Rev. Edward Hamer, for example, knew of a case where a 'Calvinistic Methodist' read a portion of the scriptures over a bewitched horse, with apparently beneficial results.[47]

There is no doubt that the supernatural aspects of Methodism appealed to many potential converts, and it is not surprising that in the early nineteenth century the more sober, 'respectable' Wesleyan ministers lost popular support in some quarters to the Primitive Methodists, who were reviving the supernatural phenomena of Wesley's day. Yet, for all the apparent associations between Methodism and supernaturalism, it should be noted that Methodism was far from being a united movement. After Wesley's death in 1791, the Methodist establishment, who were attempting to trans-form the Methodist movement into a more organised, structured and respectable Church, attacked the activities of the grassroots revivalists, who had been heavily influenced by the visit of the American evangelist Lorenzo Dow in 1806. The Methodist authorities were obviously well aware of the supernatural beliefs held by many of their members, and, even though the movement's founder had been a devout believer in witchcraft, by the nineteenth century they were trying to distance themselves from any supernatural activities or expressions of belief which might tarnish their nascent respectability. For the nineteenth-century Methodist authorities the supernatural beliefs of its founder had for too long been used as a stick with which to berate the movement for its credulity. Thus, in 1801, for example, the Welsh Methodist leadership warned its members against involvement in sorcery, magic and witchcraft.[48] In 1816, around fifty members of the Portland Methodist Society, including two prominent lay preachers, were struck off the class register by the Rev. Francis Derry, for holding to the belief in witchcraft. Writing of the events at Portland, some eighty years later, the Methodist Robert Pearce expressed the opinion that 'a firm policy was necessary to deal with this mischievous superstition', but he questioned the wisdom of Derry's high-handed methods.[49] When considering the role played by Methodism in nourishing the belief in witchcraft and magic, therefore, one must be careful not to overgeneralise about the movement. While some of Wesley's generation, and the early Primitive Methodists, obviously believed in witchcraft and embroiled themselves in the popular struggle against witches, the nineteenth-century Methodist hierarchy actively denounced such beliefs. By the second half of the nineteenth century even the Primitive Methodists were discarding those supernatural elements, such as visions, trances and oracular dreams, which originally marked them out from other Methodist groups.

There is little convincing evidence to suggest that eighteenth-century Wesleyan Methodism and early-nineteenth-century Primitive Methodism were sufficiently popular or influential to have made a significant impact on the strength of supernatural beliefs, either among its members or on the wider populace. Witchcraft beliefs survived equally long in areas little influenced by Methodism. Besides, the popular belief in witchcraft was still so widespread during the eighteenth century that it would have been difficult to raise the level of belief significantly further. The claim that Methodism fostered superstitious ignorance often came from Anglican clergymen, who, when confronted by the supernatural beliefs of their own parishioners, found it convenient to lay some of the blame for such a 'deplorable' state of affairs on their religious rivals. When, for example, in 1817, the Rev. Richard Lyne, Rector of Little Petherick, Cornwall, was shocked to find his flock resorting to charms, he blamed Methodism for its pernicious propagation of such 'superstition'. Lyne considered Wesley to be the 'Magus of England', and damned him for his 'surprising power to bewitch' the people.[50] Similarly, the Rev. Edward Hamer, in lamenting

the continued belief in witchcraft in his parish of Llanidloes, Montgomeryshire, could not but help point an accusatory finger at the
Methodists who did so little 'to uproot this pernicious belief, while it did
much to remove more innocent pastimes.'[51]

Yet, while Methodists were accused of peddling 'superstition', much to
the annoyance and surprise of the Anglican clergy, the Christian services
they provided, and the fabric of the church and churchyard in which
those services were enacted, continued to remain a focal point for popular magic.[52] Up until the present century consecrated wine was considered a magical cure-all, and confirmation was thought to be an infallible
remedy for rheumatism. Churchyard earth was also thought to possess
strong curative powers. Sacramental rings made out of a shilling taken
from the offertory were commonly worn as a remedy for fits. Around
1853 a Berkshire vicar had to dismiss his parish clerk for exchanging
coins for this purpose on behalf of fellow villagers.[53] There was also a
widespread belief that clergymen had the power to cure the bewitched.
So, whether the Church liked it or not, until the tradition of popular
magic itself declined, the church remained an integral element and focus
of popular magic. Thus the Church of England, unwillingly, and often
unwittingly, certainly contributed more to the survival of witchcraft and
magical beliefs than Methodism ever did.

Furthermore, just as not all Methodists accepted everything Wesley
believed in, so not all Anglican churchmen were sceptical concerning the
reality of witchcraft. One such man was Robert Stephen Hawker, vicar
of Morwenstow, Cornwall. As his fellow clergyman Sabine Baring-Gould
remembered him, Hawker shared some of the 'superstitions' of his parishioners: 'Living as he did in a visionary dreamworld of spirits, he was
ready to admit without questioning the stories he heard of witchcraft and
the power of the evil eye.' There was an old woman in Morwenstow
whom he thoroughly believed to a be a witch, and whom he had
witnessed bewitching his own pigs. When anyone objected to his claim
that she was a witch he would answer, 'I have seen the five black spots
placed diagonally under her tongue, which are evidences of what she is.
They are like those in the feet of swine, made by the entrance into them
of the demons at Gadara.'[54] Hawker, like some of his Methodist counterparts, obviously interpreted literally at least some of the Bible's pronouncements on witchcraft. When a companion one day asked him if he really
believed in 'such rubbish', Hawker replied, 'I do not pretend to be wiser
than the Word of God. I find that the evil eye is reckoned along with
"blasphemy, pride, and foolishness," as things that defile a man.'[55]

However, Hawker's interpretation of witchcraft was formulated on a quite different intellectual level to that of his parishioners. The historian J. F. C. Harrison wondered if the Anglican clergy of the late eighteenth and nineteenth century were 'all completely innocent of neo-Platonic influences'.[56] In the case of Hawker at least, the answer is no. He believed that an imperceptible atmosphere surrounded men, which was the medium in which angels and devils moved, and which vibrated with spiritual influences affecting the soul. Envious and bitter thoughts rippled through this atmosphere and could penetrate into the mind and body, and in this way envy turned itself into a true disease. His ideas certainly smacked of Renaissance Neoplatonism, which, to put in very simple terms, claimed that the world was enveloped in a medium of spirits that infused everything, and that could be influenced for good and bad. Unfortunately we do not know where Hawker got his ideas from, or even whether he would have defined them as Neoplatonic. What is certain is that he considered them to be on a different philosophical plane to the theories of the spiritualist movement which was then in vogue, and which he criticised for its credulity. Writing early this century, the Rev. Charles Kent, Rector of Merton, Norfolk, also expressed his belief in a similar, but more simple, theory of witchcraft: 'My own belief in witchery, as they term it about here, is possibly not so crude as that of some of my older parishioners ... I believe in the actual power of hate so working on the power of faith that evil results. Witchery is hate made manifest.'[57]

While Hawker and Kent interpreted witchcraft from a philosophical view of the power of faith and envy, the belief in witchcraft held by the Rev. William Ettrick, vicar of Affpuddle and Toner's Puddle, Dorset, was very much grounded on the same level as his parishioners. Like many of his social inferiors, Ettrick was persuaded of the reality of witchcraft, not as a result of theological or philosophical persuasion, but as a consequence of a series of distressing misfortunes which befell his household. Ettrick's progression from a position of scepticism to the conviction that his gardener was a witch can be traced from entries in his diary for the years 1804–5.[58] On 14 November 1804 he described the strange illness of his child as 'like a demonical Possession and began immediately after the child was snatched out of the Mothers Arms, by a Hag & reputed witch. ... I was once incredulous about the power of Witchcraft, but have no doubts remaining.' On 1 December he continued:

> WITCHCRAFT ... Untill Susan Woodrow has come again for some Days to wash &c. we have reasons very strong and many to ascribe to this ill looking & worse tempered wretch, the sufferings of this Child, the Curse upon the

> Horse &c. ... While her connections with the House remains, we shall remain under Power, and are come to a determine to dismiss her.

Several days after her dismissal, Susan Woodrow, obviously distressed by her treatment, came to deliver two letters to Ettrick:

> I wd not receive the Letters from her, but threatened a Warrant if she did not carry her self off from hence directly – with great Reluctance, after, much previous boldness and repeated demands what have I done? ... her Crime admits of no legal proofs, being all works of darkness, and I must say nothing until somebody else suffers, and then my allegations will seem not altogether visionary.

The legacy of Woodrow's supposed witchcraft continued long after her dismissal. The last rather plaintive mention of her in Ettrick's diary was on 11 September 1805: 'Bees – have but one stock now left and those we are taking on – they have dwindled away unaccountably, Susan having had hands upon them last yr ... Keep no more Bees.'

Hawker and Ettrick may seem like exceptional examples, eccentrics perhaps, but one must be cautious about overgeneralising about the clergy. As will become quite apparent later in this chapter, the Anglican clergy were far from being one homogenous group following the same orthodox position. Like their Methodist counterparts, on an individual level they were a diverse group of people open to influences from outside the Anglican orthodoxy, and ready to develop their own personal philosophies regarding their faith.

Possession, religion and spiritualism

One of the aims of this chapter is to question the notion that after 1736 educated society completely rejected the belief in witchcraft and magic. Certainly, for much of the eighteenth century there was a conspicuous lack of interest and involvement in popular manifestations of witchcraft. However, there were other forms of related supernatural beliefs that continued to engage the minds of many educated men and women. Spirit possession and related diabolic phenomena attracted considerable curiosity, not only in the eighteenth century but also in the nineteenth century, when new intellectual interpretations of the supernatural emerged.[59]

Only two years after the passing of the Witchcraft Act, great excitement was aroused in Portishead by a case of bewitchment that exhibited the suspicious signs of spirit involvement. According to a newspaper report, 'An Outcry was daily made of this Prodigy by Droves of People who visited the House, where the Witchcraft was supposed to be in full Power'.[60] The house in question belonged to an old tailor and his wife, who nursed parish children for 18d. a week. At 'every Instant either one or the other had a Bang on the Head, or some other Part of the Body, with large Stones, Spoons, Knives, &c. ... the two old People, in order to drive the Dilemma from them, were constantly at Prayer, by the Advice of the good People.' Spirit voices also seem to have been heard. Not only were the local villagers fascinated by the case, since a gentlewoman, who happened to be staying in the area, also went to see the goings-on herself. The gentlewoman, who had no faith in 'such Chimera's', suspected the old couple's twelve-year-old granddaughter of being behind the manifestations. She was searched and two pockets full of stones were found under her petticoats. It was also discovered that 'she had a Knack in changing her Voice to several Tones'. According to the newspaper reporting the case, the Gentlewoman 'had the Thanks of the whole Parish for laying this young Witch'.

Neighbouring Bristol was the scene of a more controversial case of spirit possession in 1762.[61] The daughters of Richard Giles, the innkeeper of the Lamb Inn, suffered from strange fits, had crooked pins stuck into them, saw visions, and heard voices. Giles himself later became ill and died. After this tragedy the girls' fits subsided for a while before returning again. A local cunning-woman was consulted, who confirmed that witchcraft was responsible, and said that a rival waggoner had paid a witch to torment them. The cunning-woman advised that a witch bottle be boiled. This was duly carried out, and the children recovered. The events at the Lamb Inn attracted considerable newspaper attention, and provoked a number of respectable gentlemen, including doctors and clergymen, to investigate the affair. Some of them became convinced of the genuineness of the spirit manifestations. A series of questions was put to the spirit in a number of languages to remove suspicion of fraud, and they were apparently competently answered using a series of raps. From this they found out that the spirit was actually tormenting six people at the same time. All the Anglican clergymen involved declined to conduct prayers for the girls except for a curate with Methodist leanings named Thomas Rouquet. This should not be considered surprising. While some Anglican clergymen undoubtedly believed in diabolic possession, they were forbidden under Canon 72 (formulated in 1604) to conduct fastings and prayers for the possessed.

Twenty-six years after the Lamb Inn affair, the Bristol intelligentsia were once more debating the nature and reality of spirits and diabolic intervention in relation to the possession of George Lukins of Yatton, Somerset. While the former case attracted a lot of interest, apart from newspaper letters, it did not lead to any significant published exchanges of opinion at the time. The Lukins affair, however, led to a flurry of both vitriolic newspaper exchanges and pamphlets akin to those from earlier in the century.[62]

At Christmas time, in 1769, George Lukins was among a band of young men and women performing a mumming play around the neighbourhood. When performing late one night at the house of a Mr Love, they were generously plied with strong beer, and Lukins became greatly inebriated. As the company left to go home, Lukins fell down drunk. Two of his next-door neighbours, named Avery and Read, picked him up and helped him home. Shortly after this drunken escapade, Lukins began to exhibit dreadful fits, during which he was sometimes rendered speechless. He would leap, howl, distort his body, dance upon burning coals, and on one occasion attempted to leap into a nearby pond. These fits occurred periodically for several years, but Lukins still managed to pursue his work as a tailor and various other occupations. In May 1775 his situation got so bad, however, that he was sent away to a hospital, where he remained for several months until he was pronounced incurable and sent back home.

During this period of Lukins' affliction, his own view, and that of others in Yatton, was that his fits were caused by witchcraft rather than direct satanic influence. According to the sceptical Yatton surgeon, Samuel Norman, 'To prove himself bewitched, he gave me and others many relations of the power of witches, their iniquitous practices and punishments for them.'[63] Several cunning-folk were consulted, but without any positive result. A cunning-woman of Bedminster, for example, prescribed several packets consisting of rolled up brown paper with pins driven through it, which were to be burnt in the fire during Lukins' fits. Several 'indigent and infirm old people' in the neighbourhood were accused of bewitching him, and Lukins himself attempted to wound one old woman, presumably to draw blood.[64]

On returning to his brother's house at Yatton after his stay in hospital, Lukins once more began to exhibit the same strange behaviour. His brother eventually grew tired of this, and one Richard Beacham of the same parish agreed to house him, though only after first consulting Samuel Norman. Lukins' fits subsided during his stay with Beacham, and even when he left Beacham's house he suffered no more fits until the year 1787. It was during this relapse into his old behaviour that there occurred a definite shift of emphasis concerning Lukins' own interpretation of his affliction. He now fully attributed it all to the invisible influence of the Devil, rather than local witches.[65] It was probably during this phase of Lukins' possession that several persons had heard him repeatedly say that he was possessed with seven devils, and if seven ministers could be got to pray with him, in faith, the devils would be cast out. It is possible that Lukins got this idea from the Bible, where it is said that Mary Magdalene was possessed by seven devils. Finally, on 7 June 1788, Lukins was brought to Bristol to be exorcised. 'Such an extraordinary case soon became the topic of the day, and many religious persons of different denominations, reading of the account in the papers were induced to visit him, for several days prior to his deliverance.'[66] The Devil would insult and taunt these visitors. On one occasion, for example, a group of ministers began singing a hymn, to which the Devil declared 'Thou fool! – thou unbeliever! – thou mayest pray to eternity – I will not be conquered – I am the Devil – I am Supreme – Governor – Thou mayest pray for ever and ever – I will torment this fellow to his life's end.'[67] A Methodist minister and schoolmaster, T. M'Geary, adjured the Devils in Greek and Latin, but the 'pretended Devils were so unclassical as not to be able to reply'.[68]

The Rev. Joseph Easterbrook, Vicar of Temple, called upon some Anglican clergymen to assist in the exorcism of Lukins, but, although they were apparently sympathetic, they all declined to help. So the group of seven ministers which gathered in the vestry of Temple Church to defeat the seven devils, was made up of Easterbrook and the following six Wesleyan Methodist ministers: Messrs J. Broadbent, J. Valton, B. Rhodes, J. Brettel, W. Hunt, and T. M'Geary. This solemn gathering rather appropriately took place on Friday the thirteenth. The company prayed and sang hymns, while the Devil 'bid them defiance, cursing and vowing dreadful vengeance on all present'. Finally, one of the ministers stood up and repeatedly commanded, 'In the name of Jesus, and in the name of the Father, the Son, and the Holy Ghost, the evil spirit to depart from the man!' This was too much for the Devil, who, with much dreadful howling, quit George Lukins' body. The following week public thanksgiving for his recovery was conducted in Yatton Church.

The arch-critic of Lukins and those clergymen who gathered around him was Samuel Norman. He considered Lukins' possession to be a fraud, and his supporters superstitious enthusiasts.[69] From his close knowledge of Lukins over many years, Norman also dismissed the idea that he was a victim of epilepsy, and instead diagnosed that he was an outright impostor. Norman's was far from being a lone voice of scepticism. Mr Box, surgeon of Wrington, visited Lukins before his journey to Bristol, and also declared him to be a cheat. The following humorous poem, dated 1794, hand-written on a slip of paper and inserted into a copy of *A Narrative of the Extraordinary Case of Geo. Lukins*, portrays the ministers involved in exorcising Lukins in a rather unflattering light:

> Lo Lukins comes, and with him comes a train,
> of parsons famous for a lack of brain,
> With vol-like faces and with raven coats;
> Their solemn stile their solemn task denotes;
> By exorcisings, prayers and pluckings,
> To drive some sturdy devils out of Lukins.[70]

The preface to the pro-Lukins pamphlet in which this was inserted referred to the 'several erroneous accounts ... now in circulation'. This was undoubtedly an allusion to those sceptical attacks written by Samuel Norman, who, like many contemporary opponents of 'enthusiasm', could not resist warning his readers against the return of pernicious Catholic superstitions, and felt obliged to guard 'the public against the long since exploded tricks of Jesuits and Popish Priests'.[71] As a counterblast to such opinions, the pamphlet advised that 'If any person, after reading this account, ascribes it to enthusiasm, delusion, or a juggling trick ... then ask them, if it is not equally as possible for such things to be permitted now as then, seeing the hand of the LORD is not shortened, nor his power diminished!'

The above cases were among the few well-publicised accounts of possession at the time, but, as Wesley's journals show, similar possessions were periodically occurring up and down the country throughout the century, particularly in relation to Methodist proselytising.[72] It is worth noting in connection with the Lamb Inn and Yatton cases that Bristol had been a key focus of the Methodist Awakening during the late 1730s and 1740s. As Clarke Garrett has pointed out, the area was also remarkable during the period for the number of vivid manifestations of divine and satanic possession at Methodist meetings.[73] Accounts of these happenings must have spread around the area, and knowledge of the behavioural symptoms of satanic possession entered into the pool of popular knowledge. As far as we know, neither Lukins nor the Giles girls had any firm contact with Methodism, and their initial behaviour was popularly understood to result from witchcraft, but it is possible that their performances were also influenced by the tradition of Methodist possession in the area.

As well as Methodists, Catholic clergymen were also prepared to wrestle with the Devil in cases of possession, though there is little documentary evidence of priests conducting exorcisms at this time. What is certain is that during the eighteenth and nineteenth centuries there lingered a popular memory of the spirit-laying powers of the Catholic clergy. The Newcastle clergyman Henry Bourne wrote in 1725, that 'it is common for the present vulgar to say, none can lay a spirit but a *Popish priest*.'[74] One hundred years later, the Yorkshire clergyman John Atkinson encountered an old woman who believed she was being tormented by spirits, and requested him to 'lay them'. Atkinson gently informed her that he could not 'lay spirits', to which she retorted, 'if I had sent for a priest o' t' au'd church, he wad a' deean it. They wur a vast mair powerful *conjurers* than you Church-priests.'[75] However, Catholic worshippers and priests were rather thin on the ground during the eighteenth century. In 1780 the vicars apostolic counted only 54,000 Catholics in the country, though, over the next sixty years numbers grew substantially as the population increased and large-scale Irish immigration took place.[76] One rare and extraordinary account of a Catholic exorcism was faithfully chronicled by the exorcist himself, the Rev. Edward Peach (1771–1839).[77] His early life had been somewhat eventful. He had been at Douay College when the French Revolution broke out, but managed to escape back to England in 1793, and several years later he was rewarded with his first mission at the Turvile family seat in Husbands Bosworth, Leicestershire. In September 1806 he was appointed to establish a mission in Birmingham, and three years later he built St Chad's chapel in Bath Street.[78] It was during his tenure at St Chad's that he was called upon to exorcise a young Protestant woman of King's Norton parish, a rural area at the time, though it is now part of Birmingham's suburban sprawl.

Some time after Easter, in 1815, the Rev. Peach heard rumours that a woman named White, whose family occupied a small farm, was suffering from an extraordinary illness. He was told that its cause arose solely from the malice of a rejected admirer who had employed a wizard at Dudley (a town some ten miles away) 'to do her mischief'. Peach initially 'paid but little attention to this story'. Not long afterwards, however, he

was informed by a sister who frequents our markets, and supplies with butter a respectable family of my congregation, Mr. P★★★l, Suffolk-street, that the young woman was married in the beginning of the preceding Lent, – that her former admirer repeatedly declared, that if she did marry any other she should never have another happy day, – that the day after her marriage she was seized with an extraordinary kind of mental complaint, – that she became suddenly delirious, – that she raved, and declared that a multitude of infernal spirits surrounded her, – that they threatened to carry her away,- and that she must go with them.[79]

This had gone on for about two months, during which time she had been attended by a doctor who declared that her illness arose more from a mental than a corporeal cause, and incorrectly concluded that she would probably not survive another day. The Anglican clergyman of the parish was also called in, 'but he found her in a state not to be benefited by his assistance, and he departed'. Among the neighbours who offered to help the family was a sympathetic Catholic woman. She acquired some holy water, dipped her finger into it, and made the sign of the cross upon White's forehead. White instantly exclaimed in a faint voice 'You have scalded me', but subsequently fell into a gentle sleep. When she awoke, more holy water was dropped into her mouth, which this time caused convulsions and suffocation. When she recovered her breath she exclaimed violently, 'You have scalded my throat; you have scalded my throat.' Shortly after she again fell into a comfortable sleep. The same procedure was adopted several times and the danger of death seemed to decrease by degrees.

At the time of being informed of these facts, Peach was asked whether he might be of any assistance in the case. He replied that he knew nothing of the family, but said he would go if he could be of service. This news was relayed to White's family, who expressed their desire that he come: 'However, I still delayed: till at length, on Tuesday in Rogation Week, May 2, 1815, a special messenger came over to inform me that Mrs. White was in a worse state than ever … I obeyed the call: and I may say with truth, that it was the most awful visit I ever made during the whole course of my ministry.'[80] The journey to King's Norton was some six miles, and the weather did its best to deter him from ever getting there. No sooner had he left the outskirts of Birmingham than he heard the sound of distant thunder approaching. By the time Peach had gone two miles the storm was right overhead: 'During the remainder of my walk, and during the time I was with her, there was hardly a cessation of one minute between the claps of thunder. I do not say that in this there was any thing supernatural; but knowing the business I was upon, it was truly awful.' Peach found White in a terrible state, and requested the gathered family and friends to leave him alone with the young woman. In one of her calm periods he asked her the circumstances of the illness, which corresponded exactly with that given by her sister. He later recalled that she had told him she was 'continually annoyed with the most criminal temptations, of almost every description, and that she felt an almost un-interrupted inclination to utter the most dreadful imprecations, and the most horrible blasphemies.' Peach explained to her some of the articles of the Catholic faith, and assured her that she must believe in the Catholic Church before she could obtain relief. White declared that from the moment she was sprinkled with holy water, and the devils possessing her receded, her belief in the Catholic faith had been sealed. The stage was set for a drama of gothic proportions. Peach and the Devil prepared to do battle over the young woman writhing in her bed, the stormy heavens above rent by lightening. The exorcism began:

> She fell into a state of convulsive agitation … every limb, every joint, seemed to be agitated and convulsed, even her countenance was distorted: it required constant attention to keep her covered. – Now it was that I felt in a particular manner the awful situation in which I was. – All alone, with a person in her distressed condition – the lightening flashing, and the thunder rolling – and I with an imperative voice commanding the evil spirit to reply to my interrogatories, and to go forth from her. I acknowledge that my flesh began to creep, and my hair to stand on end.

Peach struggled on valiantly, and after finishing the exorcism White suddenly became calm, and before long was talking normally to him. He then discovered that she had either not been baptised or the essential rites of baptism had not been performed properly, so, before leaving he baptised her. He went to see her again the next day, and found her in good health.

Peach, obvious impressed by his own success, wrote an account of White's illness and exorcism for the *Catholicon*, which was duly published in June 1816. He returned to White's farm on 8 August 1816, and was pleased to find her in full health and with a baby in her arms. He was even more happy to find that by his successful exorcism he had seemingly made a convert to the Catholic faith. White told him she had only been to the Anglican church twice since, and then only to attend two christenings. Her neighbours had also frequently solicited her to attend a Presbyterian meeting, but she declined. Peach asked if her husband was willing to let her attend the Catholic chapel, and she replied 'that at first he was very unwilling, on account of the many prejudices which he had imbibed against the Catholic religion'.[81] Her husband had eventually agreed, but she had not been able to attend because she had been too busy making and looking after the cheeses. They hoped, however, to take a small farm nearer to Birmingham, which would mean she should have more time to attend chapel. Peach was convinced of her earnestness, and gave her two copies of his account of her exorcism, and promised to send her books of Catholic instruction. Not long after this encounter, Peach decided to publish a complete account of events in the form of a tract, in the conclusion to which he claimed: 'I may without hesitation assure my readers that in the space of a short time she will be a member of that church whose ministers, as she learnt by experience, have inherited the powers granted by Christ to his true believers.'

The public stir caused by the affair subsided, only to be rekindled briefly twenty years later. In April 1836, the *Birmingham Advertiser* made reference to the case in far from complimentary terms. Peach denounced it as a violent diatribe which 'would have disgraced a Pagan persecutor of the Catholic religion'. He thought the events of 1815 had passed 'into the gulf of oblivion', although his publisher and bookseller, R. P. Stone of Bull street, had informed him that over the years a few people had enquired about purchasing a copy of the tract. Because of the 'unchristian interference of the fiery zealot, the *Advertiser*', Peach decided to have a new edition of the 1816 tract printed so as to set the record straight.

Most possession cases show similar characteristics, and, as James Sharpe has commented, 'we are looking at very stereotyped patterns of behaviour'.[82] Two distinct groups of spirit possession can be detected: those which concerned bodily fits, and those which involved mischievous spirit activities such as object throwing and pinching. Both were, of course, open to imposture. The two types of manifestation can be conveniently labelled as internal possession and external possession ('obsession') respectively. The victims were usually either adolescents or young adults, and mostly female. Unlike in the previous century when the daughters of the gentry were afflicted, the eighteenth- and nineteenth-century victims of possession were commonly from modest social backgrounds.[83] In most of these cases, when the victims started suffering from fits, or objects started being thrown, witchcraft was usually suspected, and cunning-folk were either consulted to identify who was responsible, or were accused of having been the agency via which the evil spell was effected. During this initial phase of the possession, then, the origins of the affliction and the means of countering it reflected popular modes of thought and action in response to suspected witchcraft. The pattern was that of other forms of supposed misfortune caused by simple *maleficium*.

In the folk framework of supernatural belief, witches were thought able to control and direct spirits to occupy the bodies of those they had a spite against. These spirits were usually described by those so afflicted, or their family, as 'evil', though it is worthy of note that the term 'possession' seems to have been used rarely in popular discourse. The symptoms of being so 'possessed' did not necessarily lead to the classic, extreme behaviour of Lukins or White. Straightforward epileptic attacks and various forms of mental illness could also be interpreted in this way.

One of the sons of William and Jane Davis, a labouring couple of Puddletown parish, Dorset, suffered from what doctors identified as 'idiocy and epilepsy'. In the opinion of William Davis, however, 'there was something curious about the boy, something different from God Almighty, and that some evil spirit was about him.' This he believed was the result of having been overlooked by a witch, and so he consulted a cunning-man.[84] Jemima Maxted, an elderly woman of Belting, Kent, who, it seems, was generally considered 'a little deranged', believed that a local witch had sent an 'evil spirit' into her. She also consulted a cunning-man to drive out the evil spirit, or 'devil', as she also referred to it.[85] A rather more unusual case of possession was that of a 'poor, half-crazed' woman who lived near Penzance, who requested a local clergyman to exorcise the ghost of her dead sister, who had entered into her and tormented her in the shape of a small fly which buzzed in her ear.[86]

Thus, while many of the clergy, Methodists and Catholics in particular, shared with folk culture the same belief in the power of possession, it did not necessarily share the same expressions, etiological concepts, and healing rituals pertaining to that basic belief. Clerical perceptions of witchcraft and possession were based on the old elite, theological conceptions of diabolism. When confronted by instances of witch-induced possession, the clergy saw the witch merely as an instrument of the Devil, and thus directed their attentions more towards Satan than his earthly vassals. On the other hand, in the folk conception of witchcraft, the Devil was largely in the background, and was not generally cited directly as an agent in cases of popular witchcraft. When attributing blame for their possession by evil spirits, people looked no further than the witch. When it came to the curing of possession, therefore, Methodists and Catholics, following the old Puritan tradition of supernatural healing, resorted to prayers and exhortations in order to expel the Devil from mind and body. However, while one folk avenue of cure was, indeed, recourse to the clergy, it was more likely that cunning-folk would be consulted, or magical remedies such as scratching and witch bottles employed. The general aim of such folk remedies was to inflict pain on the corporeal witch, rather than on the abstract devils of theology. Although it was popularly believed that a clergyman could cure for witchcraft by saying 'a few words' over the victim, the popular reasoning behind this belief differed radically from the conception of exorcism. People invested the clergyman himself with the magical power to cure, whereas according to Methodist beliefs it was only the power and the word of God that could heal supernaturally inspired illnesses.

It was generally with the intervention of religious interests that cases of folk possession were transformed into classic, full-blown satanic possession. As anthropologists and psychologists have emphasised, possession cases can be seen as forms of popular theatre enacted out for a wondering audience.[87] People were often encouraged, either by the possessed or by their families, to come and witness the unusual behaviour, either for potential financial gain, or purely as an act of attention-seeking. First neighbours and fellow villagers would tramp into the house of the possessed to offer their advice and opinions. The news would spread to neighbouring villages, and the Sunday holiday would draw visitors from further afield to see the unusual antics of the bewitched. Mundane cases of witch-induced illness certainly also attracted local attention, but the phenomena associated with possession eventually brought forth doctors and clergymen seeking to advance their understanding of both the disembodied spirit world and the human body. Thus the audiences who gathered in the confined theatre of the bedroom or cottage of the possessed changed in their cultural composition, and it would seem that the possessed, mindful of engaging the interest of their audience, exhibited different behaviour in response. Clergymen and doctors were largely uninterested in the popular diagnosis of possession as witchcraft because it was an unsuitable avenue of 'rational' discourse. They sought more to explore and confirm their ideas about the nature and reality of the Devil's intervention in earthly affairs. Questions were put in classical languages not only to detect fraud but also to converse on an overtly intellectual level with devils, who, although the essence of evil, were considered to be far more cultured than the people they possessed. In order to maintain their performance the possessed had to try and respond to this. They would begin to talk less of witches and more and more of devils, usually multiple devils, conversing in different voices, or supposedly communicating in different languages.

A distinctive aspect of possession cases in general was the contagious effect of such vivid displays of supernatural assault. The seventeenth-century examples of mass possession among the nuns at Loudon and elsewhere are the most obvious illustration of this phenomenon, but even in the more staid atmosphere of late eighteenth-century Somerset limited contagious possession could occur. A servant named John Young, of Yatton parish, went to see Lukins during one of his fits, and shortly after claimed that he too was bewitched, and began to perform similar feats, distorting his face and limbs, leaping, collapsing, bellowing, singing, and talking in different voices. A girl of Chelvey who visited Lukins also subsequently exhibited the same symptoms. Samuel Norman was consulted concerning both cases, and proceeded to treat them roughly with powerful emetics. Not surprisingly, perhaps, after several days of vomiting their witchcraft-induced fits ceased.

It was undoubtedly the case that religious adherence to the doctrine of possession and exorcism created an environment which allowed the possessed to expand and develop their performances. It is no coincidence that accounts of diabolic possession during the nineteenth century were more common in predominantly Catholic France than in Anglican England. In France epidemic possessions could still break out, such as the famous case at Morzine, in Haute-Savoie, during the late 1850s and 1860s, when over one hundred women and children were affected.[88] Because exorcism was permitted and widely practised by the Catholic clergy the possessed knew they were likely to become the focus of interest beyond their own social group. In England and Wales cases of classic as opposed to folk possession usually developed in association with Methodist involvement. In this context, Anglican linking of the 'superstitious' similarities between Catholicism and Methodism during the eighteenth century, was not actually too wide of the mark. By exorcising the possessed, Methodists were, indeed, filling a role in popular culture which the pre-Reformation Church had once occupied, and which the Anglican clergy felt uncomfortable with.

In this discussion on possession the reader has probably recognised that some of the phenomena described, primarily those which related to external possession, were classic examples of what are currently attributed to poltergeist activity.[89] The term has been avoided up until now so as to provide some sense of the changing religious and intellectual context within which these phenomena were interpreted. The German term *Poltergeist*, meaning 'noisy or knocking ghost', was first introduced to the English reading public in a large collection of ghostly encounters published by Catherine Crowe in 1848.[90] In her book, Crowe dedicated a chapter to 'The Poltergeists of the Germans, and Possession' in which she suggested that the two phenomena were remarkably similar. However, 'poltergeist' did not really enter the popular vocabulary until the 1920s when the press widely reported the investigations of the psychical researcher, Harry Price.[91] To understand the significance of the introduction of the term into our vocabulary it is necessary to place it in the wider context of the development of spiritualism during the nineteenth century, and its relationship to the religious establishment and popular beliefs.[92]

The doctrine of spiritualism concerned the communication of information from the spirits of the dead to the living via the channel of a gifted medium. Many of the various beliefs, tenets and manifestations that constituted spiritualism were, however, by no means new when the embryonic movement was introduced to Britain from America during the mid-nineteenth century. One of the reasons why spiritualism was embraced so enthusiastically by the educated classes was because communication with spirits had been attested by respected religious and secular sources from the Bible onwards. In 1862, for example, G. Slade Butler, commenting on a documented case of spirit appearance in seventeenth-century Rye, Sussex, remarked that the case was

> interesting at the present time, from the similarity it bears to many of the recent cases recorded in the *Spiritual Magazine* … the fact remains that at various periods of the world's history, from the story of the Witch of Endor down to the record in the *Cornhill Magazine* of Mr. Hume's marvellous feats, it has by a great variety of observers been asserted that appearances of the dead have come to them, or other similar events occurred out of the range of known physical laws.[93]

It was also the case that during the first half of the nineteenth century certain sections of educated society, particularly educated and often radical artisans, had already been attracted to new and rejuvenated forms of pseudo-science such as phrenology and mesmerism. It was often these same people who also embraced spiritualism in their quest to explore those hidden aspects of the human condition untouched by medical and religious orthodoxies.

Spiritualism as a distinct movement was born out of the famous spirit-rappings which plagued the Fox family of Hydesville, New York State, in 1848. As with many possession cases, the focus of the spirit noises were two adolescent girls, who began to converse with the spirit by means of taps on the wainscot. When the family subsequently moved to Rochester the rappings followed them. Instead of the rappings being attributed to witchcraft or devils, however, it was conceived that the girls were actually communicating with the spirits of the dead. The news of this soon spread, and it was not long before people flocked to pass on messages to deceased friends and relatives, and financial gifts to the girls piled up. Before long, many more people suddenly discovered they could communicate with the dead in a similar way. The first wave of spiritualist activity in Britain was triggered by the well-publicised visit in 1852 and 1853 of two American mediums, Mrs Hayden and Mrs Roberts. They brought with them the craze for table-tilting and table-rapping, which were performed as much for drawing-room amusement as for serious experimental communications with the dead. But, as with phrenology and mesmerism, it

was not long before spiritualism became absorbed into a wider philosophical and religious debate about the meaning of existence. Clergymen
from across the religious spectrum embraced spiritualism as an invigorating
affirmation of Christian doctrine on life after death, and also, as with
mesmerism, saw in it a potential avenue of spiritual healing. Officially,
both the Anglican and Catholic hierarchies condemned spiritualism outright, but Anglican clergyman who openly supported spiritualism were
generally left to their own devices.

During the late nineteenth century a new branch of spiritualism called
theosophy developed under the charismatic guidance of Madame Blavatsky,
née Helena Petrovna Hahn, the daughter of a Russian colonel.[94] Her
spiritual philosophy, which was a mix of eastern mysticism, western
spiritualism, and occultism, was divulged in several turgid but influential
books published during the 1870s and 1880s, and proved to be a popular
and enduring movement amongst the middle classes. Theosophy flourished
because it had both a unifying charismatic leader and a governing body
in the Theosophical Society. For the same reason, however, Theosophy
became an easy target for critics, who saw in it similarities with the old
pernicious 'superstitions' of witchcraft and magic. Thus an editorial in *The
Times* complained that the 'astrologer or the witch may be discredited;
but in their place arise the palmist and theosophist to minister to human
credulity'.[95] The central element of theosophy, which led to the equation
with witchcraft, was the belief that there existed in the mountains of
Tibet a brotherhood of holy men named the Mahatmas who had dedicated themselves to a special relationship with the Theosophical Society.
These Mahatmas, the most communicative of whom was Koot Hoomi –
or, as *Punch* satirised him, 'Koot Hoomiboog' – had extra-ordinary occult
powers. They could travel in astral form, transport objects, and could
communicate by instantly producing writing on paper anywhere in the
world. As with spirit communications, however, the Mahatmas, for all
their power and wisdom, usually seem to have been called upon to
perform rather trivial tasks.

Not surprisingly, spiritualism in all its forms had its vociferous critics,
and while some clergymen were seduced by the immediacy and imagery
of spiritualism, a large group of their brethren, again from across the
religious spectrum, saw the spiritualist movement as an unwelcome refor-
mulation of ignorant, pernicious 'superstitions'. The Rev. Edward Hamer
wrote in 1877 that his Welsh parishioners' continued belief in witchcraft
was, unfortunately, nothing remarkable, 'for witchcraft in the present
decade of the nineteenth century is not only rampant among the upper

classes in the United States, but in our own country, as set forth in the history and reception of Spiritualism.'[96] Twenty years later, the Bishop of Salisbury was provoked into expressing his general concern over the influence of spiritualism after a Dorset farmer had openly laughed at him for doubting the existence of witchcraft. The Bishop complained that

> there was a great revival of that form of belief. If they read the spiritualistic journals common enough in some parts of England, and especially in Yorkshire, they would see the revival of these superstitions in gross form … He had no doubt at all that the germs of superstition were still existing among the people of this country, especially in the modern form connected with Theosophy and nervous forms of belief, and he was sometimes afraid they would see a recrudescence of the old miserable business.[97]

Even the Rev. Robert Hawker, with his classical philosophy of an enveloping spirit world, sneered at 'a day when the spasms and raps and bad spelling of a familiar spirit are received with acquiescent belief in polished communities and even in intellectual London'.[98] In the second edition of her large compilation of witchcraft texts from early modern books and pamphlets, the author Elizabeth Lynn Linton stated her hope that the book would help to establish 'wise scepticism and philosophic tolerance', for 'still we have our necromancers, who call up the dead from their graves to talk to us more trivial nonsense that ever they talked while living, and who reconcile us with humanity by showing us how infinitely inferior is spirituality.'[99]

A second group of clergymen, and other devout persons, thought that the mischievousness of spiritualism went far beyond the propagation of popular 'superstition', and was, in fact, acting as a channel for demons rather than the benign spirits of the dead. In 1853 an excited debate was generated by the publication of three pamphlets denouncing the newly introduced craze of table-turning and table-rapping as satanic dabblings. The first two to be published, *Table-Moving Tested, and proved to be the result of Satanic Agency* (London, 1853) and *Table-Turning, the Devil's Modern Master-piece. Being the result of a course of experiments* (London, 1853) were written by the Rev. Nathaniel Stedman Godfrey, vicar of Wortley, Leeds. The third, *Table-Talking; Disclosures of Satanic Wonders & Prophetic Signs* (Bath, 1853), by the Rev. E. Gillson, curate of Lyncombe and Widcombe, Bath, was written to corroborate Godfrey's findings.[100] Both men's convictions were confirmed by attending 'table-talking' sessions where the satanic origin of such communications was revealed. Gillson, for example, organised a session with some friends and another family 'who had been accustomed to table-turning as a mere amusement'. It was not long before a spirit began to communicate by lifting up the table leg and rapping. Gillson asked, 'Are you a departed spirit?' The answer was yes. He then asked the following questions in succession:

Are you a fallen angel?   No answer, which indicated a negative.
Do you know the fallen angels?   Yes.
Are they more powerful than you?   Yes.
Are you obliged to obey them?   Yes.
Do you like their society?   Yes.
Do you know Satan?   Yes.
Is he the Prince of Devils?   Yes.[101]

In a further set of questions Gillman attempted to ascertain the where-abouts of Satan's earthly headquarters – with predictable results:

Are they in Engand?   There was a slight movement.
Are they in France?   A violent movement.
Are they in Spain?   Similar agitation.
Are they at Rome?   The table literally seemed frantic.[102]

The alarming information was also communicated that there was a veritable nest of devils in Bath itself. Gillson recounted that he had already heard of one case of insanity arising from table-turning, and although he allowed it might have been caused by overexcitement, he was more inclined to consider it a case of diabolic possession. One of the tests that Godfrey and Gillson tried in order to confirm their suspicions of satanic agency was the placing of a Bible on the table. This was similar in essence to attempts by seventeenth-century clergymen to confirm the guilt of a witch by trying to make him or her recite the Lord's Prayer or other Biblical passages. Both Godfrey and Gillson found that the table ceased to move as soon as the Bible was laid on it. Other books of a similar weight and size did not have the same effect. This was conclusive proof that the communicating spirits were evil, for they could not stand the presence of the word of God, just as seventeenth-century witches could not utter Holy Scripture. Other spirits were also contacted who acknowledged they were sent by Satan himself, and one actually admitted he had been charged with deceiving and ensnaring Gillson and his friends. 'I left the scene more deeply solemnised than I can express', wrote Gillson; 'I always knew that we were surrounded by innumerable devils, because I believe it on the testimony of the divine word. But to have their agency thus sensibly manifested, I confess was overpowering.'[103]

For Gillson the sudden and widespread communication of satanic spirits through the medium of table-talking in the middle of the nineteenth century was a prophetic sign of an imminent spiritual struggle. Satan's reign was drawing to a close, and, as predicted in the Bible, he would make one last effort to ensnare the people. Satan, it would seem, hoped to achieve his aim through the medium of the Catholic Church and Spiritualism. It was the duty of the likes of Godfrey and Gillson to sound the alarm regarding this final assault. Indeed, seven years before spiritualism was brought to Britain, Gillson had published a similar warning against the return of Catholicism entitled *The Relapsed Demoniac*.[104]

Such alarmist talk of devils stalking the land inevitably provoked an immediate response from both laymen and senior clergymen, such as Francis Close, the Dean of Carlisle.[105] Despite such eminent rebuttals, accusations of demonism continued to be directed at spiritualists over the next few decades. In 1871, for example, the Rev. John Jones, a Liverpool Congregationalist minister, published a sermon entitled *Spiritualism the Work of Demons*, in which he warned that through the vehicle of spiritualism Satan was ensnaring the people, and that they must wake up to the imminent danger.[106] In response, the Christian Socialist and spiritualist Thomas Shorter published a riposte in pamphlet form under the pseudonym Thomas Brevior, in which he observed that while many scientists were impressed by the evidence of spiritualism, 'when the same facts are brought home to a clergyman or Congregationalist Minister, he in general is equally confident that it must all be the work of the devil or of evil spirits.'[107]

Towards the end of the nineteenth century the public discourse concerning diabolism and evil spirits continued in a vein not far removed from that of the seventeenth century. Possession was by no means considered a relic of the past. As the Rev. Henry Parr, curate of Tunbridge parish church, affirmed in a general sermon upon satanic agency, 'possession did not cease with the time of Christ ... I have yet to learn that it has ceased to this day.'[108] Parr was not responding to the growth of spiritualism like many of his fellow clergymen, but rather wanted to convince his parishioners that there was a variety of other insidious ways, such as propagating disease and causing storms, in which the Devil continued to plague the human world. The witch was undoubtedly an absent if not forgotten figure of satanic agency in all these discussions, though several critics of spiritualism did condemn the movement as a modern form of witchcraft. Thus, in a sermon attacking spiritualism, preached at St Paul's Cathedral, the Rev. J. A. V. Magee, vicar of St Mark's, Hamilton Square, reminded those present: 'we denounce this witchcraft, not because there is nothing in it, but because there is something in it.'[109] It would be rather remiss not to mention here that the popular witchcraft historian and fervent Catholic, Montague Summers, wrote in the 1920s that spiritualism was but 'Old Witchcraft'. In saying this, Summers was not criticising spiritualism for being mere superstitious nonsense; he actually believed that witches had been guilty of the devilish crimes of which they were accused. Witches were the earthly vassals of Satan, and there was nothing in spiritualism which could not be found in the records of the witch-trials.[110]

The phenomena associated more specifically with poltergeists remained somewhat problematic for the critics of spiritualism. For those who accused the spiritualists of dabbling with the Devil, the capricious and sometimes malicious poltergeist was proof of the diabolic nature of the spirits that mediums were meddling with. However, even some of those who saw in spiritualism mere pernicious 'superstition' were less sceptical and mocking when confronted with the more puzzling poltergeist-type manifestations. It was well known that this type of spirit appearance had a long-attested history and was independent of the spirit manifestations 'conjured' up by mediums. Despite the fact that some cases, such as the Cock Lane Ghost, had been exposed as frauds, the weight of history favoured more serious contemplation of the phenomenon. While for the sceptics, parlour-room table-rapping, ectoplasm, and the mindless antics some spirits were requested to perform were considered infantile and ludicrous, poltergeists presented something less explicable, something more unsettling.

The various strands of thought on the nature of poltergeist manifestations – popular, medical, theological and spiritual – were brought together in a case of spirit disturbance that occurred in 1889 at the cottage of a labourer named Hewlett who lived near Homington, a village a few miles south of Salisbury. It may come as no surprise to find that Hewlett was a Primitive Methodist preacher, and prayer meetings were regularly held at his home. The events which unfolded, and the interest they attracted amongst all sections of society from the local area, were similar in many respects to the Lamb Inn affair nearly 130 years earlier. The obvious difference between the two cases was that by the late nineteenth century spiritualism and psychical research had entered the discourse concerning spirits.[111]

The focus of the manifestations was Hewlett's nine-year-old daughter, Lydia, who seems to have been ailing for some time, and had been attended in her ill health by Dr James Kelland of Salisbury. According to Lydia, just before her condition became a lot worse she had caught a gypsy stealing onions from a neighbour's garden, and the gypsy had threatened that she would suffer for it if she told anyone. This undoubtedly seriously frightened the young girl. It was not long after this that she entered into a semi-conscious state, and rapping noises began to occur in her bedroom. Lydia's parents and many of their neighbours believed that the gypsy had bewitched their daughter. Not surprisingly, these events caused quite a stir in the village, and it was not long before the news spread to Salisbury where it excited interest in educated circles. It is important to make clear, though, that it was not the fact that the girl was thought to be bewitched that generated so much middle-class interest, but the nature of the manifestations, which conformed to the tradition of spirit communication. Among the visitors to the Hewlett's house were Canon Kingsbury, one Colonel Pepper, the Rev. J. Harper, who was pastor of the Salisbury Primitive Methodists, other unspecified clergy-men, two police superintendents, and many other inquisitive people from Salisbury.

The most detailed account of the scene in the Hewlett's cottage comes from a *Salisbury Times* newspaper correspondent who accompanied the Rev. Harper and his son on a visit to the Hewletts. On the road to Homington they fell in with a villager who told them that his father had recently also seen a strange apparition. He, however, believed his father had merely seen a flash caused by the erection of a marquee near by. On arrival at this man's cottage, his mother came out and joined the conver-sation concerning the Hewletts: '"It's been on all day," said she, in tones which certainly did not indicate that she belonged to the unbelievers anent witchcraft.' The party was also given an account of how a cunning man had countered the ill-will of another gypsy. It would seem that the bewitchment of Lydia had triggered the collective memory of Homington, with previous encounters with the supernatural being circulated around the village.

The party of three continued on their journey to the Hewlett's cottage, which was situated in an isolated spot some distance from the main village. On the hill up to the cottage they met the Rev. Canon Kingsbury and another clergyman, who had just been with the Hewletts. 'It's quieter now', said Kingsbury, and went on to inform them that he had put a number of questions to the rapping spirit which had been answered. Canon Kingsbury, it was evident, 'was not inclined to the belief that there was any shamming about the affair, but the gentleman who accom-panied him was not, it appeared, a very firm believer in spiritualism'. Not far from the cottage, the party met another visitor, who informed them in a confidential tone that 'the cause of the mysterious knockings was known. The girl was bewitched'. On entering the cottage they found that the place was crowded, mostly with Salisbury folk. As another account records, one young man among them, named Ernest Moody, was engaged all afternoon in putting questions to the spirit, and he had written down a list of all the questions and answers, which was afterwards handed to Superintendent Stephens. According to the knocks given in answer by the spirit, it had been discovered that the gypsy had stolen nine onions, she was dark, wore her hair in a plait, and was married with seven children. She was 4ft 8in in height, and was twenty-eight years of age. It was also communicated that her name was Smith, that she was a witch, and had 'power from the devil'. She was said to be at Breamore, some six or seven miles away, and the spirit instructed that the policemen of Coombe, Charlton and Breamore should be sent in search of the gypsy, and that they should start at three o'clock on Sunday morning, and travel via Charlton. Rev. Harper suggested that prayer should be offered in the hope of banishing the spirit, and a group of those present engaged in earnest supplication. Snatches of hymns were sung, one of which contained the words 'Angels and men before Thee fall, And devils fear and fly'. This induced a double-rapping sound, whereupon Harper uttered some words, and the knockings grew fainter. However, the arrival of some new visitors disturbed the calm and the raps began again with renewed vigour.

A discussion took place among the visitors concerning the apprehension of the gypsy: 'that it might be rather awkward to apprehend a woman on a charge of witchcraft was realised by some, at any rate, but there was the question whether she could not be tackled for stealing onions'. The police constable present, who was deeply impressed by the rappings, promised to do the best he could, but said he had to obtain a warrant first since he was not in close pursuit. As instructed by the spirit, on Sunday morning a search party was duly organised. However, they did not set off at three o'clock, and did not go via Charlton as directed. At Godshill, near Breamore, they came across an encampment of around one hundred gypsies and were told that a woman named Smith, resembling the description given by the spirit, had set off for the New Forest several hours before. The search was, therefore, called off. The failure of the search was attributed by some to the fact that the spirit's instructions had not been adhered to correctly. The manifestations continued for another nine days until Lydia, who looked very ill, was brought to the Salisbury Infirmary, where the knockings finally ceased for good. Afterwards she spent some time at the Herbert Convalescent Home.

The fairly wide newspaper coverage of the case attracted the interest of spiritualists and psychic investigators, who expressed their views in an exchange of letters to *The Salisbury and Winchester Journal.* A Mr Gillingham of Chard, Somerset, believed the case proved that humans were 'on the threshold of mighty discoveries ... We seem to be ascending from the gross into the more sensitive and sympathetic.' He went on to suggest that 'In psychical natures like Lydia Hewlett's the nerve sphere ... becomes a media for all kinds of extraordinary phenomena beyond the range of human observation, and yet explicable on higher natural lines verging on the supernatural, without having recourse to witchcraft or superstition.'[112] In the same issue a letter from an anonymous member of the Society for Psychical Research stated that, from his own personal inquiries into the case, he believed that no fraud had taken place, and outlined all the recent research on similar manifestations. In response to this letter, James Kelland, the doctor who had been attending Lydia, felt it necessary to set out the medical facts of her condition. Kelland believed that her physical state was an ordinary attack of catalepsy, which was not uncommon in girls and young women. As to the rappings, Kelland asserted that they were either the result of a cruel hoax by unknown persons, or were noises caused by rats in the walls or under the floor. Kelland then outlined the natural environment which had been conducive to Lydia's condition: 'Poor Lydia Hewlett, living in a lonely cottage near those great black yews, in bad health, and exhausted by a long daily tramp to Coombe school was just the person to make a good "medium," or a good anything else which required weak nerves as the essential element of success.' 'All medical men', he went on to observe, 'have seen what strange things hysterical children will do. I do not call them impostors, but one peculiarity is common to all, they will not play to empty benches.' In his concluding sentence, Kelland, probably referring to Canon Kingsbury, wrote, 'I refrain from saying anything more about it lest I should hurt the feelings of certain persons whose conduct in this matter has not been marked by a great amount of common sense.'[113] This flurry of letters to the newspaper seems to have marked the end of the whole affair, and the lives of the Hewletts and the people of Homington returned to relative normality.

The Homington affair was by no means the only example of supposed spirit or poltergeist manifestations among the lower classes during the late nineteenth century. Several years later, a similar case occurred in the neighbouring county of Dorset, concerning which the *Somerset County Herald* reported that, 'there are suggestions that the causes are associated with spiritualism; and of course there are people who believe that witchcraft is at the bottom of all these strange experiences'.[114] But the Homington affair was undoubtedly one of the last in which popular conceptions of witchcraft were still prominent, and the shape of the informal discourse surrounding the phenomena followed, to some degree, that of the eighteenth century. From the mid-1880s onwards, particularly with the founding of the Society for Psychical Research in 1882, poltergeist phenomena became more the concern of the enthusiastic and growing band of psychical researchers, and less the focus of religious interest. As the popular belief in witchcraft declined, so the interpretation of poltergeist activity in terms of bewitchment became obsolete. Similar phenomena continued to be recorded, usually focused around adolescent girls, as they had always been. However, both popular and educated discourse on the subject gradually changed from one based on traditional folk beliefs and Christian theology, to the present-day media-dominated one concerning fringe scientific concepts such as parapsychology and psychokinesis. Religious involvement never entirely ceased, though, and even in the present day exorcisms are still occasionally performed in houses purportedly plagued by poltergeists.

Whether one believes in poltergeists or attributes their activities to adolescent attention-seeking, no one can fail to recognise the striking uniformity of the associated phenomena over the centuries. We are looking at a tradition of supernatural expression that was well known to all social groups, the knowledge of which must have been handed down through both oral and printed channels of transmission. While much of educated society had extricated itself from the popular world of witches and witchcraft, a two-way dialogue was still maintained between upper and lower levels of society concerning evil spirits. In cases of possession two worlds met – not just the human and spirit worlds, but the worlds of folk and theological supernatural tradition. Belief in spirit intervention remained widespread; only the way it was interpreted changed over the centuries.

Witchcraft and insanity

Not unconnected with the interest generated in pseudo-sciences and psychical research during the nineteenth century was the growth of psychology as a serious branch of medicine. Important developments in the diagnosis and classification of mental illness came to influence the medical and legal discourse concerning the popular belief in witchcraft. It was French psychology, in particular, that turned its attention to analysing the belief in witchcraft and demonic possession from a psychiatric point of view. Some of the most famous medical psychologists of the nineteenth century, such as Esquirol, Macario and Charcot, sought to explain the marked physical manifestations of such 'irrational' beliefs as forms of hysteria, neurosis or monomania.[115] In contrast, British medical psychology, which was heavily influenced by the French, was far less interested in interpreting popular manifestations of belief in witchcraft and magic.[116] The political and religious conditions that fostered such interest in France were certainly not present in England and Wales, and cases of the extreme behaviour exhibited by the possessed, which particularly fascinated medical psychologists, were far less common.

Mental asylums and hospitals provided the French psychologists with relevant case studies of possession and bewitchment, and British asylums also contained inmates whose illness found expression at least partly in notions of witchcraft or possession. The Rev. Henry Parr was of the opinion that among the 'unhappy inmates' of English asylums there were those who, although a puzzle to the physicians, were undoubtedly possessed by devils.[117] There were certainly those who were mentally disturbed by the dread of bewitchment. In 1871, for example, James Carslake, a shoemaker of Sidbury, Devon, was admitted to a lunatic asylum after he was found hanging from a tree. He believed his daughter had been bewitched by her mother, and unable to cope with this knowledge he tried to kill himself. In the same county twenty-two years later, a labourer's wife residing in a village near Ashburton became depressed and suicidal, and so an application was made for her to be sent to the county asylum. She told a magistrate who visited her that her husband and neighbours had bewitched her by means of a looking-glass, and thereby taken away her power of will.[118] In 1905 several members of John Markey's family of May Hill, Gloucestershire, who considered themselves plagued by witchcraft, were pronounced insane. One of Markey's daughters, Mrs Barnes, was removed to Gloucester asylum, and her daughter was taken to Newent Workhouse Hospital. At the same time, John's second son, George, became deranged and it took three men to hold him down. He had recently married his second wife, the first having died in an asylum. The night he became deranged, George ran off without his boots, and was arrested shortly after on suspicion of being a wandering lunatic. He was examined by Dr Carleton of Newnham and pronounced insane. During this time he continually referred to the 'witchery' that he blamed for all the trouble that had come upon the family.[119] It is quite likely that other such sad cases could have been found among the inmates of asylums up and down the country.

It was assumed by some educated commentators that the adherence to such a strong belief in witchcraft was inherently a sign of insanity. The magistrates who heard the case of Ann Davis, who had scratched a woman she accused of bewitching her, suggested that perhaps 'the lunatic asylum was the best place for a person entertaining such dangerous notions'.[120] The nineteenth-century psychiatric category of 'monomania', coined by Esquirol, and defined as an 'insanity with one particular delusion and obsessive preoccupation', was potentially applicable to many people who believed themselves bewitched. The term was, in fact, applied to one witch-believer, John Bird, who was tried at the Dorset assizes in 1871 for severely beating an 85-year-old woman named Charlotte Griffin.[121] Bird, a farmer, twenty-three years of age, believed Griffin was bewitching him by 'hag-riding' him at night. One day Bird confronted Griffin about her evil activities, words were exchanged, and Bird struck her repeatedly with a stick. Realising the serious consequences of his actions, he fled to Liverpool, where he was subsequently arrested. Bird's defence lawyer, Mr Collins, argued that his client was 'labouring under a delusion', and he called Mr Good, surgeon of the Dorset county prison, who described Bird as a 'simple, weak-minded, monomaniac'. Judge Brett then asked Good whether Bird's 'being bewitched as he thought is the reason of your thinking him a monomaniac?' To which Good replied in the affirmative. Judge Brett was not at all impressed with the medical evidence, and in summing up the case he rejected the claim that Bird was a monomaniac. The available evidence would suggest that Brett was right to do so. If all those who considered themselves bewitched at the time were to be diagnosed insane, then hospitals and asylums would have been bursting at the seams with inmates.

Many perfectly sane people believed themselves bewitched, and quite a few, like John Bird, went and assaulted those they accused of being witches. That is not to say that expressions of belief in witchcraft were never indicative of mental illness though. A more likely monomaniac was James Haywood, of Long Compton, Warwickshire, who in 1875 killed an old woman called Ann Tennant with a pitchfork because he believed she had bewitched him. Haywood was tried at the Warwick winter assizes, where it was heard in evidence that he had at one time received a head injury when a bough fell on him, and that he was looked on in the village 'not much otherwise than as a madman'. In his defence Haywood made the not improbable plea that he had not meant to kill Tennant, but only wished to draw her blood in order to break her power over him. However, at another time he told Mr Anderson, the governor of the gaol in which he was imprisoned, that 'it was his duty to kill her', and that there were still fifteen or sixteen witches left in the village who were harming him. Anderson stated that Haywood's conduct was that of an eccentric man, although he was shrewd in some matters: 'He was a quiet, inoffensive man, except on the subject of witchcraft.' He even offered Anderson a sovereign to let him out of gaol. Dr Parvey of the county lunatic asylum, and Mr Winn, surgeon of the gaol, considered that Haywood was of an imbecile and unsound mind, and said they would sign a certificate to that effect after the trial. They further believed he would never be cured of his insanity. Judge Bramwell informed the jury that 'the prisoner was not suffering under a delusion of a character to justify him in killing the woman, but they must consider the medical testimony in the case as to the prisoner's sanity.' He said it would be 'a shocking thing that this miserable creature should be put to death, and if they found the prisoner guilty they would return a verdict very few people would regret.' The jury were sympathetic and acquitted Haywood on the ground of insanity.[122]

Another area of medical and legal debate over the link between insanity and the belief in witchcraft derived from disputes arising from contested wills and deeds. In 1886 the Probate Division of the High Court of Justice heard the case of *Westren* v. *Westren*. The dispute concerned the will of the late Thomas Westren, a retired farmer of Barnstaple, Devon, who left all his property, valued at £700, to his widow, Mary Thomas. Westren's children contested the will on two accounts. First, that Mary, whom he had married only a couple of years before his death, had exercised undue influence. Second, because Thomas claimed his own daughters had bewitched him, and so was obviously of unsound mind when he altered his will. After some debate, Mr Inderwick QC withdrew the charge of undue influence, and relied on the statement that the deceased considered himself 'witched'. Witnesses were then called to testify that Thomas Westren was a believer in witchcraft. However, other witnesses also testified to the deceased's competency in his business matters, which effectively dispelled the idea that the belief in witchcraft rendered him incompetent. Both Westren's doctor, Dr Harper, and his solicitor, Mr Bencraft, said they could give undeniable proof of his sound mental disposition. A compromise was recommended, and Sir James Hannen, presiding over the case, concluded that 'it was very difficult to say that to believe in witchcraft meant insanity'.[123] Another Devonshire case arose out of a disputed deed. It was deposed in the Court of Chancery, in June 1893, that the person who executed the deed had said the Devil was after her, and on one particular occasion when tormented by the Devil she desired that she be locked in her room. The doctor who attended her stated in court that 'she was as competent as any person of her age to execute a deed.' He went on to observe that it was not uncommon with people in Devonshire to think they had evil spirits in them when they were ill.[124]

One of the most unusual cases ever to be heard in the Probate Division concerned the contested will of Morgan Jones, a gentleman of Chapel Street, Rhydyfro, a small village north of Swansea. He died on 27 May 1903, leaving his property to a variety of charities including Dr Barnardo's, the National Society for the Prevention of Cruelty to Children, and the Royal Society for the Prevention of Cruelty to Animals. The will was dated 13 August 1902, and was contested by several relatives on the grounds that it was not executed properly, and the deceased was of un-sound mind at the time. Evidence for the latter plea was based on the following eleven alleged delusions:

> (1) That the slates on his father's house were red and would bewitch him; (2) that people were purposely disturbing him by making a noise in the house; (3) that he had been bewitched by being tied round with chains by some tailors who had been working with his father when he was a boy; (4) that the front door was bewitched; (5) that he was very poor; (6) that he had been bewitched by Harris, Cwrtycadno; (7) that some stone houses and places were bewitched; (8) that the front door of Llanquicke [Llangiwg] Parish Church was bewitched; (9) that he could foretell any one's future by astrology, by examining the shape of their head; (10) that he was surrounded by thieves and cheats, and that he was always overcharged by tradesmen; (11) that he was accused of sheep-stealing.

As further proof of Jones's insanity it was heard that in one of his almanacs, found after his death, he had written 'Morgan Jones, Esq., has been a slave, a nigger, and is working in the gutter, and bewitched, indeed, I am sure, no doubt.' One of Jones's former landladies, Mrs G. Williams, was also called to tell of his unsoundness of mind. By way of evidence she recalled that Jones 'would eat a bloater with apple-pie. He also ate bloater and eggs together, and when she told him to eat them separately he said he would run a knife through her.' Not surprisingly, this rather absurd piece of evidence provoked laughter in the court.

Morgan certainly seems to have been an eccentric character who had had a traumatic and troubled childhood, having been sent to a home for imbeciles in Bristol by his father. But the beliefs he held concerning witchcraft were definitely not a symptom of insanity; they were quite reasonable beliefs in the context of Welsh rural society at the time. Several respectable professional men also attested in court that Jones seemed quite sane. Richard Rees, from the Capital and Counties Bank, Swansea, gave evidence as to Jones's capacity in business matters. His solicitor, Mr Lloyd, was of the opinion that the deceased's intellect was good. Dr Griffiths Griffiths, a magistrate of Pontardawe, said he had known Jones for many years and had always considered him pretty intelligent. The Rev. Rees Rees, one of the executors, described Jones as an eccentric man, but he had heard him discuss agriculture, astrology, theology, and other subjects quite rationally. The presiding judge considered that there was not enough evidence to suggest that Jones was insane, and pronounced for the will.[125]

It must be stressed that, as far as I know, no one was ever incarcerated for expressing a zealous or even obsessional belief in witchcraft. Although the occasional legal attempt was made to classify witch-believers as insane, with the exception of James Haywood they largely failed, and normal sentencing was passed. It was only when that belief manifested itself in certain clinically recognised forms of extreme mental illness, such as suicidal tendencies or violent derangement, that they were taken away to asylums and hospitals because they were considered a danger to themselves or others.

As modern psychiatric studies have found, non-delusional fixed beliefs concerning witchcraft can be distinguished from psychosis expressed in terms of witchcraft.[126] The problem in the nineteenth century was that psychiatric knowledge was not sophisticated enough to be able always to tell the difference. Those medical men who were often called to pronounce on the mental state of prisoners at criminal trials involving witchcraft worked in urban environments, and probably knew little of the culture in which the crimes took place. In rural areas the belief in witchcraft was widespread and the threat of witchcraft taken very seriously. The anxiety and suffering of those under the impression they were bewitched was quite understandable, even if their actions seem strange to us. It is noticeable that in the probate disputes the doctors who were called to give evidence were those who knew the people concerned and the culture in which they lived, and were able, therefore, make the distinction between monomania and normal fixed beliefs concerning witchcraft. Many of those who considered themselves bewitched may have been obsessive in their belief, but everyone has their own obsessions, doctors and psychologists included.

Reforming the popular mind

Up until the mid-eighteenth century the Church authorities had sought to guide public morality and chastise moral and religious transgressors, not only from the pulpit but also through the ecclesiastical courts. As part of this process, during the sixteenth and seventeenth centuries the courts dealt with numerous cases involving popular magic and slanderous accusations of witchcraft. By the eighteenth century, though, the range of business brought before the Church courts had dwindled significantly. This process of limitation began in earnest in the 1720s when the Church stopped presenting Catholics before the courts, and in subsequent years the courts also stopped dealing with matters such as Nonconformist offences, clandestine marriages, blasphemy, the licensing of professionals, and defamation. As recent research has shown, by the mid-eighteenth century the Church courts' business was overwhelmingly concerned with the sexual transgressions of its members, and little else.[127]

As defamation presentments before the church courts declined considerably during the latter half of the seventeenth century, so those involving witchcraft obviously became infrequent as well, as did cases involving other magical practices such as divination and charming. One rare late case was that of a woman of Winwick, Cheshire, who, in 1725, was presented 'for occasioning Several young people on ye Lords day to come to her under a pretence of telling them their Fortunes'. Jan Albers, commenting on this case, observed that 'the thrust of the proceeding seems to have been that the fortune telling was done on the Sabbath, rather than that it was done at all', which suggests that the church felt more concerned with religious laxity than the resort to popular magic at the time.[128] Most of the handful of relevant cases brought before the courts during the first half of the eighteenth century came from the more peripheral areas of the country. At the Llandaff Consistory Court, in 1722, for example, Mary Rees of Peterstone-super-Ely, Glamorgan, was alleged to have described her neighbour, Catherine Nicholls, as 'Y slwtt, y slwtt frowt, y witch goch, y witch bengoch, yr whore buttain bengoch' ('The slut, the nasty slut, the red witch, the red-headed witch, the red-headed whore and harlot).[129] Nowhere were the ecclesiastical courts more active and powerful in the eighteenth century than on the Isle of Man.[130] The spiritual courts there, like the Scottish kirk sessions, continued to deal with a wide range of social transgressions, including witchcraft and magic, well into the eighteenth century.

Although in the early eighteenth century the Church was prepared to act on request, or occasionally on its own behalf, against magical practices and expressions of belief in witchcraft, on the whole there seems to have been remarkably little ecclesiastical activity to reform those who held such beliefs. However, there were a few expressions of concern as to

the corrupting effects of the popular resort to magic, like that uttered by
Bishop Wilson during the perambulation of the Manx parishes in 1741:

> Many complaints have been brought into our courts against people using fool-
> ish and wicked charms and arts, either to injure their neighbour in his goods,
> or to transfer them to themselves, to the great dishonour of God, who alone
> can increase the fruits of the earth to our comfort, or withhold them for our
> sins; and, indeed, it is for want of true faith in God's power and goodness that
> makes men afraid of what such wretched instruments of Satan can do.[131]

But as the ecclesiastical jurisdiction over public morality and spirituality
waned, a vacuum was left behind that secular organisations such as the
Society for the Promotion of Christian Knowledge and the Societies for
Reformation of Manners attempted to fill, but with hardly the same level
of organisation and success.[132]

After a long period in which the Church expressed little public concern over the tight grip magic still held over many of its members, in the
first two decades of the nineteenth century several Anglican ministers,
from quite different parts of the country, were so shocked by the strength
of magical beliefs among their flocks that they felt it necessary to speak
out publicly and condemn such 'superstitions' in the strongest terms. In
1808, the Rev. Isaac Nicholson (1780–1839), curate of Great Paxton, in
the old county of Huntingdonshire, was moved to publish a sermon on
the subject after a local woman was viciously attacked for being a witch.
He began by stating that

> The better informed part of the community may believe that the doctrine of
> witchcraft has been long exploded, and that it does not, in this enlightened age,
> disgrace even the lowest orders of the people of England; but the following
> statement of facts, will convince them of their mistake, and, allowing for the
> difference of science and civilisation, will shew that Great Paxton, in the same
> county, is more than upon a level with Warboys for ignorance, credulity, and
> barbarity.[133]

Nicholson called the belief in witchcraft a 'stupendous monument of
national weakness, ignorance, and disgrace', and evidently considered that
such beliefs could no longer be tolerated.[134] In the same year, the Rev.
Thomas Hawkins delivered two sermons at Warley church, near Halifax,
after several recent cases of witchcraft had 'made a considerable stir in the
whole neighbourhood'. Three parishioners, a child about ten or twelve
years old, a middle-aged man, and an elderly man, all suffering from
debilitating illness, had consulted a cunning-man who had told them that
they were bewitched, and subsequently applied various magical charms

and remedies to cure them. In the preface to his sermons, Hawkins admitted that 'witchcraft is that at which heretofore I generally smiled with contempt, but shall henceforth treat it with serious severity and decided opposition.'[135] Hawkins delivered his condemnatory sermons, full of the old Biblical arguments against such practices, and also publicly admonished the guilty members of the congregation. In the face of this clerical censure, those involved continued to express an obstinate adherence to their belief in witchcraft and magic, and as a result the highly unusual step was taken to suspend them from the 'Christian privilege of regular communion' – a step which Hawkins confessed was a 'matter of grief and trial' to himself and friends.[136]

Hawkins's previous contemptuous connivance at the belief in witchcraft, and the activities of cunning-folk, was symptomatic of the eighteenth-century elite's attitude towards popular magical beliefs. The 'superstitious' state of the lower orders was viewed as something regrettable but not threatening. Only when such popular beliefs were thought to impinge on the interests of church or state were they considered seriously; and in Hawkins case it was only when he recognised a perceived threat to his own religious interests that he became concerned. Like a number of his contemporaries, Hawkins did not deny the reality of witchcraft, but seemed unsure as to whether it still existed, and preferred to sidestep the question. 'Whether there may be any *real* witches now, or only *pretenders*', he remarked, 'is a matter I will not at this time discuss'. But what was certain was that God abominated such persons and practices. According to Hawkins, cunning-men, wizards, witches and fortune-tellers offended 'against the letter of the law and the spirit of the gospel. They lay a stumbling-block before their brethren. They bring religion into reproach … Using their singular prescriptions, submitting to their decisions, and complying with their orders and directions, is tacit obedience to Satan, and to put on their charms (however concealed) is to wear, at least, a part of the devil's livery.'[137]

Nine years after the events at Warley, the rector of Little Petherick, Cornwall, the Rev. Richard Lyne, also felt it necessary to castigate his flock for resorting to charms after one of his services was interrupted by a woman suffering from fits. It subsequently transpired that she was in possession of a charm against such attacks. Lyne felt himself called upon, 'as the Minister of God and his Watchman' in that parish, to show 'that to work or use charms of any kind, for the relief of bodily or mental disorders, for recovery of stolen goods, or for any other purpose, is an abominable thing, contrary to the gospel of Christ, and therefore injurious to true religion'.[138] Lyne cited three arguments with which people defended the use of charms: namely, that 'only scripture words, or only very good words, are used in their charms'; 'that many cures have followed upon the use of them'; and that many people had 'died, or still remain uncured, who would not be charmed'. But Lyne dismissed such 'ancient and inveterate excuses', and was of the opinion that, if cures were wrought by charms, 'it must be by agency of the Devil, with a curse, and not a blessing'.

In 1814, the Rev. William Vowles, of Tiverton, Devon, was driven by local events to decry from the pulpit the 'abominable and prolific brood of vices [which] has been hatched and fostered by this foul bird of night, POPULAR CREDULITY!'[139] His sermon was occasioned by the sensational case of Ann Taylor, the daughter of a respectable yeoman from the parish of Tiverton, who lay six days in a state of insensibility, during which she had a dream that abounded with 'excessive absurdities' and was interspersed 'with a few pious reflections', and that was subsequently printed and circulated widely. Like his fellow clergymen above, Vowles was shocked at the level of 'superstition' which apparently he had hitherto been rather unaware:

> in the nineteenth century we see professing Christians, nay *Protestants* clinging to the relics of heathenism. We had imagined that the thick shades of superstition which had clouded the world for ages, were now well nigh dispersed by the speeding effulgence of the gospel … it is distressing to learn our mistake … the tendency of this pagan notion is dangerous; its influence is truly baleful, and calls for the strongest reprobation … it is, indeed, a hydra, leading in its train disease, fatuity and madness, and when it has seized on a mind constitutionally gloomy, not unfrequently has it reduced the miserable sufferer to a premature death.[140]

There was even a worry in some quarters that if no attempts were made to suppress such 'pagan notions', then there was a danger of a popular relapse into idolatry and paganism. When in 1821 the government finally got around to repealing the Irish Witchcraft Statute of 1587, an anonymous writer, obviously an anti-papist of evangelical persuasion, wrote a 'solemn appeal' for the statute to remain, since, according to the writer, 'the practice of Witchcraft is the certain mark of people abandoned to confusion, and popular tumult; and the permission of it in a government, the positive mark of infatuation'.[141] The author spoke of his deficiency,

> in that CHARITY 'which thinketh no evil of SATAN'.- I have an *unfashionable* belief in HIS existence and influence, as 'THE SPIRIT THAT NOW WORKETH IN THE CHLDREN OF DISOBEDIENCE' … the word of God, which cannot lie,

declares witchcraft to be one of his instruments of delusion ... [and] as the *divine* law punished that sin with death, and nations addicted to it, with destruction; such offences, I must deem not unworthy the notice of *human* legislators.[142]

The conclusion to *ANTIPAS* warned that a 'Papal relapse may terminate in a Pagan crisis: it is not so remote as some imagine.'

The clergy's attempt to show their 'superstitious' flock the errors of their 'credulous' ways seems to have been marked by a singular lack of success. We have already seen what came of Thomas Hawkins's attempt to make his witch-believing parishioners see the folly of their conduct, and Isaac Nicholson experienced a similar failure. One Sunday, just before church, the accused witch, Ann Izzard, sought out Nicholson and 'In tears, and greatly agitated, she told me, her neighbours pretended they had discovered by means of certain charms that she was a witch ... she said, they threatened to punish her, abused her children, and frightened her so much that she frequently dropped on the ground in fainting fits.' She wanted Nicholson's protection, and to his credit, after the day's sermon, he addressed the congregation upon the subject. He 'pointed out the folly of their opinions', and 'tried to persuade them, that, although they might be weak enough to suppose there was no harm in laying violent hands on a woman, they madly called a witch, yet the laws of their country would view their conduct in a very different light'. But all his words were to no avail: 'argument, explanation, and remonstrance, were in vain; the mania had taken full possession of them, and was only to be cured, or restrained by the powerful arm of the law.'[143] Not long after, Izzard was badly assaulted, and nine people were subsequently prosecuted and sent to gaol for a month.

Nicholson's own reputation among his parishioners suffered from his act of intervention on Izzard's behalf: 'I have been repeatedly told, that eleven people out of twelve in this neighbourhood, condemn me for taking Ann Izzard into my house.' He also recorded the following conversation between two old men, one a parishioner and the other from St Neots, which took place the day after he preached his sermon. He simply calls them Abraham and Richard, but in a copy of the sermon held in Cambridge University Library a hand-written note in nineteenth-century style refers to 'Abraham Barber' and 'Pedlar Paxton'.

ABRAHAM. (of Little Paxton.) I say, Richard, you was at our church yesterday. (Richard was very unwilling to own it.) I say, Richard, I know you was there.
RICHARD. Well, I was − what of that?

ABRAHAM. I knew what the parson intended to be at – I knew he would tell a parcel of confounded lies, so I would not go.

RICHARD. You are right – he did it rarely – I never heard a man tell such lies in all my life – but *we let him go on!*

According to Nicholson, the conversation was not deficient in 'disgusting oaths and curses'.[144] Several decades later, the Rev. William Keary, vicar of Nunnington, North Yorkshire, similarly aroused the wrath of his parishioners when he attempted to point out the foolishness and dangers of believing in witchcraft. Owing to several cows having allegedly died of witchcraft in Nunnington, the village elders had consulted a cunning-woman about the identity of the witch responsible. Keary, in an attempt to enlighten his parishioners, preached a sermon on the subject. That evening, a leading farmer called at the rectory to express his anger at being preached at, and remarked, 'Ye're mebbe very wise, passon, an' Ah knaws ye're larned, but in this matter ye knaws nothing whatever, an' ye're altogether mista'en; ye're sadly wrang, passon, ye're sadly wrang; Ah knaws, Ah knaws it, – seed it wi' me own eyes.'[145] Parishioners did not generally go about telling their vicars and curates what to think, and expected the same sort of respect in turn. They would attend church, listen, sing and pray, but they would not be lectured to about being ignorant and foolish. They knew that witches and witchcraft were every-day realities, and the vicar had no right to criticise them for believing in what the Bible plainly stated existed.

As has already been mentioned, in the first sixty years after the repeal of the Witchcraft Act there appears to have been remarkably little attempt by either Church or state to pay any particular attention to the belief in witchcraft and magic, or any vigorous attempt to suppress it. But as the new century dawned, so too did the realisation that the belief in witchcraft and magic had by no means died out, and was, in fact, posing a social and moral problem. Previously, there seems to have been a some-what *laissez-faire* attitude towards popular superstition, it being supposed that the enlightening effects of scientific and philosophical progress would somehow trickle down to the masses in due course, without there being any need for direct intervention. By the early nineteenth century, however, it was becoming obvious to the likes of William Vowles that they had made a 'mistake' in being so presumptuous. It also became apparent, to those who attempted to chastise or to try and reason with the witch-believers, that religious and moral arguments issued from the pulpit had little or no effect at all: 'personal contact was no longer enough. It was now realised that the process of cultural transmission was too complex

and began too early to be controlled by a weekly sermon and an occasional home visit.[146] With their new-found awareness of a forgotten
problem, figures of authority believed that the only way to counter such
pernicious beliefs was through a concerted two-pronged strategy of
popular education and legal coercion.

After the Restoration, elite fears concerning the political threat posed
by mass literacy and popular polemical literature created a widespread
revulsion against the idea of popular education. Between 1680 and 1780
there was actually a marked slowing down of growth in basic literacy as
a result of this elite perception that popular education, as in the 1640s,
would lead to revolutionary tendencies amongst the masses.[147] The dominant view for much of the eighteenth century was that ignorance was the
most appropriate state for those whose role in life was bestial toil; for to
educate such men and women would be to give them aspirations above
their station, and so, as was observed in 1763, make them 'contemn those
drudgeries for which they were born'.[148] This obscurantist ideology was
still held to by many in the early nineteenth century. Davies Giddy, for
example, wrote in 1807 that 'giving education to the labouring classes or
the poor would be prejudicial to their morals and happiness; it would
teach them to despise their lot in life'.[149] However, by the nineteenth
century a nascent opposition was growing to obscurantism, which argued
that limited popular education would actually instil a stronger sense of
discipline and deference amongst the lower orders than a state of ignorance was effecting. As the Chartist William Lovett perceptively explained:

> While a large portion of the hawks and owls of society were seeking to perpetuate
> that state of mental darkness most favourable to the securing of their prey,
> another portion, with more cunning, were for admitting a sufficient amount of
> mental glimmer to cause the multitude to walk quietly and contentedly in the
> paths they in their wisdom had prescribed for them.[150]

With the growing radicalisation of the workforce during the last two
decades of the eighteenth century, and especially with the fears aroused
by the French Revolution, it became obvious to some that 'ignorance'
was patently not acting as a proof against radicalism. Instead, it left the
mass of the people in a dangerously vacuous mental state in which they
could be easily influenced by forces threatening order and stability – not
only political radicalism but also religious dissent. Therefore, according to
the likes of Adam Smith, 'The more they are instructed, the less liable
they are to the delusions of enthusiasm and superstition, which, among
the ignorant nations, frequently occasion the most dreadful disorders.'[151]

In practical terms, it was not until the second half of the nineteenth century, and particularly after the Education Act of 1870, that mass education under government funding and control really began to make a substantial impact on the level of popular education. Before the 1850s much of the schooling of the labouring classes had been informal or semi-formal, provided by religious groups, charity schools, dame schools, and individual tuition. But even at this stage hope was high among reformers that education was providing a swift and powerful antidote to popular 'superstition'. As early as 1831 a Yorkshire contributor to William Hone's *Year Book* confidently remarked that 'Witches and wizards are not so common as they were a few years ago amongst us. The spread of education, by means of National and Sunday Schools, goes a great way to destroy superstition.'[152] The 1870 Education Act inspired particular cause for optimism. In 1884, the president of the *Dorset Natural History and Antiquarian Field Club* could look back and assert that 'Superstition received a severe blow by the Education Act ... the schoolmaster will prove the best exorcist, and School training will help to eradicate the belief in witchcraft.'[153] However, those more closely involved in education were aware that such confident claims concerning the progress of popular 'enlightenment' were rather premature. When in the 1840s the newly formed Council of Education sent its inspectors around the country to report on the education and general moral state of the nation, it was discovered that educational provision was totally inadequate in many areas, and consequently the belief in magic was still widespread and deeply ingrained, especially among the rural population.[154] Common schools and haphazardly recruited teachers were particularly singled out and criticised for failing to educate properly, since, although they were giving children a certain competence in elementary subjects, they were failing to instil in them the sense of morality which society expected of them.

In general, educationalists seem to have considered education's effect on popular magical beliefs as something akin to a good dose of salts, quickly purging the mind of all absurd notions. This stemmed from a widespread assumption that there was a direct link between illiteracy and criminality in general. Ignorance was considered a primary cause of criminality, and schooling was designed to eradicate ignorance, and, there-fore, by a simple equation it was thought that as educational provision expanded, so there would be a concomitant decrease in vice and crime.[155] The continually expressed surprise that 'superstition' had not diminished in the face of increased schooling was partly born of an inadequate knowl-edge of, and contact with, the mentality of the labouring classes, and partly because there was a general overestimation of the level and quality of school provision. Aspirations concerning the progress of popular education exceeded the reality on the ground.

By the end of the 1850s it was beginning to dawn on a few that education and the popular belief in magic were not diametrically opposed forces, and that such beliefs were not declining at a steady rate concomitant with rising literacy levels. James Augustus St John, in *The Education of the People*, devoted a chapter to the problem of education and 'superstition'. St John had no illusions about the strength of magical beliefs in Britain, or about the difficulties of eradicating them. He 'fairly doubted whether the savage races of the earth' equalled many Englishmen 'in moral and religious ignorance', and considered superstition as 'a vice, and the well-spring of other vices'. 'The belief in witchcraft', St John declared, 'hardens the heart, and leads to the persecution, and often to the murder, of the most helpless and innocent portion of our species.'[156] According to St John, one of the reasons for the ineffectuality of education in uprooting superstition was that superstition was not just a mode of thought but 'a disease of the mind as fever or small-pox is a disease of the body'; and disease was, of course, impervious to the power of words – unless one happened to believe in magic. He also cited the argument that those who believed in witchcraft and the like, were not, unfortunately, naturally endowed with the mental faculties to embrace pure reason:

> education cannot eradicate such opinions from the mind, because we cannot by education create in men faculties not bestowed on them by nature: we can only develop, elevate, and refine their understandings. Some persons, therefore, whatever they may be taught, will continue to cherish the belief in certain superstitions, witchcraft amongst the rest, to the end of their days.[157]

While St John believed that superstition was 'indestructible', he still expressed the hope that 'its empire' might at least 'be diminished by education'.

St John was a realist in an age when popular education was seen as an integral element of the inexorable march of progress against which no retarding force could withstand. Yet, as the decades went by, so it became increasingly evident that the almost magical ameliorative power which had been attributed to popular education was not a strong enough force to overthrow the belief in witchcraft and magic. In 1880, for instance, a member of the Board of Guardians of the Shaftesbury Union, after receiving an application from a Gillingham man claiming he was bewitched, reported that Gillingham was a parish 'blessed with a School Board and every appliance of the most scientific education, yet even this is not enough to eradicate this most ancient of superstitions'.[158] As late as 1926, the presiding magistrate at Tipton Police Court, in sentencing two men for threatening a suspected witch, stated that he thought 'education and improvement in the ideas of the people had driven all that sort of thing out of the people's minds'. What they needed, he thought, was 'instruction and enlightenment', and expressed the hope that 'someone, ministers of religion and others, will try to eradicate such ignorance from people'. He suggested that the Court Missionary, a Miss Edwards, should visit those involved to see what she could do to that effect.[159]

If those who believed in witchcraft were guilty of credulity, so, to a certain extent, were those who believed that education, and religious and moral inculcation, would suddenly free the popular mind from such notions. Education was not the guaranteed, quick-fix remedy for 'moral sickness' that it was simplistically believed to be. The attempt during the nineteenth century to suppress the popular belief in witchcraft and magic by smothering it with the blanket of education was a failure which was difficult for contemporaries to contemplate. That is not to say that the education system that was gradually put into place during this period did not contribute to an undoubted decline of magical beliefs during the late nineteenth and early twentieth centuries, but other forces, not directly controlled by the state or Church, were at work during the same period, which were to have a far more profound influence on the popular belief in witchcraft and magic.

In 1824 the little invoked fourth clause of the Witchcraft Act was given fresh emphasis in the newly passed Vagrancy Act (5 Geo. IV., c. 83, s. 4). Under section four of the new act, 'persons pretending or professing to tell fortunes, or using any subtle craft, means, or device, by palmistry or otherwise, to deceive and impose' were to be considered as 'rogues and vagabonds', punishable with three months' hard labour, or by a fine of £25. The clause was aimed primarily at suppressing fortune-tellers, particularly gypsy fortune-tellers, who were said to be 'infesting' the streets of the capital and defrauding its inhabitants, but it was also widely used in prosecuting rural cunning-folk. Fortune-tellers had been prosecuted under the old vagrancy laws, but the 1824 Act now allowed them to be punished for what they practised, rather than for their itinerant status. Apart from the general law-and-order aspects of the clause, there were also implications for the suppression of magical beliefs; for occult practitioners were also thought to be pernicious in that they sustained and strengthened such beliefs, and encouraged moral degeneration. The Rev.

Richard Phayre, rector of Raynham St Mary, Norfolk, complained, for instance, that the activities of a local astrologer were 'eating' into his community 'like a canker'.[160] To strike out against occult practitioners, therefore, was to strike at the heart of popular 'superstition'.

Before the legislature and judiciary began a more concerted and organised campaign against occult practitioners after 1824, the Society for the Suppression of Vice, which was founded in 1802, had been running its own private war against the capital's fortune-tellers.[161] In its first public address, the Society laid out its objective 'to diminish the gross mass of public enormity, to circumscribe the wasting contagion of vice; to bring back a sense of public decency and morality, and by a temperate enforcement of the laws, to effect a general respect for civil order and religion'.[162] The Society certainly considered fortune-telling as an affront to both public decency and morality, and they listed among their first successes the prosecutions of several such offenders. There was 'Samuel Best, a Fortune-teller and Impostor, Surry, committed as a vagrant'; also, 'Several Fortune-tellers, and notorious impostors, in Norwood, committed till the ensuing sessions, and then dismissed with a severe Reprimand, except one who was sent to serve in His Majesty's Navy'; and, finally, 'one other Fortune-teller and Impostor, six Months Imprisonment; it appearing that she had been the Means of Seducing Females to Prostitution'.[163]

It is worth focusing on the Norwood fortune-tellers for a moment, since the history of this famous band of gypsies mirrors changing elite perceptions concerning occult practitioners.[164] The parish of Lambeth, in which Norwood lies, had been a popular gypsy encampment back in the seventeenth century. On 11 August 1668, Samuel Pepys recorded in his diary that his 'wife and Mercer and Deb went with Pelling to see the gypsies at Lambeth, and have their fortune told'. By the mid-eighteenth century Norwood Common had become the focus for the gypsies, and people from all levels of society flocked there to have their fortunes told. Not surprisingly, at a time when fear of lawlessness was high on the political agenda, the gypsies' nefarious activities caused concern in some quarters. In 1726, for instance, *Mist's Weekly Journal* warned its readers that a gypsy gang was going 'about the City and Suburbs pretending to tell Fortunes, and ... thereby cheat and impose upon young People, and the Ignorant and unwary'.[165] But no concerted action was taken to suppress the Norwood fortune-tellers, and well-to-do ladies, like Pepys's wife, continued to enter the gypsies' huts until the late eighteenth century. It was in 1797 that the fortunes of the fortune-tellers took a turn for the worse. In August of that year, the authorities, apparently for the first time, attempted to suppress the Norwood gypsies. On a Sunday morning, at about five o'clock, ten police officers drove to Norwood in three hackney-coaches and arrested some thirty men, women and children under the Vagrancy Act.[166] Five years later, the newly formed Society for the Suppression of Vice also targeted the Norwood fortune-tellers. At their trial at the Surrey quarter sessions, the fortune-tellers 'were examined, and the charge of fortune-telling proved against them'.[167] Faced with police repression and subsequent enclosure of the Common, the fortune-tellers finally deserted Norwood. The Society and the police may have considered the quashing of the Norwood gypsies as a success, but all they really succeeding in doing was dispersing the itinerant fortune-tellers over a wider area, and thus making it much more difficult to control their activities. In the Society's account of the prosecution of the astrologer Joseph Powell, in 1807, the difficulty of suppressing occult practitioners was recognised: 'the secret manner in which these astrological deceivers carry on their traffic is, too generally, such as to elude the notice and detection of common observers, or at least those who more particularly watch over and protect the public morals.'[168]

The Society was the object of considerable criticism and even ridicule for its apparently hypocritical position in going to great lengths to suppress the often harmless 'vices' of the humble but not the real vices of high society. The Society was particularly reviled by the newspapers for its prosecution of Joseph Powell, whom they pictured as a decrepit old man who was to be pitied rather than prosecuted. The Society complained bitterly of the account of the trial reported in papers such as the *Morning Chronicle* and *Statesman*, to which were annexed 'the most virulent and insulting observations, intending to expose the prosecutor to the contempt and indignation of every humane reader'.[169] Twenty or thirty years later the newspapers themselves would be condemning the activities of the fortune-tellers and praising the authorities for prosecuting them.

The passing of the 1824 Vagrancy Act does not appear to have led to a sudden rise in prosecutions against occult practitioners around the country, partly because the new law only reflected what was already happening – that fortune-tellers were being convicted for vagrancy, and also because the fourth clause of the Witchcraft Act already allowed for their prosecution. It was not until the 1840s, and particularly from the late 1850s onwards, that there was a real nation-wide upsurge in prosecutions as represented by the increased frequency of newspaper reports. This rise reflects not only increased newspaper interest in popular magic but also landmark developments in the creation of a national police force. In 1839 the County Police Bill was passed, which empowered magistrates at quarter sessions to establish county police forces, though the number of constables appointed was not to be in excess of one to every 1,000 of the population. Under the Bill the establishment of a police force was not obligatory and by the early 1850s only a minority of counties had done so, but even so, the effects of the Bill in the localities were quite considerable, especially in rural areas. Under the County and Borough Police Act of 1856 the establishment of county police forces was made compulsory, and they were to be subject to stringent inspection. In the following year the number of reported prosecutions concerning occult activities can be seen to have risen quite substantially.

With hindsight, it is obvious that the prosecution of occult practitioners actually did little to damage their trade. As police suppression of their activities became more intense, particularly in urban areas, occult practitioners, rather than be put off, simply resigned themselves to sporadic fines or terms in prison. Thus the 'Newbury Cunning Woman', Maria Giles, notched up an amazing tenth conviction for false pretences in November 1871, and was finally given a hefty five-year prison sentence.[170] Another recidivist practitioner, James Ball, the 'Wise Man of Stepney', was convicted no fewer than six times between 1878 and 1894. One of the practical problems facing the authorities in their attempt to suppress occult activities was that it was difficult to catch the occult practitioner in the act of defrauding a client. Furthermore it was not easy persuading people to stand as witnesses, either for fear of magical reprisals in the case of cunning-men and women, or for fear of appearing foolish in public. When the Birmingham police called for witnesses to come forward in the prosecution of a fortune-teller, they found 'a great reluctance on the part of the fair victims of the "sorcerer" to admit they had consulted the oracle'. Two women were finally summoned but only one actually turned up.[171] To counter this problem, the urban police used paid informers, usually women, sometimes policemen's wives, who visited the practitioners and then reported everything back to the police, who would then raid the premises in question. The Society for the Prevention of Vice had been roundly criticised for employing the same artifice at the beginning of the century. The old trick of using marked coins was also used to prove that money had exchanged hands. Such techniques could be easily employed in urban areas where the police operated daily in close proximity to the fortune-tellers, and where the fortune-tellers dealt with such a high turnover of customers that informers could enter without attracting attention. In rural areas, however, occult practitioners often operated within a more closed, police-free environment, where it was difficult for the police to set up an organised information network, and so had to rely on people to lodge complaints before taking action. The Rev. Sabine Baring-Gould, writing of the activities of Devon cunning-folk in the early twentieth century, noted the difficulty of bringing prosecutions against them, and observed that 'on this immunity they trade'.[172]

That the campaign against London fortune-tellers, which began in the last few years of the eighteenth century, met with a singular lack of success is evident from the thriving state of the fortune-telling business over a hundred years later. In 1912 *The Times* observed that the number of fortune-tellers in London had actually increased rapidly in previous years, and estimated that some six to seven hundred fortune-tellers were operating at that time. Under the subheading 'The Evil in the Country' it remarked that the problem was common throughout the provinces as well.[173] In the same year the Metropolitan Police Commissioner issued an order that fortune-tellers of all types within his jurisdiction must remove all words such as 'palmist', 'clairvoyant' and 'astrologer' from their door-plates, window signs, and other public advertisements. The concern over fortune-tellers even led to a number of questions being asked in the House of Commons in 1911 and 1912. Most of these were put by the Liberal Member of Parliament and Fellow of the Royal Geographical Society, John Cathcart Wason. On 9 May 1911, Wason complained to the House that while fashionable West End fortune-tellers drove a thriving trade with relative impunity, the more humble fortune-tellers were being persecuted by the police. He wondered whether 'there is one law for the rich and another for the poor?'[174] Six days later, Wason asked the Secretary of State for the Home Department, Winston Churchill, if the Executive would 'take immediate steps to ensure equal administration of Justice' regarding the prosecution of fortune-tellers. Churchill replied by merely referring him to the nature of the Vagrancy Act. Not so easily brushed aside, Cathcart Wason responded by asking Churchill if he was aware 'that vice practised behind curtains with soft music' was 'infinitely worse than when practised in the open?' Churchill opined that he could not 'pronounce upon these finer shades', and the House moved on to discuss the Truck Act and the forthcoming coronation.[175] Wason actually supported the suppression of fortune-tellers but wanted the law equally applied. Taking advantage of Churchill's appointment as First Lord of the Admiralty later in the year, he took the opportunity to ask the new Secretary of State, Reginald McKenna, whether he would take rigorous steps to stop the practice.[176] On 26 June 1912, Wason again brought the matter before the House, and on 10 October, Josiah Wedgwood, a fellow Liberal, also asked the Home Secretary about recent prosecutions.[177]

Five years later, the Metropolitan Police carried out another of its periodic clampdowns on fortune-telling, reporting on which the *Justice of the Peace* observed that 'the effort has been one of unusual thoroughness, no doubt because the extent to which the evil had grown within the past two or three years called for stringent measures if it were to be successfully grappled with.'[178] Despite initial success, though, the periodical's editor doubted whether police suppression would succeed in the long term: 'no infliction of penalties upon the impostors will stop them in their lucrative frauds, or eradicate in their dupes a belief in the occult. What the severities of the early Christian emperors and the cruelties of the Spanish Inquisition failed to do, is not likely to be effected by our mild punishments.'[179] It had become obvious by the early twentieth century that the suppression of occult practitioners in both town and country was not having a significant impact in reducing the problem of the popular resort to fortune-telling and magic. In fact, it even had a reverse effect in that it galvanised fortune-tellers into organising themselves as a countermeasure. In the 1890s a national 'Occultists' Defence League' was set up to help those fortune-tellers and astrologers being persecuted by the police. Its secretary and legal advisor was Joseph Dodson, a solicitor, astrologer, and proprietor of 'The Occult Book Co.', 6 Central Street, Halifax. For the payment of an annual fee, members would be defended by a solicitor and counsel specially trained for the work. During the police search of the premises of the London fortune-tellers, the 'Keiros', in 1904, several letters were found from Dodson, which referred to certain magistrates as 'bigoted, incompetent, and leather-headed'. In another letter it was advertised that only four members of the league had been prosecuted, and that most of the charges had been dismissed.[180]

At the same time as it was becoming clear that the half-hearted attempt at suppressing fortune-tellers was patently ineffectual, fortune-telling was becoming a fashionable amusement among the middle and upper classes. There was a growing sense that fortune-telling, when performed as a form of entertainment without financial gain, was neither pernicious nor criminal, but a mere diversion which all levels of society could indulge in without fear of descending into a state of moral turpitude. As early as 1873, *The Treasury of Literature and the Ladies' Treasury* felt at ease to advise its refined female readers:

> Christmas is a fitting time for play ... Whatever the games afloat, fortune-telling is found to be the most seductive, and an attractive 'witch,' the most

sought after. So let every young lady learn to tell fortunes … If the play of fortune-telling is to be well carried at an evening party, a small room appropriately decorated with cabalistic signs cut in silver paper, an hour-glass, a rod or staff, and a young lady dressed in character, as Mother Shipton, help to make a great deal of fun.[181]

The writer Gertrude Konstam admitted to playing the fortune-teller at charity bazaars: 'I have myself been guilty of "laying cards" for a considerable fee under the very nose of the stalwart policeman who was keeping order in the queue outside the oracle's enclosure.'[182] In fact, by 1900, fortune-telling for charitable purposes had become a staple of well-heeled fund-raising events. As one lawyer defending a fortune-teller remarked in 1896, 'Nowadays no fête or bazaar was complete without a person, generally a lady, who practised palmistry.'[183] Indeed, one popular-selling book on palmistry, first published in 1901, included a chapter on 'Palmistry as a Society Amusement'. The author shrewdly observed that 'Superior people may scoff, but few can restrain their curiosity when the search-light of Palmistry is turned upon themselves. As a drawing-room entertainment Palmistry never fails.'[184] By 1914 the popularity of such fortune-tellers among the middle and upper classes was so considerable that *The Times* devoted a whole column to the subject, observing in a light, mocking tone that 'no gentleman's "variety" show is complete without one. They are the most popular form of occultism. From what "charity" bazaar, from which of those other charities that "begin at home," is the palmist absent? She or the crystal-gazer is a certain "draw." Her tent in the garden, her throne on the landing or in the boudoir, is thronged with worshippers.'[185]

Nevertheless, there was some debate as to the legality of the phenomenon of 'society' fortune-telling. In 1903 the following query was sent to *The Justice of the Peace* for instance: 'A young lady at gatherings for charitable purposes professes, by means of palmistry, to delineate character (not to tell fortunes or divine the future) for which a sum of sixpence or a shilling is paid, and which goes to augment the charitable fund. Is she in any way liable to proceedings under the Vagrancy Act, 1824, or otherwise?'[186] The vogue for charity fortune-telling certainly made the suppression of professional fortune-tellers appear a little unseemly. Depending on which way the Vagrancy Law was interpreted, charity fortune-tellers were potentially open to prosecution. However, many of those doing the fortune-telling were middle-class women, and it would have been a foolhardy policeman who attempted to arrest a well-heeled lady performing for charitable purposes.

The legal debate over the Witchcraft and Vagrancy Acts

As has already been mentioned, prosecutions under the fourth clause of the Witchcraft Act for the 'more effectual preventing and punishing' of those who pretended to have powers of witchcraft, conjuration and fortune-telling were not common in the eighteenth century, and its utility was largely superseded by the Vagrancy Act. Yet the Witchcraft Act continued to be invoked sporadically right into the twentieth century. In 1894, for example, a Cornish cunning-man, William Rapson Oates, was charged at the Bodmin assizes with obtaining money by 'false pretences, and with pretending to exercise witchcraft and sorcery'. It was observed, however, that the latter charge 'was framed on an almost obsolete statute', and Judge Vaughan Williams advised the jury to treat the case as one of false pretences only.[187] In the Keiro case, ten years later, charges were initially brought under both the Larceny Act and the Witchcraft Act. Mr Plowden, the magistrate at their initial hearing, admitted that

> with regard to the second charge under the Witchcraft Act, passed nearly 200 years ago, he confessed to having some misgivings whether that Act really applied under the altered circumstances in which they now lived, especially when the serious import attached to fortune-telling in past ages was contrasted with the frivolous spirit with which it was regarded in modern times ... He thought the Act aimed at persons professing witchcraft and supernatural powers, and that there was doubt whether the somewhat rubbishy predictions of the defendants really came within the dignity of supernatural predictions. The more doubt he had as to whether the Act meant and could mean to make fortune-telling an offence the more reason there was for him to leave the matter for a jury to decide.[188]

The impression gained from such accounts is that there was a certain legal embarrassment about dealing with the Witchcraft Act. The wording of section four of the Act was more explicit and relevant to the charges laid against cunning-folk and fortune-tellers than the Vagrancy Act, but the presence of the word 'witchcraft' seems to have been off-putting. The law was considered to belong to a bygone age when belief in witchcraft and magic was widespread, and was unsuitable for the modern industrial empire of turn-of-the-century Britain. Thus, in 1917, *The Justice of the Peace* presented its readers with a potted history of the laws against fortune-telling and witchcraft, in which it was stated that 'it would be idle to pretend that such a state of the law is satisfactory. A change is long overdue which would bring it more into line with the present state of human knowledge.'[189]

While the implementation of the Witchcraft Act rarely intruded upon the sensitivities of the 'modern' Victorian and Edwardian legal mind, the

Vagrancy Act was frequently employed in courts up and down the country. Not surprisingly, section four had generated criticism from early on. Fortune-tellers and cunning-folk were certainly unlikely to have given it a warm welcome, but these people rarely published their views, and had little influence in the circles of society which mattered. Those who did complain publicly were middle-class astrologers who found themselves just as open to prosecution as the lowliest fortune-teller. One of the foremost astrologers of the day, Richard James Morrison, otherwise known as Zadkiel, the author of the best selling *Zadkiel's Almanac*, was at the forefront of attempts to amend section four.[190] Following the conviction of a Manchester astrologer in 1844, Morrison formed the 'British Association for the Advancement of Astral Science &c., and the Protection of Astrologers'. By the following year he claimed it had 107 members, but despite the enthusiastic response, it seems to have folded not long after. Several years later, Morrison was motivated to attempt a more serious challenge to the law, after the high-profile prosecution, in January 1852, of the Bath astrologer, Francis Copestick.[191] By this time, Morrison had become acquainted with Lord Robert Grosvenor, who was sympathetic to the idea of amending section four. Morrison hoped to make it legal for enfranchised householders, as opposed to 'idle and disorderly persons', to practise astrology professionally in their own homes. Morrison, with the advice of Christopher Cooke, a solicitor and astrologer, wrote a petition which Grosvenor and William Ewart, a radical Member of Parliament, agreed to present as a Private Member's Bill on 16 March 1852. Not unsurprisingly, perhaps, it failed to make it on to the parliamentary timetable, and it sunk without trace.

It is important to remember that these middle-class astrologers did not necessarily want to abolish section four, but to change it in their favour. They were severely critical of common fortune-tellers and pseudo-astrologers, and accused them of debasing and demeaning their 'science'. The fact that under section four they were tarred with the same brush as fortune-tellers irritated them considerably. Christopher Cooke sought to make this clear: 'The science has been so long unpopular, that its real principles have been much lost sight of; and the charlatan has been confounded with the real artist.'[192] He even printed two accounts of 'pure fortune-telling, meriting punishment'. The error of the courts, he asserted, was in 'mixing up such cases as these with those connected with real astrology'.[193] Astrology was a science offering 'unadulterated ingots of truth'; palmistry and the like was 'rubbish'.[194] It was not just a question of the integrity of the fortune-tellers, though, since palmists may have had as much faith in their methods as the learned astrologers in theirs. It was also an attempt to disassociate themselves, in both the legal and public spheres, from the perceived vulgarity of the fortune-tellers with whom section four lumped them. Under Morrison's amendment, an earnest but poor astrologer or cunning-person, who did not earn enough to be a franchised householder, would still be punishable as a rogue and a vagabond.

With the failure of Morrison's endeavours to reform the Vagrancy Act in favour of middle-class astrology, vociferous opposition to section four subsided for the next twenty-five years. It was rekindled not by a new generation of middle-class astrologers, but by the far more influential spiritualist lobby. The educated and often highly respected adherents of spiritualism became concerned about the police persecution of mediums. As Christopher Cooke had observed back in the 1850s, 'the spiritual rappists now-a-days take upon themselves a portion of the odium which formerly attached to the adherents of Urania.'[195] In 1877 spiritualists expressed much vocal concern over the prosecution of the medium Henry Slade. The case was well-publicised in the national press, and led to a flurry of letters and comments in dedicated publications such as *The Spiritualist*. Just as the prosecution of the astrologer Bradshaw had goaded other middle-class astrologers into organising themselves, the Slade trial fostered a 'Slade Defence Fund'. One of Slade's fellow mediums, Stainton Moses, was moved to write an essay on the trial in which he condemned the law. In Moses' florid words, when the ridicule and 'supercilious scorn' of the opponents of spiritualism failed, they resorted 'to obsolete and rusty lances dragged from the armoury where they have long hung un-used, and rapidly furbished up to meet exigencies for which they were never constructed.'[196] Those 'rusty lances' were the Witchcraft Act and Vagrancy Act, the contents of which Moses outlined for his readers. Moses did not 'venture to guess' what the past societies which created these laws 'were afraid of', but he was certain they should be consigned to that vague period of time when an unenlightened populace had not yet realised the humanity of the spirit world. The legal persecutions of the past had no place in the present. Spiritualists must defend themselves from the 'men who have tried to revive, in the nineteenth century, the bigotry and inquisitional tactics of mediaevalism'.[197] Several years later, a correspondent to the spiritualist publication *Light* similarly expressed his astonishment 'that the trials for sorcery and witchcraft which blackened the seventeenth century should be revived in the metropolis of England so near to the close of the nineteenth, with Mr Gladstone for Prime Minister and Sir William Harcourt for Home Secretary'.[198] Thus while one section of educated society saw in spiritualism the recrudescence of the 'superstitions' of previous centuries, the spiritualists viewed their prosecution as a return to the dark days of the witch-hunts.

The furore over the Slade trial also had ramifications for fortune-telling. Not long before, a fortune-teller named John Ball had been sentenced to the full three months' hard labour under the Vagrancy Act.[200] His conviction emerged as a debating point in relation to the merits of the Slade prosecution. An editorial in the *Haverfordwest Telegraph*, for example, noted the comparisons which had been made, and bravely suggested that, 'at the risk of differing from many of our readers, we venture to question the defensibility of this enactment, either on the grounds of abstract justice or of ultimate expediency.' The paper challenged the legal assumptions concerning fortune-telling, and suggested that the act was applied 'with the same arbitrariness of decision as that with which in laws long since abolished, witchcraft was assumed to be an undoubted fact … in no other instance that we can call to mind does our law interfere with the course of action to which any man's opinions may lead him, provided he stops short of causing serious peril to the public.' The editorial was not defending fortune-telling and spiritualism on the grounds that they were in any way worthy pursuits; it was purely a matter of individual rights. In any case, the interference of the law would be counterproductive, and 'by creating a sense of grievance, only confirm the delusion and multiply the numbers of the dupes of such persons as John Ball and Dr Slade.'[199] Thus the high-profile prosecution of spiritualists brought into question the whole legal basis of section four, and also, to a lesser extent, the 1736 Witchcraft Act. These laws which had been implemented many times without question against fortune-tellers and cunning-folk, who had no influence in high society, became the focus of serious legal debate, which can be traced through the pages of *The Justice of the Peace*, a publication for those involved in the judiciary.

A year before the Slade trial another less notorious but prominent spiritualist, Francis Ward Monck, was sentenced by the Huddersfield magistrates to three months' hard labour under section four of the Vagrancy Act.[200] The substance of the charge was that Monck gave a seance for a fixed sum, at which he informed the company present that certain writings on a slate held by him and another under a table came from departed spirits. Monck lodged an appeal, similar in substance to that of the middle-class astrologers of mid-century. His argument was that the Vagrancy Act 'was intended to apply to gypsies and other wandering and homeless vagabonds', and that his practice was no offence within the meaning of section four. The facts of the case were sent to the Queen's Bench Division of the High Court of Justice for the magistrates' ruling to be assessed. The Queen's Council, Henry Matthews, then sought to untangle the exact nature of the offence in relation to the palmistry referred to in section four. Matthews observed that palmistry was defined in *Cowell's Law Dictionary* as 'a kind of divination practised by looking at the lines and marks of the fingers and hands'. Such divination did not, therefore, profess to be by supernatural means, and so the alleged offence was not *ejusdem generis*. There was also no vagabondage, as Monck had been living in the same house for four years. However, if Monck pretended to call spirits into the room, 'this would be conjuration, an offence of a totally different, and, as it was formerly regarded, a much more serious nature', and he might be convicted under the Witchcraft Act of 1736. On the other hand, Mr Poland thought the magistrates were correct: 'The essence of the offence is the using subtle craft, means, or device, and palmistry was mentioned because it was a common mode of deceit.' He also cited several other more relevant dictionary definitions of palmistry, such as an 'action of the hand', and a 'trick with the hand'. The words 'or otherwise' should not be restricted he thought. Finally, Mr Cleasby concluded that the clause encompassed 'all persons who pretend to tell fortunes, which imports that deception is practised by doing so'. The conviction was upheld and the case set a precedent, becoming a standard reference in future prosecutions under section four of the Vagrancy Act.

The next key case was in 1887 when Richard Henry Penny lodged an appeal against his conviction under section four. Penny was no common fortune-teller. He was a respected astrologer who contributed to a variety of periodicals and was on friendly terms with W. T. Stead, editor of the *Pall Mall Gazette*.[201] Part of Penny's defence was that he practised astrology which was far divorced from mere fortune-telling. Astrology, it was argued, was bound by fixed rules, which when properly applied would give an indication of what was likely to happen. Penny professed no 'mysterious personal power of divination such as might impose on the credulity of the superstitious which was the mischief aimed at by that portion of the statute'. Furthermore, there was no intent to deceive since Penny had the most implicit faith in the science he professed to apply. Penny's counsel argued that the intention to deceive must be the gist of the offence, otherwise anyone who foretold the future could be prosecuted. By way of example, he cited the well-known story of Sir Edward Bulwer Lytton casting Disraeli's nativity. 'Could he have been found guilty of an offence under the statute?' enquired the counsel. 'What, too, of *Zadkiel's Almanack*, which deals with the science of the stars and futurity.' This was a good point. You had to pay for astrological almanacs to find out about future events, just as the astrologer had to be paid. In fact, in 1828 there had been calls for the Stationers' Company to be prosecuted under the Vagrancy Act for the astrological almanacs it issued. However, this cogent point was lost on the presiding legal minds. Judge Denman ruled that the case was quite clear, that there was ample evidence to justify the conviction, and that it was unnecessary to decide whether the intention to deceive was an essential part of the defence. In his own opinion, it was 'absurd to suppose that in the present age anyone could believe that merely by knowing the state of the heavens at the date of the birth of a person he could foretell the fortune of that person'. So Penny's appeal was dismissed with costs.[202]

The main legal point to emerge from these rulings concerned the interpretation that the word 'pretend' implied there was an intention 'to deceive and impose'. This suggested that the act of fortune-telling was by its very nature a deception. This point was brought up in a similar ruling on the prosecution of the fortune-teller Georgina Jones (*Reg.* v. *Entwistle*).[203] The solicitors who lodged the appeal against the ruling was Jacques and Company on behalf of Dodson and Company, Stainland – in other words, Joseph Dodson, legal advisor to the Occultists' Defence League. Their representative in court was T. P. Perks, who had also defended other fortune-tellers, presumably on behalf of the League. This led to one of the justices observing that he appeared 'to be a sort of standing counsel to these fortune-tellers throughout the country'. Perks contended that the conviction was bad, as it did not allege an intent to deceive: 'People might honestly believe that they could foretell the future; pretending does not necessarily involve deception, many people believe in palmistry.'

The appeal was heard by Judge Charles John Darling (1849–1936), who was the Conservative Member of Parliament for Deptford until his elevation to the bench in 1897. This move became the subject of rumours at the time that his appointment was made on political grounds rather than on the basis of his questionable legal talents. It was said that 'in a murder trial he was very good', but in 'charges of less gravity he often allowed himself to behave with a levity quite unsuited to the trial of a criminal case'. He apparently 'frequently lost the respect of the jury to such an extent that they ignored or paid little attention' to him.[204] As we shall see, this summing up of his handling of less serious criminal trials provides an accurate reflection of the legal confusion he sowed by his opinions and judgements in both the Jones trial and later fortune-telling cases. Darling, following the argument of Cleasby in the Monck ruling, was of the opinion that the only way the law would not apply to fortune-telling was if a person were to say 'Well, I am not a real fortune-teller, I cannot tell fortunes, what I am about to tell you by means I am about to take must not deceive in any way, but now I will pretend to tell your fortune or I will profess to tell your fortune; I will make use of the ordinary means which people take to do it.' In this situation there would be no intention to deceive, but, instead, it would be 'done in fun, and done to amuse the people at a concert, or in a drawing-room'. Darling's colleague, Justice Channell, believed that for a conviction to be upheld 'the thing should be done in order to deceive', but that in the case of Jones the offence was sufficiently proved. However, in order to make a clear distinction between the activities of the common fortune-teller and the entertaining *salon* fortune-teller, he averred that 'persons who are acting do not pretend', and gave the following example: 'It is a serious offence I believe to pretend to be a policeman, but I do not think when a man acts the part of a policeman in a pantomime he pretends to be a policeman.' The prosecution case was again upheld.

Dodson seems to have learned from the trial, and by the time of the prosecution in 1904 of the London fortune-tellers, Charles Stephenson, *alias* Professor Keiro, and his wife Martha, the Occultists' Defence League had formulated a printed document for their members, to be signed by each client. It was hoped that this would absolve them of charges under section four, presumably in the way that Judge Darling had suggested. When the police searched Keiro's premises they found 550 signed and 700 unsigned copies of the following 'protection form':

> Keiro hereby gives notice to all who wish to consult him that he has no intention to deceive or impose upon any one; that any consultant is at liberty to believe or not his statements as to character, past life, or prediction, of foretelling of the future; and any one who consults him must do so on the understanding that he has no intention to deceive or impose upon any one or to obtain money by false pretences ... Having consulted you, I hereby declare my belief that in all you have said and written you have had no intent to deceive or impose upon me or to obtain money by false pretences, and I pay your fee accordingly.

A footnote printed in small letters appeared on the notice stating: 'N.B. – The copyright of this form is the property of the Occultists' Defence League, and is reserved to the exclusive use of its members. – J. Dodson, secretary to the league. (Entered at Stationers'-hall.)'[205] These disclaimers did not prevent the Keiros from being convicted. Five years later, though, two palmists did avoid prosecution under section four by issuing a similar notice to potential customers: 'Notice to patrons.– Characters will be read as delineated on the hands, and no profession of ability to tell fortunes is made. Whatever is stated as a probability from the character revealed by the hand is so stated without intention to deceive, and for the purposes of amusement only.'[206] However, at the same trial another fortune-teller was convicted despite displaying a disclaimer notice. In this case the notice was differently worded to that above, and the justices felt that the way it was written did not prevent the application of the statute. With hindsight, the town clerk who conducted the prosecutions wrote to *The Justice of the Peace* to ask, '*First.* Would a notice in the form above described, assuming it to be clearly visible, prevent a conviction being obtained. *Secondly.* Should not the palmist actually say to the customer "I am not a real fortune teller, etc." before he can be protected?' In reply it was suggested, 'We do not think that the palmist need do more than bring it home to the mind of the person consulting him that he does not tell fortunes.'

Despite the legal arguments against the validity of section four, and the voices of protest from spiritualists, astrologers and well-to-do charity fortune-tellers, prosecutions occurred regularly throughout the years of the First World War. The trials in this period continued to wrestle with the legal interpretations of the words 'to deceive and impose', and over the matter of belief with regards to deception. It was not until the appeal case of *Stonehouse* v. *Masson* in April 1921, though, that an attempt was made to clear up some of the confusion. Stonehouse was an invalid spinster living at Primrose Hill, who claimed to tell fortunes by psychometry.

One of the presiding judges at the King's Bench was Charles Darling whose previous contradictory rulings had caused some of the confusion concerning the word 'pretend'. At the appeal hearing on the case of Georgina Jones, in 1899, Darling had decided that the word 'pretend' implied that there was an intention to deceive and impose. However, at the appeal hearing of *Davis* v. *Curry* nineteen years later, Darling had modified his views somewhat. He now decided that an intention to deceive was an ingredient of the offence of fortune-telling, and the accused was, therefore, entitled to call evidence that he honestly believed in the powers that he claimed to possess. 'Many persons honestly believe in nonsense', he said, 'but we do not punish them for it'. Following this rather enlightened decision, in October 1919 the case against Ellen Lucy Bloodworth was dismissed on the grounds that the magistrate, Mr Bankes, was 'absolutely satisfied that she believes she has these powers'.[207] The

Stonehouse ruling overturned that of *Davis* v. *Curry*. Lord Chief Justice Lawrence concluded in his summing up that 'The thing which the statute aimed at was a public mischief, because it affected the lives and happiness of those people who were weak enough to patronize such people, and the thing itself was the thing which ought to be repressed'. Justice Darling then admitted that his judgement in the Davis case had been wrong, and he had come to the conclusion that 'the Legislature had decided that fortune-telling and professing to tell fortunes was a fraud, and that it was a deception in itself'.[208]

As the editor of *The Justice of the Peace* observed, this ruling simplified the task of the magistrate a good deal. He need not now attempt to divine 'the real state of mind' of the fortune-tellers as to the belief in their supernatural powers. They could simply be prosecuted for what they practised. This was a relief because, as was pointed out by several legal commentators, 'many highly educated people, who are certainly not insane', believed things which others found incredible and absurd.[209] It was 'an age when men of high reputation and exceptional ability subscribe to a belief in fairies, when photographs of deceased persons arm-in-arm with angels, or of children with fairy companions, are solemnly discussed by learned men.'[210] This was largely an allusion to Arthur Conan Doyle, creator of Sherlock Holmes and enthusiastic spiritualist. Several months previously, in December 1920, he had caused a national sensation by publishing photographs in the *Strand* of two girls posing with what Doyle genuinely believed to be fairies.[211] The front cover described it as 'An epoch making event'. The girls had taken the pictures several years before, and the fairies were quite clearly paper cut-outs, but Doyle and a number of spiritualists and theosophists claimed they were genuine. With such eminent people publicly expressing their belief in fairies, there was, indeed, a certain incongruity in penalising those of a lower class for holding to rather more mundane supernatural beliefs.

The Stonehouse case may have clarified the legal position of fortune-telling to the relief of magistrates on one hand, and to the detriment of fortune-tellers on the other, but post-First World War Britain was going through a period of social liberality which cast a more sympathetic light on their plight to the world outside the legal establishment. There was definitely a further shift in educated opinion, which is evident from the more permissive editorial tone of *The Justice of the Peace* concerning fortune-telling. In 1917 it had described fortune-telling as an 'evil' which had to be tackled, but by 1928 it was actually sticking up for fortune-tellers, and severely criticising the police for prosecuting them:

the Vagrancy Act, 1824, which was passed for the purpose of dealing with the
hooligan type of gypsy fortune-teller of that day is still being used as a means
of harassing the harmless woman fortune-teller of to-day … within the last
hundred years many people by no means illiterate have become convinced that
there is matter for serious investigation in the old 'superstitions' of astrology,
palmistry and the like, and that the present state of the law makes anything like
a scientific inquiry impossible.[212]

The *Justice of the Peace* went so far as to suggest that a bill altering the
Vagrancy Act would be more valuable than one to restrict Sunday trading.[213]
After the war, the intermittent campaign to reform popular supernatural
beliefs by suppressing occult practitioners lost momentum, although it did
not cease entirely. It was deemed by some that society had provided
enough reforming measures in terms of education and welfare to ensure
that the lower orders could do without state intrusions into their moral
well-being. As Gertrude Konstam wrote in 1919, 'in what way can anything told under such conditions be so much more injurious than a book,
a play, or evil companionship that Authority feels itself obliged to interfere
… in point of fact, the Legislature takes it upon itself to decide on what
the poor shall or shall not waste their means, for the fortune-tellers who
are prosecuted are generally those who charge low fees.'[214] It was up to the
dissatisfied clients of fortune-tellers to decide whether they wanted to
prosecute, and not the state.

As the nineteenth century drew to a close and an exciting new century beckoned, there was also a growing sense that society had progressed
to a state of sophistication far beyond that of the beginning of the century. The country had entered a new epoch of enlightenment. Throughout the nineteenth century, the Middle Ages and the period of the
witch-trials had been the standard comparative metaphors for credulity,
but as the century ended people even began to make similar allusions to
the antiquated period of their grandparents. Thus in 1896 a solicitor made
the case that section four was an anachronism and that it no longer per-
tained to the present time when people were too knowing to be duped.
'In the time of George IV', he affirmed, 'there were so-called wizards
and witches, and fortunes were told by the stars, &c. The Members of
Parliament at that time considered that a Bill should be passed to protect
the people, who were not so enlightened then as they were now.'[215] Two
years before, a similar statement was made in defence of two women
prosecuted under section four for 'pretending' to procure the love of a
man for a young woman. Mr Weldron, the defendants' solicitor, contended that 'it could not be said the prisoners had used a subtle device or

craft. The Act was passed at the time when there was a great deal more of superstition than now existed.'[216] Finally, during the trial of a clairvoyant fortune-teller in 1919, the presiding magistrate mused that the Vagrancy Act was a relic of a more simplistic age, 'when anyone who talked about railways, telephones, airships, or votes for women would have been looked upon as a lunatic'.[217] Judging from their use of language, one would have thought these people were referring to the time of James I and not George IV. It would seem, then, that for a new generation the period of the early nineteenth century had become a yardstick for popular credulity and 'superstition'. Society had changed and it was time the law caught up with it.

In 1930 this new ethos manifested itself in a serious attempt by spiritualists to lobby Members of Parliament for the reform of the Witchcraft and Vagrancy Acts. They seem to have received a sympathetic hearing, and on 26 November William Kelly, Labour Member for Rochdale, stood up in the House of Commons and requested 'That leave be given to bring in a bill to relieve spiritualists and mediums from prosecution under the enactments relating to witchcraft and vagrancy whilst genuinely exercising their psychic powers whether in religious practice or scientific investigation.'[218] The proposal was entitled the 'Spiritualism and Psychical Research (Exemption) Bill'. Kelly was not actually a practising spiritualist but thought it 'a blot upon the country' that the Witchcraft and Vagrancy Acts be used to persecute people who were doing such 'splendid work'. He highlighted the incongruity that such great public figures as the recently deceased Conan Doyle and Sir Oliver Lodge were potentially open to prosecution as common 'rogues and vagabonds'. However, to protect the public from any fraudulent mediums 'operating under the title of Spiritualism and psychic research' the bill proposed that the Home Secretary would issue certificates to those spiritualists who agreed to undergo and pass an official examination to prove their genuineness. The only vocal opponent of the bill was Frederick Macquisten, a solicitor and Conservative Member for Argyll. He was not against the spiritualist movement, but objected to the idea of licensing, which would, he thought, reduce spiritualists to 'the state of the canine species'. In consideration of this, he said the bill was 'a mere abuse of legislation'. The bill was backed by a group of Labour Members, including the author and journalist Oliver Baldwin, the Nonconformist Minister Gordon Lang, and Ellen Wilkinson, one of the few female Members of the House. They were joined by just one Conservative, Daniel Somerville, Member for East Willesden. Despite Macquisten's opposition, the bill was accepted and given a second reading.

At this stage the bill was endorsed by one of its original backers, William Carter. It was again opposed by a Conservative Member of Parliament, this time Lieutenant-Colonel Francis Fremantle. In his blustering military manner he initially professed his complete ignorance of spiritualism, and claimed the bill was 'a most fantastical proposal'. He freely admitted he 'associated spiritualists and mediums with the fairy stories of Hans Andersen and the like'. Happy in his unenlightened state, Fremantle expressed his sorrow at attempts to spoil 'the connection hitherto existing between spiritualists and mediums on the one hand and the picture of witches sailing on brooms in the sky, with the law on the other hand.' However, Fremantle also saw some serious cause for concern in allowing spiritualists legal freedoms. He had been made aware of its associations 'with a certain perversion of the uninformed mind of the young', and believed it had 'had most disastrous effects in many cases'. He concluded, therefore, that 'whether they were prosecuted under laws as to witchcraft or whatever else, nothing could be too much for these people'.[219] Fremantle was a member of both the Church Assembly and the Ecclesiastical Committee, and it is possible that his opposition to the bill was also motivated by religious considerations as well as ignorance. The House was poorly attended and the bill was counted out.

As with previous calls for the reform of the Witchcraft and Vagrancy Acts, whether they came from middle-class astrologers or spiritualists, the bill was designed to disassociate 'respectable' occult practitioners from the 'vulgar' breed of fortune-tellers and cunning-folk. It was not designed to abolish section four of each act but to exempt spiritualists from them. While general attitudes towards fortune-telling had softened considerably, the spiritualist movement still objected strongly to being in any way connected with those who they still considered to be 'rogues and vagabonds'.

Despite the failure of the Spiritualism and Psychical Research (Exemption) Bill, the spiritualist movement did not give up its struggle, and continued to lobby for the reform of the law. What with economic and social instability at home, and growing concern over developments in Europe, the legislature obviously felt it had rather more pressing matters during the 1930s to consider than repealing the laws against occult practitioners. That did not stop fortune-tellers and spiritualists from being prosecuted still. As late as 1949, Home Office statistics record that thirty-nine fortune-tellers were prosecuted under the Vagrancy Act. Even the Witchcraft Act continued to be used. In 1927, for example, a gypsy was prosecuted at the Cornwall assizes for pretended witchcraft. She had been given large sums of money by an old gardener to remove a spell from him. She had also threatened him with blindness and death if he did not pay her. The presiding judge, Justice Shearman, sentenced her to six months' imprisonment. Twelve years later another gypsy, named Bessy Birch, was charged under the act at the Portsmouth quarter sessions. Her crime was fraudulently to claim she could remove a curse from a woman's ring. The last successful conviction under the Act was that of the medium Helen Duncan in 1944. The case generated considerable public attention, and much sympathy was expressed for her plight.[220]

The spiritualist movement's pressure on Parliament to reform the Witchcraft and Vagrancy Acts even continued during the period of the Second World War. In 1943 the Under-Secretary for the Home Office, acting on behalf of the Home Secretary, received a deputation calling for a reform of the law. It was made up of leading spiritualists, three Members of Parliament, and Air Chief Marshal Lord Dowding. They received a sympathetic hearing, but the government was rather more concerned with protecting the nation against Nazi Germany at the time. However, the spiritualists were certainly not lacking in tenacity. During the general elections of 1945 and 1950 the Spiritualists National Union and other organisations submitted a questionnaire to parliamentary candidates asking them their views concerning a bill to reform the law. Apparently two hundred elected Members pledged their support for such a move. In 1946 another deputation was despatched to the Home Office, which included the Dowager Duchess of Hamilton and Leslie Hale, the Member for Oldham West. It was only in 1948, though, that the first signs emerged of serious government intent to repeal the Witchcraft Act, and modify the Vagrancy Act. During a committee discussion of the Criminal Justice Bill, the Home Secretary remarked that it was 'anomalous that in these days proceedings under the Witchcraft Act should be taken against people in this country'. He further suggested that some rephrasing of the old law might bring it 'into line with modern conditions and modern requirements'.[221]

Finally, in 1950, thirty years after the first Spiritualism Bill was formulated, and 215 years after the Witchcraft Act was first debated in the House of Commons, the Fraudulent Mediums Bill was presented to Parliament, and given a second reading on 1 December. The Bill's proposer was Walter Monslow, Labour Member for Barrow-in-Furness. He was a Methodist and not a practising spiritualist, but believed that spiritualism should be guaranteed the same freedoms as other religious faiths. The Bill generated a lively and sympathetic debate, provoking some long-winded philosophical reflections, and also some humorous recollections. Geoffrey de Freitas, Under-Secretary of State, for example, recalled attending a public meeting

during the 1945 election discussing the mass production of household
equipment. Out of the blue, somebody suddenly asked him about the
Witchcraft Act: 'I said facetiously that the way to solve the witch problem
was not by legislation. The proper way was to mass-produce household
equipment such as vacuum cleaners – get away from brooms and broomsticks and ground the witches.' Mr Mellish, Member for Bermondsey,
mused that he could well understand why foreigners thought the British
a peculiar lot: 'last night we were discussing a matter of great importance
– the crisis in Korea ... and now we are discussing the Witchcraft Act.'[222]
The Secretary of State, James Ede, had obviously done some homework
on the subject of witchcraft. He gave a long speech in which he presented
a potted history of the laws against witchcraft and fortune-telling, made
reference to James Frazer's *Golden Bough* in relation to the prevalence of
the belief in spirits, and cited the case of Temperance Lloyd, one of the
last women to be hanged for witchcraft in England. Ede portrayed the
1736 Witchcraft Act as 'a most enlightened measure, well in advance of
public opinion'. Regarding the Fraudulent Mediums Bill, he stated that
the attitude of the government was 'one of benevolent neutrality, but we
do commend to the House the necessity of keeping alive the great spirit
of toleration in these matters which has been increasingly shown in this
House during the last 200 years or so.'[223]

Although the debate was dominated by the concerns of spiritualists,
John Parker, Labour Member for Dagenham, brought up the question of
fortune-telling in relation to the law. He began by asking whether under
the bill it would still be illegal for a gypsy at a fair to tell fortunes.[224] He
went on to observe that prosecutions had been 'brought in the past against
people who have attempted to tell fortunes, which is not always done for
the purpose of entertainment. Many people take it semi-seriously.' Arthur
Colegate, Conservative Member for Burton, responded by pointing out
that no proceedings could be taken under the bill without the consent of
the Director of Public Prosecutions, 'who is not likely to act so frivolously
as to allow prosecution of music hall performers, gipsies at fairs, and
people of that kind.'[225] Parker was not convinced, and reiterated his concern that the proposals in the bill were inadequate to prevent people
being deceived, 'especially those who may not be very well educated'.
Later in the debate the Home Secretary turned his attention to the subject, and attempted to differentiate between casual gypsy fortune-telling,
and the activities of professional urban fortune-tellers. In recent years, he
said, prosecutions under section four of the Vagrancy Act had been 'confined to palmists, fortune-tellers and the like, and may I say that these are

not the gipsies on Epsom Down or Hampstead Heath, but the people who set up establishments in which they undertake, in a very different spirit, to be able to advise young women about their matrimonial ventures and carry on similar practices.'[226] To continue to protect the public from such people, therefore, the bill would not abolish section four, but substitute a new penalty for the offence of trying to impose on the public for reward. George Deer, Labour Member for Newark, welcomed this safeguard but wondered whether the act of reward would apply to those 'selling herbal remedies after the service and doing a bit of fortune-telling on Mondays'. He hoped that the bill would provide adequate safeguards against 'charlatans of this kind.' 'I believe in religious toleration', he said magnanimously, 'but I also believe it is bad that many decent people should be imposed upon.'[227] The journalist and Labour member for Nottingham South, Henry Norman Smith, expressed a personal interest concerning the application of the Vagrancy Act. His great grandparents were itinerant gypsies and were greatly impeded by the Act. His great-grandmother used to 'practise the art of clairvoyance', which was probably Smith's polite euphemism for fortune-telling. Smith seemed to have been satisfied with the Home Secretary's categorisation of fortune-tellers, and said he would support the bill.

The bill was successfully voted in and was passed on to a standing committee for further consultation. During the committee stage Geoffrey de Freitas introduced two amendments, which were readily accepted. The first made it clear that the onus of proving that a person acted for reward would be on the prosecution, and the second covered rewards of gifts or valuable property.[228] The bill as it stood now provided for the repeal of the Witchcraft Act and the amendment of section four of the Vagrancy Act, but still made provision for the punishment of persons who 'fraudulently purported to act as spiritualistic mediums, or to exercise powers of tele-pathy, clairvoyance or other similar powers'. The bill excluded from its provision anything done solely for the purpose of entertainment. The penalties proposed were a maximum fine of £50 or four months' imprison-ment, or both on summary conviction, or £500 or two years' imprison-ment, or both, on conviction. On 3 May 1951 the bill was brought before the House of Lords for endorsement, and on 22 June the bill received royal assent, thereby erasing the concept of witchcraft from the statute books once and for all.[229]

This chapter ends where it began, with the passing of a law in response to the emergence of a new educated consensus concerning the interpretation of the supernatural. Both laws were considered in their day to be edifying measures responding to advances in human knowledge and tolerance. In the period between the two Acts of 1736 and 1951, several general shifts in attitude towards the continued popular belief in witchcraft and magic can be detected. The first was a shift in the ruling elite's perception of popular beliefs, from a position of perceived social irrelevance in the early eighteenth century, to a point at the end of the century when the belief in witchcraft and magic was once more thought to pose a considerable social and moral problem. The second was the subsequent attempt during the nineteenth and early twentieth centuries to reform the popular mentality which fostered such beliefs as part of a more general campaign to reshape popular morals and social activities. Finally, there developed a more relaxed and pluralistic attitude towards unorthodox beliefs, and a shedding of old attitudes and preconceptions concerning the state's responsibilities in relation to the private beliefs of its citizens. Of course, during each of these phases there were those whose views ran counter to the prevailing trend.

It is no coincidence that the rediscovery of popular 'superstition' as a social problem roughly coincides with what has been termed the 'discovery of the people' in the late eighteenth century.[230] The sea-change in elite attitudes towards the reality of witchcraft and magic, which began in the late seventeenth century, inevitably broke one of the strongest remaining social and psychological bonds that had bound together lord and labourer, barmaid and bishop, with a shared perception of the unstable balance between the natural and supernatural worlds that governed their everyday existence. The elite denial of witchcraft signalled the final severance of cultural ties between learned and popular culture. But as we have seen, due to their continued adherence to biblical authority, the conservative elite did not completely reject the concept of witchcraft. This, more than a complete denial, perhaps further contributed to the general elite reticence to address seriously the continued popular belief in witchcraft and magic, and its reluctance actively to reform popular beliefs. Those learned men who maintained that witchcraft *had* existed would have found it most uncomfortable to have to vindicate such a view while at the same time actively denouncing the lower orders for believing that witches *still* existed. The most convenient and least embarrassing stance to take therefore, was simply to turn a blind eye to the situation, and leave the people to wallow in their own mental 'ignorance'. During the mid-eighteenth century, the break with their witch-believing past was still too recent for many members of the elite to examine the popular belief in witchcraft with detached circumspection. The follies of the recent past rendered indecent any attempt to punish those who still believed in witches and who continued to act upon such beliefs. Only after the passing of the generation whose fathers had been a part of the witch-prosecution era, and after a period of conscious elite detachment from the beliefs of the 'people', do we begin to discern a renewed awareness of the continued popular belief in witchcraft.

One of the reasons for this renascent interest in popular occult beliefs towards the end of the eighteenth century, and the growing perception of it as a problem, was undoubtedly the rise of Methodism. Increasing anxiety over the popularity of Methodism led to a closer examination of the spiritual and moral state of the labouring poor, particularly by members of the Church of England, whose religious interests were threatened. Once they began to examine popular beliefs, and the more they began to look, the more apparent it became that they had been deceiving themselves about the religious condition of the people. With growing anxiety over not only active religious dissent but also popular radicalism, the 'superstitious' state of the people was now seen to be a real problem. If people could be influenced by such 'absurd' and 'credulous' beliefs as witchcraft, swayed by the prophetic messages of an Ann Taylor, or duped by the oracular utterances of a fortune-teller, then how easily influenced they could be by other dogmas and creeds which threatened ecclesiastical and secular authority.

The recognised failure to reform the popular mentality through instruction and coercion over a period of one hundred years was singularly frustrating to cultural reformers, especially in respect of their successes in other areas of popular culture. From the middle of the eighteenth century, when, as we have seen, popular mentality was still low on the reforming agenda, people of authority began successfully to suppress and sanitise those physical expressions of 'uncivilised', popular culture such as blood sports, which were deemed 'inconsistent with the laws of nature, the laws of religion, and the laws of a civilised nation'.[231] By the end of the eighteenth century, opposition to traditional popular recreation was meeting with considerable success, and by the 1840s once-widespread sports such as 'throwing at cocks' had been well and truly suppressed. During the nineteenth century, many other customary cultural activities such as harvest celebrations, wakes, May Day revels, and boisterous hiring fairs, either disappeared or were transformed into more decorous, sober occasions under authoritarian guidance. In the area of popular custom the reformers achieved much, despite numerous failures. More significantly, though, the results of their achievement were visible, and success could easily be measured. However, when it came to the eradication of popular magical beliefs, the reformers were not just dealing with the physical manifestations of a culture, or a way of behaving, but also a belief system – a way of thinking. In many respects the popular mentality remained remarkably unscathed by the forces of authoritarian repression, inculcation and elementary education. First, because attempts at repressing those ministers of 'superstition', cunning-folk and fortune-tellers, were fitful and half-hearted efforts which only began seventy years after the Witchcraft Act made much of their trade illegal. Second, because the rising level of popular education, which the authorities encouraged as an antidote to 'superstition', actually gave people greater access to magical knowledge.

In the same period as the popular belief in witchcraft and magic became a 'social problem', there also developed in educated circles new forms of semi-respectable occult beliefs. In essence, many aspects of phrenology, mesmerism, spiritualism, theosophy and astrology were no less 'superstitious' than the popular occult beliefs that were so widely condemned as the relics of ignorance. While the critics of these movements did, indeed, equate them with the 'old' beliefs in witchcraft and magic, the spiritualist, theosophist and middle-class astrologer looked down upon and despised the lower-class practitioners of fortune-telling and magic. The main difference between the two groups, however, was that the spiritualists and occultists dignified their belief-systems by developing coherent if not necessarily rational philosophies. Although the vogue for charity fortune-telling, and later the rise of newspaper astrology, signalled the demise of the old attitude that fortune-tellers presented a danger to public morals, they continued to attract some authoritarian opprobrium. Despite calls in some circles to let the people decide if they wanted to waste their money on fortune-tellers, the more patronising, paternalist section of the legislature continued to believe that the pockets of the ignorant poor, if not their morals, still needed a protective hand. As was highlighted by the parliamentary debates, it was all right for the legislature to condone the consultation and payment of mediums, because it had been decided that it was an intellectually and morally valid pursuit. The same group of people also decided that fortune-tellers were frauds, and their clients uneducated dupes. The decision was purely a value judgement rather than one based on any convincing, rational consideration of the relative nature of supernatural beliefs and their exploitation.

CHAPTER 2

WITCHCRAFT AND POPULAR JUSTICE

> And be it further enacted, That from and after the said Twenty-fourth Day of June, no Prosecution, Suit, or Proceeding, shall be commenced or carried on against any Person or Persons for Witchcraft, Sorcery, Inchantment, or Conjuration, or for charging another with such Offence, in any Court whatsoever in Great Britain.
>
> Witchcraft Act of 1736

So ended the era of official persecution and prosecution of witches. By 1736 the statute of 1604 had become something of a dead letter. The last execution for witchcraft in England and Wales had been in 1684, and the last indictment in 1717. From the late seventeenth century onwards, Parliament and the judiciary had been taking an increasingly sceptical attitude towards the existence of witchcraft, resulting in a gradual process of secular and ecclesiastical detachment from popular concerns over the problem of witchcraft. The fear of witchcraft, which had once united both the people and the state, increasingly became a concern of the people only. The state no longer protected its people from the evil influence of the witch, but for the majority of people the threat of witchcraft remained. How, then, did the people respond to the break up of this once solid partnership against witchcraft? And what effect did the closing of the criminal courts to the witch-persecuted public have on popular perceptions of justice? In the previous chapter we looked at responses towards the belief in witchcraft and magic from above; it is now necessary to look at how those below responded in turn.

The decline of witchcraft prosecutions

Attempts at explaining the significant decline in witch prosecutions that began during the 1670s have been frustrated by the fact that there is so little reliable, quantifiable contemporary information relating to witch-craft accusations that did not result in prosecution, and to the reasons why they did not. However, based on the information we have, and drawing inferences from the paucity of relevant evidence, two possible interpretative models of declining witch prosecutions can be put forward. (1) Faced with an increasingly sceptical judiciary, people who tried to institute prosecutions against witches were continually frustrated. As a consequence, the witch-believing populace gave up on official means of justice, and either contented themselves by grumbling into their pint pots, or resorted to unofficial justice instead. (2) The flow of indictment requests to justices of the peace during the late seventeenth and early eighteenth centuries continued at a similar level as before, but no official action was taken. I would suggest that, for several reasons, the second of the two models provides a more accurate picture of events.

First, as will be examined in detail later, applications to authority figures to act against suspected witches continued to be lodged well into the nineteenth century. This suggests that there was a considerable level of popular ignorance concerning the legal rejection of witchcraft as a criminal offence. In the mid-nineteenth century, for example, Arthur Chichester reported to the folklorist Mrs Bray that a farmer had come to him as a magistrate to consult how he should best proceed against an old woman who had bewitched himself and his cattle. Some years later, in 1875, an old woman living at Chelston, Devon, applied to Mr Hearder, the magis-trates' clerk at Torquay, for a warrant to apprehend a witch whom she believed had killed her husband. In 1879 the Caergwrle magistrates heard a petition from a woman asking them to restrain a neighbour who per-sistently bewitched her butter-making.[1] Thus well over a hundred years after the Witchcraft Act of 1736 people still continued to expect official succour against the malicious power of the witch.

Second, examining witch prosecutions as a series of individual cases, rather than as a general phenomenon, reflects adversely on the notion of a widespread popular disillusionment among the witch-believing public with the effectiveness of the justice being offered to them by the end of the seventeenth century. If, for example, we take the ten-year period from 1587 to 1597 from the Surrey assize records, as a comparatively intense period of witch prosecution (in English terms), we find that only eight cases of witchcraft were brought to trial over this period. Further-more, these cases were spread over a wide geographical area: Leigh, Southwark, Effingham, Woking, Battersea, Great Bookham, Bletchingley, Kingston-upon-Thames.[2] What I am attempting to convey is the sense of individuality and isolation of each witchcraft drama, even at a time when prosecutions were in full swing. Furthermore, this sense of isolation is heightened when we consider the lapse of time between each case, and also the poor level of contemporary communications. The idea of a general disillusionment with the efficacy of the courts, therefore, presupposes a degree of uniformity in the popular experience of justice, which did not exist.

It is regrettable that Alan Macfarlane in his study of Essex witchcraft declined to 'attempt an explanation of changes in the intensity of witch-craft beliefs'.[3] His caution is our loss, for the prosecution statistics for Essex in the latter half of the seventeenth century cry out for an expla-nation. This county had by far the highest number of assize indictments for witchcraft (this is still undoubtedly true when the poor survival rate of assize documents for some other counties is taken into account), yet the last presentment of a witch at the quarter sessions was in 1664, and the last at the assizes in 1675. Surrey, by comparison, had only one-sixth of the number of presentments as Essex, but assize indictments occurred as late as 1682 and 1701, and just across the Thames a warrant was issued by the magistrates at the Brentford petty sessions in June 1683 to appre-hend one Jane Dalton accused upon oath of being a witch.[4] Further-more, at least seven trials for witchcraft were held in Somerset and at least eight in Devon after 1675. Why, then, did no presentments occur after 1675 in the county that thirty years before abounded in witches? The answer to this would seem central to the question of decline from above or below.

Macfarlane noted that there were only thirty-nine presentments be-tween 1647 and 1680, twenty of which were rejected as *ignoramus*. This, he comments, 'seems to reflect a great change in attitude on the part of the minor gentry, of whom grand juries were composed. It seems to have been an important factor in the decline of witchcraft prosecutions in Essex some fifty years before the official repeal of the Witchcraft Act.'[5] There was undoubtedly a growing sense of caution among grand juries as to the reliability of much of the evidence presented to them at witch-trials, and this is well reflected in a charge given before the general Surrey quarter sessions of 1692:

> you are to enquire and present all Persons that have invocated, entertained or employed any wicked Spirit, or have used any Witchcraft, Charm, or Sorcery; this is a sin of a very deep die, being directly against the first Commandment, and is punished with Death both by the Law of God, and by a Statute made in the first Year of King *James* the First; but it is so hard a matter to have full

proof brought of it, that no Jury can be too cautious and tender in a prosecution of this Nature. However, where the evidence is clear and undeniable, you must proceed according to your Oaths.[6]

Yet, I do not believe that the circumspection of the grand juries in throwing out indictments more frequently actually affected the flow of popular requests for new bills to be drawn up. The key to declining prosecution lies, I suspect, outside the courts themselves and with the justices of the peace in the local setting. By the late seventeenth century, growing parliamentary scepticism concerning witchcraft, and the increasingly cautious attitude of many influential members of elite society towards the evidence presented at witchcraft trials, was undoubtedly putting pressure on justices to exercise their discretionary powers to nip potential witchcraft prosecutions in the bud. But while the justices were exhibiting increasing circumspection in response to informal pressure from above, they also had to contend with the continued pressure for prosecution from below.

It is possible that the growing influence of the petty sessions was influential in the decline of witchcraft prosecutions. As Norma Landau has observed, a plaintiff who managed to instigate a recognisance binding his or her persecutor to appear at the quarter sessions might feel satisfied that retribution had been gained.[7] The defendant had to pay a fee for the recognisance, and undertake an often lengthy and expensive journey to the sessions, while the plaintiff need not appear at the sessions unless he or she actually intended to prosecute. So to the plaintiff the adoption of the warrant to petty sessions may have seemed like a poor return for their troubles, and discouraged potential plaintiffs from requesting judicial aid in the future. In the context of declining witch prosecution such a scenario would certainly bolster the theory that the flow of applications for indictments dried up from below. Unfortunately, though, so few petty sessions' documents exist from the seventeenth and early eighteenth centuries that such a theory remains completely unsubstantiated. Besides, the victim of witchcraft would gain little satisfaction from an accused witch merely having to present his- or herself at court. What the victim wanted was to be physically rid of the witch, preferably permanently through execution, or at least temporarily through imprisonment.

In many instances having a witch executed or incarcerated was a means to effect a cure rather than an act of retribution or punishment. For example, it was only when the witch Edmund Hartley of Cleworth, Lancashire, was finally hanged in 1596/7 that his victims began to recover.[8] It should also be remembered that unofficial means of negating the effects of witchcraft were often tried before legal aid was sought, and sometimes afterwards if the witch escaped hanging or a lengthy spell in gaol. In this respect, the prosecution record does not necessarily reflect the true level of witchcraft accusations within any given area or period. Secular justice was just one way of ridding oneself of witchcraft among a number of other 'popular' methods. However, the most certain way of removing a spell was to be rid of the witch permanently. Although one could not just go out and murder a witch without being prosecuted for it, by using the legal process the same aim could be effected with impunity. But that outcome was by no means certain. For example, of those indicted for witchcraft at the Surrey assizes between 1560 and 1700 only 9.2 per cent were actually executed. In Kent over the same period 17.5 per cent of those indicted were executed, and the execution rate for Essex was 27 per cent.[9] One presumes, then, that the victim of witchcraft was still satisfied if the witch was imprisoned, and therefore removed from the community for a while if not for good. Of course, there was always a chance that the witch might die in prison.

Authority's role in the persecution and prosecution of witches

The justice of the peace was the most powerful representative of authority that most people were likely to have contact with. A justice could be a 'petty tyrant or a benevolent ruler';[10] his wide-ranging jurisdictional powers enabled him to intervene directly in the lives of the individuals within his hundred. As Peter Virgin has pointed out, the only contact which many people had with their government was made through the magistracy.[11] The solitary justice could conduct the preliminary examination of suspects and witnesses in felony cases, bind people over to be of good behaviour, take recognisances and commit suspected criminals to prison. Two justices acting together could further tackle cases of riot. By the late seventeenth century, however, the justices' main involvement in crime control was through the exercise of their extensive powers of summary conviction, so that a wide range of offenders were being tried before one or two justices without any trial by jury. The growing importance of the petty sessions through the latter half of the seventeenth century further augmented the justice's role as extra-legal arbiter within the community. Although justices could, and did, exercise their own judgement as to whether or not a given individual was to be prosecuted, it is important to remember that they by no means operated within a vacuum. Their decisions were open to influence from both above and below in the their respective communities, and also from wider political and religious interests.[12]

It has usually been taken for granted that by the end of the seventeenth century justices of the peace, *en masse*, became increasingly sceptical concerning witchcraft; yet each justice should really be considered individually concerning his personal beliefs, and his interaction with those in his jurisdiction. By 1700, where one justice may have been sceptical of witchcraft, a neighbouring one might not have been, and this is reflected in the prosecution statistics. It is quite likely that the last indictments for witchcraft brought before the courts only got there because the complaints of the victims of bewitchment fell on the ears of justices who still believed in the existence of witches. This seems to have been the case in such late prosecutions as that of Sarah Moredike of Southwark, Surrey, in 1701.[13] She was accused of bewitching one Richard Hathaway, who suffered from fits, and who, on being discharged from hospital as incurable, thought himself the victim of witchcraft. After much persecution, Moredike moved to Paul's Wharf, where the trouble continued. It was during a mobbing she received there that a local magistrate, Sir Thomas Lane, intervened and ordered that Moredike be scratched by Hathaway. She was then sent to the magistrate's house where she was stripped and searched for witch's marks by two women and a doctor. No such suspicious marks being found, Sir Thomas proceeded to commit her as a witch to the Wood Street Compter, refusing bail to the extent of £500. Brought to trial at the summer assizes at Guildford, the grand jury endorsed the indictment *billa vera* but she was later acquitted by the petty jury. The prosecution of Jane Wenham of Walkerne, Hertfordshire, is even more indicative of the way in which the attitude of the justice could be decisive.[14] In early February 1712, one John Chapman, believing Wenham had bewitched some of his livestock, called her a 'Witch and Bitch'. On the 9th of that month, Wenham applied to the magistrate Sir Henry Chauncy for a warrant against Chapman for his abuse. Chauncy, however, referred her to the arbitration of the Rev. Gardiner, who ordered the farmer to pay one shilling as a punishment. A potential court case had been avoided against the wishes of Wenham, who was apparently heard to say that, 'if she could not have justice here, she would have it elsewhere'. A few days after, a servant of the Rev. Gardiner became afflicted with fits. On 13 February Wenham refused to come to the sick girl to be scratched, and was apprehended under suspicion of felony and witchcraft by a constable wielding a warrant issued by Chauncy: there was to be no arbitration this time.

The clergy were not only involved in cases of witchcraft in their common role as justices but also in their role as representatives of religious authority in their parishes.[15] Although the trial of witches could only be conducted in the secular courts, the clergy were often involved in the pre-trial process of establishing the guilt of suspected witches. The detailed report concerning the suspected witch Widow Comon, written in 1699 by the Rev. James Boys, rector of Great Coggeshall, Essex, illustrates how involved the clergyman could get in cases of witchcraft accusation. The Widow Comon, her husband having recently drowned, became demented and began to speak of her relationship with the Devil. The Rev. Boys visited her several times, questioning her as to her diabolic acts and requesting her to repeat the Lord's Prayer, which she was unable to do. The widow was subsequently swum and some months later died. It was upon Boy's request that her cadaver was searched for witch marks.[16] In the case of Jane Wenham, the Rev. Strutt and the Rev. Gardiner also tested the suspected witch's knowledge of the Lord's Prayer. The two clergymen further advised the magistrate, Henry Chauncy, to apprehend three other women whom Wenham had named as confederates. Both also gave damning evidence at her trial. Thus the clergy were far from hesitant in embroiling themselves in the tangle of accusations, assaults, swimmings, weighings, and prosecution of suspected witches. It is no small wonder, then, that in the subsequent two centuries clergymen continued to be applied to in cases of witchcraft.

Although accused witches usually found themselves in court as defendants, they also appeared as plaintiffs, both in the ecclesiastical courts and occasionally in the secular courts, prosecuting those who made slanderous accusations of witchcraft against them. In 1661, Mary and Morris James of Haverfordwest brought an action for £200 damages against Peter Davids and his wife for having publicly stated 'Thou Mary hast bewitched my child and my drinke, and my child is yet sick and thou did'st doe it.' Nearly seventy years later, in 1730, Margaret Richards was brought before the magistrates at Neath charged with slandering William Williams of Llansamlet. She had accused him of bewitching her oxen and had threatened 'to have his blood for fear that he should come to bewitch them tomorrow again'.[17] So, although both the secular and the ecclesiastical authorities were anything but sympathetic to suspected witches, there was an official channel, albeit restricted, through which suspected witches could successfully achieve justice on their own terms. Evidence from the case of Jane Wenham suggests, though, that justices were not keen to allow access to the courts to those slandered by the imputation of witchcraft, preferring instead to deal with such cases informally.

As will become evident later, 'official' participation in the popular struggle against witchcraft was to have a lasting impression on the popular perception of the role of local authority over the next two centuries. For nearly two hundred years the victims of witchcraft had had easy access to official means of justice, and had been accustomed to the active support and close co-operation of both judiciary and clergy in their fight against witchcraft. The benefits were not just one-way; elite authority and popular justice maintained a symbiotic relationship with regard to the threat of witchcraft. Though the witch-accusers were more concerned about getting rid of the particular witches who tormented them, elite authority was far more concerned about the threat of witchcraft to its own grip on power, and was quite happy for the lower orders to root out witches for them as part of a general campaign against witchcraft. One of the best ways to examine the nature of this symbiotic relationship between local agents of elite authority and popular justice, and how that relationship changed over time, is by examining the history of the water ordeal from its inception in the early seventeenth century to its demise in the mid-nineteenth century.

Swimming: the popular adoption
of a continental practice

The first known use of the water ordeal as a test for witchcraft in England occurred in 1612 when Mary Sutton, of Milton, Bedfordshire, was swum in a local milldam. These events, and the subsequent trial, were recorded in the pamphlet *Witches Apprehended* (1613), which for the first time explained in detail the process of witch swimming in a popular format.[18] I have come across no evidence that corroborates Keith Thomas's statement that swimming 'was being used in witch cases in England by 1590'.[19] Prior to 1612, the use of the water ordeal to try witchcraft was obviously known by the educated elite, but only as a practice employed on the Continent.[20] It can be implied from Scot's *Discoverie* that it was not being used in England in 1584, while William Perkins only referred to its use 'in other countries'.[21] Undoubtedly influential in the introduction of the water ordeal for witchcraft was James VI's endorsement of the method in his *Daemonologie* (1597). In it he referred to the 'fleeting' of witches 'on the water' as a good help 'that may be used for their trial', and explained that 'God hath appoynted (for a super-naturall signe of the monstrous impietie of Witches) that the water shall refuse to receive them in her bosom, that have shaken off them the sacred water of Baptisme, and wilfullie refused the benefit thereof'.[22] As Stuart Clark has commented, *Daemonologie* is 'neither original nor profound', its significance largely lying in its 'being one of the first defences of Continental beliefs about witch-craft in English.'[23] In the year of James's accession to the English throne in 1603 a new edition of his *Daemonologie* was published, and it seems likely that it was through the circulation of this new edition among the educated elite that the continental practice of swimming witches came into vogue. The directions on how to swim a witch contained in *Witches Apprehended* undoubtedly further helped introduce the ordeal to a wider, more popular audience. The pamphlet also contained a woodcut depicting Sutton's swimming, which for those who could not read provided a good pictorial demonstration of the method.

The water ordeal was not, however, a new concept to English popular culture. In the early medieval period both the ordeals of cold water and hot iron were employed in the trial of crown pleas of felony; though in 1215 a decree of the Fourth Lateran Council put an end to both prac-tices. That the resumption of the water ordeal in seventeenth-century England was not a direct resurrection of this indigenous tradition is indi-cated by the fact that in medieval England women were never subjected to the ordeal of cold water. Thus, in 1198, an alleged sorceress was freed after passing the ordeal of hot iron.[24] The successful introduction of witch-swimming in England was, therefore, an early indicator of the increasing influence of continental theories of witchcraft. But its success was not merely due to James I's influential endorsement of the practice, and its subsequent judicious adoption by the educated elite in the provinces, for it obviously also struck a familiar chord with the populace at large. At first, the speed of the assimilation of the practice into popular culture seems somewhat surprising. According to John Cotta, writing in 1616, it was by then already fairly widespread. But a closer examination shows that swimming fitted in well with existing, long-held popular practices and preconceptions concerning trial and justice.[25] As Clive Holmes has observed, 'The swimming ordeal was functional but, equally, it was deeply rooted in the symbolic world of popular culture.'[26]

Prior to, and during, the seventeenth century, ducking- or cucking-stools had been fairly widely employed, particularly in towns, to punish a variety of minor offences such as the wearing of inappropriate dress on feast days, violation of the laws of weights and measures, and scolding.[27] By the seventeenth century ducking had become a punishment to which only scolding women were subjected. This probably reflects more upon the diminution of the offences punishable by ducking than evidence of some patriarchal campaign of female repression. The ritualised ducking of women was, therefore, a custom already established within popular culture before the influence of *Daemonologie*.

Like the ducking-stool, witch-swimming was a practice which was originally (though not always by the end of the century) sanctioned and organised by local authority figures. In other words it was a truly popular practice in that it involved the co-operation of the whole community. This is evident from the first two recorded cases of swimming, where the initiative was taken by educated figures of authority rather than villagers. This is hardly surprising when we consider that it was the educated elite who were instructing the largely illiterate masses in the new practice. In the case of Mary Sutton and her mother the accusations against them were generated after a 'difference' arose between Mother Sutton and a 'gentleman of worship' named Master Enger. Following this dispute Enger suffered a number of misfortunes including the death of his horses, pigs, and seven year-old son. Enger related his woes to a friend, who advised him to take the two women to his milldam and have them swum.[28] Mary Sutton was swum twice, and at the second test she floated, notwithstanding Master Enger's men 'tossing her up and down to make her sink'. Still denying all the charges against her, she was taken before a magistrate, put on trial, and subsequently both she and her mother were hanged. In the same year justices and 'other officers', presumably the parish constables, caused Arthur Bill and his parents, of Raunds, Northamptonshire, to be swum; all three floated but only Arthur was prosecuted and later hanged on 22 July.[29]

Swimming quickly came to be seen as a definitive test for witchcraft. After the first few years, when accused men and women were dragged to the local pond or river, probably uncomprehending of the ordeal they were about to be subjected to, so rooted had the practice become that by the mid-seventeenth century the accused themselves were requesting to be swum in order to clear their names in the eyes of God, the law and the community. In 1645, for example, the suspected witch Jane Hott, of Faversham, Kent, whilst languishing in gaol, declared to a gentleman that if they tried her in the water she would certainly sink. However, on being subjected to the ordeal she floated.[30] The witch-hunter John Stearne asserted, 'That [swimming] hath been used and I durst not goe about to cleere my selfe of it, because formerly I used it, but it was at such time of the yeare as when none tooke any harme by it, neither did I ever doe it but upon their owne request.'[31]

Until the end of the century, justices, constables and clergyman continued to sanction or at least tolerate the swimming of suspected witches. In 1660 Widow Robinson, her two daughters, and another man were taken from Worcester gaol to be swum in the River Severn. In 1699 the Rev. James Boys allowed a witch to be swum several times on different dates. A rather unusual case occurred in 1716, when the Worcestershire justice, John Goodere, was removed from the bench after his highly unusual attendance at a swimming. After the alleged witch had been swum, Goodere stripped, jumped into the water, and 'swam about it on his back, exposing his nakedness to the Men and Women that were present'. On emerging from the water he pulled on his breeches 'before several women that were present and asked which of them would be kn——kt'.[32]

From the first appearance of swimming, learned men of the period such as William Perkins, John Cotta, Richard Bernard, and later Thomas Ady, had expressed their disapproval of the ordeal as a true test of witchcraft. Cotta, writing in 1612, stated: 'Neither can I beleeve (I speake it with reverence unto graver judgements) ... floating of bodies above the water, or the like, are any trial of a witch.'[33] Ady was sceptical in that 'few men or women being tied hand and feet together can sink quite away till they be drowned.'[34] Such opinions did little to quell the enthusiasm for swimming, either among those accused of witchcraft, the justices and constables who countenanced sanctioned its practise, or the judges and juries who accepted it as proof. The elite acceptance of the water ordeal as evidence only began to crumble following the excesses of Matthew Hopkins and John Stearne, who organised many swimmings with the connivance of local justices over the two-year period 1645–46. In 1645 Parliament organised a special Commission of Oyer and Terminer to examine the many extraordinary confessions extorted by Hopkins and Stearne, and one of the first things the special court did was to condemn outright the use of swimming.[35] Such condemnation may have influenced justices and judges, but, as evidence already cited suggests, minor officials do not seem to have taken much heed. In 1694, though, a rare action was brought against witch-swimmers when a suspected witch named Margaret Waddam of Rode, Somerset, prosecuted three men, who, without any authority, had swum her in the River Avon 'until such time as she was near dead'.

In 1712, judicial condemnation of the water ordeal was further underlined by Lord Chief Justice Parker. According to the Rev. Francis Hutchinson, at the summer assizes held at Brentwood, Essex, Parker gave

'all Men Warning, That if any dare for the future to make use of that
Experiment, and the Party lose her Life by it, all they that are the Cause
of it are guilty of Wilful Murder.' Hutchinson added that he wished he
could 'proclaim it so loud, that every Man in *England* might hear it; that
if any Man hereafter uses that ungodly Trial, and the Part tried be drown'd;
neither King *James*'s Book, nor any other past Precedents will save them
from an Halter.'[36] Parker's warning probably influenced Sir Henry Chauncy's
refusal, in the same year, to sanction the swimming of the suspected witch
Jane Wenham, even though it was she who made the request. Chauncy
was by no means a sceptic: he himself resorted to scratching Wenham six
or seven times in order to break her power, but he refused to let her
undergo the water ordeal, pronouncing it illegal and unjustifiable.[37] However, in 1717, Parker's threat did not prevent the swimming of Jane Clarke,
and her son and daughter, of Great Wigston, Leicestershire. The swimming
may not have been 'authorised' but the accused's failure to sink was still
cited as evidence of their guilt during their trial.[38] It was eighteen years
later, in 1730, that Parker's threat was actually carried out, when three men
were charged with manslaughter after swimming an old woman of Frome,
who subsequently died. Around forty people had participated in the swimming, yet only three people were charged with manslaughter because no
one was willing to give evidence against the organisers of the swimming.
The defendants had dragged the old woman, 'shiv'ring with an ague out
of her house, set her astride on the pommel of a saddle, and carried her
about two miles to a millpond, stript off her upper cloaths, tied her legs,
and with a rope about her middle, threw her in, two hundred spectators
aiding and abetting the riot ... when almost spent they poured in brandy
to revive her, drew her to a stable, threw her on some litter in her wet
cloaths, where in an hour after she expired.'[39] Five years later, in 1735, a
poor shoemaker named John Kinsman, of Naseby, nearly died from his
repeated immersion in a great pond in Kelmarsh lordship. Apparently,
around one thousand people turned out to watch. In this instance no
action seems to have been taken, perhaps because, unlike the victim of the
Frome tragedy, Kinsman survived.[40]

Ironically, in the space of a hundred years an ordeal that the King of
England and the educated elite had injected into popular culture became
a popular practice that was severely censured by that same elite. By 1736
those figures of local authority who had originally sanctioned the swimming of witches, namely the gentry, justices and clergymen, were now
obliged, perhaps against their own judgement, to condemn those in their
communities for taking the law into their own hands. This shift in

educated opinion was not just a result of the declining belief in witch-craft, since, as we have seen, there had always been a measure of circum-spection concerning the validity of the ordeal, but also a response to new fears over law and order.

By 1736 what might previously have been described as a 'gathering' at a swimming was now termed a 'mob', and what was once a quasi-official proceeding could now be construed as a 'riot'. The Riot Act of 1714, which reaffirmed an earlier act of 1549, made it a capital offence for twelve or more persons to assemble riotously and tumultuously to the disturbance of the public peace, for more than an hour after a justice had read a proclamation specified in the Act ordering them to disperse. How-ever, as has been discussed in the previous chapter, there was a disparity between the harshness of the new legislature of the early eighteenth century and the realities of its application. As Thomas Skyrme has ob-served, justices found it difficult to enforce such rigid new laws, particu-larly in cases where the sympathy of the local population lay with the offenders.[41] Thus in a series of rulings made by the Court of King's Bench towards the end of the seventeenth century, that other form of popular justice, the skimmington, was also deemed to constitute a riot, but prosecutions for what was a fairly common practice remained extremely rare.[42] As will be shown later, justices were also loath to take any action against 'mob' swimmings, and usually acted only in the rare instances when the suspected witch died from her ordeal, in which case man-slaughter charges were brought as in the Frome case. What is important, though, is not so much the lack of application of the law, as the fears which generated the laws, and the terminology in which such popular gatherings were described.

The Witchcraft Act of 1736 was passed with little controversy. For Mem-bers of Parliament the issue was rather *passé* and provoked little uproar: there were new secular and religious causes to get excited over in the 'Age of Enlightenment'. But what about the great mass of the population – how did they get to hear of the new law? And what did it mean to them? Considering the continued popular resort to swimming through-out the eighteenth and early nineteenth centuries, one wonders whether people were never made properly aware of the illegality of the actions resulting from their beliefs, or whether they were properly informed and simply chose to ignore it.

From where, or whom, could people hear of the new law? For the literate only two pamphlets responding to the Act were published, and little debate seems to have raged in contemporary journals and magazines although the news of its passing was reported. The problem lies in discovering the channels along which this information could have been passed down to the semi-literate, who had no access to such written sources, and the plain illiterate. A glimpse of one such possible channel can, however, be gained from the sermon of the Rev. Joseph Juxon, vicar of Twyford, published shortly after the passing of the Witchcraft Act.[43] Juxon was not actually inspired to give his sermon because of the new Act, but because some of his parishioners had performed 'foolish unwarrantable Experiments' by swimming witches. A large portion of the sermon was taken up with a discussion of the usual biblical arguments against the existence of witchcraft, but also central to Juxon's sermon was his attempt to underline the secular denial of witchcraft as spelled out in the new Act. In his sermon, Juxon echoed the final clause of the 1736 Act, explaining to his audience the new legal distinction concerning those who could and could not be prosecuted:

> if there are any amongst you who professedly declare that by their Art in consulting evil and seducing Spirits, they can procure you that Favour and Protection, which Heaven above can grant; these, and these only, are the Witches the scripture knows any thing of, and whom you have any Warrant or Authority from thence to cut off. But then this you are to do, not upon any uncertain fallacious Experiments, not upon your own private Judgement or Conviction, but by appealing to the Laws of your Country, by prosecuting 'em in a fair and legal way.[44]

Towards the end of his sermon, Juxon proceeded to spell out the possible fate of those who would continue to resort to unofficial justice:

> In our own Country there is no Fear indeed, that in our Days, whilst Truth and Knowledge prevails, and after the good Care that our Legislature has taken of us, any should now suffer by the hands of Publick Justice, on the score of Witchcraft any more. But when private Persons, without any Authority, and by vain and deceitful Tests, take upon 'em to determine the Guilt or Innocence of Persons unjustly suspected, it is high time to put a stop to such Proceedings, which must at best cast a lasting Odium on the Name of those who are accused, may possibly end in the Death of some of 'em; and if it should, must expose those who are the Cause of it, to the Punishment due unto Murderers, both in this World, and in the World to come.[45]

Juxon's aim in delivering his sermon seems to have been threefold. First, to affirm from a biblical point of view that 'modern Notions of Witchcraft' had 'no other Foundation than Ignorance or Superstition'.[46] Second, to make his parishioners aware of the implications of the Witchcraft Act. Third, to condemn the resort to 'Publick Justice' in terms similar to those of Chief Justice Parker a couple of decades before. If any of the congregation at Twyford church were still paying attention, or had indeed remained awake, after the previous twenty-five pages of dull prose, then Juxon's warnings may have sunk in. No doubt the gist, and purpose, of the vicar's discourse would have been subsequently communicated informally around the parish at least. But, as we have seen in the previous chapter, we should not assume that Juxon's condemnatory words were treated with anything but indifference or annoyance by his parishioners.

Apart from the odd sermon, there is remarkably little evidence of the transmission of the Witchcraft Act down to the general public. After 1736, one would assume, though, that justices and clergymen would have informed those who continued to apply to them of the legal reasons why they could no longer take any action. Despite such possible attempts at informing the public, the historical record shows that for the next 150 years people continued to apply to figures of local authority to restrain witches, and continued to resort to 'Publick Justice'.

According to Wallace Notestein, 'with the nullification of the law the common people began to take the law into their own hands. We shall note that, as a consequence, there was an increase in the number of swimming ordeals and other illegal procedures.'[47] This is, I believe, a misguided assumption. First, because it implies a widespread popular understanding of the Witchcraft Act, for which there is little evidence. Second, because throughout the period of witch prosecution there was a constant background level of unofficial action taking place which was largely overshadowed by the reports of official action. In 1718, for example, Francis Hutchinson remarked concerning witch-swimming, 'Our Countrey-People are still as fond of it, as they are of Baiting a Bear or Bull.'[48] Once witchcraft was removed from the statute books we are left with this background of extra-legal redress, except that now it comes to the foreground of attention. Furthermore, there is no reason, in a technical sense, why there should have been an initial increase in the number of swimmings after 1736, for swimming was not a punishment in itself but a test to prove that a person *was* a witch, who could then be brought forward for justice to be served, whether officially or unofficially. Though, as we shall see later, swimming was applied as a punishment in a later period.

Although it only takes two to duck a witch, hundreds could actually turn out, either to stand back and watch, or to join in with the manhandling that the suspected witch often had to endure. As Juxon opined, 'I know not how it happens, but there is so much superstitious Fear, and this is so deeply rooted, in the Minds of Men, that whenever the Alarm is given, there is always a Party formed, a very powerful one too, against these poor ignorant and helpless Creatures.'[49] If the event was well publicised, then inhabitants of other villages could turn out to enjoy the entertainment. After all, to those of that frame of mind, a witch-swimming was probably the next best thing to a public execution. Entries from the diary of Rev. Humphrey Michel illustrate only too well the nature and popularity of the spectacle.

> June 11, 1709, being St. Barnabas' Festival and Whitsun Eve, one Thomas Holmes, of Horninghold, a labourer, was dowsed three times for a witch, and did not sink, but swam, though his hands and feet and head were all tyed fast together; and all this was done in the Dungeon Pit in Blaston, before 500 people (they say) … June 17, being Whitsun week, one Elizabeth Ridgway and Jane Barlow, of Horninghold, were both by consent dowsed for witches, and did not sink … before some thousands of people at the Dungeon pit.

The following day the vicar himself was present:

> June 18. The said Jane Barlow, 40 years old, would be dowsed again to clear herself, but in the great close pond, because she said that was not enchanted as Dungeon Pit (she said) was; and yet, in the sight of many hundreds of people and myself she did not sink … Mary Palmer, her sister, a cripple from her cradle, almost 42 years old, was dowsed there for a witch several times, and, though bound hands and feet, did not swim, but sank immediately, like a stone, before us all.[50]

It is probably no coincidence that this series of mob duckings occurred between 11 and 18 June, for this was Whitsun week under the old calendar, traditionally seven days of celebration and festivities, often fuelled by the distribution of Whitsun ale.

Only a year after the passing of the Witchcraft Act the swimming of a married woman in her sixties took place at Oakley, Bedfordshire, in circumstances which suggest either a general ignorance of the statute amongst the villagers, or a defiant display of popular justice in contravention of the Act. The parish constables, rather than upholding the law, actually promised the woman a guinea if she should willingly undergo the swimming ordeal, and the vicar who apparently believed in the witch's guilt, was also present. The poor woman was tied up in a wet sheet, her thumbs and big toes bound together, and then swum in the River Ouse with a rope tied around her middle. She floated three times, and there were cries of 'A witch! Drown her! Hang her!' from the crowd. On being dragged out of the water half-dead, a member of the crowd suggested she also be weighed against the church Bible, which was about twelve pounds in weight. Not surprisingly she passed this test, though many of those present counted her acquittal unsatisfactory, including the vicar of Oakley.[51]

Only a decade on from the above events and no churchman in his right mind would have been seen idle among the crowd at a swimming, though he might still, however, turn a blind eye to the proceedings. The parish register of Monk's Eleigh in Suffolk could record quite calmly that on 19 December 1748, Alice Green, a labourer's wife, was 'swum, malicious and evil people having raised an ill report of her being a witch'.[52] In fact the scant evidence would suggest that after 1736 many swimmings took place without the authorities intervening and prosecutions ensuing. When the justices and clergymen withdrew from such proceedings after 1736 – if they had not done so before – they seem to have largely washed their hands of anything connected with it, and were unwilling to institute proceedings against those who took the law into their own hands concerning a crime which, in legal terms, no longer existed.

I have come across only two confirmed cases of prosecutions resulting from the swimming of suspected witches during the period from 1736 to the end of the century. The first of these trials, the Tring case of 1751, became something of a national sensation. The trial and subsequent execution of Thomas Colley for his part in the swimming of Ruth and John Osborne, aged fifty-six and sixty-nine respectively, was not only recorded in journals and newspapers of the time, but was also the subject of two pamphlets.[53] The Osbornes were accused of bewitching a local publican named Butterfield, who, it seems, was the main organiser of the plan to swim his supposed persecutors in the glare of maximum local publicity. The town cryers of Winslow, Leighton and Hemel Hempstead were paid to announce that the Osbornes were to be ducked at Longmarston on 22 April. On the day, a vast concourse gathered, and the parish officers acted to remove the Osbornes from the workhouse to the church for security. Angered by this move, the 'mob' began vandalising the workhouse, and even seized the governor and threatened to drown him and set fire to the town. Under such duress the Osbornes were handed over and swum, and Ruth subsequently died from her ordeal. Only one of the ringleaders, Colley, a chimney sweep, was subsequently arrested. From his 'confessions' we find that Colley's knowledge of witch-swimming was informed by a story he had heard about another swimming that had apparently taken place in the neighbouring county of Bedfordshire sixteen or seventeen years before. It is almost certain that this was a folk memory of the Oakley affair, though the facts of the case had become somewhat distorted over the years. According to Colley, two women had been swum on that occasion. One 'swam like a Cork', and the other, who had been paid to undergo the ordeal, sunk and was drowned, 'after which, they murdered the supposed Witch; and no Harm coming upon it, he thought he might lawfully serve these two People [the Osbornes] in the same Manner.' We need not doubt Colley's statement that he believed swimming to be a legally acceptable process. After all, it would have been foolish of Colley, Butterfield and their conspirators to advertise publicly the event all over the countryside if they believed they would be punished for it. This continuing popular notion concerning the legality of swimming is also apparent from the ducking of an old woman of Aston, Leicestershire, in June 1776. The organisers of the 'event' pretended to have an official warrant ordering that the old woman be swum.[54]

In the second prosecution case, in 1760, the villagers of Great Glen and Burton Overy, Leicestershire, carried out a series of swimmings similar to that recorded by the Rev. Michel. The swimmings began after two old women of Glen accused each other of witchcraft, and challenged each other to be swum. They accordingly stripped to their shifts, had their thumbs and big toes tied across, and with a cart-rope tied around their middles suffered themselves to be thrown into a local pond. One of them was unable to sink, and in defence of her reputation claimed that there were several other women in neighbouring Burton as much witches as she was. At the same time a local girl was pronounced bewitched by a 'student in astrology'. In consequence, on the following day a 'mob' repaired to Burton where they gathered outside the cottage of an old woman on whom suspicion had also fallen. She refused to come out and be swum, and so the 'mob' forced their way into her cottage, dragged her out, and swum her in a nearby gravel pit. Another woman was tried on the same day, and another the following day. The *Annual Register* reported that 'Several of the ring leaders in this riot, we hear, have been apprehended, and carried before a Justice; two of which have been bound over to the sessions, and others ordered to pay small fines.' In July two persons were sentenced at the Leicester quarter sessions to stand in the pillory twice, and to lie in jail for one month.[55] It is not certain who actually instigated the prosecutions. It is possible that one of the women who was subjected to a swimming lodged a complaint, or maybe the authorities, in a rare display of legal enforcement, instigated proceedings for riot.

A third possible prosecution may have occurred in 1761. In late December 1760, Sarah Jellicoat, of Wilton, Wiltshire, was about to be swum by townsfolk for bewitching a farmer's servant and a tallow chandler's soap. Fortunately for her she was saved 'by the favourable inter-position of some humane gentlemen & the vigilance of a discreet magis-trate, who stopped the proceedings before the violence thereof had gone to a great pitch'. The aggressors were apparently bound over by recognisance to appear at the next assizes to justify their actions.[56] Whether a prosecution ensued I have been unable to find out.

In general, prosecutions seem to have been the exception rather than the rule when it came to attempts at suppressing and punishing communities for swimming suspected witches. It appears from the evidence that when magistrates and other conscientious members of the elite intervened in attempted swimmings, they preferred to deal with the situation informally without resorting to force or instituting legal proceedings. Thus, when a few weeks after the Tring affair, some people gathered together at Leighton (Leighton Buzzard) market cross, proclaimed Jane Massey and Catherine Haukes to be witches, and proceeded to go and have them swum, they were successfully prevented 'by several gentleman who advised them to return home'.[57] In the Wiltshire village of Seend around one hundred people gathered to see an old woman being ducked in a mill pond in 1773. A rope was tied about her middle and she was thrown into the pond two or three times. Her clothes kept her afloat, and her guilt was thereby evident to all those present. The following day she was to be ducked once again, but the local justice of the peace intervened to prevent it taking place.[58] A year later an old couple named Hart, who were accused of bewitching some cattle, were swum by some 'illiterate blockheads'. They were rescued not by the local constable, but by some brave members of the public.[59] In a case from the early nineteenth century, an old woman named Warden, living in St John Street, Wellingborough, had to be rescued from a swimming by her son, who was a master at St George's School, Leicester.[60] Finally, when, in July 1825, Isaac Stebbings volunteered himself to be swum a second time at Wickham-Skeith, in Suffolk, the clergyman of the parish and two churchwardens intervened, the swimmers were kept away, and no further action was taken.[61]

The contemporary newspaper and journal evidence indicates a continuing but sporadic tradition of witch-swimming. Evidence from the oral record suggests, however, that many more instances of swimming probably went unrecorded at the time. The childhood recollection of a swimming related to a Norfolk magistrate in 1857 is likely to have been one of many such instances around the country which were never brought before the courts as cases of assault, or brought to the attention of the newspapers:

old Mrs. Pointer – when I wuz a boy – she wuz a real witch! Har they swum.
A long ladder was put across the river, and old Mr. Loveday stood on it, pushing
her under water, but 'twas no use – up she came every time. Then they pulled
her out, and began to mob her. Then she called out to be weighed against the
church book but the churchwarden swore with a great oath that she should not
come near the Bible and told her 'to go home, for a —— infernal old witch
as she was.' And so she was, sir.[62]

Around the same time in neighbouring Suffolk, an old man of Polstead
claimed to have seen a witch swum in the village pond. He remembered
that 'she went over the water like a cork'. The parish clerk of Seend,
Wiltshire, who died in 1891 aged eighty-three, also remembered as a boy
another old woman being swum in the village stream.[63] We have to be
careful, therefore, not to underestimate the vitality of the tradition. The
evidence already presented here certainly contradicts Robert Malcolmson's
view that 'Plebeian attempts to punish witches became rare', and his
citation of the Tring case as one of the 'last public exercises in witch-
hunting'.[64] Even as late as 1880, two labouring men of High Easter, Essex,
were presented at the petty sessions for confronting one Susan Sharpe,
and asking if 'she would consent to be thrown in a pond, to test whether
she were a witch'. When a summons was served upon one of the defendants, he told the policeman that nothing would satisfy him 'unless she
would submit to be thrown into a pond, and if she sank he would be
satisfied she was not a witch, for witches could always swim'.[65] As will be
discussed later, though, by 1880 changes in communal policing made it
near impossible for witch-swimmings actually to take place any more.

With the withdrawal of officials from the swimming of witches, communities had to rely on their own knowledge of the swimming tradition,
rather than the knowledge and procedural guidance of educated figures
of authority. In the seventeenth century, 'officially' conducted swimmings
followed a set procedure as laid out in books and pamphlets of the period,
with the suspected witch's thumbs being bound to his or her toes in a
cross-wise fashion, and with a rope tied around the witch's middle, which
was held between two men.[66] Until the mid-eighteenth century, unofficial
communal swimmings were still being conducted in the same manner. In
the Oakley, Tring, and Glen and Burton cases, for example, the suspected
witches' thumbs were tied to their toes. By the nineteenth century, however, the oral transmission of knowledge concerning swimming procedure
seems to have attenuated to the point where it was still commonly known
that witches floated in water, but knowledge of the original procedure
had been lost, and communities were left to devise their own unorthodox

operations. Thus, in the case of Mrs Pointer, mentioned above, a ladder was placed across a river from which a man pushed her under. In the Wickham-Skeith case (1825), four men accompanied Stebbings into the water, and when the water was breast-high they 'lifted him up and laid him flat upon his back on the water'. The magistrate who recorded the account of the swimming of Mrs Pointer was also given the following account of the unorthodox swimming of Betsey Norris: 'once a woman named Huggins, a wonderful strong woman, swore she would try whether Betsey Norris was a witch or not. She took and put her on to a faggot and shoved her into a pond, and turned her over and over with a pitch-fork, but she came up again every time, and swam like a duck or a goose.'[67]

As Clive Holmes has noted, there is a sense in which swimming 'could become a punishment, a popular replacement for the official sanction formally abandoned in 1736'.[68] Thus in the Aston case (1776) we find swimming apparently being used more as a punishment than as an ordeal. The witch was initially scratched by her supposed victims, but no cure having been effected, she was swum seven days later.[69] This corruption of the swimming ordeal is most apparent in the case of the swimming of a deaf and dumb cunning-man, nick-named 'Dummy', at Sible Hedingham, in Essex, in 1863. Emma Smith, wife of a beer-shop keeper in the nearby village of Ridgewell, believed herself to have been bewitched by Dummy, and one night she accosted him at the Swan Inn at Sible Hedingham, in front of some forty or fifty people, and requested him to come home with her in order to remove his spell. Dummy refused, and began to be jostled by Smith, her husband, and a master carpenter named Samuel Stammers. A woman's voice was heard to say, 'Put him, or swim him, on the Millhead', and Dummy was then dragged down to a nearby brook where Emma Smith caught hold of his shoulders and Stammers grabbed his legs, and they threw him into the sluice. When Dummy tried to clamber out, Stammers shoved him back into the water where he was 'kept a quarter of an hour muddling in the water.' Stammers eventually pulled Dummy out and laid him on the bank, and two women helped him home. A month later he died from inflammation of the lungs and brain.[70] As Christina Hole has pointed out, though, no one seems to have paid any attention to whether Dummy floated and sank.[71] Dummy was not swum to prove his guilt but to punish him for his supposed crime. However, I do not think that Hole was right to extrapolate from the evidence that, of those present, 'practically every one had forgotten what swimming really meant'. Once swimming was freed from 'official' guidance, and in the subsequent absence of harsh repressive measures against its practice, it could be more freely employed as a form of popular justice. As such, it served a dual purpose. When there was a measure of public doubt concerning the guilt of a suspected witch, then swimming could be employed for its original purpose as a test. But when the community was already convinced of the guilt of the witch, then swimming could also be used as a ritual of public chastisement, a means of coercing the witch into stopping his or her witchcraft, just as scolds were ducked to silence their tongues.

The continued resort to figures of authority and their response

For many, even in the late nineteenth century, the threat and extent of witchcraft were as potent a reality as they had ever been in the sixteenth and seventeenth centuries. In 1857, a Norfolk farmer, 'J. B.', confided in his local magistrate that the problem of witchcraft had actually got worse: 'They do say, your worship, that such folks are increased about in the world, and if you have so many as even one in this or any other parish, they do a sight of harm.'[72] Even in 1897, Mr Mitchell, the blacksmith of Piddlehinton, in Dorset, remarked to a folklorist concerning witchcraft that 'It do seem a bad job should be such works about, *but there be*, and a terr'ble sight o' it too, *there be, indeed*.'[73] Considering the continued strength of belief in the power of witchcraft it is not surprising that accusations continued to be made, and communal action against witches continued to take place, well into the nineteenth century. What is surprising though, is the extent to which people, over a hundred years after the passing of the Witchcraft Act, still considered agents of state authority as allies in the continuing popular struggle against witchcraft. In the popular mind, witchcraft remained a crime against the individual and the community. If a crime such as witchcraft had been committed, therefore, then it was perceived that the state was obliged to act against it if so requested. After all, people paid their taxes and tithes and expected to see some positive official response if their lives or livelihood were being threatened by witchcraft. As the Norfolk farmer, J. B., pointed out to his local magistrate: 'Sir, if our squire knew there was any such bad things as witchcraft in the parish, he would have it altered; because, you know, Sir, I have to pay rates and taxes, hard and fast.' This indignant assertion by the taxpayer that he should expect some return for his contributions was echoed by a Cornish farmer in conversation with the Rev. Robert

Hawker. Visiting the village of Morwenstow, Cornwall, the day after a violent thunderstorm, Hawker came upon a local farmer and his men standing in a ditch beside a dead horse, the death of which was attributed to 'that wretched old Cherry Parnell's doing, with her vengence and her noise'. After explaining to Hawker the particular background to this instance of *maleficium* the conversation took a new turn:

> 'And I do think, sir,' he went on to say, changing his tone to a kind of indignant growl, 'I do think that, when I call to mind how I've paid tithe and rates faithfully all these years, and kept my place in church before your reverence every Sunday, and always voted in the vestries that what hath and be ought to be, – I do think that such ones as old Cherry Parnell never ought to be allowed to meddle with such things as thunder and lightning.'[74]

There are several possible reasons why people might have resorted to magistrates. As in the seventeenth century, it is quite likely that those who sought the law to act on their behalf may already have resorted to both private magic rituals and cunning-folk, but finding no relief decided, finally, to fall back on the legal process. Thus Farmer J. B. had already been to a local cunning-woman, and employed a witch bottle, before beating a path to the magistrate's door. It may have also been the case that some victims of witchcraft were also unable to resort to their own unbewitching actions, such as scratching, because the witch lived some distance away, as was probably the case in the application to Mr Trafford cited below. Another possible reason for turning to the magistrate was because it did not cost anything, whereas the employment of an occult practitioner could be expensive.

The pattern of applications to justices concerning witches, in both the prosecution and post-prosecution periods, may also have been directly influenced by the relative distance that had to be travelled to see the local justice. In this context it is worth considering the observation of a nineteenth-century diarist, grandfather of Cecil Torr, who wrote on 24 May 1852: 'We never before had a magistrate nearer than xxxxx, and if any little paltry squabble happened between parties, their courage invariably cooled down on crossing the water, and almost invariably they returned home without a summons. But now whilst passion is up they have only to go to xxxxx, and a summons is granted, I find, much to the regret of many after cool reflection.'[75] Of course, for those who could write, or get someone else to write for them, complaints could also be lodged by letter. In 1825, for example, a note bearing five signatures was sent to the chairman of the Talgarth petty sessions, alleging that one Thomas Ralph was a troublesome witch.[76]

It is difficult to ascertain what fate applicants to magistrates had in mind for those they accused of being witches. The reason for this was, perhaps, that the people themselves were often unsure as to what they wanted to be done, and rather depended on the authorities to decide for them. Thus an old Somerset woman, who fancied her neighbour had bewitched her two drunken sons, requested the local squire 'to exercise his powers as a Magistrate *somehow* [my emphasis] to restrain this witch'.[77] Another elderly woman, who applied to Mr Trafford, the stipendiary magistrate at the Manchester police court, in May 1863, requested that the witchcraft practised against her 'must be stopped by some means'.[78] When Mr. Trafford asked what she wanted, she replied, 'A summons for a kind of witchcraft; my husband has died from it, and I want it put a stop to.' The applicant claimed that a Glossop man had been tormenting her by witchcraft, and asked 'Maister Trafford' if he would write to the witch to make him stop:

> Mr Trafford: Well, come to me at Salford Town hall to morrow morning.
>
> Applicant: But will you protect me till to-morrow? – my life is in danger from witchcraft, and I want protection.
>
> Mr Trafford: How can I protect you unless you come and live with me, and I'm sure I don't want that …
>
> Mr. Trafford: Well, I will write to him and tell him to be quiet.
>
> Applicant: No, you must write to him and tell him to stop it – (laughter) …
>
> Mr Trafford: Well, I will send over in some shape or other, and see if I cannot get it stopped.

Trafford was unusually patient and obliging, and he even suggested to the woman that a horseshoe nailed over the door was 'a very good protection' – a suggestion which would undoubtedly have brought censure upon him from some fellow magistrates for encouraging superstition. Farmer J. B. of Hockham parish, Norfolk, was equally adamant that the magistrate must test and subsequently restrain the witch who tormented his wife, but again he seemed rather unclear as to what fate should ultimately await the witch. He did at least think that her incarceration in the Union House, if not in prison, would prove beneficial:

> J. B.– 'I do hope your worship will grant the police to take old Mrs. C. all of a sudden – by surprise like – and take her to a pit, and swim her (not to hurt her).' …
>
> J. B. – 'What, Sir! arn't you going to have it proved? Can't you at any rate have her hitched to the Union House? That might be a benefit.'
>
> 'I will make enquiries, and will do what is advisable.'

(Exit applicant, protesting against anything short of full proof by 'swimming her.')[79]

The same Norfolk magistrate, in another letter to *The Times*, described how he had elicited a rather more categorical response from one young woman, as to what should have been done with the Hockham witch. On accompanying a wedding party at the time of J. B.'s request, he humorously 'asked the bride and her smart friend "how they would like their own characters to be tested in the river, with their present buoyant-looking petticoats?" They declined the trial. I then asked them, "What was I expected to do with old Mrs. C—— if she had floated?" Answer (with the gravest look) "Why then, Sir, of course she would have to be made away with."'[80] The idea that a witch could simply 'be made away with' is also evident from Thomas Colley's acceptance of the story in which the Bedfordshire witch, once proved as such by swimming, was murdered with impunity. At a time when, from a modern perspective, trivial crimes were punishable by death or transportation, perhaps it is not surprising that people believed that witches deserved to be 'made away with' for their crimes. Unfortunately we do not know whether the bride believed that the witch should be executed by the legal authorities, or, like Colley, thought it acceptable that the witch be lynched by the community. Witches, of course, could also be killed by counter-magic. After the second swimming of Isaac Stebbings was prevented, a local cunning-man was paid £3 on the assurance that Stebbings would be 'killed by inches'.[81]

An examination of applications to figures of authority in the community reveals that those accused and persecuted as witches, as well as applying to a magistrate to have their tormentors bound over, often sought succour at the door of the rectory. Writing in 1847, the Norfolk clergyman John Gunn commented that applications had often been made to him 'for advice by persons feeling themselves aggrieved by the imputation of sorcery'.[82] When, in 1883, an accused witch was scratched severely in the neck and in four places on her arm, she went to complain to the Rev. R. F. Meredith, rector of Halstock, Dorset. Meredith advised her to take out a summons before the justice, but she did not follow his advice, perhaps fearing that the justice would have little sympathy. In 1895 a Herefordshire woman also felt it necessary to go to the local vicarage to deny a village rumour that she had bewitched two old people. 'Indeed, indeed, I did no sich thing', she asserted, 'I never ill-wished them nor nothin.'[83] This resort to clergymen who were not also acting magistrates may reflect two preconceptions in the minds of the accused witches. First, the continued belief that the magistrate was a partner in the fight *against* witchcraft may have led some of those accused of witchcraft to consider that the magistrate would be naturally prejudiced against them. Even when an accused witch did instigate a prosecution for assault, there still remained the worry that the court would be ill-disposed towards them. When Charity Furzer, a suspected witch, appeared before the Chard bench of magistrates to give evidence against her assailant, 'she seemed very anxious to impress upon the magistrates the certainty of HER not being one [a witch], and the tears ran down her cheek as she asseverated her innocence.'[84] Therefore, those suspected witches who were apprehensive concerning the attitude of their local magistrates turned to the only other significant member of authority in the community, the clergyman. Second, applications to the clergy may also be linked with the folk memory of the old church courts, where up until the eighteenth century accused witches could prosecute their accusers for slander, and so have their names cleared before the community.

If those who applied to magistrates and clergymen to act against witches felt themselves ill-served by their unsympathetic reception, then those who applied to the same gentlemen to protect them from the imputation of witchcraft often received little better treatment. The Rev. John Gunn admitted in 1847 that, 'In one instance, a labourer asked me what steps he should take to protect his wife from being called a witch. I persuaded him to let her treat the matter with contempt.'[85] Such precious advice was of little comfort in the face of hostile accusations and the labourer returned a few days later to declare he could bare it no more. Similarly, in June 1792, an old woman of Stanningfield, Suffolk, who could no longer face the accusations of witchcraft being made against her, received little comfort from the local magistrates, and had to resort to popular justice to clear her name. In the course of an examination relative to a pauper before Sir Charles Davers, Bart., and the Rev. John Ord, at the Angel Inn, the old woman charged another with having called her a witch, which she said had very much disordered her head. The justices told her, however, that they could take no cognisance thereof and she was dismissed. Having received no legal help, she handed herself over to the community to prove her innocence by extra-legal means. First it was suggested that she be weighed against the church Bible, but the clergyman refused to lend it, so she was forced to undergo the far more dangerous procedure of swimming. She was swum in a local horsepond, was found to sink, and was then dragged out 'almost lifeless'. Her husband, who along with her brother and another man, held the rope at her swimming, was reported to have said that he thought it better to indulge her therein, than to suffer her to destroy herself, which she would otherwise have certainly done.[86]

To justify their belief in witchcraft and the actions they wished to subject suspected witches to, some witch-believers made reference to the Bible as providing them with the authoritative sanction to deal with them how they would. After centuries in which the state and ecclesiastical authorities had held up the Bible to the people as the repository of wisdom, truth and moral probity, nineteenth-century magistrates and churchmen found it extremely difficult to start arguing successfully that the witches in the Bible were not *really* witches. Victims of witchcraft had little time or patience for lectures about Biblical mistranslation: was it not plainly written in the Bible that 'Thou shalt not suffer a witch to live'? Thus a Berkshire folklorist found that the belief in witchcraft was constantly justified by reference to the story of the Witch of Endor. Similarly, when the folklore collector Boys Firmin 'expressed a doubt or seemed inclined to be incredulous, my informant confronted me with the "Witch of Endor" – was I going to deny that story?'[87] Farmer J. B., in arguing with his local magistrate, also 'brought forward the witch of Endor, the demoniacs of the New Testament, &c.' The interview ended with the farmer 'being apparently "convinced against his will," and, therefore, "of the same opinion still".'[88] During the inquest on the death of Mary Jane Saunders, eldest daughter of George Saunders, labourer of Lufton, Somerset, in June 1892, the coroner turned his attention to Saunders' belief that his daughter had been bewitched: 'do you seriously believe that any person could have this influence? Witness: You read in the Bible about witchcraft.'[89] At the trial of James Haywood, charged with the murder of the suspected witch Ann Tennant at the winter assizes in Warwick, 15 December 1875, Mr Anderson, the governor of the gaol in which Haywood had been incarcerated, told the court how Haywood was a quiet, inoffensive man except on the subject of witchcraft. Haywood had told him it was his duty to kill Tennant, and referred to Acts viii, 9–11, and Leviticus xx, 27, to show that he was justified in his crime, and had marked those pages in his Bible.[90] The popular belief in the authority of the Bible as an arbiter of justice was also manifest in the practice of weighing witches against the church Bible.[91] The Rev. Robert Forby noted that 'many instances might be cited of persons who had been accused of witchcraft applying to the clergyman of the parish to be allowed to prove their innocence by this ordeal'.

The growth of popular literacy in the nineteenth century, which most members of authority were busy promoting as an antidote to the belief in witchcraft, seems to have had an opposite effect to that intended. The Bible was the single most popular literary work, and although it was promoted as a manual of spiritual and moral guidance, it was also a reposi-tory of occult knowledge. As the naturalist A. R. Wallace once observed, amongst the 'peasantry' superstition 'rather increased than diminished in those who are able to read by their confining their studies almost wholly to the Bible'.[92] Considering that the Bible condemned witches and sanc-tioned retributive justice, it is also no wonder that people legitimised their actions by reference to it.

Witch-mobbing as an act of folk justice

Communal or mob action against witches, whether inspired by the desire to swim or weigh a witch, or to draw blood, should be seen in the same context as those other forms of communal, extra-legal justice which have received far more historical attention – rough music, skimmingtons, stang-riding, *ceffyl pren*, and their other regional variants.[93] The central feature of these manifestations of communal disapprobation was the ritualised public shaming and ostracism of those members of the community who were perceived to have transgressed the bounds of communal norms and accepted social behaviour. There are, of course, a number of significant differences in the nature of the social transgression, the external appear-ance of the communal action, and the ultimate intent of the crowd. But witch-mobbing and communal shaming rituals were both expressions of communal justice, as opposed to – and in spite of – state concepts of public order, and their focus was specific individuals who were deemed offensive to the community if not always to the state. E. P. Thompson's description of rough music serves equally well for witch-mobbing: 'Rough music belongs to a mode of life in which some part of the law belongs still to the community and is theirs to enforce … it indicates modes of social self-control and the disciplining of certain kinds of violence and anti-social offence.'[94]

An apposite point made by Thompson concerning rough music, which needs to be born in mind when considering the nature of folk justice in general, is that such punishments were 'not automatic' and were 'not always visited upon an offence. We do not have a "pre-industrial society" in which "community norms imposed themselves with steely force"'.[95] Not every village witch would find him- or herself being scratched or ducked each time they were suspected of having performed an act of evil, and many undoubtedly lived their unusual lives to the end without ever being assaulted. As is only too obvious from the sixteenth- and seventeenth-century evidence, accusations could build up over many years before official, or unofficial, action was taken. It was only when certain individuals reached a certain pitch of frustration, resentment or desperation that the suspected witch found him- or herself confronted by the force of popular justice. Such actions may have been communal in the sense that a good proportion of the community sanctioned the proceedings and turned out to join in or watch, but such events had to be initially suggested by someone, and there were always going to be a motivated few, the victims usually, who organised the proceedings. Significantly, though, neither individual nor group actions against witches (as well as other communal transgressors) were usually undertaken unless they were sanctioned by a considerable portion of the community. As Rosemary Jones has observed, folk justice was only dealt out 'if popular consensus regarding the gravity of the offence, and the legitimacy of the prescribed punishment could be firmly established'.[96]

Considering that there were well-defined, ritualised methods of chastising a witch, it is rather surprising to find other forms of ritual justice occasionally being employed to force suspected witches to stop their witchcraft. In the spring of 1857, for example, a Surrey labourer called upon his local magistrate and told him he had better look after the rough music they were giving M——, or some mischief would result. The magistrate accordingly visited M—— and asked him if he had anything to complain of?

> 'Oh, they make a noise and clatter with bones and cleavers and hammers and all manner, and neither I nor my neighbours can sleep.'
> 'Do you know any of their names?'
> 'Oh yes, but what's the use of that? It's E—— sets them on.'
> I returned home and sent for E——, and told him that M—— was much annoyed by people making a noise, and that he said that he E—— set them on.[97]

It emerged that E—— believed that M—— had bewitched his wife and magically disturbed her at night; an itinerant herb-gatherer having shown him M——'s face in the steam given off from a red-hot horseshoe being plunged into some dirty water.

The use of rough music to chastise a witch may not have been as exceptional as the historical record suggests, but it is still highly unusual, and it is interesting to speculate on why E—— turned to this particular form of justice to deter M—— from bewitching his wife, instead of resorting to swimming or scratching. Perhaps the rough music would have culminated in just such an assault, and this is what the labourer who initially informed the magistrate meant by 'some mischief coming of it'. Perhaps E—— thought he might deter M—— from continuing his malign practices by utilising a public display of ritualised disapprobation, before resorting to more violent means which might land him in serious trouble. This would seem to be the case, for E—— told the magistrate that he would 'shoot 'un next time he comes'.

In a number of cases of witch-mobbing we find that the public house played a significant role. The assault on Mary Nicholas of Abergavenny, in 1827, began when two of her assailants came out of the Bull public house, took hold of her under each arm and dragged her down the road, a crowd of people in tow.[98] Those involved in the attempted mobbing of Mrs Mole in 1858 were said to have been drinking. In the case of the Tring ducking of 1751, Thomas Colley related how 'he left his Work, and went to Butterfield's [public] House, who gave him and others that were there with him, Gin, and other Liquors, and encouraged them to proceed in their Design of Ducking the two People.'[99] The public house not only dispensed drinks but also acted as a communal talking shop, and the mixing of shared grievances and ale combined to create a heady brew of excitement, perceived injustice and violent resolve. It was in the ale house that the victims of witchcraft could relate their woes, canvass public opinion, and garner support for communal action against the suspected witch. In a sense, the public house could serve as a communal court where 'public justice' could be sanctioned and organised. E. P. Thompson found that in nineteenth-century Woking, where rough music was institutionalised 'in unusual strength', there was known to be a village court that was 'put into shape at an alehouse … but when, who by, and how, was kept a profound secret'.[100] Communal justice dispensed from the taproom was not without official precedent. Petty sessions were originally held in public houses, and inquests continued to be held there until the late nineteenth century. As one writer described in 1700, the justices' business was conducted 'amidst the smoking of Pipes, the cluttering of Pots, and the noise and ordure of a narrow Room infected with Drinking and a Throng'.[101] Thus taproom courts, whether official or unofficial, seem to have played a significant role in the functioning of communally sanctioned justice.

In reporting the Sible Hedingham swimming case of 1863, *The Times* noted the 'somewhat singular fact' that 'nearly all of the 60 or 70 persons concerned in the outrage which resulted in the death of the deceased were of the small tradesman class, and that none of the agricultural labourers were mixed up in the affair.'[102] Considering that it is often assumed that 'labourers were the chief bearers of superstition',[103] this may seem surprising to social historians as well. But we see the same dominance of tradesmen, and also small farmers, in other examples of witch-mobbing as well. For example, in the case of the Abergavenny mobbing of 1827, we find that those prosecuted were a farmer and his farm servant, a shoemaker, and a blacksmith.[104] If we look at witch-mobbing in the same context as folk justice and rural riot, we find that this phenomenon is not so surprising. Tradesmen can often be found to be prominently involved in cases of rough music,[105] and it was the small farmer/tradesman class which was influential in fomenting many of the Swing riots of 1830–31.[106] As Mick Reed has found from his close study of nineteenth-century Lodsworth, in Sussex, in every dispute that 'power' was opposed in the community, 'The main *visible* opposition came from groups that were neither wage labourers nor capitalist' – in other words 'local tradespeople and small farmers'.[107] In the context of Reed's discussion, 'power' relates to political and economic forces, but perhaps we should also consider it in supernatural terms as well.

Witch-mobbing, the parish constable and the coming of the new police

As we have seen, after 1736 the vicar and the justice, if they had not already done so, disassociated themselves from popular attempts to test and arrest witches. But the third member of the triumvirate of parochial justice in the parish, the constable, continued to maintain a very ambiguous position towards the peoples' demand for action against witches.

The parish constable was usually a long-established member of the community in which he served. Although originally chosen by the courts leet or manorial court, an Act of 1662, promulgated in response to the declining authority of that court, also enabled any two justices of the peace to choose constables if a leet had not been held. Those chosen were normally from the more 'respectable', literate members of the community and were usually small property owners.[108] Although the office carried some prestige, many constables were not particularly grateful for the responsibility and authority placed upon them as they risked a loss of time and money in pursuing their duties properly. A loophole did exist, however, which enabled constables to deputise their duties to another for a fee. As a contributor to the Second Report of Commissioners on County Rates (1836) remarked, if respectable persons were sometimes chosen at the leet, they 'find substitutes for a small sum, and these deputies blunder through the year, and when they are most wanted are never to be found'.[109] Increasingly during the eighteenth and early nineteenth centuries, this aroused increasing concern as to its influence on the effective maintenance of law and order, and was cited as a reason for the necessity of a paid, uniformed police force.

As Robert Storch has observed, 'Being local men, rooted in their communities, tied by kinship, friendship, and economic relationships to those they lived among, constables often reflected popular or "folk" conceptions of crime.'[110] The deputy system meant that in many cases those who actually performed the function of constable were from the lower, less-educated members of the parish, and had far less knowledge of their legal duties. It is also likely that the deputy constables were more immersed in the traditional village culture of custom and popular sanction than their more respectable employers, and were more influenced by the laws of communal custom than those of the state. The constable would often act, or not act, according to what the community believed to be a punishable crime, as opposed to what the state law defined a crime. According to John Rule many legally defined crimes were not regarded as such by the poor in society.[111] Rule labels these as 'social crimes' which were sanctioned by the community but condemned by the state. They can be divided broadly into three groups. First, they were customised economic crimes such as poaching, smuggling, wrecking, wood-gathering and violation of licensing laws, which somehow benefited the labouring community at the expense of 'alien' external agents, whether it be wealthy individuals or the state. The second group consisted of popular activities deemed offensive to orthodox elite views of morality, such as gambling, fighting and blood sports. The third group consisted of forms of popular justice performed to punish and ostracise individuals such as adulterers, scolds, and witches, who had transgressed shared social values but not necessarily the legal code. In such cases where constables was bound by state law to act against community members who had committed a communally sanctioned 'social crime', we often find them singularly sluggish and ineffective in carrying out their duties. In contrast, in cases where criminal acts were condemned by both state and community, such as burglary, rape and murder, the constable was often far more active.

The constable in attempting to juggle his dual responsibilities to community and state, often found himself caught between conflicting interests. As Joan Kent has shown for the seventeenth century, when 'the interests of the state and those of the village diverged', as happened in cases of rough music, or the collection of taxes, 'his office would be a focus of conflict'.[112] The constable found himself dealing with a similar dilemma when the community took it upon itself to inflict some form of trial or punishment upon witches. As we shall see shortly, in such cases the constable usually resolved this dilemma by either making himself scarce so as not to compromise himself in the eyes of either his fellow villagers or the authorities, or actively participated on the side of folk justice. I have not come across any instance where the parish constable fulfilled his legal obligations by defending the witch against the wrath of the community. Only in the Tring case of 1751 did parish officers make some attempt to protect the suspected witches, but in the end, for their own safety, they eventually handed the Osbornes over to the mob. This suggests that when it came to the test, constables were more beholden to the will of the community than to that of the state. To interfere when the community's blood was up could lead to opprobrium being heaped upon the constable, even to a risk of physical assault, and also, if a tradesman, lead to some financial loss through boycotting. Besides, it seems that in a number of cases the constables themselves believed in the guilt of the witch and condoned the proceedings.

The first case illustrating the behaviour of the constable in cases of witch-mobbing occurred in 1808, when the accused witch, Ann Izzard, of Great Paxton, Cambridgeshire, was badly beaten by villagers. On the evening of Sunday, 8 May, a mob broke into the cottage of Wright Izzard, which stood some way from the village, restrained him, dragged his wife out of bed, threw her naked into the yard and scratched her arms with pins, and beat her stomach, face and breast with a length of wood. When the mob, having drawn blood to negate Izzard's witchcraft, and satiated their blood lust, finally dispersed, Ann crawled back into her house, put her clothes on and went to the parish constable. Not surprisingly, the constable reneged on his responsibilities as a state agent, giving the excuse that 'he could not protect her, because he was not sworn'. Ann then called on a compassionate neighbour, Alice Russel, who saw to her wounds and gave her a bed. On hearing of this, the incensed villagers turned on Russel as a harbourer of witches: "'the protectors of a witch, are just as bad as the witch, and deserve the same treatment," cried the infatuated populace the next morning.' The widow Russel, who Nicholson had known well for twelve years, died shortly after on 20 May, 'a martyr to fear and apprehension'. On the evening of 9 May, Ann was again mobbed and scratched. The next morning it was put about the village that she would be swum as soon as the working day was over. On hearing this she took refuge in a neighbouring village, and instituted legal proceedings. Nine villagers were subsequently tried at the Huntingdon assizes and afterwards at the court of King's Bench, where eight of them were sentenced to one month's imprisonment, and one to two months'.[113] Considering the treatment that was doled out to Alice Russel, one can perhaps understand the constable's reluctance to help Izzard on the night of 8 May, but the constable's inactivity seems to have spread over the two following days when it was obviously widely known that further mobbings were to take place. Furthermore, he apparently made no effort to inform the local magistrates of the situation, leaving the villagers partially to achieve their aims by driving Izzard out of the community.

In the above case, the constable adopted a strictly neutral position, distancing himself from both mob and witch. However, in the case of the swimming of Isaac Stebbings, in July 1825, the parish constable resolved his conflict of interests by participating in the swimming in order to 'keep the peace' and ensure the proceedings did not get out of hand. His presence presumably gave the swimming a sense of legitimacy. Within the context of old-style village self-policing he was undoubtedly conducting himself respectably: Stebbings asked to be swum, and was probably reassured to see the constable present, the villagers were happy to oblige, and as long as the participants acted in an orderly manner, then the constable, probably in all sincerity, believed he was doing his job.[114]

Two years later, another constable made no pretence of impartiality during the mobbing of a witch, and found himself in court for his role in the affair. John Prosser, shoemaker and parish constable; William Watkins, a farmer in 'good circumstances'; Thomas Jenkins, Watkin's servant; and Henry Evans, a blacksmith; all of Abergavenny, were indicted before the Monmouth assizes for riot, and for committing an assault upon Mary Nicholas, a woman over ninety years of age.[115] On 10 March, Watkins and Jenkins seized Mary Nicholas, and, followed by a gathering crowd, dragged her the distance of one mile to Watkins' farm at Llanfoist. Once there, she was forced to kneel down at the heels of a sickly colt she was accused of bewitching, and compelled to bless it. In front of some 80–100 people, Watkins took a stick of briar rose and scratched her arms until they bled. Not being satisfied with this, Nicholas was then taken to the beast-house where she was stripped down to her waist and searched for any sign of a witch's teat. On finding a wen upon her head they brought everyone into the beast-house to confirm their discovery. Clumps of hair were also pulled out of her head to see if it would burn;

'many talked of ducking her'. Prosser was present as the old woman was jostled, humiliated and assaulted, and when Nicholas's daughter, Mary Philips, interposed and remonstrated with Watkins, Prosser spoke up and asserted his authority on behalf of Watkins, saying: 'Watkins, do not be bullied by her; I am the constable of the parish, and I'll make her mother do it again.' Not surprisingly, the judge, Baron Vaughan, censured Prosser in particular: 'I am sorry to observe a constable amongst the prisoners – a man bound to preserve, and not to disturb, the peace, who should have been any where else, unless he had been present to assist the old woman.' The defence lawyer successfully attempted to persuade the jury that Prosser and company were not guilty of the more serious crime of riot, in that whereas a riot was 'a meeting, with acts done to the terror of all His Majesty's subjects', in the prisoners' case there was only 'one defined object, the blessing of the colt'. The defendants were found guilty only of assault.

Prosser obviously had few doubts as to the advisability of his involvement in what the community saw as Nicholas's criminal act. His presence gave the proceedings a sense of official sanction in the eyes of those present, a point which he himself reaffirmed. This case suggests that in some rural areas the popular conception of justice, and the popular perception of the constable as the overseer of that justice, had changed little between 1612 and 1827. Whether Prosser was aware of the illegality of his actions in the eyes of the state we do not know, though he was certainly aware of his duty to the community.

The parish constable, like the non-stipendiary justice of the peace, had long been an integral element of the community structure. Neither official was a full-time agent of law enforcement, and they both had to juggle their official duties with their other occupations. Because the constable lived alongside those he policed, it was in his interests, and those of the local justice, to keep prosecutions to a minimum (often by not reporting communally sanctioned 'crimes'), and to mediate in disputes as much as possible. In many areas the local justice lived at a distance from the main parish community and was often unaware of criminal disturbances, or connived at them, and in such cases the constable's task was made easier in this respect. In this way the constable system, in rural areas at least, helped to minimise the level of recorded crime. It also oversaw that, within certain bounds, disputes arising from accusations of witchcraft or other social transgressions remained strictly an affair of the community and not of the state, thereby creating an appearance of harmony out of the habitual petty crimes and neighbourly discord of village life. Thus while the constable system had its many detractors, and was undoubtedly badly defective in expanding urban centres, it also had its defenders in rural areas. The Norfolk clergyman C. D. Brereton argued that a professional police force would alienate the lower classes, and therefore parish constables drawn from and rooted in the community would continue to be more effective in the countryside. Another Norfolk commentator expressed the opinion that the imposition of a rural Police Act would 'lead to a great deal of irritation, and the destruction of that kind of feeling which for 3 or 400 year past had kept the people together in harmony and peace'.[116]

The constable was the crucial linchpin in the continued but uneasy coexistence and operation of both folk and state systems of justice. With the inception of a more centralised, paid and uniformed police force, that fragile balance tipped considerably one way. The constable had long been a figure in the social landscape, had long been involved in the chastisement of social transgressors, and in the trying and prosecution of witches, and the folk memory of this involvement had lingered on in many minds. The uniformed policeman, on the other hand, was a wholly new element in the community, and one which had accrued no such sense of folk sympathy. The new police were trained and sent out into the community with the idea that their function was to suppress any attempts to subvert the state law. The policemen, unlike the constable, was not beholden to the community, but to the state and the victims of 'crime' as defined by the state. As most studies of the police have shown, one of the most obvious effects of their introduction was the sudden rise in the suppression of rowdy public behaviour, and the prevention of public gatherings and communal recreations which contravened either the law or middle-class sensibilities.[117] In the case of the mobbing of a suspected witch named Mrs Mole, we can clearly see the different approaches to such communal events under the old and new systems of parochial policing.

In September 1858, Mrs Mole, a labourer's wife, aged seventy-five, of East Thorpe, Essex, was accused by the Brazier family of bewitching their daughter and some of their livestock. In order to remove Mole's spell the Braziers consulted a cunning-man named Burrell, who resided at nearby Copford. Burrell was unable to help, however, and so they then called in the well-known cunning-man, James Murrell, to stop Mole's witchery; and it was the expected arrival of Murrell in East Thorpe which led to the ensuing 'disgraceful scenes'.[118] The rector of East Thorpe had been absent for a few weeks and returned to find his parishioners in a state of high excitement over the affair. The shocked rector attempted to defuse the situation by calling in the parish relieving officer to recommend that the bewitched girl be removed to the union-house for examination by the parish surgeon. However, the overseer of the poor refused to act, stating that they were expecting Murrell to come and cure her. Displaying an unusual level of resolve, the rector then applied to the local magistrate and obtained a promise that the police would be present on the day of Murrell's visit. Despite the fact that the County and Borough Police Act had compelled all counties to establish a rural police force, a parish constable still functioned in East Thorpe, though the rector obviously expected little help from him. At eight o'clock on Monday evening Murrell arrived, and some two hundred people gathered near Mrs Mole's cottage to serve justice upon her. The gathering took place right in front of the constable's house, but he kept himself out of sight, and made no attempt to dispel the crowd, many of whom were drunk. To prevent any violence being done to Mrs Mole the rector was obliged to mount guard at the Moles' door until the arrival of the requested policemen. When two uniformed policemen finally appeared in the village, the crowd dispersed quietly.

Had the rector, unlike many of his fellow clergymen, not actively involved himself in the defence of Mrs Mole, then folk justice would have undoubtedly won the day on that Monday evening. The local magistrate was either unaware or unconcerned as to the build-up of hostility towards Mole; the constable, not surprisingly, was not going to interfere with the threatening crowd; and the nearest new police were apparently stationed some distance away. That the mere presence of two uniformed policemen was enough to dispel an excited and drunken crowd of two hundred shows just what an unsettling impression the new police could initially have on a small rural community.

The new police were little liked in communities, which had long been allowed to police themselves to a certain degree. Despite attempts by the like of the Kent County Constabulary to station married men with families in rural districts, hoping that they would quickly become integrated into the local community, the policeman was often considered an alien and intrusive figure.[119] He may have been 'of the people' but he was not 'of the community'. The policeman was far less prone to local pressure than the parish constable, and equally less sympathetic to communal concepts of order. What must have been a commonly held opinion of this new interfering force was expressed at the trial of six men accused of 'disgusting exhibition' during a skimmington interrupted by the police, which took place at Potterne, Wiltshire, in February 1857.[120]

Admitting the charge before the Devizes petty sessions, the six men justified their actions by claiming that 'breaches of morality in the immaculate village of Potterne … had from time immemorial been celebrated in this way; it was a Potterne custom, as old as the church itself.' Furthermore, they considered the police interference an infringement of the ancient rights of the village, and they asserted that they could bring several respectable farmers to confirm the antiquity of the custom, and that no attempt had been made in the past to put a stop to any similar event. To show their disregard for the workings of state justice, the villagers organised a general 'carousal' on the return of the defendants, and a subscription was raised among the 'pot-companions' of the defendants to defray their expenses.

A community could also express its unity in the face of state censure against an act of folk justice by refusing to give evidence which could incriminate those involved. This happened in Otterton, Devon, in 1858. An old half-witted woman named Mary Ford was accused of bewitching a young man and his intended, who were both taken with fits. One evening after dark, friends of the young couple 'raised a mob' outside Ford's house and induced her to come out, whereupon they attacked her, stabbing her in several places. When the mobbing reached the ears of the local authorities 'every exertion' was made to find out the guilty parties 'but unfortunately with little success', due to the fact that everyone believed in the guilt of the witch and refused to divulge the names of the organisers.[121]

While the general decline in the practice of folk justice from around the mid-nineteenth century onwards was, in the words of Rosemary Jones, 'multifarious and complex', most historians of the subject generally agree that the inception of the new police force was a significant factor.[122] Robert Storch has also shown how many nineteenth-century commentators linked the coming of the police with the decline of many traditional customs and amusements.[123] Similarly, I believe that the imposition of the police force on communities also acted as a significant deterrent to communal action against witches. Previously, as I have illustrated, mob actions against witches only came to court after the fact, and usually only when the victim died or sustained serious injuries. With the inception of the police force the authorities had the manpower to suppress such actions before a finger was actually laid on the witch, and could arrest those involved on the spot, instead of attempting to detain people after the fact. Thus in Middlesborough, in August 1853, when a large mob, shouting 'pull her out' and 'burn her', assembled outside the door of an old woman accused of bewitching two children, four police officers were swiftly sent from nearby Stockton. On their arrival, they promptly arrested six or seven of the 'rioters', and placed them in 'durance vile', thereby preventing the assault from taking place, and deterring others from repeating the mobbing of the woman on another occasion.[124]

There is some evidence to suggest, though, that in some rural areas at least, inadequate policing and magisterial lenience meant that non-violent expressions of folk justice continued to take place without police suppression.[125] Carolyn Conley has shown how, even after 1856, some Kent justices 'rarely punished demonstrations in favour of widely accepted standards of morality'. Even when the police or the victims of rough music brought charges, justices 'usually announced that such conduct was disgraceful and could not be tolerated, and then dismissed the case for lack of evidence that anyone had been annoyed or disturbed'. Therefore 'the discretionary powers of the magistrate made it possible for technically illegal incidents of rough music and even more serious crimes to be dismissed for lack of evidence.'[126] Though it would be unwise to overgeneralise about this continuing complicity between the justice and the community after the demise of the parish constable, we do gain the impression that some non-stipendiary rural magistrates continued to respect the 'unwritten law' of the community.

However, in the case of witchcraft, the intent of mob actions was always to enact some form of physical violence upon the body of the witch, rather than to enact ritualised symbolic violence, which characterised other forms of folk justice. Even though mob assaults upon witches nearly always followed prescribed, ritualised violent actions governed by supernatural beliefs, the manhandling involved in attempting to scratch, swim or weigh a witch often led to other unwarranted blows and kicks. Such violent intentions obviously made witch-mobbing a far more obnoxious communal action to the authorities than those based on shaming and deriding, and as such could not be as easily connived at in the new atmosphere of policing. What made witch-mobbing even more unacceptable, compared with other forms of ritual ostracism, was that it was born out of 'ignorant superstition'.

While the old informal relationship between community, constable and justice meant that such mobbings often went undetected or ignored by the justice of the peace, with the inception of a full-time police force, and the extension of state control which that led to in rural areas, it was much more difficult to enact such violence without detection. Under the new system, justices of the peace, especially the increasing numbers of

stipendiary magistrates, also had to be seen to be more assiduous in suppressing riotous and violent behaviour. It is surely significant, then, that
after 1860, when, following the 1856 Police Act, a nationwide county
constabulary was effectively up and running, I have come across only one
case of witch-mobbing (Sible Heddingham, 1863), while other forms of
folk justice continued to operate despite some police repression. It could
be argued, of course, that the decline of witch-mobbing in the mid-
nineteenth century was actually an indication of the declining belief in
witchcraft, in that there were not enough believers to generate a mob.
There may be an element of truth in such a proposition, but when we
consider the extensive evidence that in rural society such beliefs remained
prevalent and strong until the end of the century, and that private, individual assaults upon witches, which attracted communal sympathy, if not
open participation, continued with considerable frequency after 1860, then
the police factor remains the most convincing.

The continued vitality of swimmings, weighings and mob-scratchings until
well into the nineteenth century owes more to the deliberate disengage-
ment of the elite from popular culture in the eighteenth century than it
does to any notion of a popular assertion of rights in the face of elite
infringements upon aspects of that culture.[127] Unlike other gatherings of
the period that contemporaries perceived as 'riots', witch-swimmings were
not directed against symbols of legal or economic authority within the
community. Conversely, people often actually requested members of authority to sanction such 'riots'. Because witch-swimming was not actually
directed against the structure of elite authority, and because of the
educated disdain for getting involved in anything associated with 'vulgar
superstition', its practice survived and even thrived in rural popular culture.
The general lack of elite suppression of the practice was in itself probably
interpreted by many as tacit acceptance of its use. Furthermore, the
authorities' unwillingness to intervene in cases of witchcraft accusation,
even when those persecuted as witches directly pleaded for succour, also
indirectly contributed to the continuance of popular ordeals. Faced with
both the justice's and clergyman's reluctance to come to the official defence of suspected witches, those accused of witchcraft looked upon swimming and weighing as the only form of justice that was available to them,
and in volunteering to undergo such ordeals they also helped perpetuate
the popular notion of the legitimacy of the practice.
    The old system of local justice, which centred around the relationship
between community, parish constable and the non-stipendiary justice,

created an environment in which the community itself was able to enact its own form of justice against social transgressors, with little direct interference from the state. But with the inception of the new police force and the creation of a stipendiary magistracy in the mid-nineteenth century, that local autonomy began to break down. By the 1860s, the new magistracy was no longer being perceived as a compliant arbiter in cases of witchcraft. The non-stipendiary justice no longer acted as an agent of local authority, but rather as an intrusive extension of state authority. With increasing worries over the extent of popular superstition, justices became more sympathetic towards those abused and accused of witchcraft, who were now perceived as the victims of unacceptable, brutal 'ignorance', and as a result this led to an increasing number of witch-assaulters being prosecuted from the 1850s onwards. For those who considered themselves the victims of witchcraft, the increasingly hostile magisterial attitude towards popular action against witchcraft was not well received. In 1885, for example, the Lincolnshire clergyman R. M. Heanley was told by a 'respectable wheelwright' that his pig had been overlooked, and the latter went on to assert: 'thou and me knaws the party that hes dun it ... Ef I nobbut could draa blud of she it 'ud be aal reight, but then shea hev the law on me, and they magistrates up to Spilsby be that iggnerant they 'ud mak' mea paay.'[128] Thus by the late nineteenth century, some 150 years after the Witchcraft Act, the popular expectation that members of the local authority were either somehow responsible for controlling the problem of witchcraft or would connive at popular action against witches had been extinguished.

The community was no longer able to police the enemy within with impunity. After three hundred years of persecution, those accused of witchcraft finally received sympathetic treatment from the authorities, and were allowed, and even encouraged, to seek full legal redress against their persecutors. Although this new atmosphere did not completely stop individual assaults against alleged witches from taking place, it certainly prevented communal mobbings, and as a result inhibited the free and active expression of a community's belief in witchcraft. This resulted in the creation of new social and psychological barriers within communities, between witches, witch-believers and agents of law enforcement, which inevitably had an impact on the generation of witchcraft accusations.

CHAPTER 3

WITCHCRAFT, MAGIC
AND POPULAR LITERATURE

Both in the past and in the present, literacy has been seen as a gift enabling people to free themselves from the shackles of 'ignorance' and 'erroneous' belief-systems. During the eighteenth and nineteenth centuries some of the educated, ruling elite desired to keep a monopoly on the written word. Knowledge was power and was therefore guarded jealously. Increasingly, though, these obscurantists were outnumbered by the social and moral reformers who sought to educate the masses in a carefully controlled manner, and who attempted to oversee the literature available to the burgeoning new readership. Literacy was lauded as a force for overthrowing the oral culture of tradition and belief, a culture which could not be controlled, and was viewed as a spring of vulgarity, credulity and ignorance. Yet, the closer we look at that oral culture the more it becomes apparent that the written and printed word were in many respects inextricably bound up with it. Particularly with regard to popular magic it is becoming clear how important the written word was, and how little reformers realised the extent to which literacy and the printing presses were contributing to the culture they were attempting to transform.

Before 1695 government had restricted printing to London, Cambridge, Oxford and York. The lapse of restrictions in 1695 led to a rapid increase of print-shops across the country. Gradual improvements in road travel and later the rise of the railway gave these burgeoning publishers easier access to their customer base. They tapped a popular appetite for simple, cheap literary forms such as broadsides, chapbooks and almanacs, the contents of which appealed to many of the interests and sentiments found in the oral folk tradition. The demand for these popular forms of literature was, by all accounts, insatiable. As Alfred Wallis wrote in 1881, in the days when his grandmother was young and '"railway libraries" were undreamt of', chapbook kitchen romances, children's toy-books, almanacs, calendars and fortune-tellers were '"thumbed" out of existence' by the populace.[1] For those living in towns, such works could be obtained from booksellers, but for many people in rural areas the only way of obtaining these repositories of accessible knowledge and entertainment was from pedlars and chapmen. These peripatetic figures who criss-crossed the countryside with their packs acted as a conduit for the printed word, linking publisher and consumer. They trudged the roads earning their pennies by successfully enticing 'the old dame or the young one with their Pamphlets, Books of Dreams, fortune telling, Nixon's prophecies, books of fate, ballads, etc.'.[2]

Referring to the above types of publication, Alfred Wallis wondered what part they had 'played in the history of civilisation', but his thoughts on the matter were fleeting, since the question could 'scarcely be conjectured by busy people in these high-pressure times'.[3] The present day may arguably be even more pressured, but several historians have fortunately found the time at least to examine the role of almanacs. However, fortune-telling books and other such printed ephemera containing a supernatural content have been rather neglected. Now is the time, then, to rummage more thoroughly through the pedlar's pack to see just how much the magical and the supernatural appealed to the people, and in what ways the literary and oral traditions interacted.

Literacy and literature

The study of the growth of popular literacy, and of the uses to which it was put, is an interpretative minefield which has to be negotiated in order to understand the nature of the reading experience in the past, and the type of literature people were buying. Trying to establish firm ground on which to reconstruct the nature of popular literature is not made any easier when the framework is being shaken by historians such as Roger Chartier, who repudiate the very concept of the 'popular' in 'popular literature'. He sees it as a blunt and monolithic tool of social analysis, as it lumps the experiences of all those outside the sphere of the dominant elite group into one amorphous mass.[4] Yet, while the plurality of cultures in society and the individualistic experience of reading need to be recognised, in consideration of what was being read, 'popular literature' still functions as a useful label. In terms of content, chapbooks and broadsides in general, and some almanacs in particular, were deliberately published to appeal to the mass of the population. They were in every respect popular, or, to take a dictionary definition of the word, they were 'easy to be comprehended' and 'pleasing to the people'.[5] The minority of the literate who derived no pleasure from these literary forms scornfully referred to them as 'vulgar literature', not just to convey their common appeal but also to designate them as coarse and worthless. 'Vulgar' is certainly too value-laden a term to be used by the historian, but we must recognise the perceptions of the past, and the distinctive nature of broadsides and chapbooks in particular, and the term 'popular literature' serves that purpose.

A constructive way of looking at popular literature in the period is to consider it in terms of 'popularised' reading matter, for the contents of chapbooks and broadsides were very often little more than extremely simplified versions of 'high brow' literature. While the well-educated minority could read Chaucer's *Wife of Bath*, the literate or semi-literate poor had access to the chapbook version, *The Wife of Beith, Reviv'd Once More*. Similarly, while the learned could peruse Marlowe's *The Tragical History of Dr Faustus*, and in 1808 the first part of Goethe's *Faust*, the chapbook readership had their own version in *The history of the wicked life and horrid death of Dr John Faustus*. The gypsy folklorist, Charles Godfrey Leland, experienced this process of 'vulgarisation' at first hand. He recalled:

> I was once myself made to contribute, involuntarily, to this kind of literature. Forty years ago I published a Folk-lore book entitled "The Poetry and Mystery of Dreams," in which the explanations of dreams, as given by ASTRAMPSHCHIUS, ARTEMIDORUS, and other ancient oneirologists, were illustrated by passages from many poets and popular ballads, showing how widely the ancient symbolism had extended. A few years ago I found that some ingenious literary hack had taken my work (without credit), and, omitting what would not be understood by servant girls, had made of it a common sixpenny dream-book.[6]

So, simplify the story, add a woodcut to excite the imagination, print it in large, bold type on poor-quality paper, fold, cut, and stitch into twenty-four pages, and sell it for a couple of pennies, and we have an elite form of literature transformed into popular literature: it largely comes down to a difference in presentation.

It has been estimated that there was a slow but substantial rise in literacy throughout the first half of the eighteenth century, resulting in literacy rates of 50–75 per cent for men and 15–40 per cent for women throughout England. As industrialisation accelerated, so this adversely affected the growth of popular literacy, but literacy rates are thought to have picked up again in the early nineteenth century, and by the early twentieth century at least 90 per cent of the adult population possessed basic literacy skills.[7] Most studies of literacy rates have based their evidence around the functional definition of literacy as the ability of people to write their signatures. Yet the fact that someone could write a signature does not necessarily mean that they could write well, and it certainly does not prove that they could read. The opposite is also true. Many people could read but not write. The ability to read is a different skill to that of writing, and in the past they were not necessarily taught together. Reading was generally the first skill to be acquired, and was often taught informally by neighbours and friends. The desire to learn to read was probably greater as it gave access to new sources of entertainment and information, whereas the ability to write was a more formally taught vocational skill. This is why it is generally assumed that the ability to read was more widely distributed than the ability to write. As Flora Thompson observed of village life at the turn of the century, 'It was surprising to find how many of the old people in the hamlet who had no regular schooling could yet read a little. A parent had taught some; others had attended a dame school or the night school, and a few had made their own children teach them in later life.' Another of Thompson's social observations is also worth mentioning in relation to the literacy statistics: 'Some who could write their own name quite well would make a cross as signature to a document out of nervousness or modesty.'[8]

For these reasons the functional definition of literacy, although a very important tool, is only a rough and sometimes misleading guide to the actual experience of reading and writing in eighteenth- and nineteenth-century popular culture. This is well highlighted in Barry Reay's local study of literacy in Kent. Reay suggests that instead of dividing people up into the literate and illiterate we should realise that 'there was in fact a diversity of literacies in the nineteenth-century rural world'.[9] Reay also stresses that in the nineteenth century, orality was still important, and that in a cultural context literacy and orality were not mutually exclusive. In a society in which the oral tradition was still strong, those who could read were expected to read aloud, whether to family and friends, or in the house, pub, or open-air.[10] Despite all the interpretative problems, though, it can be safely assumed that in the period concerned a large and ever-increasing proportion of the population had access to the written word in one form or another. In this sense, in comparison with rates of literacy, the written and printed word probably had a disproportionate influence on popular beliefs. This may seem odd, but that is because literacy is sometimes viewed in a simplistic way. It is the concept of access rather than ability which is most important here.

Growing literacy has often been equated with the spread of rational thought, but this is an equation of which we need to free our minds. As David Vincent has forcefully affirmed, the written word was a storehouse of supernatural knowledge, and an integral element of many charms and rituals.[11] Books have always been surrounded by a powerful magical aura. Witches were believed to have their books and parchments of harmful spells, and cunning-folk impressed their customers with their awe-inspiring old tomes. Some simple healing charms were preserved through their written transmission, and were only deemed effective in that form.[12] Protective talismans with their garbled mix of occult words and symbols were treated with profound respect by their owners, and provided a profitable source of income for those cunning-folk who could copy them out. The ability to read and write gave people access to supernatural power, therefore, and provided the illiterate with the means of curing and protecting themselves from evil and misfortune. The following case serves well to illustrate the importance of the written word in popular magic. In October 1866, a Nottinghamshire labourer named Bellamy was prosecuted before the Retford petty sessions for having assaulted a suspected witch. In his defence he remarked, 'There's witching the same now as ever there was, only they durst not show it; and there's the same books as there always was.' On his arrest the man was searched and a Latin charm was found upon him, and a further copy was also found in his watchcase. The charm was produced in evidence, and on being questioned about it Bellamy explained that he had obtained the charm from 'a man at the railway station, who wrote them out of a book'. Bellamy attached so much importance to his charms that after being sentenced he stated to police constable Cooper that 'he would sooner give £2 more than lose them', and they were duly given back to him. Here, then, we have all three elements mentioned in one instance; the dreaded witches' book, the cunning-man's book from which the charms were copied, and the written charms themselves. For Bellamy and many like him, both illiterate and literate, the written word was a means of obtaining magical power. A few scribbled lines of poor Latin on a scrap of paper was perceived to be of more value than probably anything else he owned.

Broadsides

During the seventeenth century, the broadside had been the most popular medium for the dissemination of news, opinions and entertaining nuggets of information, and in the subsequent century-and-a-half it continued to maintain its popularity.[13] Cheap and ephemeral, the broadside was a single sheet of paper printed on one side only and usually headed by a woodcut. By its broadest definition, the broadside encompassed a range of literary material: handbills, proclamations, advertisements, ballads, songs, and news sheets. They changed little in content, although the 'black-letter' Gothic typeface of the sixteenth and seventeenth centuries gave way to the 'white-letter' Roman typeface of the eighteenth century. Although this change may appear insignificant, it has affected their survival as historic documents. Normally discarded after being read, those examples which survive today are the result of active collection on the part of a handful of eighteenth- and nineteenth-century collectors. Since there was a certain snobbery concerning the assumed superiority of the older black-letter form, the later white-letter broadsides attracted less interest and scholarly attention. The broadside collections that exist today, such as that of Sabine Baring-Gould, which contains nearly twelve thousand examples, consist largely of ballads and song sheets, and although this most certainly reflects the popularity of these broadside formats, they also, however, mirror the educated antiquarian interest in popular ballads. These collections may not, then, truly reflect the popularity of broadsides containing a supernatural content, and certainly do not accurately represent the huge output of advertising handbills during the period.

The handbill had long been a popular means of advertising among astrologers, but the expansion of provincial presses after 1695, and improvements in communications and printing techniques during the eighteenth and early nineteenth centuries, meant that far more people could take advantage of the handbill and considerably more people could be reached. Vast quantities of handbills could be printed quickly and for a fairly reasonable price. The utility of the handbill as a means of advertising was that it could be targeted at quite specific sections of society. The intended recipients of astrologers' handbills were usually members of the servant classes, who formed a large portion of their clientele. Although, unfortunately, the broadside collectors were not particularly interested in advertisements, we can gain at least some idea of their content and employment from reports of the prosecution of astrologers and fortune-tellers which occasionally resulted from a misplaced handbill. Although these handbills attracted new clients, they were also open invitations to the police. Thus, in October 1807, a surgeon named Mr Blair, living in Great Russell Street, reported the London astrologer Joseph Powell to the police after finding the following handbill, which had been given to his maidservant by a match-seller presumably employed by Powell:

SCIENTIAL INSTRUCTIONS.

A. B. Professor of the Sidereal Science, No. 5, Sutton Street, Soho Square, teaches Astrology and calculating Nativities, with the most precise accuracy, at 2s. 6d. per lesson.

Application to the courteous reader. – Who will not praise and admire the glory of the sun and stars, and the frame of heaven, and not wish to know their influence and operations upon the earth? For fear of the ridicule of revilers and vilifiers of the science, who understand it not, and so deem it fraud and iniquity.

Oh happy world! If they did not a hundred thousand times more hurt by the baits of pleasure, honour, pride, authority, arrogance, extortion, envy, covetousness, and cruelty! and thereby make, or ruin themselves by grasping, and wantonness; and others by deception, craft, fraud, and villainy? but that is gilded over, and so such pass for good respectable people. Some may start and rave at this, but who can confute the truth of it?

Can any suppose that the stars, the celestial bodies, are designed for no other purpose than for us to look at heedlessly, as being of no worth, nor having any effect on us? Daily experience and the most learned of all ages have proved it, and testified it to us that they have, and in a great degree do, determine over fate; which I and all other professors have experienced and proved in thousands of different nativities. Who then, by means of such a noble inestimable science, would not wish for a precognition of the events of their most sanguine hopes and fears, which alternately alleviate or depress their minds? Is the praising and magnifying a work, a wrong to the workmen? Is knowing, manifesting, and experience the power and operations of the created wronging or dishonouring the Creator? Though this be a persecuted science, yet, happy world! What blest a state if nothing worse was practised in it! No letters, unless post paid, will be taken in.[14]

Powell had already been arrested several times for fortune-telling, and took the opportunity in his handbill not only to advertise himself but also to indulge in a thoughtful if rather melodramatic defence of the noble science. Nevertheless, one doubts if the unfortunate Powell was still proclaiming 'Oh happy world!' in prison. In 1857, a Liverpool astrologer, Joseph Railey, alias Henderson, was also arrested in a similar fashion. One of his handbills was placed under the door of the residence of the Rev. P. T. Forfar, minister of the Oldham Street Scotch church, in Sandon Street. After reading its contents, Forfar wrote to the local magistrate, Major Greig, enclosing the handbill, and subsequently two detective officers were sent to arrest Railey.[15]

Apart from advertising, the only other significant use of the broadside for occult purposes was as a vehicle for disseminating versions of apocryphal letters said to have been written by or to Christ. During the eighteenth and nineteenth centuries these were being peddled around the countryside as protective charms. They usually consisted of either the

Sunday Letter in which Jesus promised protection to all those who observe the Sabbath, or the correspondence between Jesus and Abgarus King of Edessa. Often compilations were printed that included both the above texts, as well as an 'Epistle to the Senate of Rome, containing a Description of Jesus Christ', supposedly sent by a Roman named Lentulus. Some editions also included a brief list of Christ's cures and miracles. Most versions were headed by a woodcut of Jesus or the crucifixion.

The origins of these texts apparently date back to the early centuries of Christianity, but to what extent oral or written versions of these apocryphal legends circulated among the people of western Europe in pre-modern times is impossible to say.[16] Were such stories a part of folk tradition in Britain before the advent of printing? We know from the study of healing charms that fragments of old apocrypha had been embedded in folk culture as far back as the early medieval period, but whether complete apocryphal stories about Jesus circulated in oral form is a completely different matter.[17] My own feeling is that it was only with the circulation of large numbers of printed broadside copies that the tradition of the Abgarus correspondence and the Sunday Letter entered English popular culture. As we shall see from their content, these accounts were meant to be read, transcribed and passed on. The tradition depended on written transmission.

The earliest surviving English broadside edition of a Saviour's Letter that I have come across dates from around 1720, though several eighteenth-century hand-written versions of the Letter have also been found. Although these were correctly identified as charms at the time of their discovery, their significance and apocryphal history were not recognised. For example, a 'curious document' found among the title deeds of a Cumbrian gentlemen (the earliest of which was dated 1705) turns out to be a copy of the Sunday Letter written upon coarse paper.[18] Another unidentified copy of the Sunday Letter, dated 6 October 1793, was found in the possession of a farmer's wife of Saltfleetby St Clements, Lincolnshire.[19] Judging by their style and wording, both hand-written examples were copied from other hand-written versions rather than directly from broadside copies. Thus the city of 'Iconium', mentioned in the broadside versions, is referred to as 'the citty Isundiagndiagna' in the Cumbrian example, and 'Indiconia' in the Lincolnshire version.

The reason for the circulation of both printed and hand-written copies of the Sunday Letter lies in a passage in the text which, in the Lincolnshire copy, states that 'he that hath a copy of this letter and doth not publish it abroad to others, shall be accursed.' In a nineteenth-century broadside edition printed in Hereford, we similarly find the passage: 'he that hath a Copy of this Letter, written with my own Hand, and spoken with my own Mouth, and keepeth it without publishing it to others, shall not prosper.'[20] In other words the Sunday Letter was an early form of chain letter. It is quite possible that there was a popular circulation of hand-written copies before the Letter was distributed in broadside form, but the huge numbers of Letters which could be printed and disseminated in the eighteenth century undoubtedly led to a massive increase in the popularity of the charm. The broadside version must therefore have also generated quite a number of hand-written copies, as those who could read the Letter would have feared not 'publishing it to others'.

In 1844, Edward Jesse reported that broadside Saviour's Letters were very common in Suffolk. He found they were pasted on cottage walls or folded and carried in pockets for protection when undertaking a journey. A decade later, a Wiltshire vicar observed that printed copies of the Abgarus letter were pasted up in most of the cottages he visited, and was told it was 'of great efficacy in diminishing the sufferings of women in child-birth'. At the turn of the century a Berkshire folklorist came across an old woman who possessed two broadside copies of the 'Saviour's Letters'. Her mother and grandmother had considered them as charms against illness, and had pinned them inside their dresses to ensure safety in childbirth. In Herefordshire, too, women hung copies above their beds for greater ease and safety during childbirth. An old lady of Tillington parish, West Sussex, kept her copy of the Letter 'with religious care'. She had bought it from a pedlar, who told her that if she stuck it up on her kitchen wall it would protect her house from witchcraft and the evil eye.[21] A correspondent to *Notes & Queries* reported that in parts of Devon the apocryphal correspondence was looked upon as a preservative against fever, and proceeded to give a detailed description of one example he found in a cottage at Bolham:

> They were surmounted by a rough woodcut of Our Lord's head, purporting to be a reproduction of the likeness imprinted on the handkerchief at Veronica, under which was a detailed description of Our Lord's person: middle height, blue eyes, fair curls, &c. I begged to be allowed to take the whole thing home to copy, when, to my surprise, I found the owner looked upon the idea as sacrilegious. She bid me read what was printed below the letters, which had escaped me before. This proved to be a declaration (put into Our Lord's mouth), that in whatever house those letters hung fever should never enter.[22]

This declaration of protection usually appeared at the end of Jesus's letter on the observance of the Sabbath day. Thus an early edition printed in

London around 1720 states: 'whosoever shall have a copy of this letter, and keep it in their houses, nothing shall hurt them – neither lightening, pestilence, nor thunder;- and if a woman be in labour, and a copy of this letter be about her, and she firmly put her trust in me, she shall safely be delivered.'[23]

The folklorist William Henderson was in possession of an unusual edition of the Letter, bought from a pedlar by the Rector of Kenn, near Exeter, which was apparently 'curiously interpolated with Methodist hymns'.[24] It was possibly produced by a local printer, as Saviour's Letters were certainly being printed in Exeter during the nineteenth century. A copy of one edition from the 1820s can be found in the Harvard University Library. It may seem odd, though, for someone to insert Methodist hymns into what was essentially a magical charm, and one might have expected most Methodists to have condemned the Letters as relics of 'Papist superstition'. However, the Letter could be interpreted on two levels, which is one of the reasons why it was so popular and publishers felt comfortable about printing it. Visually these broadsheets were overt pieces of religious iconography. The innocent clergyman espying a Saviour's Letter pasted on a cottager's wall might well have been heartened at such a display of religious devotion. A closer inspection might have modified his opinion. Then again, the thrust of the Letter's text was a commendable command for Godly behaviour and strict religious observance of the Sabbath:

> You shall diligently and peaceably labour in your respective callings, wherein it hath pleased God to place you. You shall love one another with brotherly love; and cause them that are baptized to go to church and receive the sacraments, baptism and the Lord's supper, and to be made members of the church: in so doing I will give you a long life and many blessings; and your land shall flourish.

Those whose lives did not conform to these standards were liable to bring upon themselves serious divine retribution: 'I will send my own plagues upon him, and consume both him, his children, and his cattle'. In this respect, then, it is not so surprising that a Methodist printer might disseminate versions of the Letter as a piece of religious propaganda – an exhortation to the masses in a popular form. The printing press of the entrepreneurial Primitive Methodist, Hugh Bourne, certainly disgorged numerous brief tracts reporting 'wonderful dreams, visions, warnings, judgements, and deliverances',[25] and, considering his strong belief in the healing power of prayer, it is not impossible that men like him also utilised the Saviour's Letter tradition.

There was obviously a big market for such documents, and it is likely that some entrepreneurial printers produced similar magical ephemera for rural consumption, though admittedly there is little trace of them in the historical record. One regional example which hints at a possible wider tradition of printed charms is the 'witching cards' that were sold at Lancashire markets for sixpence during the nineteenth century. These small printed cards, which were meant to be hung in the home or in farm outbuildings, consisted of the following passage:

> PRAYER FOR DELIVERANCE FROM WITCHES AND EVIL SPIRITS
>
> As it is said in the seventeenth chapter of St. Mathew. At the twentieth verse 'By faith ye may remove Mountains'. Be it according to my Faith, if there is or ever shall be, Witches, or Evil Spirits that haunt, or trouble this person, or this place, or these beasts, I adjure thee to DEPART without disturbance, molestation, or trouble in the least. In the name of the Father, and of the Son, and of the Holy Ghost. Amen.[26]

Again, for the publishers, the religious content of these cards presumably legitimised them to a certain extent. There was certainly a fine line between the dissemination of piety and magical protection.

Chapbooks

The chapbook really reached its zenith during the eighteenth century with the expansion of regional publishers, and it remained a hugely popular literary format up until the mid-nineteenth century. Victor Neuburg has identified over 240 chapbook printers in London alone during the period, and another 140 in the regions.[27] Chapbooks were cheap, written in a simple style, and, due to their size, were easily hawked around the countryside, and so made available to new markets.[28] In physical terms they could be considered as large broadside sheets, folded into a booklet form of normally eight, sixteen, or twenty-four small pages, and which, like the broadside, were usually headed by the obligatory woodcut. They differed, however, in the range and content of the information they contained, and in their emphasis on escapist and fantastical subject matter. Realising the large and insatiable appetite for fortune-telling and the supernatural, publishers were all too ready to turn such topics into cheap literature for public consumption. As Chancellor Ferguson remarked in 1897, 'judging from the number of chap-books devoted thereto, the supernatural and the superstitious must have had great charms for readers.'[29]

The production of chapbooks and broadsides must have been a highly profitable business, and so printers who were capable of producing work of a high standard were quite happy to turn out chapbooks of appalling print quality. Putting profit before principles, some printers who produced chapbooks with a magical content were careful to insert provisos explaining that the contents of their chapbooks were merely produced to highlight the ignorance and 'superstitious' folly of a past society. One Glasgow printer, a prolific producer of fortune-telling and dream books, added the following paragraph to a number of his publications:

TO THE READER

The foregoing pages are published principally to show the superstitions which engrossed the minds of the population of Scotland during a past age, and which are happily disappearing before the progress of an enlightened civilisation. It is hoped, therefore, that the reader will not attach the slightest importance to the solutions of the dreams as rendered above, as dreams are generally the result of a disordered stomach, or an excited imagination.[30]

While the above preface was intended to discredit the content of the pages that followed, some chapbook authors adopted a more ambiguous tone in their introductions. They neither condemned nor condoned their subject matter, but presented it to the public as a form of harmless diversion. The author of the popular chapbook *The High German Fortune-Teller* stressed to the 'Courteous Reader' the innocuous nature of its contents, which included advice on palmistry, interpreting the dice, dreams and moles, as well as a secret alphabet and a list of happy days in each month: 'I must let you know, there is nothing in it fixed and certain, but Providence can avert both the good and bad Omens thereof. In fine, it being a Recreation in itself innocent and harmless, it need not discourage any, but rather it will serve to divert and please all, at times, when, perhaps, otherwise they'd be acting more debauched and vicious Exercises.'[31]

When examining the nature of popular literature, not only must the readership be considered but also those who printed such literature. It was the publishers who decided what to print and in what format: demand influenced supply, but that which was supplied also influenced the type of literature that was demanded. The publishers of magical chapbooks knew full well that they were treading on rather unstable moral ground as far as the influence their subject matter had on their readers was concerned. Therefore, the above provisos were added more to deflect any educated criticism they may have incurred by producing and reinforcing the belief in such 'nonsense' than as a conscientious effort to reform popular beliefs. Indeed, the author of the *High German Fortune-Teller* presented the argument to potential critics that it was preferable that the lower orders were ensconced in their homes figuring out the future, than out on the streets or indulging in vice.

These publishers were shrewd businessmen who knew exactly the tastes of their respective readerships, and how to repackage information according to the relative reading abilities and desires of their customers. A good illustration of their marketing skills can be drawn from the printing history of the spurious works on human reproduction attributed to Aristotle.[32] Entitled *Aristotle's Master Piece*, *Aristotle's Last Legacy* and *Aristotle's Midwife*, only a few passages from them can actually be ascribed to the writings of Aristotle. Although the earliest Latin edition was printed in Rome in 1475 under the title *The Problems of Aristotle*, in England it was from the latter half of the seventeenth century until the late nineteenth century that 'his' works achieved great popularity. By attributing these writings to Aristotle, they gained a dubious respectability in a period when the ancient philosophers were held in greater esteem than their modern counterparts. During the eighteenth century, the three works were usually sold in one edition, and, to spice it up a bit, collections of remedies were often tagged onto the end. The contents of the various editions were not always the same, and so in some editions we find chapters on 'Judgement drawn from several parts of Man's Body' and 'Palmistry, shewing the various Judgements drawn from the hand' which closely resemble the contents of contemporary fortune-telling chapbooks. *Aristotle's Masterpiece* was a lengthy work of around 140 pages, and by no means a book for the basic reader. The publishers knew this, and, realising the potential of exploiting Aristotle's name further, produced a 24-page chapbook version for the popular market. First printed in London around 1690, *Aristotle's Legacy: or, his golden cabinet of secrets opened. In five treatises … Translated into English by Dr. Borman*, was still being reprinted in Newcastle one hundred years later. It contained none of the medical content of *Aristotle's Masterpiece*, and is little more than a run-of-the-mill fortune book containing information on palmistry, physiognomy, dreams and moles. A 1790 edition contains a woodcut of a card-dealing fortune-teller being consulted by a couple of clients. Aristotle was not the only Greek philosopher to enter the fortune-telling market, since Pythagoras's name was also used to promote a 'Wheel of Fortune'.[33] The ancient Greek connection is also evident in another eighteenth-century fortune-teller, entitled *Dreams and Moles, with their interpretation and signification … to which is prefixed, a collection of choice … receipts concerning love and marriage. First compiled in Greek, and now … rendered into English by a Fellow of the Royal Society*.[34] Needless to say, the learned fellow's name is not divulged.

Writing towards the end of the nineteenth century, Charles Godfrey Leland was 'convinced, from much inquiry, that next to the Bible and the Almanac there is no *one* book which is so much disseminated among the million as the fortune-teller, in some form or other.'[35] Certainly the number of titles churned out by the chapbook printers during the eighteenth and nineteenth centuries would tend to confirm Leland's opinion. Charles Mackay estimated that two popular early-nineteenth-century works, *Mother Bridget's Dream-book and Oracle of Fate* and the *Norwood Gipsy*, had run through as many as fifty editions in as many years in London alone. Sold at sums varying from one penny to sixpence, upwards of eleven thousand copies were being sold annually.[36] In mid-nineteenth-century Lancashire it was reported that hawkers and small shops sold a 'vast quantity' of 'Dream Books' and 'Books of Fate', and in Holderness, Yorkshire, it was observed that 'Sellers of dream-books must formerly have driven a fair trade … even now a dream or fortune "interpreter" is often to be found amongst the literary valuables of the cottage'.[37]

The fortune-telling chapbook with probably the longest and most successful print history was *Mother Bunch's Closet Newly Broke Open*.[38] According to the chapbook, wise Mother Bunch was an 'old woman who lived at Bonny Venter in the West', but in early literary references she actually hails from London. As mentioned in *Pasquil's Jests* (1604), Mother Bunch was a well-known London ale-house hostess. Her name was also used as an early London-slang euphemism for 'water', which was presumably a comment upon the quality of the ale she sold. This is evident from a passage in Dekker's play *The Shoemaker's Holiday*, performed in 1599: 'Am I sure that Paul's steeple is a handful higher than London Stone, or that the Pissing-Conduit leaks nothing but pure Mother Bunch.'[39] The earliest edition of *Mother Bunch's Closet* seems to have been printed in 1685, and continued to be reprinted until well into the latter half of the nineteenth century.[40]

A rival to Mother Bunch was Mother Bridget the Norwood Gypsy. Among the numerous fortune-telling chapbooks attributed to her was *The True Fortune-Teller; or Universal Book of Fate*.[41] Like *Mother Bunch* this twenty-four page chapbook, printed in Glasgow around the middle of the nineteenth century, provides us with some fictitious biographical information about its supposed author, who had magnanimously left her work 'for the benefit and instruction of the world'. Bridget's parents apparently died when she was young, and she was left to ramble abroad, begging as she went. She was gifted at reading people's features and

manners, and she would also sit up whole nights gazing at the heavens,
'as intent on considering the stars, as the greatest astrologers would be
with their glasses'. She began to develop a reputation for her accurate
predictions, and before long became the topic of conversation within the
politest circles. As she grew old she became doubled up with age, 'which
together with her enormous length of nose and chin, her pipe, and the
number of animals about her, made her cut a most hideous figure'.
According to the 'editor' of *The True Fortune-Teller*, Mother Bridget

> had never been taught to write, yet by long practice she had formed to herself
> a kind of hieroglyphical characters, in which she decyphered her observations,
> knowledge, and remarks; these I found concealed within the thatch of her cave
> … as I am rather of a studious turn, I thought as I had made it my business
> formerly to transcribe the Egyptian hieroglyphics, which, when they were as
> unintelligible to me as these, I might by perseverance get at the depth of this
> valuable manuscript, or at least it would serve to deposit in the British Museum.[42]

The translator achieved his purpose, for, in chapbook form, Mother
Bridget's valuable work has, indeed, been deposited in the British
Museum. Like other fortune books, it contains such information as 'evil
and perilous Days of every Month of the Year' and 'Judgements Deduced
from the Nails'. More unusually, though, it also provides the reader with
some quite complex astrological information. On page 8, for example,
we find 'An explanation of the Circles of the Sphere, and some other
Terms of Astrology, for the easier Understanding of this Book'. This does
not mean that some of its astrological predictions were of great portent,
telling the reader, for instance, that 'on the seventh day the child that is
born may live many years; on this day it is good to shave the head, to
tame wild beasts, and buy hogs'. It is unusual, however, to find such
complex astrological detail in chapbooks. Despite its attempt at explanation
it must have remained rather incomprehensible to many of its readers.

   In name at least, Mother Bridget was not a fictional character. She
was the niece of Margaret Finch, 'The Queen of the Gypsies at Norwood'. After Margaret's death in 1740, Bridget succeeded her as 'Queen',
until her own death in her hut on Norwood Common on 4 August
1768. She was a very successful fortune-teller, having accumulated a considerable sum of money in her lifetime, varying in estimates from £200
to £1,000.[43] There is no evidence that she ever wrote any fortune-telling
manuscripts, and the earliest surviving, and probably the first, edition of
a fortune book ascribed to her is from around 1790, over two decades
after her funeral. Obviously the reputation of Mother Bridget's fortune-
telling prowess, even after her death, was such that London chapbook

producers thought her name, and that of Norwood, a marketable commodity. Through the medium of the chapbook, Mother Bridget and Norwood subsequently became familiar to people hundreds of miles from the capital.

A significant portion of most fortune books was devoted to love magic, usually consisting of various rituals for discovering one's future partner, or, as *Mother Bunch* put it, 'how you shall know and see the persons that shall ease you of the simple thing so much talked of called a maidenhead, by him that must be your husband, collected from the Twelve Sybils, Trismajistus, and Cornelius Agrippa'. The first method of divination that *Mother Bunch* recites is as follows:

> You that desire to know it this way must wait till Midsummer Eve, then at night three or four of you, or more or less, must take your smocks and dip them in fair water, then turn the wrong side outwards, and hang them on chairs before the fire, and have by you a vessel with drink in it and lay some salt in another before the fire, and be sure not to speak a word whatever you hear or see. In a little time the likeness of those persons you shall marry will come and turn your smocks, and drink to you; now if there be any of you that will never marry, they will hear a bell, but not the rest but whoever hears this bell none of my authors is positive that she shall dye a maid.

More simple variations of this popular divinatory ritual have been recorded from around the country by nineteenth-century folklorists. In west Wales, for example, young women would wash their shirts or some other garment they were wearing close to their skin, turn them inside out, and place them before the fire to dry. If they were to marry they would see the spirit of their future husbands, but if they were to die single they would see a coffin move along the room.[44] Depending on region, this charm was also performed on Christmas Eve, New Year's Eve, St Mark's Eve and All Hallow's Eve. Another form of love divination present in the folklore record was given in *A New Fortune-Book* (Cirencester, *c.* 1770):

> Take an Onion call'd St. Thomas's Onion, peel it and put it into a clean handkerchief, put on a clean smock, and lay it under your head, have the Room clean swept then lie down and spreading your Arms abroad say:
>
> > St. Thomas, pray do me right,
> > And let my true Love come to Night,
> > That I may behold his Face,
> > And him in my kind arms embrace.
>
> then fall asleep and in your dream you shall see him come to you, be not coy, but get hold of him and then you will be sure 'tis he, but if he gives you the slip, try again.

During the early nineteenth century, the daughter of a respectable trades-man inquired of an old dame what she knew about a love invocation to be said on St Thomas's Eve (20 December). All that the woman could remember at the time was the following verse, which is obviously a version of that from the chapbook:

> Good St. Thomas, use me right,
> Bring to me my love this night,
> In his apparel, his array,
> The clothes he walks in every day.[45]

Another tradition that also appears in both chapbooks and oral folklore sources was the making of the Dumb Cake on St Mark's Eve. The cake was actually a form of bread, which was baked just before midnight. It had to be made in complete silence and while fasting. At exactly twelve o'clock it was believed the future husband would appear to turn the bread over.[46]

These analogies lead us to the question as to the extent to which the circulation of chapbooks influenced the oral divinatory tradition. Concerning the above examples, it is most likely that the authors of these chapbooks were putting into print what were already popular and wide-spread rituals. In other words, the print tradition was borrowing from the oral tradition. Yet this does not preclude the possibility that the chapbook helped maintain, and perhaps further popularise, these methods of divina-tion during the eighteenth and nineteenth centuries. If this was the case to any great extent, we might expect to see some evidence of standardi-sation of practice around the country. As the folklore record shows, however, not only were there numerous local variations of the same charm but there were also numerous other popular and widespread methods of love divination which were not present in chapbooks. This would suggest that during the lifetime of the chapbook the oral tradition was healthy enough to prevent any significant trend towards standardisation occurring.

Another indication that the chapbook did not have a profound impact on the oral tradition of love magic is that chapbooks also printed other alien rituals of which there is no trace in the folklore record, and which do not share any of the motifs common to the catalogue of known native divinatory types. Thus *A New Fortune Book* tells its readers how 'To make the inchanted Ring that will cause love': 'Take a hollow ring of Ivory, horn or any convenient Metal, steep it in the Juice of Rue a night and a day, then draw thro' it the hair of a young Heifer cut between the Horns, then steep it again in Water of Fennel 24 Hours, and the first on whose Finger you put it, or who wears it, will be strangely Inchanted.' We also find a more simplistic vernacular variation of this charm in *Aristotle's Legacy* (Newcastle, *c.* 1790): 'get a hollow ring, and goats hair taken from the beard; steep it in the juice of nightshade or wakerobin, an herd [*sic*] so called; pull it through the ring, and whoever wears it shall cause them to fall in love with you.' There is no evidence of this charm type ever being employed. Such rituals were printed in chapbooks time and time again throughout the eighteenth and nineteenth centuries, and the fact that they do not appear in the folklore record would suggest that they did not originate from oral tradition, but instead were either concocted by the chapbook authors or taken from old books of inventive magic. Consequently, because they lacked the familiar elements of existing divinatory forms they did not appeal to the chapbook readership. It would be extremely unwise to suggest, however, that the chapbook made no impression at all on the oral divinatory tradition. We really know too little about the range and content of popular divination in the period before the widespread popularity of the chapbook to draw any firm conclusions. It is quite possible, for instance, that charms such as the dumb cake were of regional origin, and that their inclusion in chapbooks led to their more widespread adoption around the country, with localised variations developing afterwards.

Apart from these rather innocent charms to divine the identity of future partners, secure their affections, and gauge their faithfulness, chapbooks did not generally dabble in other more explicit charms concerning love and sex. Nothing is said about impotency or abortion for example. The only sensitive subject tackled by a few eighteenth-century chapbooks concerned the problem of 'How to know whether a female be a pure virgin or not'. *Aristotle's Legacy* gave the following advice: 'Take of Alabaster a quarter of a ounce, powder it, and sift the powder very fine, steep it in Aqua Vitae; then dry and powder it again; put a dram of this to any liquor the party is to drink, and if it make her not blush, or change colour, she has lost her virginity; if she does, she is a maid.'[47] I have not come across any case in the ethnographic sources of divination to identify a virgin. But then again, if such rituals were practised it would be equally surprising, perhaps, if any folklorist or antiquarian had published accounts of them.

Next to love magic, the most common feature of these chapbooks was oneiromancy, or, as the chapbooks termed it, 'the signification of dreams'. In the nineteenth century the popularity of this form of divination led to a flood of dream-books, some of which developed quite complicated systems of analysis. The common folk rule of interpretation was that whatever one dreamt of, the contrary would come true. The same tradition is also reflected in the chapbooks. *The New Infallible Fortune Teller* tells us, for instance, that 'to dream of dead relations promises the seeing some friend'.[48] However, this rule of thumb was not always observed by the dream-books, and sometimes we find that what one dreams will actually happen. In some instances the dreams mentioned are of a rather unusual nature. According to the *Infallible Fortune Teller*, 'to dream you see an egg hang by a string at your bed head, denotes finding hidden treasure.'

The most successful of these dream-interpretation chapbooks was *Napoleon Bonaparte's Book of Fate*, which seems to have first appeared in the 1820s, and subsequently enjoyed numerous reprints and editions.[49] One frequently published edition informs us that it was, 'formerly in the possession of and used by Napoleon, rendered into the English language by H. Kirchenhoffer from a German translation of an ancient Egyptian manuscript found in the year 1801, by M. Sonnini in one of the royal tombs near Mount Libycus in Upper Egypt'. Another edition tells us that the book was subsequently captured at the Battle of 'Leipsic'. The air of mystery surrounding the book continued into the twentieth century. One of the first newspaper astrologers, Edward Lyndoe, who worked for *The People*, included a version of the book in one of his fortune-telling publications, and told the following tall story regarding its origin: 'I came by a very old document some years ago … The old French professor who lent it me used often to talk about this Oraculum as we travelled together in the train, and I gathered from him that he had the original from his grandfather, whose father in turn had held a position in the Imperial Court.'[50]

The popularity of the book undoubtedly stemmed from what it grandly called its 'oraculum', a system of randomly written rows of ciphers or crosses which were counted; the number of even and odd numbered rows then corresponded to a tabulated index headed by astrological symbols, which explained the meaning of the dreamer's dream. For simple, easily remembered dreams the reader was also supplied with the usual list of short-cut interpretations. The oraculum was not an original concept, being but a variant of geomantic fortune-telling known and written about for centuries. It undoubtedly lent the *Book of Fate* an air of learned, pseudo-scientific respectability, and editions of the *Book* were found among the belongings of two astrologers, Joseph Railey and Sarah Owen. In *Redburn*, a sailing novel by Herman Melville, we find a revealing description of the awe in which the character, Jack Blunt, an Irish Cockney, held his dream-book:

Now, Blunt revered, adored, and worshipped this *Bonaparte Dream Book* of his; and was fully persuaded that between those red covers, and in his own dreams, lay all the secrets of futurity ... he would steal out of his bunk before the rest of the watch were awake; take out his pamphlet, and a bit of chalk; and then straddling his chest, begin scratching his oily head to remember his fugitive dreams; marking down strokes on his chest-lid, as if he were casting up his daily accounts. Though often perplexed and lost in mazes concerning the cabalistic figures in the book, and the chapter of directions to beginners; for he could with difficulty read at all; yet, in the end, if not interrupted, he somehow managed to arrive at a conclusion satisfactorily to him.[51]

This system was obviously popular, and later in the century 'Raphael', who already produced a successful almanac and a successful run of fortune-telling books, also used a similar system for his *Dream Book*, which in its third edition had a print run of 10,000.

Dream interpretation was undoubtedly taken seriously within the context of the existing body of oral folk knowledge. This is evident from an inquest conducted by the Walsall borough coroner on the body of a little girl who drowned in a canal in September 1884. The child's mother told how she had kept her daughter at home because she had 'a dread' upon her in consequence of having three nights in succession dreamt of baking bread. She had lost other children, and on each occasion had similar dreams before the child died. Owing to the dream, she had kept the girl away from school.[52] What with the flood of dream books in the nineteenth century, and their apparent popularity, there would seem to be a case for assuming that they were widely used as a reference work. At any rate, their influence upon the populace was seen as pernicious by the likes of T. Sharper Knowlson:

> Of course it is easy to say 'bosh,' and to declare this interpretation of dreams is a more [sic] amusement. It is more than that. Deep down in their hearts many people fear 'there is something in it;' and although they never openly acknowledge the fact, they – women especially – shew their curiosity and their superstition by harbouring the dream book and pondering its interpretations. A lively sense of humour is the best antidote ... the authors and publishers of dream books should have the attention of the Censor.[53]

After love divination and dream interpretation, palmistry and card reading were the chapbook subjects most represented in the ethnographic record. However, despite the fact that knowledge of these two methods was available to all for a penny or so, few instances can actually be found of people telling each other's fortune in this manner. Both types of divination were more likely to be practised by fortune-tellers or cunning-folk, who were obviously thought to have a gift for prescience. Chapbooks also included a variety of other methods of fortune-telling which were less traditional to English and Welsh society in the period concerned. Any self-respecting fortune-telling chapbook had its section on the signification of moles, though this hardly appears at all in the folklore sources. *The New Infallible Fortune-Teller* tells us, for instance, that the lucky owner of a mole on the left side of the forehead will 'get riches by tillage, building and planting', and that a mole 'on the left buttock denotes a pleasing person, and one much delighted in the work of generation'. But woe betide the person with two moles 'answering equally on either side of the gullet', for this 'threatens untimely death'. *A New Fortune Book* (Cirencester, *c.* 1770) further informs us that 'a mole on the lip signifies a very happy marriage', and that 'a mole on or near the Privities shews a man vigorous in love, in a woman barrenness of children'. Another, more complicated divinatory method elucidated for the benefit of readers, was the wheel of fortune, in which people generated a number, either from rolling dice or calculating the numerical value of the letters in their name. The number corresponded to a compartment within the 'wheel', which tallied with an allocated prediction. Similar in style were pricking tables, which consisted of a grid of numbers and letters covered by a piece of white paper. The squares in the grid corresponded to a list of future outcomes. A pin would be randomly stuck into the paper, and was then removed. The grid number of the square which had been pricked would be identified, and then the pricker would turn to the corresponding prediction.[54]

From around the middle of the nineteenth century the 'Art of telling Fortunes by the Grounds of Tea or Coffee' was added to the contents of a number of fortune books.[55] Charles Mackay, writing in 1852, stated that there were 'thousands and tens of thousands of humble families in which the good-wife, and even the good-man, resort to the grounds at the bottom of their tea-cups, to know whether the next harvest will be abundant, or their sow bring forth a numerous litter'.[56] If Mackay is accurate, then tea-cup divination was a widespread practice before it appeared widely in the chapbooks. If this is so, then the chapbook publishers obviously picked up on what was a popular divinatory method, knowledge of which had been transmitted and diffused orally. Prognosticating from the patterns of dregs was by no means new, and for centuries the lees of wine had been interpreted in a similar manner. With the popularity of the coffee house and reductions in the price of coffee during the second half of the eighteenth century, fortune-telling by the use of coffee grounds became an established practice by the end of the century.

In 1762, for example, it was asserted that there were those who imposed upon the credulous by casting 'coffee-grounds', and a chapbook dating from around 1815 referred to fortune-tellers who 'make you twirl the coffee cup, to see by the grounds at bottom how long you are to live'.[57] Tea gardens sprang up during the mid-eighteenth century, but tea only achieved widespread popularity during the first half of the nineteenth century when prices had dropped sufficiently, and my own feeling is that Mackay somewhat overstated the populariy of tea-leaf divination at the time.[58] I have come across very little evidence that tea-cup divination was extensively practised until the second half of the nineteenth century. By 1911, though, the folklorist Jonathan Caredig Davies could observe that in Wales tea-cup divination was 'very much practised', though he also asserted that it was far more popular in the colonies, especially Australia, than it was in England.[59] Based on the evidence, I would suggest, therefore, that the present widespread knowledge of the method is partly attributable to its inclusion in mid-nineteenth-century chapbooks.

People undoubtedly purchased such literature for its simple entertainment value. The woodcuts of heads and hands which accompanied sections on palm-reading and physiognomy were a source of enjoyment in themselves. The familiar forms of love divination were also probably performed as much for their entertainment value as for any serious desire to confirm future partners. But the contents of these books were also put to serious use. Weather omens, and lists of good, bad or happy days in each month were likely to have been considered seriously and actions adjusted accordingly. Decisions concerning agricultural tasks, financial speculations or legal action may, perhaps, have rested on a wheel of fortune, an oraculum, or the dregs at the bottom of a cup. Consulting a fortune book also had its benefits over a visit to a cunning-person or fortune-teller. It was cheaper and less arduous, and could be conducted in the strictest privacy. In at least one instance, a court heard how a woman consulted a fortune book to confirm what she had been told by a cunning-man. The woman, Mary Passant, was informed that one of her neighbours had bewitched her. After hearing this she 'sent to Mr Wray, bookseller, for two fortune-telling books' to see if it was true.[60]

The fortune book was, then, a divinatory tool-kit for the masses. The extent to which they were used depended on a variety of factors: on the sophistication of the reader, on the relative availability and personal attitudes towards fortune-tellers, and on the depth of existing oral divinatory knowledge. In consideration of these factors, it can be conjectured that fortune books were more influential in urban society than in rural areas. As folklore sources show, in rural England and Wales there was a huge pool of divinatory knowledge to which the whole community had access. In urban areas, where communities were more fragmented and old oral traditions were in decline, the fortune book became a more important source of knowledge, and in the absence of competition from well-established patterns of divinatory practice, methods such as card-reading were adopted more readily. Thus one Welsh folklorist observed that divination by cards was more popular in towns than in country places.[61] Fortune books were also influential in that they were invaluable training guides for budding fortune-tellers and cunning-folk. Police found the *New Universal Fortune-Teller* and *Raphael's Witch or Oracle of the Future* among the books and papers of Clayton Chaffer. John Major, a London fortune-teller, also owned a copy of *Raphael's Witch*, as well as *Aristotle's Masterpiece*, *Mother Shipton* and the *Fruits of Philosophy*, among a variety of other fortune-telling publications.[62]

Prophecy

Closely related to the fortune-tellers and dream-books were prophetic chapbooks, of which there were two main types: those based on scriptural prophecies or couched in religious terms, and those based on the utterances of various non-religious lay prophets. Examples of the former were *The Royal Fortune-Teller: with the signs of the times, and scriptural prophecies* (Newcastle, *c.* 1810), the *Christian's Diary* (London, *c.* 1800), and the numerous editions of the apocryphal oracle *The Wandering Jew*, who refused to help Christ and was condemned to wander the earth until the Last Judgement.[63] Judging by their print runs these 'religious' prophetic chapbooks, with their blend of sacred and folk belief, and their emphasis on the Day of Judgement, sacred trances and miracles, had a consistent but moderate popular appeal. It is difficult to prove conclusively, but it is likely that the French Revolution provoked greater interest in such chapbooks during the late eighteenth and early nineteenth centuries. This was also the period when pseudo-religious prophets such as Joanna Southcott and Richard Brothers were attracting considerable attention.[64] By all accounts, though, the most popular prophetic chapbooks were those attributed to the lay prophets Mother Shipton and Robert Nixon. Both of these characters supposedly lived and prophesied some time during the second half of the fifteenth and first half of the sixteenth centuries, though there is no historical evidence that they ever existed, and their prophecies were first printed many decades later.

Robert Nixon was said to have been an idiot ploughman, brought up in the parish of Over, Cheshire, who developed a reputation for making cryptic, oracular pronouncements.[65] As one story goes, the fame of Nixon's oracular powers eventually reached the ears of Henry VII, who sent for him and became convinced of his powers. Nixon predicted that his own death would be brought about by starvation, and so it was. One day, while the king was out on a long hunting trip, the servants began to torment and bully Nixon. For his own safety one of the king's men locked him in a closet and made sure meals were brought to him regularly. Unfortunately, Nixon's guardian was called out on an urgent errand, and forgot about his closeted charge. On his return three days later, poor Nixon was found starved to death. Nixon's prophecies were first published by one John Oldmixon in 1714, and proved so popular that further editions were printed in nearly every decade up until the 1870s. A chapbook printed in Warrington around 1815 claimed, not unreasonably, that it was in its fifty-fifth edition. Over the years, printers from all over the country took advantage of Nixon's fame, attesting to the widespread geographical appeal of his prophecies. Extant editions in the British library were published in London, Glasgow, Edinburgh, Liverpool, Chester, Gainsborough, Aylesbury, Birmingham, Hull, Penrith, Diss, Derby, Halifax and Manchester.

Even more popular than Nixon's prophecies were those attributed to Ursula Shipton, who was allegedly born at Knaresborough in Yorkshire.[66] The earliest surviving publication of her prophecies dates from 1641. This anonymous tract, in which Mother Shipton is said to have foretold the death of Cardinal Wolsey and other political figures, was undoubtedly a product of the foment of the time when political and religious prophecy was rife.[67] It contained very little biographical information, however, and it was not until 1667, when Richard Head published his account of her life and death, that the Shipton myth was properly formed. Head's history of Mother Shipton was supplemented by another anonymous history twenty years later, and the two together formed the basis of all subsequent editions.[68] According to these histories, Ursula's mother, Agatha, was orphaned at the age of sixteen, and was forced to seek relief from the parish. One day, as the unhappy Agatha moped by the side of a river, she was approached by the Devil in the guise of a handsome man. He whisked her off to a banquet, provided her with rich garments, seduced her with wine and music, and finally bedded her. She was later to tell the midwife that his caresses were as cold as ice. Ursula was the issue of this diabolical union. Agatha's neighbours grew suspicious, and, believing her to be a witch, had her brought before the local justice, though she was later released. The unfortunate Ursula was not blessed with refined features, and as she grew older she had to put up with townsfolk calling her nasty names such as 'Devils Bastard' and 'Hag-face'. Despite her ugly appearance, at the age of twenty-four she married one Toby Shipton, and not long after she began to exercise her powers of prescience. One of her first acts was to divine the identity of the person who had stolen a new smock and petticoat from one of her neighbours. She soon developed a reputation as a cunning-woman, and people from near and far came to consult her. Before long she began to explore the very depths of her powers by prophesying on major events such as Henry VIII's journey to France, and the dissolution of the monasteries, as well as on lost property. She continued as the foremost Sibyl of her time until her death aged seventy-three. Like *Nixon's*, numerous editions of Mother Shipton's prophecies were printed by publishers around the country throughout the eighteenth and nineteenth centuries, and sometimes the work of both prophets was packaged together. The Shipton name was also used to market a number of common fortune-telling chapbooks, which were obviously in direct competition with those other eminent dames, Mother Bunch and Mother Bridget.[69]

The popular fame of Nixon and Shipton is evident not only from their printing history but also from the observations of people such as the self-educated poet John Clare (1793–1864), who recalled how his father, who could read only a little, was very fond of 'old Nixon's Prophecies, Mother Bunches Fairey Tales, and Mother Shipton's Legacy etc.'[70] According to Charles Mackay, writing in 1841, the prophecies of Mother Shipton were still considered seriously in many rural districts: 'In cottages and servants' halls her reputation is great; and she rules, the most popular of British prophets, among all the uneducated, or half-educated portions of the community.'[71] New prophecies attributed to Shipton were also generated in oral culture by communities seeking explanations for momentous local events. Thus when a railway viaduct collapsed during the construction of the line between Harrogate and York, the locals believed Mother Shipton had prophesied it would happen, though no such prophecy was heard of until after the disaster.[72] In 1879 a rumour circulated in Somerset that Mother Shipton had predicted that the great Ham Hill stone quarry would be swallowed up by a tremendous earthquake on Good Friday of that year. Great alarm was felt in the neighbourhood. Some left the area before Good Friday, while those that stayed removed all their crockery. When the dreaded day arrived, nothing untoward occurred and daily life resumed as normal. However, this false alarm apparently 'did little to dispel the faith in Mother Shipton; the calculator had made a blunder about the date, and it was not her fault, and many Somersetshire folk are still waiting, expecting to suffer from the prophesied catastrophe.'[73]

Over time the original prophecies published in the seventeenth century were also occasionally added to by chapbook publishers in order to update the relevancy of the content. In 1862, for example, Charles Hindley added a prophetic doggerel to one of his editions of *Mother Shipton* which foretold the invention of the steam engine and the electric telegraph, and ended with the apocalyptic pronouncement: 'The world to an end shall come/ In eighteen hundred and eighty-one.'[74] Hindley's mischievous tampering proved very successful, and news of Mother Shipton's prediction of the world's end soon became a topic of common knowledge and much debate, and subsequent editions gave great prominence to it.[75] Hindley's confession in 1873 that he was the author of these lines did little to stem their popular currency.[76] Not surprisingly, this prophecy was the cause of much genuine alarm as the dreaded year approached, and in at least one case the fear of the imminent demise of the world ended in personal tragedy. In November 1881 an inquest was held at Hoxton, in London, on the body of a ten-year-old girl named Kate Weedon who had died of severe shock and convulsions brought on by fright. At the inquest her mother told how her daughter had recently read the prophecies of Mother Shipton and had consequently become very much alarmed, particularly as the year was quickly drawing to a close: 'she very frequently cried and talked about the world coming to an end in 1881. On returning from school on the 17th inst., she was weeping bitterly and speaking of Mother Shipton. Her mother told her it was all nonsense, but this had not the least effect upon her, and when she went to bed at half-past 10 she was still crying and wringing her hands, saying she knew the end of the world would come in the night.' At around half-past three in the morning Mrs Weedon was awakened by a cry, and got up to see if Kate was all right, only to find her having a violent fit. A doctor was immediately sent for, but only two hours later she was dead.[77] For poor Kate Weedon the world did, indeed, come to an end in 1881.

What was it about Nixon and Mother Shipton that made them so enduringly popular and influential? Prophecy in general had obviously always held a certain fascination, but what set Nixon and Shipton apart from other forms of prophetic literature was their narrative content. Their life histories gave the prophecies a concrete social context. They were rooted firmly in the heritage and geography of England. Nixon and Shipton were also of common birth like their readers, and people could relate to them. Although they were supposed to have lived centuries before their prophecies were widely circulated, and the accounts of their 'Life and Death' were written in the seventeenth and early eighteenth centuries, for the nineteenth-century reader there was still much in these life stories that was familiar and convincing. Readers could see in Mother Shipton the cunning-folk of their own experience, and in Nixon the village simpleton. As with the traditions surrounding all folk heroes, though, the familiar merged with the fantastic. Nixon and Shipton were recognisable characters, yet their experiences were quite extraordinary.[78] This was a potent combination, and the reader was drawn into their exciting lives, which made their prophecies all the more appealing; they were left wondering what would happen next? What further role was Nixon or Shipton to play in their lives?

As society, particularly in the countryside, began to change dramatically during the late nineteenth and early twentieth centuries, so the link with the lives of Nixon and Shipton weakened and the popular belief in their prophecies waned. After 1900, publishers checking through their sales figures were obviously made aware of the changing interests of their readers, and the once continual flow of editions slowed down to a trickle. Public interest in Mother Shipton still endured in the area of her supposed origin, and the Leeds publisher Arthur Wigley continued to print her *Life and Prophecies* for a local market.[79] By the 1920s, though, the Cheshire ploughboy and the Yorkshire cunning-woman were no longer the important national figures who had occupied the minds of the labouring classes for more than two centuries.

In contrast to the popularity of Nixon and Shipton, the famous prophecies of the sixteenth-century French astrologer Nostradamus (1503–66) never really caught the imagination of the chapbook reader. His prophecies had first been translated into English in 1558, and proved rather too successful for the government, which took legal action against the booksellers who sold them.[80] Over the next hundred years Nostradamus's prophecies were known in England, but, while the French publishers churned out numerous editions, few English versions were produced until the second half of the seventeenth century. The resurgence of interest in Nostradamus at this time was fuelled by events surrounding the monarchy crisis and the accession of William III. There was obviously potential for exploiting Nostradamus's name, just as, say, that of Aristotle had been used, but chapbook publishers obviously did not think it a worthwhile proposition, though the odd attempt was made to introduce Nostradamus to the basic reader. In 1816, for example, a fortune book entitled *The Wizard; or the whole Art of divining Dreams* declared its interpretations to be based on his principles, and included a simple account of his life. However, it does not seem to have had a successful print run, suggesting that neither the fame of the French astrologer nor his prophecies appealed to the chapbook readership. English readers could not relate to Nostradamus or his life. His prophecies and his name only achieved popular recognition during the twentieth century, as Nixon and Shipton fell into relative obscurity. Public interest in his quatrains was first kindled by claims that he had predicted both the First and Second World Wars. During the latter, his prophecies were also manipulated and promoted by both German and British war departments for propaganda purposes.[81]

The witch and the Devil

When looking through chapbook collections it soon becomes apparent that in comparison with all the stories of fortune-tellers, astrologers, conjurors and prophets, the witch makes comparatively few appearances. This dearth of witches is in sharp contrast with their predominance in oral tradition. That witchcraft was a potentially very popular topic for literature is indicated by the long publication history of two chapbooks that were concerned with witches: *The Witch of the Woodlands* and *The History of the Lancashire Witches*. Samuel Bamford recalled devouring both these works as a boy, along with other romances such as *Tom Hickathrift* and *Jack the Giant Killer*. 'Of all these tales and ballads I was soon master, and they formed the subjects of many a wonder-creating story for my acquaintance both at the workhouse and elsewhere.'[82] When we look more closely at the contents of these works we find that the concept of the witch being absorbed by young Bamford and many thousands like him was not quite the same as the witch of popular experience.

The tale of *The Witch of the Woodlands; or the Cobler's New Translation* was a light-hearted cautionary tale which first appeared during the late seventeenth century, and continued to be published at intervals up until the mid-nineteenth century. It told the story of Robin the Cobbler, who was 'punish'd bad as Faustus with his devils' for his evil living. Despite its title the story does not actually concern witchcraft very much, although one section tells how four witches turn up to punish Robin for his licentiousness by transforming him into a horse and riding him through the undergrowth. One of the few other memorable impressions is a woodcut of witches dancing in a circle that appears in some editions, such as one printed in Birmingham around 1820.

The History of the Lancashire Witches. Also a Treatise of Witches in general is much more true to its title, being devoted to the history of a family of witches, 'their manner of becoming such', and 'the entertainments and frolics which happened among them'.[83] The story actually bears no relation to the history of the famous Lancashire witch-trials of 1612 and 1634, which at the time, and in later years, became the subject of a variety of pamphlets, ballads, plays, novels and even puppet shows.[84] This media coverage of the activities of the Lancashire witches of Pendle Hill meant that knowledge of their activities became ingrained in popular tradition. The author of the chapbook was certainly well aware of the popular notoriety of the Lancashire witches, since he remarks that 'the name of Lancashire witches has been so frequent in the mouths of old and young, and many imperfect stories have been rumoured abroad'. In the spirit of popular enlightenment the author then goes on to give a totally fictitious account as well. *The History of the Lancashire Witches* tells the story of Mother Cuthbert and her 'two lusty daughters', who lived at the bottom of 'Wood-and-Mountain-Hill' in Lancashire. They were very poor, 'which made them often repine at and lament their want'. One day Mother Cuthbert meets the Devil, who appears in the shape of a rabbit. He gives her a purse full of money and tells her to return to the same spot the next day. She does as she is told, and finds herself transported to a revel where she joins other witches in feasting and dancing. She enters 'the society of witches' and is given some ointment and an imp in the shape of a mole. At the end of the festivities the witches all fly away upon coal-staffs. Her daughters are subsequently initiated as well. With their newly acquired powers, the three women engage in a series of escapades such as bewitching the nasty Mayor of Lancaster, who had had Mother Cuthbert whipped, rescuing a poor man arrested by a cruel creditor, revelling in a local gentleman's house, and enchanting several thieves and taking away their ill-gotten gains.

The *History of the Lancashire Witches* does not adopt a moralising tone about the folly of believing in witchcraft. It was not meant to be a cautionary tale but a story 'Conducive to Mirth and Recreation'. Neither were witches portrayed in a bad light. Indeed, in the *Brief Treatise* attached to the *Lancashire Witches*, it is made clear that although 'many of 'em are more mischievous than others, in laming and destroying cattle, and in destroying ships at sea by raising storms … the Lancashire witches we see chiefly divert themselves in merriment and are therefore found to be more sociable than the rest.'[85] What is most striking about both this chapbook and *The Witch of the Woodlands* is that the traditional role of the witch is subverted. Instead of representing a social threat, witches actually chastise others who exhibit anti-social behaviour. Thus in *The Witch of the Woodlands* a licentious man is punished, and in the *History of the Lancashire Witches* oppressors of the poor, thieves and false lovers are chastised magically. This was a new genial and frolicsome image of the witch in contrast with the earlier account of how Agatha Shipton became a witch, written during the period of the witch-trials. The story of Agatha was one of overt Devil worship. The Devil seals his power over Agatha by giving her a mark: he 'plukt her by the Groin, and there immediately grew a kind of Tet, which he instantly suckt, telling her that must be his constant Custom with her morning and evening'. She uses her powers to commit acts of revenge on neighbours, killing their horses and cattle. The motifs and concepts of witchcraft presented in *The History of the Lancashire Witches* were more in tune with folk tradition even if Agatha's vengeful acts were more realistic in terms of the popular experience of witchcraft. As with many accounts of witches from folklore, Agatha Shipton and Mother Cuthbert were extremely poor, and lived outside the social norms, being respectively an orphan spinster and a widow. Their desire to be witches was fuelled by frustration and resentment born of the injustices they had experienced. They indulged in such fantastic activities as shape-shifting and flying. In one of the tales, for example, Mother Cuthbert's youngest daughter, Cicely, turns herself into a hare to make sport for the hounds of a gentleman she desires to make love to. As in numerous folk legends collected during the nineteenth century, she is bitten on the haunches by one of the hounds, and is found back at her cottage rubbing her sore back.

Where the chapbook portrayal of the witch diverged strongly from folk legend was in the sympathy it evoked for its subject. In the chapbooks the witch only vented her wrath at the dissolute, the cruel and the avaricious. However, in reality, most victims of witchcraft would certainly not have considered themselves to have been guilty of such shortcomings. Witches were thought to act out of malice and spite for their own pleasure, causing suffering to the innocent and the law-abiding. Witches were pernicious, capricious and a downright nuisance. Nevertheless, despite this benign portrayal of witches, these chapbooks proved popular. Maybe if they had been more realistic, more reflective of popular anxieties concerning witches and witchcraft, they would not have sold so well. People turned to chapbooks for escapism. They did not necessarily want to read accurate reproductions of their own misfortunes and daily torments.

The paucity of witches in chapbook literature is also mirrored in the broadside ballads of the eighteenth and nineteenth centuries. I have only found a few examples, two notably entitled 'Witches glee' and 'Witches' Song', among many such jolly ditties as 'Hairy gobs an' fine moose-catchers' and 'The Widow Waddle of Chickabiddy Lane'. That this was not just a result of collection bias is suggested by a parallel absence of the witch in the oral ballad tradition. According to James Reeves, 'The supernatural, as [Cecil James] Sharp and other collectors noticed, is conspicuously absent. Whether this is an Anglo-Saxon attitude, or whether it is the result of a gradual process of rationalisation, is not clear. Certainly songs about witches were rare in the south of England by the nineteenth century.'[86] There is no reason why 'rationalisation' or the declining belief in witchcraft should necessarily have resulted in the disappearance of witch-related ballads as opposed to others; after all, a good song is a good song. Besides, the belief in witchcraft was still widespread when many of the collectors were recording folksongs. A more convincing explanation relates to the absence of the witch in popular literature. Robert Thomson has demonstrated that at least 80 per cent of the folksongs collected in the late nineteenth and early twentieth centuries derived from earlier printed broadsides. Over ninety such songs were found to derive from seventeenth-century broadsides.[87] Thus the paucity of witch-related songs in the oral tradition of the late nineteenth century, could be explained by the paucity of songs in the printed tradition.

Although much of educated society saw the popular belief in witchcraft as foolish, it was also deemed deleterious, and most certainly a delusion not be nourished in any way. As early as 1718 Francis Hutchinson remarked upon the pernicious effects of witchcraft literature: 'These Books and Narratives are in Tradesmen's Shops and Farmers' Houses, and are read with great Eagerness, and are continually leavening the Minds of the Youth, who delight in such Subjects; and considering what sore Evils these notions bring when they prevail, I hope no Man will think but they must still be combated, oppos'd and kept down.'[88] The weight of educated opinion concerning this matter must have had an effect on chapbook publishers. The fear of strong reprobation largely kept the witch, and remedies against witchcraft, out of the pages of popular literature. When the witch did appear, she was not the menacing, malicious figure of popular experience but rather a hedonistic character who used her powers to positive effect. It is possible, but very unlikely, that the publishers who originally produced these reader-friendly witches did so in a deliberate attempt to subvert the perceived, morally injurious, popular belief in the harmful power of the witch.

The Devil had a much stronger presence in chapbook literature than the witch. The most enduring and popular tale of diabolical intervention was, of course, the life of Dr Faustus, which went through numerous chapbook reprints during the eighteenth and nineteenth centuries.[89] The concept of the Faustian pact was also transferred to an English context, thereby making the moral behind the story more pertinent and contemporary. One such account of the consequences of dealing with the Devil was recorded in a chapbook published around 1790 entitled *The Second Spira; or the Blasphemers Reproved. Setting forth an example of God's Judgement on Six Profane Young Men at Brodney in Somersetshire. To which is added a Sermon preached on the occasion by the Reverend Mr. Simmons.* It relates how six young men went into the churchyard at midnight, carrying with them wine and bread, with the intention of taking the sacrament in the name of the Devil. As they were preparing, a voice was heard warning them to turn and repent. The six men ignored the advice, but on continuing with their diabolic ceremony there arose such dreadful and astonishing cries, bellowing and dismal groans, that the Rev. Simmons, who lived nearby, was woken up and went to investigate. He saw the wine and bread but nothing else, and so he went back to bed. The next morning the young men were found lying about in a most deplorable condition, blood running from their mouths and ears.

It is unusual to see an account of group Devil worship presented in popular literature at this period. Usually, human interaction with the Devil was concerned with individual pacts. Nearly all of these accounts of diabolic deals, and the appalling consequences which arose from them, concerned young men, and were, therefore, presumably written for their benefit.[90] The reason for this gender bias lies in the fact that while in the seventeenth century females were accused of making pacts with the Devil in order to gain powers of witchcraft, young men were also accused of dealing with the Devil, but to obtain wealth rather than malevolent, supernatural capabilities.[91] Once the ruling elite ceased to believe in the continued existence of witchcraft, then the concept of the female diabolic pact also declined. Women were still victims of diabolic possession, but that was a completely different relationship to that of the pact. The Devil and male cupidity, however, were still realities. Although the Devil continued to be believed in by many people across the whole social range, his power to intervene directly in earthly affairs was held to be no longer credible by the majority of educated men and women. Yet tales of the Devil ripping to shreds avaricious young men still served well as educational cautionary tales for the lower classes, instructing them on the dangers of coveting a way of life beyond their natural station.

The image of the Devil presented in these chapbooks was more a figment of early modern elite theology than popular tradition, but there was definitely some absorption of the male pact tradition into popular culture, transmitted not only through chapbook literature but also through its reaffirmation by Evangelical preachers. Writing in 1871, Thomas Quiller Couch remembered one tale of a pact being made in his part of Cornwall. The man concerned was not 'actively vicious, never being known to use his supernatural powers of ill-doing, to the detriment of others, and only asked the foul fiend's assistance, when the depths of his potations had not left him enough to pay the reckoning. He was then accustomed to hold his hat up the chimney, and demand money.'[92] However, Quiller Couch also believed that by the time of his writing, 'the notion that mysterious compacts are formed between evil spirits and wicked men has become nearly obsolete.'[93] The most extraordinary example of life imitating literature with regard to the male pact can be found in the trial of William Dove, who was accused of poisoning his wife in 1856. While in jail awaiting trial, the governor heard reports that Dove had a knife on him. Dove was subsequently searched, and sewn up in his clothes was found the following letter to the Devil written in his own blood: 'Dear Devil, – If you will get me clear at the assizes and let me have the enjoyment of life, health, wealth, tobacco here, more food and better, and my wishes granted till I am 60, come to me to-night. I remain, your faithful subject, William Dove.'[94] It is quite likely that Dove got his idea of attempting to bargain with the Devil from reading or hearing of the story of Dr Faustus, since the chapbook version described how Faustus wrote a similar letter to the Devil in his own blood. No doubt if the Dove affair had occurred a hundred years previously, his sorry story would have been turned into a chapbook itself, acting as a warning to other men of the sad end that awaited all those who turn to the Devil.

By the 1860s the chapbook format had expired, and the broadsheet was drawing in its last breath. However, the gap in the market for amazing life histories and marvellous adventures was subsequently filled by new literary formats such as the penny dreadful and the novelette.[95] These were of a significantly higher literary standard than the chapbook, and in terms of content they appealed more generally to the new dominant urban society than did its rusticated predecessor. There were a few exceptions, though, most notably a penny novel entitled *A Fortune Teller's Life; or Record of Fate*,[96] which told the story of 'Dame Sibylla', the beautiful daughter of an Italian nobleman, who marries a renowned astrologer. Her husband is murdered, and Dame Sibylla flees to England with her child and takes up fortune-telling in Shropshire: 'Their slender means soon disappeared, and Madame Sibylla adopted her husband's profession, only to find herself harassed and persecuted by the police.' She soon gained a reputation, but obviously not necessarily a good one, as she was thought to possess the 'evil eye'. She died one day not long after being caught on the property of a local squire. He threatened that if he caught her again 'he would have her ducked in the horse-pond'.

Although the chapbook format declined, the popular interest in fortune-telling, for which it had catered, remained strong. Cheap fortune-telling booklets continued to be published during the second half of the nineteenth century, but they were now better produced, often used more sophisticated language, and contained more refined illustrations. By the end of the nineteenth century most such publications were written by professional fortune-tellers. Writing fortune-telling guides could not only be lucrative in itself, but could also serve as a vehicle to advertise the fortune-tellers' business. These works were no longer hawked by tramping chapmen and pedlars; in the new era of the steam train, the railway bookstall became a popular means of distributing fortune books, such as the sixpenny work *Shall I tell you your Fortune, my pretty Maid?*, which Frederick Elworthy bought at a station one day.[97] For those seeking prophetic enlightenment and information about the future there was also another literary source available which was as old as the chapbook, but which proved to have a far better shelf life: the almanac.

Almanacs

Although some chapbooks contained astrological information, it was the almanac which really sated the public thirst for stellar prediction.[98] Indeed, it has been commonly stated, and not without reason, that after the Bible the astrological almanac was the most ubiquitous form of literature. By 1660 average sales had reached around 400,000 a year, and over the next two centuries sales reached even higher peaks at times, although the overall number of almanac titles actually declined. The most successful and enduring title was *Moore's Almanack*, which sold around 107,000 copies in 1768, and reached an impressive peak of 560,000 in 1839. During the 1820s and 1830s the market was substantially reinvigorated by the appearance of a new breed of populist almanac. First off the presses in November 1826 was Raphael's *Prophetic Messenger*, which was later renamed the *Prophetic Almanac*. Not surprisingly, considering *Moore's* dominance of the market at the time, its success was modest at first, though it built up a strong following over the next few decades, and by the end of the century sales were probably not far off 200,000. Part of its success was due to the innovation of providing forecasts for every day of the year. In 1831 *The Herald of Astrology*, the name of which was changed to the now familiar *Zadkiel's Almanac* in 1836, was launched in direct competition to Raphael's publication. Again, sales grew slowly but surely, and by 1870 around 80,000 copies were being sold. Both almanacs presumably picked up some of *Moore's* readership as sales of that publication fell markedly after mid-century. Although neither of the new almanacs ever matched *Moore's* huge sales, in terms of popular fame the reputations of Raphael and Zadkiel certainly rivalled that of *Moore's*, and all three pseudonymous figures dominated the market for the rest of the century.

As has already been observed, popular literary formats were designed to entice the illiterate as well as the literate, and, like chapbooks and broadsides, almanacs also had their pictorial attractions. A humorous account in the satirical almanac *Poor Robin* describes a scene where people are debating over which almanac to buy, and in the end they finally settle on *Moore's* because it had 'a picture in it'.[99] A regular feature of eighteenth-century almanacs was the zodiac man. As its name suggests, this depicted a fully naked man surrounded by the signs of the zodiac indicating which aspect of the body they ruled, and was meant to be used as an astrological guide to the most propitious times to administer medicines and carry out blood-letting. While the astrological content of almanacs offended those who considered it mere vulgar superstition, the depiction of a naked man also offended their sense of decency.[100] Due to censure, perhaps, almanac publishers began to drop the zodiac man from their pages during the late eighteenth century, but its influence, nevertheless, lived on in folklore. Writing in 1830, the Suffolk clergymen Robert Forby observed that, although the 'progress of refinement' had divested almanacs 'of their formerly indispensable ornament', the zodiac man still had its many believers.[101] The hieroglyph was another important visual feature of several almanacs. It consisted of an engraved scene, often containing classical and biblical allusions, which was a symbolic representation of important future events. The hieroglyph was a way of conveying prophecy in a medium accessible to everyone, and it undoubtedly contributed to the overall success of *Moore's*.

The evidence suggests that at least up until the second half of the nineteenth century almanacs sold as well in urban as in rural areas. The publisher and moral reformer Charles Knight bemoaned the fact that the believers in *Moore's* 'comprised nearly all the rural population and very many of the dwellers in towns'.[102] In class terms the astrological almanac readership was generally perceived to be low in nature. Thus an editorial in *The Times* commented that, '"Old Moore's" and "Zadkiel's" almanacs, with their curious survivals of medieval astrology … yearly sell by thousands among the lower social strata of our countrymen.'[103] Almanacs were undoubtedly very popular among farmers, and during the late nineteenth century *Raphael's Almanac* appealed directly to agricultural concerns, with advertisements proclaiming: 'THE WAY OUT OF TROUBLE. If you are a farmer and your crops fail, or if you are perplexed about buying or selling your cattle, get RAPHAEL'S Almanac and it will tell you the very days and hours to ensure success in all your operations.'[104] Yet I do not think we should underestimate the middle-class readership of astrological almanacs. There were many educated people with an interest in astrology, like the clergyman poet William Barnes, who dabbled privately, and it would be surprising if they did not buy almanacs as well as the more erudite expositions of astrological practice that were available.[105]

The section devoted to weather predictions was probably the most thumbed section of almanacs. As the Dorset folklorist John Udal found, 'signs and portents in any way indicative of what the weather is likely to be are eagerly looked for and carefully treasured up, resulting in a strong belief in those superstitions to which they give rise.'[106] Numerous were the ways and sayings of folk weather prediction. Cows lying down portended rain, sheep flocking together signalled rough weather, crows flying high was a sign of fair weather, and a cat sitting with her back to the fire indicated frost or snow. The phases of the moon were also thought to have their effect on the sky. When the new moon was seen 'lying on its back' with its horns in the air dry weather was to be expected, while a new moon on a Saturday was a sign of forthcoming bad weather.[107] However, the almanac seems to have been considered the most reliable of weather oracles. The Rev. Morris observed that in Yorkshire, for instance, people maintained a remarkable faith in almanac weather forecasts, and recalled talking about the state of the weather with an old countryman who confidently asserted that, 'T'Almanack says we s'all a'e thunner at Sunda, bud wi fine infidels [intervals] during t'week.'[108] A major reason for this popular deference to almanac prediction was that, unlike folklore forecasting, almanacs such as *Zadkiel's* gave daily weather predictions for the whole year. A farmer wanting to plant his crops on 25 March, say, could look up that day and see exactly what to expect in advance. In this sense Messrs Raphael, Zadkiel and Moore were the precursors of our modern daily forecasters.

In addition to useful weather prognostications, and advice on when to carry out various agricultural pursuits, the other main use of these almanacs was in the field of medicine. As Raphael advertised, his 'Almanac will show you what herbs will cure you, and the exact days and hours to gather them, so that they may be full of strength and healing power'. Indeed, by the mid-nineteenth century, the success or failure of astrological almanacs was apparently partly dependent on the accounts they gave of the planetary influences associated with diseases and cures. The Rev. Forby found that people in East Anglia considered it imprudent to tamper with any part of the body at the time that *Moore's* showed it to be under the dominion of the ruling star, or, as it was commonly said, 'when the sign lies in it'. Forby remembered hearing a wealthy yeoman ask a farrier when he would perform an operation on a colt of his. In reply the farrier said 'he would just step home, and see how the sign lay, and would then let him know'. In another instance from the late eighteenth century, a doctor prescribed a purge to another wealthy farmer, but on enquiring later as to his health, the doctor was told by the sick man that 'he had looked into his Almanack, and seeing the sign lay in "Bowels," he thought *that*, and the physic together, would be too much for him.'[109] Writing in 1859, T. T. Wilkinson reported that in Lancashire sales of *Moore's*, which had reached a peak in 1839, was by then 'sadly at a discount', because it lacked the table of the 'Moon's signs'; 'the farmers are consequently at a loss to know which will be healthy cattle, and they prefer a spurious edition which supplies the grave omission.'[110] For the same reason editions of works such as Culpeper's *Herbal* were found to be selling more than all other works on the subject.

Almanacs were, of course, indispensable items for cunning-folk and occupational astrologers. When Joseph Powell was arrested he was found to be in possession of a number of almanacs and astronomical tables, and when police confiscated the books and papers of two other practitioners, Joseph Railey and Clayton Chaffer, the police found copies of Raphael's *Prophetic Messenger*. How they were actually used by these people is more difficult to assess. Some cunning-folk may have used the astrological data to draw up horoscopes, but the scant evidence suggests that they were also employed on a less sophisticated level. The Gloucestershire folklorist Margaret Eyre was told by one occult practitioner that he consulted

Zadkiel's Almanack to look up lucky days, and added, 'Yes, Miss, 't will help 'ee, this book will.' At the inquest on the body of Mary Saunders of Lufton, Somerset, in June 1892, it was stated that, believing their daughter to have been bewitched, her parents visited the South Petherton cunning-man, James Stacey. The father of the deceased told the coroner: 'I told him [Stacey] I did not know whether there was any such spell over her. He said he would look on the almanack, and then said no-one could "overlook" her, because she was the first born child.'[111] It would seem, then, that almanacs were used on several different levels depending on the interests and sophistication of the reader.

From lucky days to herbal astrology, hieroglyphs to weather tips, there was something for everyone in the astrological almanac. Thus an advertise-ment for *Raphael's Almanac* boasted that it could advise on 'when to buy, sell, court, marry, set fowls, fish, hire servants, seek employment, speculate, bake, brew, travel, remove, or do anything else'.[112] Almanacs professed to be able to guide people safely through all the uncertainties of life, and in doing so created a sense of order in an unpredictable world. It is no wonder, therefore, that they proved so enduringly popular.

Anti-superstition literature

When we consider the huge numbers of morally improving stories and cautionary tales that were turned into chapbook literature for the moral edification of the masses, it is surprising how few didactic reforming chapbooks seem to have concerned fortune-telling, witchcraft and magic, especially in comparison with the huge volume of fortune books printed. As we have seen in the first chapter, several clergymen had sermons printed in which they reprehended their flocks for believing in witchcraft and magic, and a few moral reformers condemned the folly of astrology in print.[113] Yet these were unlikely to have had large print runs or wide distribution, and were not written in a style or format readily accessible to the chapbook readership.[114]

One of the few surviving examples of the chapbook medium being exploited to attack popular magical beliefs was THE FORTUNE TELLER'S CONJURING CAP; or Questions and answers About Marriage and other things; shewing how to be WISE, RICH AND HAPPY (Banbury, c. 1815). This unusual chapbook was an eight-page satire upon cunning-folk and fortune-tellers, written in the style of a fortune book, and sold for the reasonable price of one penny. Its author took on the persona of a sarcastic cunning-man:

If you ask, are there no true signs by which persons may give a guess what luck they shall have, I answer, yes. And as my CONJURING CAP is as deep as any, is made with very large ears, and has a pretty jingle of bells too at top; I think I can see as far into a mill-stone as any of them. I shall set myself therefore in my great armchair, and answer some of the most usual questions.[115]

These included the following queries:

WILL MY MASTER MARRY ME?

Is a question put to the conjuror very often: which might be answered by any one else, as well as by him. No, to be sure! you did not think he would when he first began to take liberties with you, and pull you about, and you soon let him see that he need not marry you unless he pleased. After toying away your own character, do you wonder that he despises you?

HOW TO RECOVER ANYTHING LOST!

As if all the stars of heaven had nothing to do, but to run scampering about to find it. The fortune teller, is sure to make the fools who consult him, lose something more, by way of fee. This is just as it ought to be. He'll not tell fifty lies for nothing. Besides, the money they give him, and the time they lose by going after him, would half pay for what was stolen from them.[116]

The chapbook concludes with an exhortation to its readers to heed what the Bible says concerning those who consult fortune-tellers: '"Though art weaned in the multitude of their counsels: let not the astrologers, the star-gazers, the monthly prognosticators [the *Moore's Almanacks* of those days] start up and save thee." Isaiah xlvii.13. No, none can instruct thee, like the Bible.' This was a straightforward attack on occult practitioners masquerading as a fortune book, but apart from the title page it would have failed to hold the interest of those at whom it was aimed. Far more cunning in its approach to seducing the 'superstitious' reader into exploring the folly of their own beliefs was *Tawney Rachel; or, The Fortune-Teller: With Some Account of Dreams, Omens, and Conjurers*. It was written by the moral and religious reformer Hannah More, and was first published in 1798.[117] Between 1795 and 1798, More issued a series of publications under the title of the Cheap Repository of Moral and Religious Tracts, and with the help of prominent evangelicals and the gentry they were distributed to the rural poor via booksellers, hawkers and Sunday schools. More was deeply concerned about the 'unsuitable' and 'ungodly' content of popular literature. By adopting the format, style and distribution channels of popularised literature, including woodcuts and eye-catching titles, she intended to subvert the irreligious and amoral content of chapbooks and ballads.[118]

So the story goes, the eponymous Tawney Rachel was the wife of a miscreant poacher named Giles. She travelled the countryside ostensibly selling laces, cabbage nets, 'wicked ballads' and history books, but with the ulterior motive of telling fortunes. She duped many 'silly girls', who lost not only their money but also their good reputations because of their dealings with Rachel. On one occasion, she performed a classic gypsy trick on the wife of farmer Jenkins by pretending that there was a pot of money buried under one of the stones in the cellar, which she could magically reveal. At the end of the story, Farmer Jenkins reports her to a constable, and she is committed to Taunton gaol. Subsequently she is transported to Botany Bay for theft. In conclusion, More warned her readers:

> I have thought it my duty to print this little history, as a kind of warning to all you young men and maidens not to have anything to say to CHEATS, IMPOSTERS, CUNNING WOMEN, FORTUNE TELLERS, CONJURERS and INTERPRETERS OF DREAMS. Listen to me, your true friend, when I assure you that God never reveals to weak and wicked women those secret designs of his providence, which no human wisdom is able to foresee ... The Bible will direct us what to do, better than any conjuror, and no days are unlucky but those which we make so, by your own vanity, folly, and sin.[119]

The deliberate adoption of a popular literary format to beguile the 'superstitious' reader, and then denounce popular magical beliefs, is also apparent in a nineteenth-century broadside collected by Charles Hindley entitled *Fortune Telling and its Results. A True and Remarkable Account of a Most Extraordinary Occurrence that took place in this Neighbourhood*. It included a very eye-catching engraving which was bound to attract an audience, and seems to have been produced for an urban market, rather than the rural target of Hannah More's tracts. It concluded with a similar cautionary notice: 'The foregoing is a statement made by one of the young women, and is published as a warning to ALL young females not to believe in such silly and superstitious nonsense, nor encourage those wicked old hags who prey upon the thoughtless and ignorant. It is all the devil's work.'

Such cautionary tales may have been counterproductive. The actual critical content was relatively small compared to the narrative content which described the 'superstitious nonsense'. They also contained woodcuts which illustrated the narrative and excited the imagination, rather than highlighted the folly of the belief in magic. The illiterate could simply look at the pictures and wonder, while the reader could enjoy the narrative, and relate to events without necessarily paying any notice to the concluding warning. Just as with attempts at reforming popular beliefs from the pulpit, the public paid little heed to attempts at moral instruction from above. From her study of Hannah More's tracts and chapbooks, Susan Pedersen concluded that 'as an attempt to reform or replace popular literature, the Cheap Repository does not seem to have been a notable success.'[120] Speaking in more general terms, Natalie Zemon Davis has also observed that 'oral culture and popular social organisation were strong enough to resist mere correction and standardisation from above.'[121] That is not to say that More's chapbook stories were not popular in themselves, only that their intended purpose was not fulfilled. In fact, after 1798, when the Cheap Repository of Moral and Religious Tracts was wound down, some of More's more successful and entertaining works, such as *Tawney Rachel*, continued to be reprinted and pirated. In contrast, the *Fortune Teller's Conjuring Cap*, which contained no narrative and nothing but sarcastic advice, does not seem to have been reprinted. On the one hand, reformist works like *Tawney Rachel* failed to 'educate' because the 'superstitious' content of the narrative swamped the moral within. On the other hand, works like the *Conjuring Cap* contained no useful or entertaining supernatural content to interest the chapbook reader initially, despite its promising title.

While only a few modest attempts were made to exploit the chapbook and broadside format as a means of instructing the masses on the folly of magic, there was considerable confidence that the newspaper as a literary format would provide the necessary antidote instead. Whereas almanacs and chapbooks were accused of encouraging popular credulity, ignorance and moral degeneration, the newspaper was promoted as a vehicle through which the people imbibed rational knowledge, and, thus illumined, cast away their old 'foolish' beliefs. The view of W. Sparrow Simpson, Sub-Dean of St Paul's Cathedral, was typical of the prevailing attitude: 'the belief in witchcraft, too, is dying fast. The village school, the railway, and the newspaper, are its sworn foes.'[122]

With the relaxation of printing restrictions in 1695 the number of newspaper titles began to increase quickly as printers and publishers set up in business in towns around the country. In 1735 there were about twenty-five provincial papers, such as the *Gloucester Journal* and *Northampton Mercury*. By 1782 the number of titles had doubled, and by 1808 there were over one hundred. It was during the nineteenth century, though, that the newspaper really began to have a significant, widespread social impact. Two primary reasons for this were, first, the growth of literacy amongst a rapidly expanding population, and, second, new technological innovations. In the eighteenth century the wooden printing press could produce at most a hundred impressions an hour, but early in the following century the new iron-frame presses were able to print a larger sheet at double the rate. The subsequent development of the steam power press meant that some publishers were able to print up to 12,000 sheets an hour. Coupled with these innovations was the creation of a fast distribution and communications system, made possible by the expansion of the railway network and the development of the telegraph. Furthermore, expanding urban areas created potentially huge markets on the very doorsteps of the printing works, making the daily paper a viable commercial prospect; so that while in 1854 only 5 dailies were published outside London, ten years later there were 51, and by 1889 some 155 were being circulated. The repeal of stamp duty, in 1855, added a further fillip to the growth of the newspaper industry, and in the following five years 120 papers were established in 102 towns where none had previously existed.[123]

Although newspapers were important disseminators of news and information, their publication was not a charitable exercise in popular education but a commercial enterprise attempting to make money. Newspapers could not rely on cover sales alone to make decent profits, and so the selling of advertising space became an important preoccupation for the publishers. In an increasingly competitive market, newspaper editors also found that to attract bigger readerships they had to excite and entertain as well as inform. In various ways both of these pressures led to the inclusion of material concerning witchcraft and magic.[124]

Newspaper accounts of court cases and other anecdotal reports involving witchcraft and magic were often prefaced with observations and complaints about the continued hold of 'superstitious' beliefs on the populace. When, for example, the *Somerset County Herald* reported a case of witchcraft from Scotland, it felt it necessary to express its disappointment at the 'credulity and superstition of the ignorant, even in these days of education and penny newspapers.'[125] Cunning-folk and fortune-tellers were particularly singled out for their pernicious influence on public morals. In the opinion of the *Cambridge Chronicle*,

> So long as ignorance and superstition exist among us, so long will there be persons sufficiently foolish to repair to *fortune-tellers*; and hence the profession of these wicked people will be perpetuated till the dawn of more intelligence... Fortune-tellers are often persons of the most abandoned character, and (as such persons generally be) they possess a certain tact, without which it would be difficult to conceive their breathing the air of any place but a prison.[126]

By reporting cases of witchcraft and magic, newspapers were attempting to promote public awareness of the continued 'problem' of popular belief in such powers. They also hoped to make clear to any readers who might hold to these beliefs both the error of their ways and the adverse consequences which might befall them. Of course, behind these commendable expressions of concern lay the more pragmatic motive that reports on witchcraft and magic were useful, entertaining column fillers.

There is a certain irony in the fact that although newspapers ostensibly used these stories to illustrate the folly of witchcraft and magic, at the same time they were also inadvertently disseminating information about occult practices, and serving as advertisements for the very cunning-folk, astrologers or fortune-tellers whom the newspapers condemned. By way of example we can turn to the experience of the Cornish folklorist and antiquarian William Paynter, who gave himself the bardic title of 'Whyler Pestry' or 'Searcher-out of Witchcraft'. During the 1920s and 1930s Paynter wrote a variety of articles for the regional press on the continued existence of popular belief in witchcraft and magic. In 1932, for example, he penned an article for the *Western Morning News* entitled 'Witchcraft. Superstition in the Westcountry. Medieval Beliefs that Survive', in which he revealed that due to his articles he had received numerous letters from people asking for his advice and help in curing them of witchcraft and disease. Thus a woman from Somerset wrote 'I saw in the papers that you cure people that are "ill-wished." Will you cure me of rheumatism? I will pay you well for it'. Another asked, 'My husband has been ill-wished with fits ... Can you charm him or send me the name and address of someone who can?'[127] Paynter never stated that he could unbewitch or charm; his interest in the subject was purely that of the folklorist, but the title he gave himself and his knowledge of the subject led people who read his newspaper articles to believe he possessed occult powers like a cunning-man.

Although in the above case the newspaper acted as an unwitting vehicle for promoting magical practices, by accepting advertising revenue from astrologers and fortune-tellers they were knowingly advancing the careers of the same people who they often singled out for public opprobrium. During the eighteenth century, astrologers and fortune-tellers had taken advantage of newspaper advertising columns, just as they had exploited the handbill. However, the rapid growth of newspapers in the nineteenth century, and also the introduction of the penny post in 1840, led to the creation of the thriving new commercial enterprise of postal astrology during the second-half of the century. The greater accessibility to newspapers and the cheapness of the post meant that astrologers could tap a national rather than a local customer base, and could trade without ever having to see their clients. Requiring only their sex and time of birth, these postal astrologers would furnish their clients with the information they requested, which usually consisted of general speculations on future marriage partners, financial prosperity, and removals. A later development from the 1870s onwards, when photographic reproduction became cheaper, was the inclusion of photographs of future husbands and wives.

The success and also the pitfalls of postal astrology can be illustrated by looking at the trial in 1893 of a self-styled 'astronomer' named William Priestly.[128] Together with a phrenologist named Frederick George Venn, he was brought before the magistrates at Teignmouth, Devon. The origin of the prosecution lay in the following advertisement that Priestly placed in the *South Wales Echo* and other regional newspapers: 'Matrimony, photograph, future husband or wife, with position, 1s 6d; one year's events, 1s 6d; five years', 3s 6d; life chart 5s 6d to 7s 6d; sex and birth time. – Professor Priestly, Okehampton-street, Exeter, Devon.' Many people saw the advertisement and wrote to Priestly asking for further particulars and enclosing the appropriate sum in postal orders. His confiscated receipt books show that between the beginning of January and the middle of April he had received 494 letters. Unfortunately, not all his clients were happy with his astrological service, and a number of complaints were made to the police. The matter was placed in the hands of P. C. Crooke, of Exeter. Although Priestly's address was, of course, published for all to see, Crooke first had to gain proof of Priestly's fraudulent activities, so he got his wife to write the following letter: 'A lady friend of mine has sent me an old copy of The South Wales Echo of February 4th, in which I find your advertisement with regard to matrimony. Please send me a photo of my future husband, for which I send a postal order for 1s 6d with this letter. I was born on the 9th April, 1863. Frances Mary Heylner.' Priestly duly sent back a photograph and description of her future husband, and an account of their meeting. In court, a solicitor speaking on behalf of Priestly said he promised to withdraw all such advertisements and would discontinue his business. Nevertheless, he was sentenced to one month's hard labour and costs. The London fortune-teller John Major, of 48 Ambrose Street, Bermondsey, was similarly trapped by the police after receiving complaints from those who had responded to his advertisements. When the police searched his house they found a large number of postcards addressed to various newspapers, and a list of the advertisements he had placed in newspapers from all over the country for which he had paid the considerable sum of £22 4s 9d. This outlay of money on advertising indicates the profits Major must have been making.[129]

It was extremely difficult for newspapers to square their supposed role as vehicles of enlightenment with the financial necessity of promoting advertising revenue, and by attempting to accommodate both they laid themselves open to charges of hypocrisy. A paper might denounce or mock fortune-telling on one page, for instance, while containing adverts for fortune-tellers in the same edition. On 12 October 1889, for example, *The Salisbury and Winchester Journal* contained front-page advertisements for the new editions of *Zadkiel's* and *Raphael's Almanac*, yet in its editorial both publications were criticised, albeit in a humorous way: 'By the modest outlay of sixpence the simple and confiding may obtain information which (if it were only trustworthy) would be cheap at any price; while the cynic will be amply repaid by perusal of these striking annual testimonies to the credulity of human nature … There are, unfortunately, thousands of persons, however, who believe quite seriously in the "Voice of the Stars".' The paper was thus guilty of promoting the very same occult repositories that it mocked as 'superstitious'.

At the turn of this century a country-woman living near Exeter remarked that advances in education produced more witchcraft than there was in former days, 'because if so much harm could be done by ignorant folk and their "books," now that the knowledge of most folk is increased their power to harm will be increased also'.[130] This chance perceptive remark was more accurate in its observation than many of the confident asseverations of educationalists. The spread of literacy and cheap literature across all levels of society was, as Peter Burke has highlighted, a story of growing *access*: physical, economic and linguistic access.[131] Improvements in communications and technological innovations opened up whole new areas of the country to the flow of chapbooks, broadsides, almanacs and newspapers that streamed off the presses of an increasing number of publishers. A rapidly expanding market was ready to purchase printed material, and it was up to the publishers and printers to exploit it. To maximise the potential readership, printers produced work that was written simply enough for the basic reader, that contained graphic images for those who could not read, and that was affordable to the humblest members of society. Above all, the contents of such literature had to strike a chord of familiarity with the purchaser; in other words, they to reflect the concerns of the oral tradition of communication. In fact the printed word helped preserve and diffuse those elements which were already present in the oral tradition, as well as sometimes supplementing the existing store of orally transmitted knowledge. Now sixteenth- and seventeenth-century occult works on divination could be plundered of their contents and presented to a far larger readership for a penny. Learned discussions on the signification of moles, metoposcopy, geomancy, and other such methods of divination, which had been available to only a few, were now available to all: the floodgates of divinatory knowledge were opened. Furthermore, the growth of provincial presses in the eighteenth and nineteenth centuries, and the witting and unwitting advertisements they provided for magical practitioners in handbills and newspapers, created even greater access to occult sources.

Both in the past and in the present it has been argued that popular literature destroyed or debased the oral tradition. D. R. Woolf, for example, referring to the eighteenth century, remarked that as 'print infested the countryside local communities were gradually caught up in a national historical tradition which soon eclipsed, and in many places virtually obliterated, village lore.'[132] As evidence for this he cites the opinions of the antiquarian John Aubrey, who thought that traditional tales had declined significantly in his lifetime due to increasing popular literacy, especially among women. Aubrey believed that memories of Oliver Cromwell and chapbook histories had together 'frighted away Robin-good-fellow and the fayries'. Two centuries later, similar claims were still being made, though by this time new popular literary formats were being blamed. Thus, in 1901, Mabel Peacock complained that 'gossiping newspapers and penny novelettes distract the thoughts of the young from interest in the lore of "idle-headed eld"'.[133] The idea that the oral tradition concerning the supernatural was in terminal decline by the eighteenth century appears completely unfounded when we consider that tales of fairies, ghosts and witches abound in nineteenth-century oral folklore collections. As to Peacock's view that at the turn of the century popular literature was responsible for turning the younger generation away from old traditions and beliefs, I believe that popular literature, rather than being responsible for such waning interest, merely reflected the declining relevancy of that lore. This decline was symptomatic of the changing concerns and interests brought about by wider social and economic factors during the second half of the nineteenth century: the same changes, in fact, that contributed to the demise of the chapbook, with its predominantly rural concerns, and to the rise of the urban-biased Sunday newspapers and penny dreadfuls. Eugen Weber, in an imaginative discussion of the demise of the fairy tale and the supernatural in chapbooks and the oral tradition in nineteenth-century France, has similarly argued that this decline was brought about by changing material conditions. The realistic substance of these tales no longer matched experience, and 'escapist fantasies became less necessary and also less relevant because the fantasies themselves were changing with the times.'[134] The oral tradition, and the magical beliefs transmitted through that channel of communication, may have been largely superseded by literacy and literature, but it seems that they were not directly destroyed by it.

Too often it has been assumed that literacy is a step towards rationality. We should not expect the illiterate to be any more irrational than the literate. Gustave Jahoda's study of literacy and magic in Ghana, for instance, found that out of a sample of 500 literate males around 75 per cent expressed a belief in witchcraft.[135] A major reason for this high level of belief was that a large majority of the sample were first-generation literates. They were brought up in extended families consisting largely of illiterates 'wholly imbued with the traditional cosmology'. Thus they had developed in an environment in which the oral tradition dominated and witchcraft was a reality. Even though they acquired a formal education, their conscious and subconscious childhood experience had produced a lasting disposition towards supernatural beliefs. The same explanation could also be applied to the experiences of many first- and even second-generation literates in nineteenth-century England and Wales. It is axiomatic that book-learning provides access to greater knowledge, but knowledge is often erroneously equated with enlightenment. One can use one's new-found reading skills and access to literary knowledge to read, perhaps, a book on astro-physics, or one can use them to read the latest predictions of Mystic Meg: it is not the ability to read which determines whether people adopt or acquire a rational approach to interpreting and coping with life, but what people *choose* to read. Literacy in certain circumstances can lead to people consciously rejecting the patterns of belief they previously held, but equally it can reinforce those same patterns of belief – even when the reading matter in question is written with the intent of overthrowing them. As a percipient Norfolk magistrate explained in a letter to *The Times*:

> 'Education' must be peculiarly understood, when the darkness to be cleared away is that of superstition. Reading and writing may co-exist therewith, even in proficiency … We may perhaps foretell the birth of a book or two, and there may be soon a lecture here and there on the subject to which so much attention has been called. Let them be done with the greatest judgement, or not at all … Let those who write or lecture keep in view the end to be aimed at, and the 'foul' soil they have to work upon; they will then not merely dig about and manure the weed they would eradicate.[136]

CHAPTER 4

THE WITCH

So far in this book the witch has been presented as a rather passive figure: the subject of sceptical derision and occasional compassion, or the object of popular fear and aggression. It is now necessary to explore who these people were and how they were perceived by the communities they lived in. In order to do this we need to explore two different types of evidence: folklore sources and newspapers. Each presents us with a quite different perspective on the popular conception of witchcraft in the modern period, while together they provide a window on to popular beliefs about witches that is not available to early modern historians. In many ways the material confirms what has already been observed from sixteenth- and seventeenth-century depositions, pamphlets and discourses. By moving backwards and forwards in time, new light is thrown on to some shady areas of our knowledge of the witch in both periods. Yet this discussion is primarily concerned with understanding the concept of the witch during the period in which the folklore sources and newspapers were published. We need to explore in what ways popular ideas about witches were influenced by cultural and intellectual changes. To what extent, for example, did theological concepts of the diabolic witch become absorbed into popular culture? The folklore sources can give us some idea. Why did some accusations of witchcraft lead to violence against those accused, and who were those at the receiving end of such assaults? The newspapers provide us with the necessary data.

As previous chapters have already demonstrated, for many people witches were as much a dangerous reality of life in the eighteenth and nineteenth centuries as they were in the early modern period. I hope, therefore, in this chapter to rescue witches from their trite and quaint portrayal in the recycled work of some popular folklore publications, and place them in their rightful social setting. Witches in the modern period were often accused of 'overlooking', but perhaps they, themselves, have for too long been overlooked.

Witches, folklore and belief

Information concerning witches and their activities has been gathered from antiquarian and folklore sources ranging from the early nineteenth to the mid-twentieth century. These accounts have been collected from all areas of England and Wales to see if any regional variations can be detected concerning witch beliefs.[1] Many of them derive from contributions to the journal of the Folklore Society, which began life as the *Folklore Record* in 1878, and from a clutch of county folklore studies which were based on orally collected information. The proceedings of various national and county antiquarian societies, many of which were formed in the mid-nineteenth century, also provided a forum for publishing notes and articles on folklore, as did the county magazines of the early twentieth century. However, although England is quite well endowed with published folklore material from the mid-nineteenth and early twentieth centuries, there is, unfortunately, nothing to compare with the large national folklore archives formed by other European countries during the present century.[2] Substantial and detailed collection of folklore from oral sources was carried out in only a few counties by a handful of dedicated folklorists. During the 1920s and 1930s various branches of the Women's Institute also attempted to gather folk legends from their elderly members, some of which were published on a county basis. On the whole, though, due to the poor academic status of folklore in this country we do not have an embarrassment of riches with regards to oral testimony concerning witchcraft from the post-war period.

Folk-tales can be divided into two broad categories: folk narratives and folk legends. Folk narratives may deal with actual beliefs, but the stories are pure invention. Folk legends, however, are accounts of events which are believed to have occurred. It is necessary to stress that the witches in these legends were not fictional figures, and when there is enough personal detail they can sometimes be traced in parish records. The stories used here belong to the latter category, and many of them are accounts from personal experience, or what some folklorists call 'memorates'. Care has been taken to select as many examples as possible that were recorded directly from those who had either known the people involved, or had been told about them by their parents or grandparents. However, the boundary between narrative and legend is often blurred, with the same motifs appearing in both, and this phenomenon is, in itself, significant in relation to the popular conception of the witch figure.

A major consideration concerning the use of folklore sources is the reliability of oral testimony.[3] As A. L. Hayward observed in 1938, there were 'unreliable and imaginative individuals who, in the hope of a glass of beer, or a tip, or even out of the more polite desire to please and satisfy a visitor, are prepared to confirm and supplement any folklore subject'.[4] Oral historians have also found that the traditions they hear may not necessarily be old, of the locality of the informant, or even of an oral origin. It could be asked, therefore, to what extent should we believe what we read? In relation to folk legends, though, this is not necessarily a useful line of enquiry for the historian. A more informative approach is to consider to what extent the informants believed in the witch legends they recounted, and how such accounts were formed. The reliability of oral testimony is best examined in the context of the informant's relationship with the those involved in the events described, or with those among whom the story circulated. It is likely, for example, that those 'unreliable and imaginative individuals' who talked readily to folklorists were also influential in confirming and relating facts and rumours concerning witches amongst their own social group. Integral to this process of diffusion was the role of gossip – which in this context is taken to mean 'groundless rumour' – in the accretion of stories around witches. A good example of how gossip could both act as a means of confirming witchcraft, and potentially distort the historical record, is found in a conversation recorded in 1856 between a Norfolk magistrate and a woman living in the neighbourhood of Hockham:

> 'I suppose, Sir, you've heard of Mrs. S——'s case – the wife of S——, the sheep-dresser, of G——?'
>
> 'No, I have not heard of it.'
>
> 'No more had I, Sir, till a few days ago, when my neighbour, Mrs. P——, asked me, "have you heard," says she, "that the man S—— of G—— has kilt a woman?" "Kilt a woman?" Says I, – "Yes," Says she – "a witch." And then I heard all about it, just as the man S—— himself had told Mrs. P——'s husband the day before, and the whole thing had only lately happened.'[5]

S—— had been told by a cunning-woman that his neighbour had be-witched him, and that next time she came to his house he and his wife should not speak to her, and consequently she would go home and die. The magistrate subsequently inquired into the matter, and found that the witch was in fact alive and well. Similar accounts of witches having been killed – especially in animal form – are not uncommon in folklore sources.[6] There must have been an element of Chinese whispers at work in the evolution of such stories by the time they were related to the folklore collector. It is quite possible that the witch was not killed in the first version of the events surrounding the sheep-dresser, but that this was a later embellishment. In a society in which many people were more likely to travel to the local market town than to neighbouring villages, rumour could easily become fact. The above account illustrates well the workings of local information networks, which were fed by gossip, and how news of actual events was embroidered as it circulated at the various gathering points in daily life, such as the village pump and the local beer shops. Thus circumstances which actually occurred developed over time into self-confirming legends. The accretion of stories surrounding local witches continued, and became more fantastic in nature long after the death of the witches concerned. In this sense the witch never died, but became an archetype who behaved in all the ways a witch was generally thought to behave, and so became a template for the generation of new witch figures. If some of the accounts presented in this discussion were the result of rumour and 'unreliable' persons, that does not necessarily mean, therefore, they should be discarded by the historian ever conscious of authenticity. Not only were they often believed in by those who narrated the events concerned, but they contain motifs that were central to the transmission and continuation of core beliefs relating to witchcraft, which in some cases can be traced back at least a thousand years.

Many incidents concerning witches were said to have taken place several generations previously. Depending on the age of the informant, the events recounted in legends had usually occurred in their childhood, or had been passed down from their grandparents, other elderly relatives, or parents. When examining witch legends it is instructive to consider the extent to which those folk who were solicited for information still believed in witchcraft themselves. One indication of the strength of belief was the emotional reactionsof some informants when asked about witchcraft. When the Rev. M. C. F. Morris asked 'a very stolid, matter-of-fact sort of old fellow, who did not apparently take any very keen interest in anything particular', about a certain deceased witch, he was taken aback to see that the old man's 'wonted stolidity quite deserted him … his countenance, as he went on, was lit up with a degree of animation that was quite extraordinary … he fairly quivered again, and his eyes wore a wild appearance which I had never before seen in them'.[7] Such displays of agitation and excitement obviously reflected the strength of feeling about the malign activities of witches. Similar reactions could be provoked when interviewers openly expressed scepticism concerning the existence of witches. A villager of Countisbury, Devon, became 'rather indignant' when E. B. Jeune 'expressed a wonder that people should believe in witchcraft in these days'. 'Oh, no, sir. It is right enough' asserted the man. Another such example also occurred early this century when an eighty-year-old Sussex man, on hearing witchcraft described as 'All rubbish', became very excited and exclaimed, 'All rubbish! It aint. Why, I knew a witch myself in this very village. Her daughter's alive still.'[8] However, different people responded in different ways, often depending on the attitude and tone of the interviewer. Cautious or negative responses did not necessarily indicate less belief. As the Rev. Canon Eddrup found in the 1880s, 'it is not always easy to get the peasantry to open their minds and say what they really think before a listener whom they suspect may be unsympathetic and unbelieving.'[9] Writing several decades later, E. K. Venner, of Halstead, Essex, also remarked that 'belief in witches is always very cautiously admitted, and generally indirectly, so some care is necessary to catch it when it comes to the surface.'[10]

While some sceptical questioners provoked indignation in their interviewees, others received ambiguous replies. When, in 1850, Margaret Gatty asked an old lady of Catterick, 'you surely don't believe in witches now-a-days?', she was told, 'No! I don't say 'at I do; but certainly i' former times there *was* wizards an' buzzards, and them sort o' things.' Gatty laughingly replied 'but you surely don't think there are any now?' Having sidestepped the question once, the old woman once again stated ambiguously, 'No! I don't say 'at ther' are; but I *do* believe in a *yevil* eye.'[11] Around the same time, another woman, from Cornwall, similarly remarked that she could not 'altogether exackly bleve in witches', and went on to talk of a suspected witch in the following terms: 'Not as I believe the woman's a witch – no, not I; but she had a evil mind, and what's so bad as a evil mind?'[12] It is difficult to interpret such statements. They could merely be indications that the interviewees felt uncomfortable about openly admitting their belief in witches in the face of scepticism. Alternatively, they could signify the more fascinating proposition that they were genuine expressions of their own original thoughts on the nature of witchcraft. If so, then the above opinions seem to suggest that the two women could not accept the reality of much of what witches were thought to do, but still held to the core belief that evil thoughts could have a malign physical influence – a rationale which, as we have seen, several clergymen adhered to during the same period.

There was undoubtedly a gradient of popular belief in witches, stretching from outright disbelief to total acceptance of witchcraft, along which each individual could be placed, and whose position along the line was likely to shift, depending on their own changing circumstances and personal experience of misfortune. Within the context of nineteenth- and early-twentieth-century rural society, a series of inexplicable misfortunes in relation to personal health or livestock could still turn sceptics into witch-believers. An example of this can be found in Hermann Lea's account of a Dorset woman of his acquaintance, whose pigs and chickens inexplicably died one by one. The woman rejected the idea that witchcraft was involved. Finally her daughter also fell ill, and it was only at this crisis point that the woman, 'who had hitherto scoffed at the notion, took it into her head that the girl was bewitched', and consulted a local wise-woman.[13] A Yorkshire clergyman also knew of a middle-aged mole-catcher who succumbed to an ailment which the local doctor could not identify. His wife believed he 'wor under a wicked spell', and wanted to go to a wise-man. The mole-catcher, however, 'didna think as she did', until, that is, he said 'theere wor but a step atween me an' death'.[14] A rare account of popular cynicism with a cautionary ending was recalled by Edward Hamer. In 1870, two respectable farmers, an uncle and nephew, both bought a pig from the same litter. Not long afterwards, both pigs began to ail. The nephew believed the pigs were bewitched and consulted a cunning-man. The uncle, however, 'would not believe that his pig was "witched"', and refused to consult the cunning-man. The nephew's pig recovered while the uncle's died. According to Hamer these events were much talked of at the time, and 'many thought the owner deserved little sympathy for manifesting so much obstinacy and scepticism.'[15] We do not know whether the uncle's lack of belief was modified by his misfortune, but the circulation of accounts of such incidents certainly provided others in the neighbourhood with confirmation of the reality of witchcraft.

A not uncommon response to questions concerning the existence of witches was to express the opinion, like the old woman from Catterick, that there used to be plenty of witches but that they had largely disappeared. This is particularly notable from the late nineteenth century onwards. In 1892, for example, the Yorkshire clergyman M. C. F. Morris found that people confessed that 'witches are just at the present moment rather scarce articles'.[16] Ten years later it was said that in the area of Cottington Hill, Berkshire, there *used* to be 'enough witches and wizards to draw a ton load up it', and a very similar statement was heard in 1936 concerning a hill in the parish of Luppit, Devon. In a similar vein, in 1907, an eighty-year-old woman, Mary Thomas, of Bengal, near Fishguard, told the folklorist J. Ceredig Davies that 'when she was a young girl, the Gwaun Valley in that county was full of witches'.[17] It is possible, of course, that statements such as these could have been used to deflect questions about whether witches still existed, but taken together they undoubtedly reflect the decline of the witch in rural communities during this period. Nevertheless, more generalised statements about the decline of witches expressed by folklorists or other social commentators should be treated with caution, especially when they date from earlier in the century. The Welsh folklore record belies, for instance, William Howells's claim, made in 1831, that 'the days of ghosts, witches, and like "horrible imaginings" are gone by'.[18] As has already been mentioned in a previous chapter, for much of the nineteenth century it was mistakenly assumed that improved communications and expanding educational provision had eradicated or were rapidly eroding such beliefs.

From the early twentieth century onwards, the physical and emotional detachment of informants from the reality of witchcraft is increasingly evident in the folklore sources. Witch legends continued to circulate and the veracity of them was rarely doubted, but the flow of new legends was diminishing because the raw material for their creation – the witches – was disappearing. It is likely that this slowing down of witch-legend formation occurred at different rates in different areas, depending on localised changes in economy and community structure. Judging by the number of articles and notes from the 1930s, there was still a rich vein of witch-beliefs and legends circulating in many rural areas. However, by the 1950s there was a perceptible decline in the quantity and clarity of folklore concerning witches. Counties like Surrey, where old rural communities were rapidly swamped by the influx of London commuters and the creation of dormitory settlements, were probably the first to lose the last vestiges of witch-lore. Thus when the oldest inhabitants of the village of Hambledon, Surrey, were asked at a Women's Institute meeting just after the Second World War to recall any stories they knew about witches, the response was apparently disappointing. All that could be remembered was vague talk of one old woman who 'was supposed to be a witch', of whom all the children were afraid.[19] Elsewhere the situation was better. During the late 1950s Eric Maple was still able to gather a number of witch stories from the elderly residents of Canewdon, Essex. Even during the 1960s Edward Wilson managed to glean a few witch legends from farming folk in Cumbria, and John Smith found that the older people of 'the more isolated parts' of Dorset and Somerset still occasionally told 'tales of witchcraft and "conjuring"'. The area where, perhaps, the occasional witch legend lingered longest among the elderly population was in rural Wales, where Robin Gwyndaf collected some accounts of witchcraft during the late 1960s and 1970s.[20] But all these last fragmented accounts concerning local witches were perceived to belong to a bygone era. As Mr Tuck, aged sixty-eight, of Beaminster, Dorset, told John Smith: 'They used to say there's some witches 'bout here … Old people used to believe in that years ago, you know.'[21]

Characteristics of the archetypal witch

Gender, age, physical appearance and peculiar manners were all significant characteristics in the popular portrayal of witches. The vast majority of witches were certainly described as old women. Although some conformed to the archetypal image of an ugly, dirty old crone, it is, perhaps, surprising to find that such classic descriptions are not that common in popular accounts of local witches. This probably signifies that we are dealing with real people and not just imaginary archetypes. A deformity or an unusual way of moving often marked out some witches. Thus a Dorset woman explained that witches had 'a funny way in their walk – 'tis more like a wamble than a proper step', and Angelina Parker remembered an old female witch called 'Shaking Charlotte' who suffered from palsy.[22] By far the most frequently mentioned physical distinction of the witch was the possession of unusual eyes or an uncanny gaze. An old Lincolnshire woman told a contributor to *The Spectator* that 'witches had vipers' eyes'.[23] Ethel Rudkin heard a Lincolnshire witch described as having 'a winkersome eye', and another 'a very queer-looking eye' due to a cast. A witch of Buryton, Devon, was described as having 'terrible eyes', and the eyes of another at Ashreigney, Devon, 'began to waste away by a continuous discharge of matter from it; the eye completely perished … after this people became still more afraid of her.'[24] The reason for this emphasis on eyes was, of course, due to the concept of the 'evil eye'. It was widely believed that a witch could bewitch someone merely by looking at them. The gaze of a witch immediately provoked unsettling and anxious emotions in those on the receiving end. Typical of such sensations were those experienced by the victims of a Surrey witch, Mary S., who died in 1909. Mary gave one man 'an evil look which upset him for the rest of the day', while another was described as being 'knocked all of a heap' by her gaze. Similarly, a Devon witch looked at another woman in 'such a way' that 'her knees trembled and she had to go indoors and have a cry.'[25] The casting of the evil eye was nearly always a deliberate act of *maleficium* rather than an involuntary action.

A major behavioural feature of folkloric witches was their habit of begging, and the aggravating tone they adopted. This point is well illustrated by the following opinion of witches: 'they overcome people – so loving and fond, with their Judish tongue to betray people; and they come asking for butter, and cheese, and milk, and all such things, and no one dares to deny them.' A Lincolnshire woman, presumably characterising their obsequious tone, also described witches as having 'weamy wimy voices'.[26] While some witches were thought to adopt an ingratiating tone, others were obstinate and insistent. Hannah Henley, for example, 'never asked like begging, she demanded'[27] People obviously resented these begging witches, but such was the fear of them that some villagers would comply with their requests to prevent any possible retaliation.

The classic scenario highlighted by Keith Thomas of the begging witch being turned away empty-handed, and bewitching out of anger and spite, is a prominent feature in folklore accounts. Mrs Joseph Cooper, of Barton, Oxfordshire, remembered a witch named Miriam Russell, who went begging at Stowford Farm, and on being denied 'said she would remember them'. A few days later all the cows and calves started going mad. Consequently the farmer gave Miriam what she wanted, and the cows returned to normal. Another Oxfordshire witch, 'Mother Buckland', made her living by begging. When a woman called Phoebe Hawes refused to give her a shawl one day, Buckland threatened her: 'Look out! You'll know; look out!' From that time Hawes thought herself bewitched, until the shawl was eventually given to Buckland.[28] It was similarly unwise to mock or taunt a witch. As a Wye Valley farmer told Margaret Eyre, 'they old witches ... if 'ee did refuse un, or make game o' they, why ee'd be sure to be stopped.' In 1862, for example, a correspondent to *Notes and Queries*, was told by a blacksmith near Sevenoaks, Kent, that as a boy he had met the local witch one day, 'and called after her jeeringly, whereupon she threatened him in vague terms'. Afterwards, while turning hay he began to feel very giddy and could not leave the field.[29]

It is quite likely that some supposed witches consciously conformed to stereotypical characteristics by deliberately dressing and acting the part in order to exploit their reputations for begging purposes. One possible candidate was 'old Dolly', a Shropshire witch, who habitually wore a high steeple-crowned hat, 'just for all the world like the picture of an old witch'.[30] It is also feasible that some begging witches did perform petty malicious acts of revenge with the intention that they be interpreted as witchcraft by their victims. The Surrey witch, Mary S., was thought to have cast a spell over some bullocks in the following manner: 'She ran among them all night with a lantern, so that the stockman, when he arrived in the morning, found them all of a lather.' The contributor of this account thought it 'not impossible for an active and malevolent woman to effect'.[31] At least some of the cases of the sudden and strange affliction of animals could have resulted from simple poisoning. In the nineteenth century it was not unknown for disputes to arise from vengeful petty poisoning, and several court cases arose from such circumstances. In 1817, for example, an old woman of Wath, Yorkshire, applied for a summons against another woman who assaulted her after accusing her of poisoning a chicken by administering mercury.[32] It would be quite easy for a supposed witch similarly to administer some form of poison to livestock, and for the victim's owner, with the witch's visit fresh in mind, to suspect witchcraft rather than straightforward poisoning. The spoiling of the butter churn, which commonly led to suspicions of witchcraft, could also have been easily effected by simple means. An early-nineteenth-century book of charms and magical receipts advised those who wished to prevent butter from coming in the churn to 'put a little soap or sugar into the churn of cream and there will never come any butter churn as long as you please'. To prevent the making of cheese it also advised putting 'among the milk a small quantity of essence of peppermint, or strong mint waters'.[33] Although it would be rather ludicrous to suggest that witches swotted up on how to simulate acts of witchcraft from such publications, it may be that the anonymous author originally got these ideas from oral sources. Indeed, a case of soap being used for the purpose of preventing butter was recalled by the Rev. Elias Owen. He was lodging at a farmhouse in Montgomeryshire when one day the farmer's wife complained that the butter had failed to come despite churning it all morning, and stated her belief that it had been bewitched by a beggar woman. Owen spoke to the servant girl about the butter, and she told him that she had once had a similar problem, the cause of which was explained as follows:

> She was churning, when a woman came to the back door to ask for a bit of something to eat. She went on churning and speaking, and she told the woman she could not herself give her anything without first asking her mistress. The woman then requested her to go to her mistress, and she left the churn to do so. The churning was resumed, but no butter could be made. The milk frothed over, and the more it was churned the more it frothed over. Upon looking into

the churn it was thought a smell of soap could be detected, and then it was remembered that a lump of soap, that had stood near the churn when the beggar was there, had disappeared, and, it was concluded that it had been popped into the churn during the absence of the girl, by the beggar woman, and her motive for doing so was to be revenged for repeated refusals when begging at that house.[34]

One can imagine that if the presence of the soap had not been so obvious, the beggar would have been blamed for witchcraft rather than for just slipping the soap into the churn.

It would be absurd to suggest that many such cases of animal bewitchments and failed butter resulted from deliberate, malicious acts by vengeful beggar-witches, but it is possible that at least a small percentage of supposed acts of witchcraft could have occurred in this way. The beggar-witches who played on their reputations needed to maintain their position by seeming to perform such acts of *maleficium*. If they just went around being refused, and were seen to do nothing in response, there would be no motivation to give to them at all. Few people really *wanted* to give charity to a witch, and the only way they could be persuaded to do so was through the implied threat of reprisal by witchcraft.

The retaliatory threats made by begging witches were deliberately couched in vague language. They rarely seem to have responded by explicitly stating they would bewitch or overlook those who refused them. This would suggest that even those who exploited their reputations were very careful not to admit openly that they were witches. There was obviously an unspoken, self-imposed boundary which the begging witch never crossed. To breach it by confessing to being a witch would alter the carefully balanced relationship between the witch and the community she relied upon. By professing to be a witch all the suspicions and rumours surrounding her would also immediately be confirmed as facts in the minds of those who believed in witchcraft. As a consequence, the witch would potentially expose herself to more risk of physical assault and abuse. While there was always an element of doubt, a begging witch would, to a certain extent, be tolerated. Furthermore, if a begging witch openly claimed to practise witchcraft, she would appear to be acting as a petty extortioner playing upon people's fears, and thereby lose the good will of that section of the community who had been sympathetic.

We know a lot about what people believed witches did, but far less about their explanations for why and how they were thought able to do it. The notion of the diabolic origin of witchcraft, which so occupied the minds of theologians during the early modern period, is certainly present in the folklore record. Writing in 1907, for example, Hermann Lea stated that in Dorset it was 'by no means an uncommon belief that a witch has sold herself to the Devil and that "he" will very often come to fetch his "disciple" at the moment of her death'.[35] A fairly widespread tradition, also recorded in the early modern period, was that people could become witches by going to the Communion service, taking the holy bread but not swallowing it, and then placing it in the mouth of a big toad which would appear in the churchyard after the service. We can assume that the toad is meant to be the Devil in disguise, but, significantly, in most accounts the Devil is not actually specified, which suggests that the motif of the toad rather than the Devil was more important to the tradition.[36] A wide-ranging survey of folklore sources from around the country also supports James Obelkevitch's findings from Lincolnshire that the notion of sexual relations between witches and the Devil was practically non-existent in the nineteenth century.[37] The evidence suggests that diabolic witchcraft was actually only a minor theme in the popular discourse concerning witchcraft.

Yet the Devil, who was often familiarly referred to by names such as 'Old Nick', 'Old Harry', 'Old Scrat', and the 'Old One', played a major role in folk tradition, though his portrayal in folklore was quite different to that depicted by some clergymen and preachers at the time. Rather than being a dark, potent figure of evil, ever poised to cause suffering and woe to the Christian world, in folk tales the Devil was often a rather comic figure, a trickster who was easily bamboozled. When he was not occupied in such mischievous activities as moving churches from one place to another, he liked nothing better than to disguise himself, and join in that most sinful of earthly pursuits – card-playing. There was a more serious and personal side to the Devil. He often acted against his own interests by appearing before sinners and sabbath-breakers, presumably to show them in which direction they were heading, and thereby frighten them into following a more God-fearing way of life. At other times the Devil would attempt to gain power over men by tempting them with riches, but he was often foiled, and, as the Welsh folklorist Elias Owen observed, he was 'generally depicted as inferior in cunning and intellect to a bright, witted Welshman'.[38] The Devil was not just an entertaining figure of folk narratives and legends, though; people sincerely thought he walked among them, and not a few people claimed to have had personal encounters with him. When, for example, a friend of the folklorist Angelina Parker told an old labourer of Holton, Oxfordshire, that he did not believe in a personal devil, the old man replied,

'Not believe in the Devil? Why, I've sin' 'im!', and considered there was no more to be said.[39] Considering the strong role of the Devil in folk tradition one might have expected, therefore, to hear much more of his involvement with witches. The question this raises is whether the concept of the pact had always been relatively weak in popular tradition, or whether it had undergone a decline during the eighteenth and early nineteenth centuries.

In England the concept of witches having some form of acquaintance with the Devil dates back to medieval times, but the detailed framework of demonology, which was being formulated by Continental theologians during the fifteenth century, only really began to influence educated English notions of witchcraft during the Elizabethan period. Most of these Continental treatises were written in Latin and remained untranslated at the time. So, the ideas they contained about Devil-worshipping witches having bestial sexual relations with the Devil, entering pacts, and attending orgiastic sabbaths, only slowly entered the popular consciousness through the filter of publications by learned English clergymen and gentlemen. During the seventeenth century, elements of the Continental conception of Devil-worship emerged periodically in the confessions of illiterate witnesses at witch-trials, and one can only presume they had imbibed such beliefs from hearing them elucidated by local clergymen, or from public readings from pamphlet literature. Thus to a limited extent a process of acculturation was occurring by which learned theological concepts of witchcraft were entering into the popular consciousness. However, this was very much a process of fusion rather than a displacement of popular beliefs. Aspects of satanic witchcraft were absorbed and conflated with existing fairy and witch motifs, and manifested themselves in a hybridised form in trial depositions.

There is no reason not to assume that the Devil was just as important a figure in seventeenth-century folk tradition as he was in that of the nineteenth century. If in popular tradition the Devil was thought to mingle with human kind, performing various acts of mischief, it would make perfect sense that he might seek out the company of witches or be sought out by them. But such meetings had little to do with the theological belief in a satanic masterplan to destroy Christian society through the agency of witches. Without the regular circulation of references to Devil-worshipping in trials, sermons and pamphlets, the figure of the diabolic witch probably diminished in the popular consciousness during the late eighteenth and early nineteenth centuries. It is significant in this respect that the occasional expressions of popular belief in demonianism that occurred in the post-prosecution period were usually influenced by the broadcasting of evangelical doctrine. We can surely detect such an influence in one of the few clearly expressed popular accounts of the diabolic origin of witchcraft, elicited from a female parishioner by a Norfolk magistrate in 1857. On asking her, 'do you seriously believe such things, or do you not think that God rules the world?', he received the following thoughtful reply:

> I do believe that there are these bad-spirited people, Sir. Ladies and gentlemen don't often hear much about such things. I believe that the Almighty gives them up; and that, as we pray, for grace and wisdom and strength to save Him, so these people pray to the enemy to give them powers to do these evil things. God has promised His help to the smallest believer who hangs on Him; and they pray to the devil to give them their badness, and he gives it to them; and he [the Devil] have as much power over these people as the Almighty have over His own.[40]

In the nineteenth century, as in the early modern period, witchcraft was more generally believed to be an innate and hereditary power. In 1855 it was observed that in Cornwall 'the faculty of witchcraft is held to be hereditary, and it is not the least cruel of the effects of this horrible creed that many really good-natured souls have on this account been kept aloof by their neighbours.'[41] Fifty years later, Hermann Lea similarly remarked that the witch's power was 'nearly always inherited, and I have heard it argued that a certain woman of my acquaintance, who was perfectly inoffensive, must necessarily be a witch because her mother was one.'[42] Whole families could even generate a reputation for witchcraft. It would be quite misleading to suggest, though, that the children of witches were automatically labelled as such themselves – the formation of reputations was more complex than that. But, even if a witch's child was not considered to have inherited his or her malign powers, he or she might still be tainted by association. The Devon folklorist Paul Karkeek knew the daughter of a witch, who, although not considered one herself, found it difficult to attract a husband because of her mother's reputation.[43]

The passing on of a witch's power from one generation to another was sometimes thought to be facilitated by the inheritance of witches' books. As Rosalind Northcote, writing of Devon, remarked, 'the power of many evilly-disposed persons ... is supposed to lie, partly, in their "books" – mysterious books, often to be heard of in possession of some one else – and never to be seen!'[44] In 1862 the daughter of an old Kent witch, well known for her evil-doings, explained that 'the power of witchcraft had been transmitted through her family for several generations by means of "the parchment"'.[45] What these books and manuscripts were meant to contain always remained a secret, and this, of course, only increased the sense of awe and fascination concerning them. There is no evidence to suggest that they were thought to contain the witch's covenant with the Devil. More likely they were considered to be books of harmful spells that the witch employed when he or she wanted to enact some form of revenge. As one old Sussex man asserted, 'that kind of wicked old woman always has books – powerful books which have a good deal of evil written in them.'[46] This suggests that literate witches were thought able to enhance their abilities through having access to the written word. Presumably if a witch's book was removed or destroyed the witch would lose at least some of her power, and the ability to transfer her knowledge to a new generation. Witches' neighbours certainly felt safer in the knowledge that no such books were around. When the witch referred to by the Sussex man above was removed to the workhouse after being found paralysed in bed, he and several others helped a workhouse official sort out her belongings. They found a pile of books, and a neighbour asked out of curiosity if he might keep them, but the others 'said it wasn't right and anyway we didn't want anyone else learning the secrets and playing us up … we asked the workhouse chap to burn them. He looked at them and said they were rubbish anyway.' In another instance from Sussex, an old man referring to a witch's book, remarked that 'one of her daughters took it out of the village – and a good thing too! We don't want any truck with that sort of thing.'[47]

Even more intriguing was the notion that witches kept familiars. These were actually popularly referred to as 'imps', though in Essex they were also described by some as 'niggets'.[48] They were thought to be evil spirits who generally manifested themselves in the form of small or domesticated animals. Much of a witch's power was invested in these imps, and they could be passed on from one generation of witches to another. The tradition was by no means uniformly spread across the country. It is virtually absent from the Welsh folklore record, for example, and is also little mentioned in sources from northern England. In the West Country it was thought that witches kept toad companions, but these do not seem to have been popularly referred to as imps or familiars, even if the concept was similar. The tradition was strongest by far in East Anglia, where the largest body of evidence concerning imps was generated in both the early modern and modern periods.

The origin of the concept of familiars remains obscure, but the fact that they are mentioned in some early-sixteenth-century court cases certainly indicates that the concept was known before the witch-trials began in earnest. Some of the most detailed accounts of familiars come from the mid-seventeenth-century East Anglian witch-hunt promoted by the 'witch-finders' Matthew Hopkins and John Stearne. James Sharpe has calculated that seventy-eight of the 110 narratives in the surviving trial records of 1645–47 involved familiars. They came in numerous animal forms such as cats, rabbits, rats, chickens, dogs, turkey cocks, and mice. Some of the witches confessed that the Devil gave them their imps after they had pledged themselves to him. Others told how they had merely received them from mothers, grandmothers or friends.[49]

In nineteenth- and early-twentieth-century East Anglia these imps were generally described as being like mice. In 1857, for example, a Norfolk magistrate was informed how people used to see a local witch's "'little things crawling about near the clock.' "What little things?" "Har imps they Called 'em." "I want to know what an imp is like?" "I never see one, Sir; I was only a boy. But I've heard they was like little meece.'"[50] There were a few exceptions. The imp of Mrs Smith, a Cambridgeshire witch, was described rather puzzlingly as 'a black thing; it wasn't exactly a dog nor a rat, it looked more like a frog'.[51] Between the seventeenth and nineteenth centuries there would seem to have been a definite diminution in the variety of imps, with mice finally predominating. The fact that these mice were often described as being white, in other words domesticated mice, suggests that at least some 'imps' were likely to have been pets in reality.

The tradition that imps were passed on from one generation to another was widespread in East Anglia. Consequently, it was also believed that if a witch's imps were burnt then the power of witchcraft would be lost for good. A Norfolk clergyman was told by a parishioner that she knew of an instance in which a box containing little imps was given by an old witch to a young woman whom she wished to succeed her in the art, but the unwilling woman burnt them in an oven instead.[52] Catherine Parsons also recorded the belief that a witch could not die until she had found a relation who was willing to take her imps.[53] The diabolic element is still evident in the folklore evidence, though it is definitely weaker than the hereditary concept. When, for example, the Norfolk magistrate mentioned above asked an old man, 'What is an imp?' He replied, 'I don't know, Sir, unless it be some bad spirit or other from the power of old Satan; but I never seed one.'[54] The Rev. Isaac Nicholson, in recounting the case of Ann Izzard, also observed that 'it was the general opinion of the people' that the witch was 'some person who had purchased a familiar, or an evil spirit of the devil, at the expense of his own soul'.[55] It is possible, though, that this description partly reflects Nicholson's own interpretation of what a familiar was. The fact that he uses the term 'familiar' rather than 'imp' shows that his statement was couched in his own words rather than those of his parishioners.

How are we to interpret the strength and nature of the tradition of familiars or imps in the folklore of the eastern counties of England? It is possible that the tradition had always been strong in this region. It could also be argued, though, that the continued vitality of the tradition in nineteenth-century folklore was at least partly due to the cultural influence of the witch-hunt of 1645–47. Nearly 250 people were investigated for being witches during the period, and at least a hundred were hanged. Hopkins and Stearne, who quickly achieved considerabe fame, travelled around the region offering their services as inquisitors, spreading news of their findings as they went. Such an intense period of activity, and the sheer number of people involved in one way or another, undoubtedly had a considerable impact on the entire population of the region. Rumour and gossip concerning the alleged activities of the witches must have been rife. The detailed accounts of familiars that were heard at the trials, and which later circulated around the towns and villages of the area, would have made quite an impression on the popular consciousness. The triangular relationship between witch, Devil and familiar may not have been a new notion to the populace, but the trials could have also given the diabolic nature of the familiar more significance in the folk memory.

An unusual and tantalising tradition that seems to relate to the concept of the familiar was recorded in Sussex during the late nineteenth century. It was believed that witches were possessed by a spirit which provided them with their power, and that no witch could die unless there was someone ready by her bedside to receive the spirit from her, and so pass on the mantle of witchcraft. In the 1860s, one Dame Killick, of Crow-borough, was thus thought to have passed on the spirit to her daughter, who then became a witch.[56] The same concept seems to form the basis of another Sussex account concerning the deathbed of a witch called Mother Venus. Present in the witch's room during her final hours was a group of local women, including a young woman of the name of Mabel Ockley, who had an infant at her breast: 'Suddenly Mother Venus sat up in bed, cast her eyes quickly over the group of women standing near, and swiftly passed her hand to the breast of Mabel Ockley. Then Mother Venus fell back dead! "What did she give you?" questioned the women. "She gave me nothing," was the reply. But the witchcraft had been passed on!'[57] The similarities of this tradition to that of the East Anglian imp, which also had to be passed on to the next generation, is quite striking. The Sussex tradition could, then, represent another regional variation on the concept of spirit companions.

Throughout the era of the witch-trials it was a fairly common procedure for the authorities to search suspected witches for the conclusive presence of unnatural teats or marks from which familiars were thought to suck blood, but the notion is poorly represented in the folklore record. One of the few references to teats was collected by the Lincolnshire folklorist Ethel Rudkin, who was told that when a local witch named Betty died, 'the woman as laid 'er out found she'd gotten a "witch-pap" like a little pap, it were, a-tween 'er two natural ones – but that weren't at all suprisin'. A *real* witch, she were.'[58] Curiously, the tradition also appears in two sources relating to south-east Wales, though in neither are familiars or imps actually mentioned. In 1763, William Thomas, of Cadoxton, Glamorgan, recorded in his diary: 'This day was determined a wager between Wm Jenkin of Cadoxton and Evan Thomas ... in that Evan called him a wizard and waged him he had teats.'[59] During the mobbing, in 1827, of Mary Nicholas, of Abergavenny, the court was told how the mob 'fancying a witch was furnished with an unnatural teat ... stripped her down to the waste and searched for it.'[60] The evidence suggests that the concept of witches' teats and marks was an established part of folk belief during the early modern period, so it would seem that the notion must have weakened considerably by the nineteenth century. Its decline probably relates to the demise of officially endorsed strip-searching of witches. After 1736 the authorities were no longer concerned with confirming the guilt of witches, and popular attempts to strip and search a woman violently, as happened at Abergavenny, were likely to be severely punished – at least by the early nineteenth century. Without the physical confirmation of the existence of teats, the notion declined because it became an irrelevant form of proof. Not surprisingly, the last echo of this tradition was heard in Norfolk, when a farmer, whose futile request to his local magistrate to have a witch swum we have already encountered, further boldly asked, 'Well, your worship, at least I hope you'll take her to a room, and have her stripped, and see if she have anything bad about her.'[61]

Fairies, flying and shape-shifting

The image of witches that has emerged so far in this discussion is one focused firmly on the context of everyday human relations, but a further exploration of the folklore sources uncovers another plane of existence on which witches were perceived to operate. This is particularly evident from the behavioural relationship between fairies and witches. Folklorists were by no means unaware of the affinities between the two. Elijah Cope, writing of his research in Staffordshire, observed that he 'often found that witchcraft and fairy lore have been linked together'. The folklorist E. S. Hartland went further, claiming that through an examination of the similar activities ascribed to them, witches, fairies and ghosts were 'all three of the same nature'.[62] The notion that relations existed *between* witches and fairies is actually little evident in the folklore sources. What we find, instead, is that witches were often thought to behave in the same manner as fairies.

Both fairies and witches were thought to have a fondness for dancing in meadows and pastures at night. The proof of such revels was the dark green, fertile grass rings they left behind, which were popularly known as hag-tracks, or hag- and fairy-rings. We now know, of course, that these fertile rings are caused by fungi. The supernatural interpretation of these rings has a long history and was a debating point in the early modern period. Henry More, for example, took the tradition seriously, and thought it 'seasonable' 'to enquire into the nature of those large *dark Rings* in the grass, which they call *Fairy Circles*, whether they be the *Rendezvouz* of Witches, or the dancing places of those little Puppet Spirits which they call *Elves* or *Fairies*'.[63] Witch and fairy revels were also thought to take place at prehistoric sites and other prominent landscape features such as hilltops.[64] As Ronald Hutton has observed, there is a significant concentration of legends concerning these witch gatherings in the far-western peninsula of Cornwall.[65] However, instances of such witch gatherings being held elsewhere in England crop up only sporadically in the folklore sources. The Dorset folklorist John Symonds Udal found that there was no 'idea existing amongst Dorset folk as to witches being in the habit of meeting together for the purpose of working their spells'.[66] In Cambridgeshire, though, witches were thought to have gathered at night in the fields around the village of Horseheath. They frolicked and danced, and on 'returning in the early hours of the morning were seen to be in a terrible state of perspiration'. In the neighbouring county of Lincolnshire Ethel Rudkin recorded several accounts of witch meetings. When she asked one G. G., of Willoughton, where the witches used to meet, he replied, 'No, I don't know the exact spot where they 'eld their *Conventions*, but I know as they did used to meet somewhere, ter discuss their business, an' such like.' Another man knew better, saying that they

used to meet at Bliber (Blyborough) Top.[67] Contrary to the theological
notion that witches met at sabbaths to show allegiance to the Devil and
perform obscene and perverted sexual acts, it would seem that in folk
tradition these gatherings were considered as harmless social events, something akin to a workers' outing. It was a time to forget about the everyday routine of performing petty acts of malice, and, just as the fairies
enjoyed doing, to dance and make merry under the stars.

Witches and fairies also shared the ability to pass through keyholes and
up and down chimneys. In parts of Wales and Dorset it was not unknown for scythe blades to be placed up chimneys and on window sills
to deter such intrusions, while in South Lancashire a parson's wig – a
most unusual sacred object – was used for the same purpose.[68] There was
also a widespread tradition that both witches and fairies used to enter
stables and ride people's horses at night, leaving them sweating, agitated
and with tangled manes in the morning. Horses found in this state were
commonly said to be 'pixy-rided', 'hag-ridden' or 'witch-ridden'. In fact,
by the nineteenth century this was one of the few types of supernatural
torment still being attributed to the fairies as well as witches. The following dialogue between a groom and his master, Mr Bridge, a justice of the
peace living near Cerne, Dorset, describes the phenomenon well: "'John,
that mare in the field looks disgraceful! All over dirt, and her mane knot-
ted and ragged!" "Sakes! Sir, don't 'ee know what be the matter wi' 'er.
Why, her's hag-rode every night into a solid sweat! And they knots? Why,
they be the stirrups the hags do ride un wi'! Poor creature, I do clane
and clane her, but tidden no use!"'[69] Occasionally fairies might also be
accused of performing other malicious acts for which witches were more
commonly blamed. In the 1930s, an old Montgomeryshire man remembered how once every year neighbours would beat pans and march around
the farm at midnight to prevent the fairies from harming the cattle and
spoiling the milk. Elijah Cope even knew some supposed witches who
'blamed fairies for mischief reputed to them'.[70]

There was a long association concerning the colour of clothing both
witches and fairies were typically thought to wear. Writing in 1684,
Richard Bovet remarked that fairies' habits were thought to be of 'red,
blew, or green, according to the old way of Country Garb, with high
crown'd hats'.[71] When we look at seventeenth-century depositions in
which clothing colour is mentioned, we also find witches wearing the
same colours. In 1661, two Newcastle children saw a witch 'in a red
waistcoat and green petticoat, who went under the bed'. The bed-bound
Dorothy Hearon claimed, in 1664, that Isable Atcheson tormented her 'in

her owne shape, clothed with a green waiscoate'. In 1686, a Cornish boy, aged fifteen or sixteen, saw 'a woman in a blue jerkin and red petticoat, with yellow and green patches'. A year later in Dorset, a witch was seen 'upon the middle beam of the chamber window, clothed in a long-crowned hat, a long red whittle, a red coat, a green apron, and a white cloak'.[72] It is important to note that all these descriptions concern visions of witches rather than actual corporeal encounters. What were being described, therefore, were either fabrications or hallucinations. In either case we might expect accounts to be influenced by stereotypical images derived from folklore. By the nineteenth century there was a diminution of the colours associated with witches, who were now predominantly thought to have a preference for red clothing. Elias Owen remarked that children would run away 'when they saw approaching them an aged woman, with a red shawl on, for they believed she was a witch'. During the early nineteenth century, a witch living in the Rope Walk area of Hastings, Sussex, wore a red cloak. The Yorkshire witch Peggy Flaunders, who died in 1835, aged eighty-five, was well remembered for her tall hat and red cloak.[73] An elderly Dorset woman explained to Hermann Lea that she could identify witches 'fast enough, but I 'on't go so far as to say that anybody can tell 'em. They do most always wear summat red about 'em – maybe a red hat or a red cloak when they be out walkin'.' Lea also knew a man 'who utterly refused to meet or pass a woman who is a stranger to him should she be wearing anything of a red colour' just in case she was a witch.[74] We also continue to find in the nineteenth century that fairies had similar tastes in fashion. They too liked wearing red, although green was still popular. An account from early-nineteenth-century Cornwall described a group of fairies wearing 'sugar-loaf' hats and little red cloaks. In Shropshire, fairies were seen dancing in a ring wearing little red jackets, and on the Gower Peninsular they dressed in bright red at their revels. The similar dress code of fairies and witches was confirmed by an old Derbyshire man, who observed that 'fairies are always dressed in a red mantle and hood which covers the whole body, and witches are dressed exactly in the same manner'.[75]

One of the most enduring witch motifs, perpetuated in modern popular culture, is that witches flew on broomsticks. Although there is only one account of a witch flying a broomstick in early modern English trials,[76] the notion was well known on the Continent, particularly in France, and was often represented in paintings and engravings from the fifteenth century onwards. The image of the witch on or with her broomstick was also reproduced in several eighteenth-century English prints and engravings. The sensational case of the alleged abduction of a young woman, Elizabeth Canning, by an old gypsy woman, Mary Squires, in 1753, led to a flurry of pamphlets and prints in which gypsies were represented as witches. As Ian Bostridge has discussed, the Canning affair was conflated with the heated debate over the 'Jew Bill' of 1754. One print unearthed by Bostridge, which shows gypsies and Jews together, depicts Squires and three other witches flying on broomsticks. Several other prints also showed Squires astride a besom, and wearing a steeple hat.[77] Perhaps the most famous eighteenth-century depiction of a witch on her broomstick and wearing a conical hat was in Hogarth's famous engraving 'Credulity, Superstition and Fanaticism'.

We can interpret this artistic eighteenth-century representation of the flying witch in two ways. We can see it as a continuation of the European artistic tradition of portraying the witch on her broom, or we can see it as an accurate reflection of folk beliefs concerning witches' flight. The broomstick certainly makes its appearance more often in nineteenth-century folklore than it does in early modern trial material. A contributor to *The Times*, for instance, recollected that around 1900 an old Sussex woman had told her 'the day, hour, and place where, if I went, I could watch all the local witches meet and career on their broomsticks. It was midnight, in early January, and on an exposed space on Burwash Ridge.' In 1912 an old man of Dodington, Somerset, also knew of a 'wicked old witch' who would 'fly on broomsticks over they Quantocks, November night time she 'ood'. One old Essex woman was asked the rather leading question of whether she had ever seen the local witch on her broomstick on moonlit nights. She was not at all surprised by the question, but admitted she had never actually witnessed such a sight, adding matter-of-factly, 'but then, you see, she lived right at the other end of the green'.[78] The broomstick was an everyday household implement commonly seen in the hands of women, including witches. Its use as a vehicle was also probably related to its use as a hobbyhorse by children. Thus an old man of Weobley, Herefordshire, told E. M. Leather that when he was a boy he and his friends would collect all the available besoms and ride them in procession past the house of a witch named 'Old Charlotte'.[79] It is significant, though, that the broom was only one object of conveyance amongst others employed by witches, and not necessarily the most popular. Reports of witches flying about straddled on fencing hurdles are as frequent if not more frequent in the folklore material, and occasionally they were said to ride also on objects such as dough covers and grindstones.[80] The fact that artistic and literary representations tended to concentrate only on the broomstick and not the hurdle, suggests that they were rather more reflective of the pictorial than the folk tradition of flying witches.

Occasionally we catch a rare glimpse in the sources of the notion that witches were able to travel in spectral form or send their souls abroad at night. In one instance a Dorset woman, recalling a strange encounter with a suspected male witch named Vachor, stated that, 'it was Vachor's spirit, for his real body could not have done it. It was only an appearance, and his real body must have been sleeping somewhere. They do go to sleep when the soul leaves to do these things.' In a case heard before the Weston-super-Mare magistrates, in 1875, the defendant, Hester Adams, claimed that a witch named Pring was tormenting her at night by hag-riding her. Adams told the magistrates that Pring was not always present at such times, 'at least not bodily, but she came in a nasty spiritual way, making a nasty noise'.[81] The same concept probably explains several references to people seeing the shadow of a witch. In 1856, for example, a Norfolk woman, when queried about the physical impossibility of a suspected witch having appeared at a nearby farm, remarked that 'it was either she or her shadow'.[82]

The most common and ubiquitous motif in witch legends is the ability of witches to turn themselves into animals. Although hares and cats were their favourite guises, they were capable of assuming any animal shape if it served their purpose. As Hermann Lea was informed, 'Dont 'ee know, sir, as they witches be able to change theirselves into the shape o' any animal pretty near; but 'tis mostly a hare or a black cat they do hidey in.'[83] Thus in Lincolnshire witches were believed to be able to assume the appearance of magpies, dogs, and toads, and in Gwent it was reported that witches had been known to take the shape of greyhounds and rats. A Witch of Anstead Brook, Surrey, 'concealed' herself in a waggoner's leading horse, and one Harriet Wells, of the Wye Valley, went about in the shape of a pig.[84] Occasionally, witches' transformations were rather more abstract. Leddy Lister of Hedworth, Durham, was said to come out at night in different shapes, usually as a very tall woman, but sometimes as a large sheet lying on hedges. In a Devon court case of 1837 a young woman who had assaulted a suspected witch made the puzzling claim that the latter 'took the shape of a black cat, ran into the room and all over the place, and then changed herself into the "Jack of Hearts"'.[85]

A very old recorded tradition was that witches, in the form of a hare, would suck the udders of cows at night, and so leave them dry when milked the next morning. As Giraldus Cambrensis observed in the twelfth century: 'It has also been a frequent complaint, from old times as well as

in the present, that certain hags in Wales, as well as in Ireland and Scotland, changed themselves into the shape of hares, that, sucking teats under
this counterfeit form, they might stealthily rob other people's milk.' The
same belief was also widespread in Scandinavian folklore. In nineteenth-
and twentieth-century England and Wales examples of this tradition are
not widely recorded, and mostly come from Northern England. The
North Yorkshire clergyman, the Rev. Atkinson, heard numerous accounts
of witches stealing milk in the form of hares. In a variation on the same
theme, one Nancy Newgill, a Yorkshire witch, was said to turn herself
into a hedgehog and milk the local cows.[86] The tradition of hedgehogs
sucking cows was still common in parts of nineteenth-century Wales, and
as a result of this belief they were destroyed as vermin.[87] However, their
association with witches in this context is not clearly evident, although it
can be assumed that the tradition had its origin in shape-shifting. Milk-
stealing was not the only petty criminal act witches performed in animal
form. A Durham man shot at a witch-hare that he caught eating his
cabbages. Jenny Clench, a Dorset witch, was accused of stealing potatoes
in the guise of a hare, and a witch living on the Surrey/Sussex border
was blamed for damaging crops.[88] Presumably witches were thought to
carry out such minor acts of pillage as animals because they were less
likely to be seen, and to escape far more easily than in human form.

The motif of the witch being chased and injured in animal guise,
often by being shot by hunters or bitten by hounds, and then being
subsequently discovered with the same injuries in human form has been
recorded from every region of the country many times over. Many of the
nineteenth- and twentieth-century legends concerned events which were
said to have occurred two or three generations before, but the belief in
shape-shifting most definitely continued into the present century. In 1901,
Mabel Peacock asserted, for instance, that in Lincolnshire, 'the belief in
shape-shifting still exists, that is certain'.[89] Some folklorists also inter-
viewed people who claimed to have actually encountered witches in
animal form. An old man from West Sussex told how one night he saw
a local witch walking by a hedge; 'I says "Why Mrs ——, you aint no
call to be out so late as this!" And I tell you, as true as I'm sitting here,
she vanished, and instead of her I saw a hare running through a gap in
the hedge. I saw it – and you could have knocked me down with a
feather.' Similarly, one of Boys Firmin's informants, after relating an
account of a local witch having been chased by hounds, asserted 'It's no
use telling what's not true. Why, I be there myself and see it. Its quite
true. The hare was Dame Garson herself.'[90] The woman who nursed the

Surrey witch Mary S. in her final hours was of the firm opinion that her illness was caused by Mary's having been shot at, and hit, while out at night in the form of a white rabbit.[91] It is clear from these accounts that people did believe that witches wandered abroad as animals, and such stories did not necessarily accrue round witches only after their death. Some even wondered openly how witches were able to change shape. In the last decade of the nineteenth century the great-niece of a village witch from the Surrey/Sussex border, who was aware of the stories surrounding her great-aunt, asked "'How do people do it, Miss?" "Do what Anne?" "Why, how do people turn into animals?"'[92]

In comparison with the wealth of accounts concerning shape-shifting from the folklore sources, the tradition is less evident in the sixteenth- and seventeenth-century source material. Keith Thomas observed that the notion was 'seldom advanced'.[93] It was, however, introduced as evidence at more trials throughout the period than Thomas's statement suggests.[94] Furthermore, a look at sources other than trial records reveals accounts of the archetypal witch-hare very similar to those from the nineteenth century.[95] Indeed, in 1621, Edward Fairfax asserted that, 'as to the transforming of shapes in this kind the question deserveth to be written of in a whole volume … the changing of witches into hares, cats, and the like shapes, is so common as late testimonies and confessions approve unto us, that none but the stupidly incredulous can wrong the credit of the reporters, or doubt of the certainty.'[96] Robin Briggs, writing from a wider European perspective, has described shape-shifting as 'a curious mixture of ancient folklore and practical everyday fears, which lurks around the fringes of witchcraft belief without ever becoming an integral part of it.'[97] What all the above evidence suggests, though, is that shape-changing was, in fact, an important aspect of witch-lore in both early modern and modern England, but is underrepresented in witchcraft historiography due to the nature of the source materials consulted. Court cases in both periods rarely mention shape-shifting. If we only considered this type of source material we would have little idea of the strength of the tradition. It is necessary to distinguish, therefore, between public witchcraft accusations and wider beliefs concerning the nature of the witch. It is also fair to say that the lack of discussion on shape-shifting in the historiography of British witchcraft relates to the innocuous nature of the animal forms assumed by witches. If, like their Continental counterparts, witches had transformed themselves into wolves, and in such forms attacked humans and animals, then shape-shifting would undoubtedly have attracted more attention. No one was afraid of being savaged by a vicious hare, and their depredations were far less serious. In continental Europe, however, fear of the wolf was engraved deeply into the psyche of rural culture. Just across the English channel, in Normandy, where wolves only became extinct around the middle of the nineteenth century, tales of werewolves continued to circulate.[98] In England the wolf had been wiped out by the fourteenth century, and it had probably disappeared from Wales even earlier.[99] It is not surprising, then, that the wolf plays little part in the early modern and modern witchcraft tradition. Nevertheless, the English and Welsh belief in were-animals is little different in essence from that of Western and Northern Europe: it is largely a matter of varying degrees of imagery and effect.

We have seen from the folklore evidence how the witch figure conformed to characteristic human attributes concerning age, gender, physical appearance and social position. The evidence presented in this discussion so far indicates that this witch stereotype had been a part of folk tradition long before the mid-eighteenth century. As we have seen, characteristic hats and clothing appear in seventeenth-century depositions, and from Richard Bovet's observations we found that exactly the same apparel was worn by fairies. Furthermore, he referred to them as old-fashioned garb even then. That is not to say that the stereotype did not change subtly over time, but the core features remained essentially the same. Such archetypal witches undoubtedly existed in many communities, and lived their lives within the confines of their social role as both a figure of derision, taunted by children and adults alike, and a figure of fear motivated by feelings of spite and revenge. These witches were not only an integral element of the human community, though; they also operated in the realm of the supernatural. This was another level of existence, a society of fairies, spirits and ghosts, who could change their form at will and fly through the air. It was a parallel world, yet its denizens often shared the same environmental space as humans, particularly when night fell. This was the time when witches and fairies danced and socialised, and when the witch or her spirit wandered abroad, visiting neighbours' stables and bedrooms. In this sense the folkloric witch was akin to the fantastical 'night witch', a concept borrowed from African tradition and correlated with the archaic folk elements of the witch that emerge from the European witchcraft trials.[100] However, the duality of the witch in English folklore is, perhaps, better expressed by reference to the 'beggar witch' and 'fairy witch', who represented respectively the mundane and supernatural aspects of the witch figure. However, the picture of the witch we have so far reconstructed from the folklore evidence is far from complete. The process of restoration requires the resort to a new source material.

The witch in court

When we look at court reports concerning those actually assaulted or threatened for allegedly practising witchcraft from the eighteenth to the twentieth centuries, we find that a rather more prosaic, albeit socially varied, picture of the witch emerges. Most of these assault cases resulted from attempts to draw blood from the supposed witch in order to negate the effects of bewitchment. The victims of these attacks would then lodge a complaint with a justice of the peace, and their assailants would usually find themselves before the local petty sessions, or more occasionally before the higher courts of quarter session and assize. The Danish witchcraft historian Gustav Henningsen has labelled these cases witch-trials 'in reverse', in that the witch was no longer the defendant in court but the prosecutor. As he observed, these trials serve as a link between the evidence of early modern witch prosecutions and the folklore records of the late nineteenth and early twentieth centuries.[101] Unfortunately the petty session was not a court of record, and relevant, surviving documentary evidence is patchy, particularly for the eighteenth and early nineteenth century. The minute books, in which the nature of each case was briefly recorded, often mention only the names of those involved and not the reasons for each dispute. Searching systematically through the petty session archive is not, therefore, a particularly rewarding task. A more profitable source of information concerning cases heard before the petty sessions is the local newspapers that reported on many of the hearings, and often picked up on the more sensational ones, including those resulting from the belief in witchcraft and magic. These reports are usually, but not always, detailed enough to provide at least some of the concrete social data about those involved in witchcraft disputes that is often lacking from folklore sources. Judging from my own trawl through the newspaper archive I would estimate that the number of prosecutions arising from assaults or threats against witches in the period could easily number over two hundred. We are looking, therefore, at a considerable body of material waiting to be analysed in much more detail. The following preliminary discussion is based on a sample of seventy such cases, and will hopefully serve to demonstrate the potential for further research.

In sixty-four (91 per cent) of the sample court cases those assaulted for witchcraft were women. This corresponds well with various statistics produced from early modern English trial records, which reveal that women made up around 90 per cent of accused witches.[102] The similarity of the statistics over time is certainly remarkable. The reason for the predominance of female witches in the early modern period has been the subject of much debate in recent years. The two main explanations that have emerged so far concern the economic marginality of women in early modern society, and the patriarchal hostility generated towards those women such as widows and spinsters who lived outside the social norms. It might be argued that similar social tensions underlay the predominance of women in the eighteenth- and nineteenth-century trial material. However, a lot more detailed small-scale research would have to be done on witchcraft accusations and gender relations in the period before such claims could be made with any confidence. It was often actually women who accused and assaulted other women for witchcraft, so it would seem that they, rather than their menfolk, were often responsible for instigating witchcraft conflicts. At present, therefore, a more profitable line of enquiry, which will be pursued further in this discussion, is to concentrate on the relationship between gender and the immediate environment in which accusations were made.

Not all the court reports provide the age of those accused of being witches. What evidence there is suggests that the majority were older than fifty but not overwhelmingly so. We know at least some were in their eighties and even nineties because their age was highlighted in court to emphasise the heinousness of the assault. The vast majority were either married or widowed. Their status in this respect probably depended on their age, as on average women usually outlived their husbands. In contrast, a handful of those accused of witchcraft were young women in their late teens or early twenties. It must always be remembered, of course, that a person did not just become a witch on reaching a certain age in life. As we have seen from the folklore sources, there was a widely held belief that witchcraft was hereditary. We should expect, therefore, at least some of those accused of witchcraft to be young. This is exactly what we find from a case heard by the Abergavenny magistrates where a young married woman, Elizabeth Walker, was stabbed with a penknife by an elderly woman, Sybil Baynum, while they were out gleaning in the fields one day. In court Baynum called Walker 'a witch, likewise saying that complainant's mother, who recently died, was also one, and had bewitched some cows, and that the daughter was possessed of the same power'. Some forty years later, in 1879, William Bulwer, of Etling Green, Norfolk, was charged with assaulting a sixteen-year-old girl, Christiana Martins. Bulwer claimed that Martin's mother was 'a bad old witch' and that 'her daughter is as bad as she is and encourages her in it'.[103] The hereditary principle was probably also behind the wounding, in 1846, of a fourteen-

year-old boy named Richard Evans, of Appledore, Devon. The magistrates
at the Buckland Brewer sessions heard how the young daughter of the
defendant, Roger Fursdon, had been ill for some time, and for some
reason he believed that Evans had overlooked her. Fursdon first cut Evans
near the wrist with a knife, and then dragged him to his house where his
young daughter again scratched him, with a pin.[104]

The archetypal image of the dirty, gob-toothed crone is little present
in the court evidence. In fact, in several cases reporters with the witch
stereotype firmly in mind thought it worth remarking on the atypical
countenance of suspected witches. In a case from Sussex, for example,
the plaintiff was described as 'most unlike our old ideal image of a witch,
being a remarkably tall, fat, rosy, good-tempered looking woman'. Another, from Somerset, was 'a very jovial looking widow, whose plump
and ruddy countenance presented a most striking contrast to the cadaver-
ous appearance which is generally associated with the names of witch
and wizard'. Isaac Nicholson thought it worth mentioning that Ann Izzard,
the mother of eight children, was 'a little woman, about sixty years of
age, and by no means ill looking'.[105] This is an initial indication, then,
that public accusations of witchcraft were not necessarily directed at those
who conformed to stereotypical images of the witch.

When we come to look at the individual circumstances of each
accusation, threat or assault we further lose sight of the archetypal folklore witch. Notions of diabolism, familiars, witch gatherings, and shape-
shifting are rarely mentioned in court evidence, even though defendants
were often quite free with their opinions before the magistrates or judges.
It is also apparent that those accused of witchcraft were rarely of a status
to qualify them as begging witches, and begging was generally absent
from the evidence given against them in court. According to Keith
Thomas, witch beliefs lasted longest in rural areas where 'the conventions
of neighbourliness and mutual help survived into the nineteenth century'.
He further suggests that the 'majority of informal witch accusations
recorded in the eighteenth, nineteenth and even twentieth centuries
conform to the same old special pattern of charity evaded, followed by
misfortune incurred.[106] However, as Thomas's footnotes show, the 'informal
witch accusations' he is referring to were largely drawn from folklore
sources, which, as has already been discussed, do, indeed, paint such a
picture. Yet the evidence of the court reports indicates that Thomas's
account is only partially representative of witchcraft accusations in general.
It is quite true that old female witches did still go begging from door to
door during the eighteenth and nineteenth centuries, and accusations did

result from these activities. As we shall see, though, the more serious public accusations and cases of assault rarely followed Thomas's classic pattern.

Where there is a clear link between begging and witchcraft is in relation to the activities of gypsies. They had long had a reputation not only for their petty thievery, tinkering and begging, but also for their occult powers. When some gypsies were rebuffed on the doorstep they sometimes exploited their magical reputation and openly threatened to bewitch those who refused them. A not untypical case was that heard before the Teignmouth magistrates in July 1888. A gypsy named Rhoda Smith went begging at 14 Ferndale Road, where she asked the servant, Emily Johns, for some victuals. Being refused, Smith said she would 'ill-wish' Johns, 'and that would ruin her for life'. Johns was so frightened that she gave Smith 3s 6d as well as her silver earrings. In another case, this time from Hammersmith police court, in 1861, a gypsy named Reservoir Ayres threatened two servant girl that 'if she did not take home money or clothes her mother-in-law, who was an old witch, would bewitch them.'[107] The gypsies' explicit threats of bewitchment were in sharp contrast to the characteristically veiled warnings of the village witch. The reason for this difference of approach presumably derives from the itinerant nature of gypsy life. They could afford to resort to this ultimate threat of reprisal because, apart from the occasional prosecution, there was little chance of adverse consequences. These gypsy beggars were not members of the communities they camped near and could simply move on, while village witches had to maintain their carefully balanced relations with their neighbours.

An analysis of the 'reverse witch trials' reveals that in 87 per cent of cases the primary targets of witchcraft were people suffering from ill health. Of the other cases, four concerned horses, one a chicken, one a pig, one a cow, and one was a case of multiple bewitchment involving farm livestock, butter-making and baking. The most unusual case was that from Staithes, in 1858, when a woman was assaulted for bewitching a newly built house which subsequently fell down.[108] Of the human victims, nineteen (32 per cent) were men while a further four cases concerned married couples. This, combined with the fact that there seems to have been no change in the percentage of women accused of witchcraft from the sixteenth to the nineteenth century, suggests that there was no significant general trend towards the 'feminisation' of witchcraft in the nineteenth century that has been identified in other parts of Europe.[109] In other words, at a personal level witchcraft remained a predominantly female affair. However, it is quite likely that detailed small-scale studies could reveal different regional patterns in this context, depending on the nature of local economies and cultures.

As in the early modern period, young women suffering from fits during which they often claimed to see visions of their tormentors, or called out their names, continued to play a significant role in witchcraft accusations, and several witch-scratching cases arose from such circumstances. As has already been discussed, possession cases continued to attract religious interest, or, more to the point, cases of bewitchment evolved into diabolic possession through ecclesiastical involvement. However, in many cases of witchcraft centred on the fits experienced by young women the cause was rooted firmly in simple *maleficium*. The talk was of bewitchment and not of possession or evil spirits. In 1852 the magistrate at the Newark police court heard just such a case concerning the daughters of Thomas Freeman, a hawker of Norwell, Nottinghamshire. One of his daughters had been ill, and 'was reduced to a complete skeleton'. She suffered much pain, during which she frequently called out the name of an elderly woman named Ann Williamson who lived in the same village. When another of his daughters started being 'attacked' in the same manner, Freeman resolved to draw Williamson's blood. Accordingly, one night he went to Williamson's house and requested her to come and see his daughters. She refused in consequence of 'the scandal he had raised about her', to which he responded by drawing a darning needle across her arm.[110] A similar story was heard at the Warwick assizes in 1867. The invalid daughter of John Davis, of Sheep Street, Stratford-upon-Avon, declared that a woman and a man were coming down the chimney and tormenting her. On one occasion she claimed they 'cast her violently upon the ground, then tossed here up into the air'. This harassment was attributed to a local woman named Jane Ward, whom Davis consequently assaulted. The attack on the supposed witch, Ann Izzard, as recounted by the Rev. Isaac Nicholson, also had its origin in the fits suffered by two young women named Alice Brown and Fanny Amey. In February 1808 the two women were walking by the frozen River Ouse when Alice attempted to cross over the ice. She had gone only a few yards when the ice gave way and she was plunged into the freezing water. She managed to clamber out, and the two frightened women hastened back to Brown's house about a quarter of a mile away. Once at home the frozen Alice experienced a strong epileptic-type fit. Her friend, Fanny, who had previously been subject to epilepsy, also became convulsed. Not surprisingly, Alice did not recover easily from her immersion. Her fits returned at short intervals and prevented her from working. It would seem that another woman in the village named Mary Fox also began to suffer in the same way.[111] Because the girls continued to experience fits long after the initial shock of their experience, witchcraft was suspected and Ann Izzard became the focus of accusations.

It is worthy of note here that some of the more sensational bodily manifestations of witchcraft, which seem to have developed during the period of the witch-trials, had declined by the nineteenth century. The voiding of pins, nails and other sharp objects, for example, had been a prominent feature in some of the later witch prosecutions.[112] The tradition certainly continued until at least the mid-eighteenth century, when a thirteen year-old boy named Ladd, of West Langdon, Kent, pretended to void needles and pins from his body, but I have found no other account of the phenomenon beyond this period.[113] This suggests that there was a partial scaling down of some of the more striking visual phenomena exhibited by the victims of witchcraft. Such displays were modes of publicly proving the victim's bewitchment and the witch's guilt. As in cases of satanic possession, the pin-voider was performing for an audience. We can interpret the obviously fraudulent symptoms as a cry for attention and sympathy, but they were also used by unscrupulous persons to defraud well-wishers. At the beginning of the eighteenth-century one such fraud named Richard Hathaway was prosecuted for this deceit, though not before his supposed tormentor, Sarah Moredike, had been mobbed by his sympathisers. Hathaway had attracted crowds of people with his vomiting of pins and nails, and money had been collected for him. However, during one of these vomiting attacks Hathaway was searched and many packets of pins and nails were found in his pockets. When his arms were tied behind his back the vomiting ceased.[114] In the Ladd case mentioned above, the boy's parents had also collected sums of money from the crowds who came to see him 'perform'. The accused witch was also attacked by a mob whipped up by the Ladds and a man named Beard, and eventually a magistrate had to intervene. The decline of pin-voiding could be due to several factors. The fact that it was no longer taken seriously by members of authority was probably influential, and those who attempted to simulate it were increasingly likely to be officially censured. It is also possible that the exposure of the phenomenon as a fraud eventually engendered a more sceptical attitude among the general populace. The decreasing frequency of the phenomenon resulted in knowledge of it fading from the popular consciousness. Without vivid displays of its reality the belief dwindled.

After humans, the horse was the most important single animal in the community. Losing a horse was a serious blow to the functioning of any business or farm that required them either as draught animals or for transport. This probably explains why horses made up the second biggest group of bewitchment victims in the reverse witch-trials. Secondary in general importance after humans and horses, but not necessarily in individual terms, were the meat and dairy animals. Finally, at the bottom of the animal bewitchment league were pets. Accusations of witchcraft involving the bewitchment of cats and dogs, for example, are uncommon in both court cases and folklore sources. When pets were bewitched, it was usually cited as secondary evidence of witchcraft, after the primary claim of personal illness. In an assault case heard by the Barnstaple magistrates in 1870, for example, Philip Burch, aged eighty, claimed that not only had he been personally bewitched for five years, but he had lost fourteen canaries and about fifty goldfinches as well. Another witch-scratcher, Ann Davis, of Axbridge, Somerset, claimed that as well as nocturnally tormenting her, the witch, Elizabeth Williams, had also killed her donkey and cat, as well as causing her to be thrown from a cart.[115]

The very small number of dairying, cow and pig bewitchments in the reverse witch trials is in sharp contrast with their preponderance in cunning-folk prosecution reports and ethnographic sources. A sample survey of six folklore collections reveals, for instance, that out of sixty-four accounts of witchcraft, only fifteen (23 per cent) concerned humans. Of the other forty-nine cases, sixteen concerned cattle, twelve concerned pigs, seven concerned horses, six related to failed butter-making, two concerned sheep, two concerned boats, and there was one case each of bewitched geese, chickens, canaries, and failed wool dye.[116] Why should livestock and dairying be so underrepresented in assault cases? Perhaps it may indicate that in terms of counter-action against witchcraft, people responded in different ways depending on the economic cost and emotional importance of those bewitched. Drawing blood was certainly held to be the most powerful of anti-witchcraft measures, but, considering the potential legal and financial consequences of committing an assault, scratching a witch was not a light undertaking. The severity of sentencing in assault cases depended on the seriousness of the wounds inflicted on the witch, and the court in which the case was heard. Some scratchers brought before the petty sessions got off with merely being bound over to keep the peace, while others, like John Davis, were sentenced at the assizes to as much as eighteen months' hard labour.[117] Financial penalties also varied from only a few shillings court costs, to as much as £4 payment to the injured party, as happened in a Lincolnshire case.[118] Indeed, in 1769, the magistrates at the Cambridge quarter sessions ordered William Adams of Grantchester, Cambridgeshire, to pay Phoebe Haly, of Caldicot, the very large sum of five guineas compensation, and 13s 4d in fines.[119] Even if large fines were not imposed, the sureties for those bound over to keep the peace could still be considerable. In 1890, two young Cornishmen were bound over in £20 each after threatening their 71-year-old neighbour, whom they believed had ill-wished their horses.[120] It would seem, then, that the risk of incurring such penalties was usually only worth it in cases of serious and persistent sickness of family members. The evidence also suggests that drawing blood was often only resorted to after considerable consultation with friends and neighbours. In one instance a witch-scratcher said she had been 'encouraged to do so by some of his neighbours', and another told the magistrates 'he had been persuaded by more than one hundred persons'.[121] Some also only acted after being advised to do so by cunning-folk. When the effects of the scratching proved beneficial, witch-scratchers were quite content to express to the magistrates their satisfaction with the result of their actions. The hag-ridden Grace Webb remarked in court, 'All I know is, I have felt better ever since I gave the scratch; it was a lucky scratch for me', and John Davis when brought into custody stated that the witch could 'do no more for me now, I've drawn first blood'.[122]

Although cows were frequently the victims of witchcraft, it would seem that pigs were the witches' favourite target. According to Frederick Elworthy, 'In England, of all animals the pig is oftenest "overlooked".' E. M. Leather similarly remarked that 'the pig seems more frequently the victim of spite than any other animal', and Margaret Eyre observed that tales of bewitchment were 'much concerned with pigs'.[123] It is worth exploring the phenomenon of porcine bewitchment in more detail, therefore, as it indicates a social dimension to witchcraft accusations that has a wider significance.

Elworthy thought the ubiquity of pig bewitchments might possibly be related to 'the difficulty of administering physic' to them. More pertinent, perhaps, was the fact that ailing pigs were well known for their unusual behaviour, which in turn generated suspicions of witchcraft. The Surrey folklorist Edward Lovett noted that 'at certain times and under certain conditions, pigs behave in a wild and erratic manner, which has given rise to the popular opinion that they are bewitched!'[124] Thus a Dorset labourer's pig was stated as 'crying like a child'. In another instance, bewitched pigs were seen 'whirling round and round', and it was observed of one Norfolk man's pigs that 'they was barking and jumping all over the sty'.[125] The more important reason for the frequency of pig bewitchments lies, however, with Elworthy's alternative suggestion that pigs had many 'owners of the peasantry class'. This is a view shared by E. M. Leather, who thought the pig was so often bewitched 'because it is often the only live stock the cottager possesses'.[126] Although a few labourers were able to maintain a cow, most relied on rearing a pig in a sty in the back yard to supplement their meagre diets. The labourer's pig, or the 'cottager's friend',[127] was often as carefully looked after as other members of the family unit, and played an important part in the domestic economy. Flora Thompson remembered how on Sunday afternoons people would call round not to see the family, but the pig, 'and would lounge with its owner against the pig-sty door for an hour, scratching piggy's back'.[128] The cottager often bought the runt of the litter from a local farmer for a few hard-earned shillings, and carefully fed it on kitchen scraps, and fattened it up on barley before being slaughtered: 'they keep a pig nine months of the year, saving up to buy it in the other three months. They do not sell any of it, and what with pork and bacon it lasts them the whole year round.'[129] As Michael Winstanley found from oral interviews among elderly people in Kent, the pig was so heavily relied upon for meat that many of the children were put off it for the rest of their lives.[130] One can imagine the sense of loss after carefully feeding up a pig for seven months, and relying on the pork to feed the family for the next seven months, only to find the pig inexplicably dying. As the Rev. H. D. Gordon observed, 'when witches kill pigs they become serious'.[131] Presumably, for the reasons given above, though, it was not usually serious enough to lead to assaults on those witches deemed responsible, unless, say, a farmer's continual losses threatened his economic survival. Instead, labourers, who were not economically dependent on their back-yard pig but would be sorely disappointed at losing it, were more likely to spend hard-earned money on a visit to a cunning-person. They might also resort to some sort of counter-witchcraft measure such as placing a branch of rowan above the sty or employing a witch bottle.

Origins of accusations

Although we can identify who and what the targets of witchcraft were, it is not so easy to trace why suspicions of witchcraft were generated in the first place, and the exact reason why those accused became suspects. What can be said with certainty is that disputes originated from diverse circumstances, which together ultimately led to disruptions in social relationships between neighbours or family members. To provide an initial example illustrating the individualistic origins of witchcraft accusations, we can return to the story of the Norfolk sheep-dresser mentioned at the beginning of this chapter:

> I could tell you why she first set about bewitching him, for they was at one time friends. Mr. S. has not been maimed very long. When he was married he gave a party, and invited this woman and her daughter. He was silly enough to give all the company jalap in their drink, and then locked them in. These two were dreadfully offended, and nothing went right with him afterwards.[132]

Thus a rather unpleasant practical joke involving the laxative jalap turned a friendly, neighbourly relationship into a hostile one that ultimately led to accusations of witchcraft. Although in most cases it is impossible to reconstruct accurately the sequence of events leading up to a public accusation, or to untangle the thought processes of those involved, it is possible to detect some recurring themes emerging from both the ethnographic sources and the court reports.

Disputes with neighbours and landlords over tenancies were the source of a number of accusations, and this presumably indicates the insecurity of tenure for many cottagers at the time. A quite detailed account of the background to one such tenancy dispute was recounted by a Dorset woman named Mrs Pitman. When her daughter was a child she believed her neighbour, Mrs Rigg, who was also married with children, had bewitched her daughter. Relations between the neighbours could not have been bad since the children all played together until Pitman's daughter fell ill. Their suspicions that witchcraft was the cause were confirmed by a cunning-woman. Pitman's reason for then suspecting Rigg was as follows:

> It had been though that we were leaving at Lady Day, but at last we had settled not to leave, as was expected. Rigg had not a settled place like my husband. He just rented a cottage and worked for one and another as a labourer, but he wished to get a regular place. Mrs. Rigg wanted to have our house. It was better than hers, which was ruinous. So they were hoping to get our house and our place.[133]

Another witchcraft accusation arising from a tenancy dispute was heard during an inquest held at Scarborough over the body of a seventeen-month-old child. The bereaved mother claimed that her next-door neighbour had bewitched the child to death as an act of revenge after she had told their mutual landlord something which led to the accused witch being turned out of her house.[134] Similarly, Mary Lewes knew of a case where a woman was accused of bewitching her landlord after she had been evicted from her cottage to make way for a new tenant.[135]

Other witchcraft-related property disputes arose out of acts of trespass. The Caernarfon petty sessions dealt with a case where a woman named Margaret Evans went down on her knees and ritually cursed her neighbour, Margaret Griffith, after a quarrel over some hens which had wandered on to the other's property. Evans read out a portion of the Bible, and went down on her knees and prayed to the Lord 'to remove the lot from the face of the earth'. A policeman described Evans as the 'terror of the neighbourhood'.[136] It would seem that such petty arguments were often symptomatic of deeper antagonisms, though. In 1876, for example, a couple named Jackson were summoned before the Warrington magistrates for beating an 84-year-old woman named Maria Platt. The assault ostensibly arose out of a dispute over the right to place a clothes line in their yard in Dial Court, during which Mr Jackson knocked the old woman to the ground and threatened to kill her. The evidence suggests that the origin of the dispute lay in the fact that Platt was considered a witch in the neighbourhood, and had been accused of evil-doing. Indeed, the defendants' solicitor told the court that he could not get any witnesses to appear, as her 'neighbours were afraid that if they gave evidence against her she would bewitch them'.[137]

While tenancy and property disputes generally concerned friction between neighbours, another identifiable set of accusations arose from conflicts within the family group. In 1871, for instance, a young man residing near Manchester was prosecuted for abusing his mother, whom he accused of bewitching him. In a case from Norwich, in 1859, the roles were reversed, when an old woman, Mrs Turner, applied for some security against her forty-year-old son. In court the following dialogue took place:

> The prisoner — She says I am a-witching of her. The mayor — Well, are you a-witching of her? The prisoner — no, I arnt. The mayor — Is he a-witching of you, old lady? The mother — I really don't know, sir, if he isn't. Prisoner — She has been told I was a-setting of a 'spell' on her. The mother — Oh, deary me! The mayor (to the prisoner) — Never mind the spell. Will you leave her? Prisoner — I can leave her.

The son, on insisting he did not have the money to pay the court fees, was taken to the cells to 'let him think it over'. It is not clear why the old woman suspected her son, but the comment that 'she had been told' that he was witching her suggests that a cunning-person may have generated the suspicion.[138] In two other instances, grandparents were also accused of bewitching their grandchildren. In the first case, a Totnes cab proprietor prosecuted his son who had accused him of bewitching his daughter. She suffered from a chronic shaking of the hand, and had been taken to several doctors in Plymouth but to no avail. Relations between father and son had long been sour as a consequence of 'an old family disagreement'. The second case was the inquest into the death of a baby girl in Fressingfield, Suffolk, in 1890, at which the girl's parents claimed that she had been overlooked by her step-grandmother, who had died on the same day.[139]

Again, in the above instances we do not know the exact reason for the bad blood between family members, though that perennial cause of family feuding – inheritance – was obviously the basis of some inter-family witchcraft accusations. In 1847 two sisters, Mrs Cole and Mrs Leggett, both of Gorlestone-on-Sea, Norfolk, ended up before the Yarmouth police court after a violent row. One Friday, Mrs Cole, the wife of a well-known pilot in the town, went to the house of Mrs Leggett, and broke open the door by throwing a stone at it. She then hurled a volley of abuse against her sister, and threatened 'to make her wallow in her blood unless she went to Norwich, and had the witches taken off her (Mrs Cole's) husband. She would make her drink her own blood unless she unbewitched her husband.' When the mayor, who was presiding in court, asked Mrs Cole the reason for her shocking behaviour, she made the following statement:

> My sister got my father to make a wrong will, and leave all his property to her; and she now sets all the lawyers at defiance. My husband has been lately in a very low way: I have had Dr. Impey to him, the pier-master's son, and old Dr. Smith, but they know nothing of his complaint – he is never at rest night or day, and my belief is he is bewitched by Mrs. Leggett. He is never well, and yet nobody can see anything the matter with him.

The magistrates reproached Mrs Cole for harbouring such a 'fearful delusion', and made her promise not to go near her sister. Before she left the court she commented: 'Well, if there are such things as witches, my sister is one.'[140]

Considering the dangerous nature of childbirth for both baby and mother it is initially surprising that very few public accusations seem to have arisen at this sensitive time. Until the twentieth century, infant and maternal mortality remained high by modern standards. It was a period when women were susceptible to disease and infection, generally labelled as 'puerperal fever', and also psychological disturbance. Charms such as

Saviour's Letters were resorted to for protection not only from natural ailments but also from witchcraft. The evidence suggests, though, that the experience of childbirth was not a significant source of witchcraft accusations, perhaps because everyone was aware of the probability that there might be complications either for the child or the mother. In other words, misfortune was to be expected. Witchcraft accusations concerning human health were usually generated by *unexpected* complications, and often concerned inexplicable and prolonged illnesses rather than the more predictable complications occurring during childbirth. This is not to say that the misfortunes of childbirth were never attributed to witchcraft. In the early modern period, for example, stillbirths were sometimes blamed on witchcraft, and I would be surprised if such misfortunes did not occasionally attract suspicions in the later period as well.

Accusations of witchcraft were more likely to be generated in the period after childbirth. From their exploration of early modern sources, both Lyndal Roper and Diane Purkiss have identified this lying-in period as a significant source of female friction and witchcraft accusations.[141] Suspicions were likely to be generated as much by the state of the mother as of the baby. It was a time when mothers might experience what is now called post-natal depression, but which at the time would have been described more generally as lowness of spirits. It was just this sort of condition, where the sufferer felt continually exhausted, nervous and generally unwell, that generated suspicions of witchcraft. It was probably this experience which led Mary Passant to assault Ann Tipton, wife of Abraham Tipton, of Elmore Green. The case was heard by the Walsall magistrates in 1869, where the following story unfolded. Tipton, it would seem, acted as a local midwife and had attended Passant during three of her previous confinements. A few days before the assault, Tipton had gone to ask Passant how she was faring after another recent confinement. Passant responded in an unfriendly manner, saying, 'I would be much better if you would pray for me.' Tipton replied, 'I wish you well, I am sure, but, as I am not a professed prayer, I don't think I could do much in that way. But why do you ask me to do so? Surely you don't think I have done you any harm.' Passant then said, 'I do, for I saw you, that night you were sitting with me, throwing something in the fire while you were looking at my husband's watch. But if you will kneel down and bless me I will be got better.' Tipton, finding herself in a position where she was damned if she did not comply, and damned if she did, answered, 'I will do as you require me to do if you will not entertain such wicked thoughts about me. Have you told any one that you thought such things about me?' Passant said she had not, and so Tipton knelt down and asked God to bless her and her family. A day or two later, Tipton passed by Passant's door and kindly asked her how she felt. Passant invited her in and told her that she had been to a cunning-man at Walsall who confirmed that Tipton had 'witched' her and also a blacksmith at Coalpool, and recommended that she draw Tipton's blood. At that point Passant produced a knife and cut Tipton's face. The Bench, after hearing all the evidence, sentenced Passant to pay a fine of ten shillings and costs, or to be imprisoned for one month in default of payment.[142]

It has been a common generalisation that accusations were levelled against people who had long had a reputation for witchcraft in their respective communities. It is thought that suspicions of witchcraft built up over many years until one day circumstances triggered an outburst of recrimination and violence. But the pattern of accusation is not always as predictable as that. Reading through the above cases and other evidence it becomes apparent that quite a few of those accused of being witches had no previous reputation for witchcraft. The accusations were not directed at familiar scapegoats in the community as one might expect, but against neighbours, friends or family who were totally bemused by the allegations being made against them. Of course, once the accusation had been broadcast, and the circumstances surrounding it debated by the community, then a person with a hitherto clean character could suddenly find their reputation being ground down by the rumour mill. The fear of losing one's reputation in this way is only too apparent from the responses of two of the women accused in the above cases. Ann Williamson expressed her anger and fear at 'the scandal' Thomas Freeman had 'raised about her', and Ann Tipton anxiously asked her accuser if she had told anyone else of her thoughts. These women presumably had unsullied reputations to protect.

As far as can be gathered, most witches were thought to be motivated by feelings of revenge, but they were also considered to be stimulated by the sheer pleasure of causing pain and hardship. This meant that victims of witchcraft did not necessarily have to seek out a reason for their bewitchment, and in such cases they merely sought to find out who among those in close proximity to themselves was the witch. This process of deduction was greatly aided by the involvement of cunning-folk. Because they were often consulted by people who lived some distance away, it was impossible for cunning-folk to identify someone from their clients' neighbourhoods who already had a bad reputation. They might try and draw out of the clients details of whom they suspected, but in some cases the bewitched had little idea who was wishing them harm, which is why they went to the cunning-person in the first place. Under these circumstances, some cunning-folk would make vague predictions, usually along the lines that the first person who the client met after a certain time or in a certain place was the witch. This almost inevitably led to suspicions being fixed upon friends and neighbours against whom there was no imputation of witchcraft, as the following case illustrates. Around 1895/6 a man of Bodmin, Cornwall, fell ill and the doctors could not cure him. A wise-woman was called in who confirmed he was bewitched, and told the man's wife that the culprit was 'a person whom you little expect. He attends the same chapel as your husband; he will call in the course of a day or two to inquire for him.' Two days later a male neighbour kindly called to ask how he was, and consequently it was put about that the unfortunate well-wisher was more of an ill-wisher. The neighbours became estranged, and the poor man's health gave way under the distress of the accusations made against him.[143] On such a basis, then, people who did not at all conform to the stereotype of the witch nevertheless became weighed down with the reputation of being one.

Bewitchment and social space

Examination of the frequency of bewitchments among different groups of targets and the circumstances surrounding them suggests that patterns are related to boundaries of social space centred on the individual and his or her immediate environment. People's lives can roughly be divided into public, private and intimate spheres of existence, in which relationships between people are maintained on varying degrees of formality or informality. Although accusations of witchcraft and assaults against witches often occurred in public as acts of legitimation, the origins of those actions can often be traced to unwonted or unwarranted intrusions and transgressions occurring in the private and intimate social arenas.

In spatial terms a person's private area was usually defined by the home or farmstead. It has to be remembered that up until the early twentieth century, life was far less privatised than it is now. In rural communities in particular, everyone new everyone else and there was a considerable level of interdependence. Properties were a lot more accessible to outsiders. Doors were not locked and barbed wire did not demarcate boundaries. Bartering and borrowing were commonplace, and produce was collected straight from the farm. There was a continual movement of people between properties. Despite such accessibility the home or farmyard was not necessarily considered a public space, but was nevertheless open to intrusion by neighbours and acquaintances. It was certainly not always easy to prevent visits from unwanted visitors, and the resulting tensions could subsequently develop into suspicions of witchery, particularly when misfortune occurred around the same time. In 1909 a 25-year-old woman of Hascombe, Surrey, recalled, for example, how a Mrs S—— was continually troubled by the intrusions of her neighbour Mrs P——, who she did not get on well with. 'Mrs S—— used to try and keep her from coming to her house, but no matter what, she would come', but she would always make sure to see Mrs P—— out to the gate. These visits unsettled Mrs S—— so much that she began to sleep badly and saw the old woman in her bedroom at night, which led her to believe she was bewitched. A Sussex farmer was more determined regarding a local witch who 'made a great trouble of going to the farm for milk'. The farmer would not let her pass through his gate for fear she would put a spell on his cows. In response she would stand in the road outside his gate and holler at him.[144] Beggars represented the classic intruder into private space, which is partly why they figure so prominently in the ethnographic material concerning witchcraft.

The bedroom symbolised the boundary between private and intimate space. It was here that people were at their most vulnerable, where their physical and psychological defences were down. Access to the bedroom was a personal affair, and strangers who might be allowed into the kitchen or front room were most definitely excluded. One of the rare occasions when the bedroom was left exposed to intrusion was during childbirth, when female neighbours would find their way in, either to help, to express support, or perhaps more nefariously to cast a spell. Otherwise, the bedroom could only be accessed by supernatural means, which helps explain why night-time visions and sensations played a significant role in witch-accusations. Such supernatural manifestations, which enabled the witch to gain close proximity to a person, were particularly disturbing intrusions into intimate space. We can see this from the prosecution of George Nichols for assaulting his landlady, Susan Larcombe, whom he accused of bewitching him. In 1859 Nichols was lodging in Larcombe's house in Axminster while he was engaged as a stone-cutter on the nearby railway workings. At night Nichols could not sleep and heard divers mysterious sounds and saw a blue light in his room. One night he jumped out of bed in fear and apprehension. The noise caused Mrs Larcombe to enter his room, upon which Nichols cut her arm to draw blood and so break her spell.[145] Most of Nichols's day was spent in the public arena of his occupation where suspicions of witchcraft were unlikely to develop. As a lodger his only private space was his bedroom, which, it would seem from events on the night in question, was susceptible to intrusion by his landlady.

These zones of proximity were by no means fixed, and varied according to the structure of the community and environment in which people lived. As the anthropologist André Julliard has shown in his innovative research on the continued belief in witchcraft in the French region of Ain during the 1970s and early 1980s, different zones of proximity exist in different types of settlement pattern, related to different agricultural and environmental factors.[146] Julliard identified two distinctly different social environments in Ain. Bresse is a bocage landscape of hedged fields with a dispersed settlement pattern of enclosed farmsteads that fosters individualistic social behaviour. Bugey, on the other hand, is an area of nucleated settlements surrounded by parcels of open fields, and is characterised by a fair degree of communal agricultural activity. In each type of community the zones of private and public space were found to be quite different. In Bresse the farm buildings and immediate surroundings were considered private, whereas in Bugey it was thought acceptable to enter the ground floor of the home without even knocking; only the first floor with its bedrooms were considered private. Julliard found that the way in which acts of witchcraft were performed, and the manner in which *desenvouteurs* (unbewitchers) went about their work, was different in each type of community because of the respective attitudes to private and public space. Related ideas have also been expressed in a historical context by David Underdown, who has tentatively worked out an ecology of social behaviour in relation to customary activity in the sixteenth and seventeenth centuries.[147] Underdown ascribes different customary behaviour to what he broadly defines as arable and wood-pasture communities. His ideas on this have attracted criticism, notably for the rather basic dichotomy of community environments he employs. Yet, the concept of an ecological history of behaviour in relation to social space could provide a new way of looking at patterns of witchcraft, particularly when applied on a detailed local basis. As Robin Briggs has recently suggested, the arable–pastoral balance of communities might be one of the keys to local variations in witchcraft accusations.[148] The nature of local economies, which were based on local environmental conditions, and the morphology of villages, whether nucleated or scattered for example, shaped the way members of a community interacted with one another, and this in turn could influence both the frequency and the nature of witchcraft accusations and the type of action taken against witches.

Even with the more general, scattered information we have so far from newspapers and folklore sources we can at least begin to explore some of the social arenas in which suspicions of bewitchment formed and accusations were made. As recent studies have observed, many accusations of witchcraft involved tensions *between* women. To understand why this was so, we need to look at the nature of women's social responsibilities, the space in which their daily tasks were carried out, and how they interacted with one another. In the course of daily life it was women who were usually charged with nursing family members when they were ill, who looked after the back-yard pig and prepared its meals, who worked in the dairy, milking the cows and making the butter and cheese. It was in these areas of health and occupation, centred on the home or farmyard, that a large majority of suspicions of witchcraft were generated. Considering the large investment of time, labour and emotion women put into these occupations it is hardly surprising that it was often they rather than their menfolk who responded when things went wrong. Furthermore, since women thus spent much of their daily lives in the company of other women, it is understandable that when the butter failed to come, the pig would not eat its food, or a child fell ill, the witch would be sought among those they generally came into contact with in the daily round – in other words, women. That is not to underestimate the role of gender stereotyping when it came to identifying possible witches, but circumstance and spatial proximity were factors equally as important, which is why female neighbours figure so prominently in witchcraft accusations.

Witchcraft disputes between men were uncommon because male occupations often tended to be carried out away from the home environment in more neutral and formal social zones. On the rare occasions that they did occur outside the family group they usually involved competition or conflict over areas of male economic responsibility such as ploughing, fishing and herding. This is illustrated by a case heard before the Retford petty sessions in 1866. The accused witch, named Swallow, and the accuser, Bellamy, were both described as agricultural servants in the service of a Mr Ellis of North Leverton, Nottinghamshire. Both were in charge of looking after the plough-horses. Bellamy thought there was something amiss with the horses and accused Swallow of having some malign influence over them. He threatened Swallow with violence, saying he would 'bleed him and let his bowels down', and avowed he would draw his blood if he continued to use witchcraft. The frightened Swallow told his father and Mr Ellis about the threats and accusations but nothing was done. Shortly afterwards Ellis sent Swallow out into the fields where Bellamy was ploughing. Bellamy declared that there was 'some witchcraft about him' and began to beat Swallow with his whipstock. In court Ellis testified to Bellamy's good character, saying he 'paid no attention to his notions about witchcraft', but was persuaded by the magistrates to dismiss him to guarantee Swallow's safety.[149]

It is also possible to identify how attitudes towards social space influenced the frequency of animal bewitchments. It is quite obvious from the sources that sheep were rarely a target of witchcraft, even in areas where sheep farming predominated. Henry Cowper, for example, thought it 'singular' that in the sheep-farming area of Cumbria he had never 'heard any instance of a stock of sheep being bewitched'. Instead, he found that bewitchments usually took place in the cow byre or dairy.[150] Horses, pigs and chickens were all kept in the immediate vicinity of the home, and in some cases even shared the same building. Although cows were put out to graze, they were brought in for milking, and of course spent the winter months in the byre. In terms of living environment, psychological attachment and economic importance, horses, cows and pigs were integral elements of the family unit, as is graphically apparent from Sir James Caird's report on life in the Northumberland village of Wark Castle in 1850: 'horses, cows and pigs, lodged under the same roof with their owners, and entering by the same door – and many cases a pigsty beneath the only window of the dwelling – 300 people, 60 horses and 50 cows, besides hosts of pigs and poultry – such is the village of Wark.'[151] Sheep, however, were not part of the same set-up. They spent nearly all their lives on grazing land away from the farmyard, and so did not come within the boundaries of private space. It is no coincidence that in one of the rare cases of sheep bewitchment mentioned in folklore sources, the bewitchment took place when two shepherds were passing by a witch's cottage with a flock of sheep on their way to the mountain pastures.[152] In societies where communities kept communal flocks overseen by a designated shepherd there was more opportunity for conflicts and accusations of witchcraft to arise, but this custom was not common in eighteenth- and nineteenth-century England and Wales.

If boundaries of social space differed on a localised basis, depending on community structure and environment, it is also likely that they changed in response to new social and economic developments in the modern period. The large-scale enclosure of common land, the acceleration of urbanisation, and the decline of mixed farming may all have contributed in a generalised way to the decline in witchcraft accusations, but it is also possible that they led to altered patterns of response to misfortune on a localised basis. Again, it has to be acknowledged that the study of witch-craft and magic in the post-prosecution period has just begun, and such trends will only be confirmed after detailed regional studies, like Willem de Blécourt's innovative research on the Dutch province of Drenthe, have been conducted.[153]

One of the purposes of this discussion has been to indicate that the way historians perceive the witch-figure in the past, whether in the early modern or modern period, will be shaped by the nature of the sources they use. For the modern period, the folklore evidence provides impor-tant information on the diversity of beliefs concerning witches, and the way in which the popular perception of the witch was subtly influenced over time. It reveals far less, however, about those individuals who were actually assaulted or threatened for having caused serious misfortune by witchcraft. Conversely, the newspaper court reports contain very little of the extraordinary activities generally attributed to witches, but instead reveal the mundane social basis of accusations and assaults against witches. Relying on only one source material, therefore, provides an inadequate and sometimes distorted understanding of the meaning of the witch figure in the past. When the sources are examined together, however, it becomes quite apparent that the representation of the witch in oral legend and tradition did not necessarily influence the way in which people personally allocated blame for witchcraft. The significance of this point is encapsulated in Robert Rowland's observation that the bewitched person 'asks, not "Who has been behaving like a witch?", but "Who can have been wishing me harm?"'[154] Accusations were usually generated out of situations in-volving factors of proximity, circumstance and motive. If the local arche-typal witch was not relevant to any of these, then she would not be blamed. Suspected acts of witchcraft were not automatically attributed to the obvious source.

Historians of witchcraft need to broaden their horizons, and begin to consider seriously the continuation of witchcraft accusations beyond the period of the witch-hunts. Witchcraft, as a cultural phenomenon, was not bound by the rather arbitrary periodisation of the past as defined by modern academia. For too long the history of witchcraft has been re-stricted by the framework of changing elite responses towards witchcraft. As a result, academic interest in witchcraft largely evaporates with the passing of the Witchcraft Act. Yet witchcraft accusations, which form the basis of most historical analyses, did not stop after 1736, and detailed accounts of conflicts concerning witchcraft continued to be heard by English and Welsh courts up until the early twentieth century. These provide as much valuable information about the mechanisms and social dimensions of witchcraft as early modern depositions. Researching witch-craft beyond the early eighteenth century helps reveal the way in which wider social and economic factors influenced patterns of accusations, and also provides better definition of the diversity of associated beliefs and their regional distribution. Furthermore, some of the more theoretical explanations for witchcraft accusations, particularly recent feminist per-spectives on gender relations, could undoubtedly benefit from a wider temporal analysis. Finally, there is a growing body of research on the continuation of witchcraft beyond the witch-trials in western Europe, most notably the work of the Dutch historians Willem de Blécourt and Marijke Gijswijt-Hofstra, and it is important from a comparative perspec-tive that British witchcraft historians make their contribution to what should become an important new field of research.[155]

CHAPTER 5

OCCULT PRACTITIONERS

For the majority of people, life in eighteenth- and nineteenth-century society, both rural and urban, was a meagre and precarious existence dictated by economic hardship. Many people were never far from the brink of destitution. There was little welfare provision to fall back on, only neighbourly charity, the workhouse or the streets. For those ground down by hard work for little reward the only glimmer of relief was the hope of a better future through good fortune or a good marriage. Hard work might bring its rewards, but unaccountable and unavoidable misfortune, particularly in terms of rural life, was ever hampering success and threatening financial security. To cope with the misfortunes, vagaries and stress of life in such an uncertain world people turned to cunning-folk, astrologers and fortune-tellers. These were people who through their professed occult powers could provide the comfort and succour which neither the state nor the Church could satisfactorily provide. Although some social historians have acknowledged the existence of these occult practitioners during the eighteenth and nineteenth centuries, their social significance and influence has generally been underestimated and often totally neglected. They existed in large numbers because many people relied on them to help them cope with a wide range of personal problems and unfulfilled desires. By examining the role and activities of these occult practitioners we gain new insights into the culture within which they operated. It is important, therefore, to establish who these people were, what they practised, and who consulted them.

Cunning-folk

Cunning-folk were important figures in the social landscape of provincial England and Wales. Like the clergy, magistracy and constabulary they held a position of authority in rural communities.[1] Their activities impinged on all aspects of people's lives: on health, love, marriage and business. A cunning-person was a multifaceted practitioner of magic, medicine, and prognostication, employing herbalism, astrology, fortune-telling and charms to seek solutions to their clients' problems. They can be defined, therefore, by the breadth of roles they assumed, and more particularly for their professed ability to prevent witchcraft and cure the bewitched. They were known by a variety of names, all denoting the possession of occult knowledge and wisdom. The prefixes 'cunning-' and 'wise-' were the most widely used, with the latter being predominant in northern England. The titles of 'conjuror' and 'wizard' were also applied to male practitioners. Conjuror was most commonly used in western and southern areas of the country. 'White witch' was a term little used in popular discourse, although it was commonly employed by folklorists and other middle-class commentators. Among the Welsh-speaking population the title 'dyn hysbys' was applied to cunning-folk, and in Cornwall the term 'pellar' was also known. Of course, it is necessary to make a distinction between what people called cunning-folk, and how the latter actually referred to themselves. Most people designated as cunning-folk by their clients did not usually present themselves either in person or in advertisements by stating 'I am the cunning-man of Rolvenden', the 'Wizard of South Petherton', or 'Dick Spot the Conjuror', as three practitioners were popularly known. Nevertheless they must have recognised the benefit to their magical reputations of attracting such titles. Indeed, one suspects that some of the more expansive popular titles, such as 'Wizard of the North', which implied that their power and fame extended over mythic swathes of the country, were deliberately fostered by some cunning-folk for purposes of self-publicity. Most cunning-folk preferred to present themselves to the general public in a more respectable manner, and so many adopted the title of 'Doctor'.

The majority of cunning-folk were male, and usually artisans, tradesmen or farmers by profession. Many continued to practise their more mundane secondary occupations while offering their magical services. This not only gave them a second income but also provided a respectable public façade for what was essentially an illegal occupation. Most cunning-women, however, seem to have practised on a full-time basis, although a few were ostensibly employed as midwives and herbalists. Cunning-folk were largely rural-based, with the mainstay of their business being the curing and prevention of farming-related witchcraft. Although many lived in villages and hamlets, provincial towns also proved to be ideal bases, accessible to both townsfolk and the surrounding rural population. Market days were particularly profitable as country-folk poured into town to sell and buy goods, bringing with them their complaints about witches. As late as the year 1900, for example, St Stephen's Back Street in the town of Norwich was still known as 'a sort of Harley Street for white witches, who flourished there as consultants for country people on market days'.[2] It was even suggested that in western England cunning-folk based in towns like Truro, Plymouth and Exeter were the 'acknowledged chiefs' of the trade.[3] Still, reputation was more important in achieving success than location, and some of the most famous cunning-folk of the period, like the Harries of Cwrt-y-cadno, lived in small isolated settlements.

While some cunning-folk set themselves up in business with the aid of a variety of old and new occult works, and probably by the careful observation of other established practitioners, quite a few inherited the trade from parents or relatives. In such cases a cunning-person already had a recognised name and ready throng of clients. Nevertheless these novices still had to prove by deed that they were worthy of their legacy. Of course, if there were no heirs to a prominent cunning-person's practice, then it was not unknown for enterprising strangers to adopt and exploit the names of famous but deceased practitioners. A good example of this was the Cornish cunning-man William Rapson Oates, who was tried at the Bodmin assizes in 1894. Oates actually professed to be a 'Dr Thomas'. He explained to one client, of Lelant, near St Ives, that he was related to the 'old wizard', and that he had cured a number of people in the parish.[4] The significance of Oates's assumed name and supposed relationship to the unnamed 'old wizard' seems to have been lost on those in court, and it only becomes apparent now by turning to other sources.[5]

Oates was obviously laying claim to being the successor of one James Thomas, a notorious cunning-man who had practised in the region several decades earlier. Thomas had started out in life as an engine driver at one of the many mines in the area. He married a well-known pellar named Tamson Blight. The marriage was not destined to last, though, as a good deal of professional jealousy apparently existed between the two. Furthermore, the evidence would suggest that Thomas had homosexual tendencies, which found expression in his singular method of curing bewitched men by sleeping with them. On one occasion during the early 1860s, while on business in the port of Hayle, he caused a scandal by sleeping with five different male clients on five consecutive nights. It was this same peccadillo which presumably obliged him to flee west Cornwall several years before, after a man named William Paynter lodged a complaint against him with the St Ives magistrates. Thomas had told him that he could cure his bewitched wife through committing an unspecified act with William, described as 'a disgraceful offence'. Despite his unorthodox activities, and his bad reputation with the press and the local authorities, he was widely consulted, and he and his estranged wife were probably the most celebrated cunning-folk in nineteenth-century Cornwall. It was this reputation that Oates was attempting to exploit in order to enhance his own standing.

It is apparent from the examination of the activities of cunning-folk that the practice of astrology above all other divinatory arts formed a very important part of their reputations. It was a common claim of cunning-folk that they could 'rule the stars'. They talked of good and evil planets, and claimed to pick herbs according to the phases of the moon. Many professed to be able to calculate charts and nativities. The book-shelves of the more erudite cunning-folk certainly contained a variety of old and new astrological treatises. There is evidence to suggest, however, that although some cunning-folk were adept astrologers, many exploited the widespread popular fascination with astrology, impressing their clients with the display of astrological symbols, without actually having the ability to make real astrological calculations. Thomas De Quincey, who stated his belief in astrology 'but not in astrologers', was influenced in forming this opinion after having once visited the Welsh cunning-man known popularly as Mochyn Nant.[6] The meeting took place in 1802 when De Quincey was a precocious seventeen-year-old. After asking De Quincey the date and time of his birth, Mochyn Nant withdrew into an adjoining room, and reappeared half an hour later: 'He had a paper of diagrams in his hand, which was supposed to contain some short-hand memoranda upon my horoscope; but, from its smokiness, a malicious visitor might have argued a possibility that it had served for more customers than myself.' He also brought out with him a folio book, which he said 'was a manuscript of unspeakable antiquity', from which he began to read 'in the most awful tone of voice'. However, on paying Mochyn Nant his fee, De Quincey managed to catch a glimpse of the awe-inspiring tome, only to find that 'it was no MS., but a printed book, in black-letter types. The month of August stood as a rubric at the head of the margin − and below it stood some days of that month in orderly succession'. From De Quincey's account we cannot conclude, however, that Mochyn Nant was actually unable to calculate nativities. Such work was time-consuming, and some cunning-folk, to suit themselves, and, perhaps, to some extent to assuage their clients impatience, cheated or resorted to a cheap fortune-telling publication. This is quite apparent from the confession of the conjuror Richard Walton, who, in 1733, was hanged at Warwick as a 'Promoter or Encourager' of a pair of thieves who stole two black mares. Walton was able to calculate nativities and set horary figures, and in so doing he believed he 'may undoubtedly have been Serviceable to many People in a general way'. However, he admitted that he had 'sometimes made pretences of Calculating a Nativity for Half a Crown, and that too, where the Age could not be given, no not to an Hour or two, when the Truth is, such a work could not be done under a pound'.[7] It is difficult, therefore, to assess accurately the extent to which astrology was actually practised as opposed to professed.

Cunning-folk are usually discussed in relation to witchcraft. They undoubtedly played a crucial role in the identification of witches and in curing the bewitched, and had considerable influence upon the actions of many of those who believed themselves to be the victims of witchcraft. When it came to the identification of witches, cunning-folk could resort to three main strategies. First, with the co-operation of their clients, they could employ a variety of divinatory techniques. Mother Arthurs, an Exeter cunning-woman, 'saw it all in the cards'. She shuffled a pack of ordinary playing cards, then told a client to shuffle them while thinking about 'what she wanted to know'. A Surrey cunning-man revealed the identity of a witch by heating a horseshoe, then plunging it into some dirty water, and asking his client whose face he saw in the steam.[8] Scrying in reflective surfaces such as water, mirrors and smoked glass was also a popular method. Such techniques usually operated by confirming the suspicions that clients had already formed. The second strategy involved instructing clients on how to conduct their own counter-magic rituals, such as using witch bottles, that would compel the witch to reveal him- or herself physically by causing them excruciating pain. This safely distanced the cunning-person from the process of accusation, though sometimes cunning-folk also involved themselves in the proceedings. Two cunning-men, James Murrell of Hadleigh, Essex, and John Hepworth of Bradford, seem to have experimented with using iron witch bottles. The latter made news in May 1804 when his large iron bottle exploded and apparently killed the person who was consulting him.[9] The third strategy was largely random in its outcome, and was all the more cynical and pernicious as it invariably resulted in accusations being made against neighbours and acquaintances with whom the client had previously maintained good relations. It usually consisted of telling the client that the first person who accosted them within a given period was the witch. The personal tragedy this crude divinatory advice could cause is most graphically revealed in a case from Ashburton, Devon, in 1874. A couple who had been suffering from some trivial ailment for a short time began to suspect they were bewitched, and subsequently went to consult an Exeter cunning-man. He informed them that the witch would come and beg their pardon within twenty-four hours. That evening a woman who lived nearby, and who knew the couple were unwell, on passing their house as she came back late from working in the fields called on them to enquire how they were. Realising that the couple had gone to bed she apologetically replied 'Oh, I beg your pardon', and left. The next morning the couple informed their neighbours of the poor woman's words, and she soon found herself being abused and threatened by the neighbours to such a degree that the police had to intervene.[10]

Cunning-folk occasionally felt confident enough to confront suspected witches face-to-face. In December 1868, a policeman stationed at Framwellgate Moor, Durham, was asked by a Mrs Home to give his sanction for a visit she wanted to make to a woman, nearly ninety years of age, whom she accused of bewitching her daughter. Her intention was to draw the witch's blood. The constable warned her not to take any such action. Frustrated by the local official of state authority, Mrs Home subsequently turned to the representative of supernatural folk justice in the community – the local wise-man. Mrs Home, her daughter and the wise-man went to the cottage of the witch, where the wise-man demanded that the old woman give him a portion of her dress to burn in order to break her spell. The old woman refused, whereupon the wise-man seized her cap, cut off some of the ribbon and threw it into the fire. Home and her daughter then beat the woman until she bled. In Essex ten years earlier, the visit of the cunning-man James Murrell to confront a suspected witch in the village of East Thorpe attracted a crowd of some two hundred people.[11]

People usually considered themselves bewitched after suffering from prolonged or inexplicable illnesses such as fits, depression, cancer, and a variety of other medical conditions that were not easily diagnosed at the time. The evidence suggests that during the nineteenth century people suffering from such ailments often consulted orthodox doctors first. At this point patients might harbour some suspicion that witchcraft was originally to blame for their illness but relied on ordinary medicine to effect a cure. It was only after the repeated failure of orthodox medicine that suspicions hardened, and people sought out cunning-folk as a last resort. Considering the ineffectiveness of orthodox medicine at the time, it is not surprising that many people eventually repaired to cunning-folk. Thus the Norfolk cunning-man James Stagg, a stone-dresser by trade, told the magistrates at his trial in 1877 that he 'had on several occasions cured persons who had been given up by doctors'.[12] No matter what the ailment was, it would seem that cunning-folk nearly always attributed it to witch-craft. It was heard at the Penryn petty sessions, for example, that when one Joanna Bate received no benefit for her bad legs from her 'medical attendants', she was advised to call in the local cunning-woman, Jane Lacy. Upon seeing Bate, Lacy immediately diagnosed that she 'had a spell upon her, but, with the help of God, in five weeks she should be the woman she was seven years ago'. She said the spell had fallen on her 'when the planets were crossing the moon'.[13]

The methods cunning-folk adopted to cure the bewitched were numerous and, as in the case of the aforementioned James Thomas, often highly individualistic. In 1842, for example, another cunning-man named Thomas, of Teignmouth, Devon, a shoemaker by trade, attempted to cure a bewitched young woman by having her violently exercised. The woman was made to run around a field for two hours, after which she was 'well shaken', and made to jump at the four corners of the field. The girl died a few hours later. The death of the young woman was not blamed on Thomas, however, but on an elderly neighbour who was suspected of the witchcraft, and who subsequently had to seek official protection. A cunning-man of St Columb, Cornwall, would beat the walls and furniture of the dwellings of the bewitched, while at the same time violently enunciating some 'gibberish'. After this ceremony, the whole house had to be cleaned, and the walls and ceilings lime-washed. One suspects that this cleansing ritual had a psychological benefit.[14] It was more common, though, for cunning-folk to prescribed herbal remedies in conjunction with magical charms when healing the bewitched. James Stagg attempted to cure a labourer's daughter by placing a 'peculiar looking leaf on her hand' and repeating some strange words. Unfortunately this treatment proved ineffective and the girl died three weeks later. Jane Lacey gave Joanna Bate some lotion to rub on her bad legs, and also required a lock of Bate's hair to enact some counter-magic. Bate, too, died not long after. To cure a labourer's daughter named Sedgeman, William Oates wrote out a charm and directed that it be sewn up and worn under the girl's corset.

After the initial consultation it was common for cunning-folk to make follow up visits to see how their patients were getting along. These home calls gave them the opportunity to charge for further treatment, and the cost inevitably began to mount up for the families of the bewitched. In fact, the sums paid to cunning-folk were often quite considerable and far exceeded the charges made by orthodox doctors. Lacy charged Bate £1 12s 6d for her services, and the poor girl who consulted Stagg had saved £5 out of her wages, all of which was handed over to him. He even had the cheek to ask for several earthenware chimney ornaments he had taken a fancy to. The fact that people were willing to hand over all their savings indicates the depths of desperation experienced by many of the sick and their families by the time cunning-folk were eventually called in.

The evidence suggests that people continued to resort to cunning-folk for medical treatment right up until the early twentieth century. This is not really surprising when it is realised that during the eighteenth and nineteenth centuries advances in medical knowledge far outstripped the actual ability to cure even the most common ailments. By labelling an illness as witchcraft, cunning-folk opened up a new avenue of treatment by magical means, although, tragically, for many that avenue of hope turned out to be a dead end. But considering the popularity of cunning-folk it is likely that they did provide some real medical benefits. Those with good herbal experience could provide beneficial tonics, pain-killers, emollients and the like for humans, and drenches for sick animals. Cunning-folk's decisive diagnoses and confidence in their powers might also have rekindled hope in many who had given in to despair. The power of positive thinking could have proved beneficial in at least some cases.

The detective function of cunning-folk was the only aspect of their trade which was not condemned outright by contemporaries. Rare, faint praise of their ability to restore stolen property came from the Rev. Elias Owen, who endorsed the following opinion of a fellow clergyman: 'of course the conjurer could do nothing, but the dread of him had often a restraining influence, and it was good that the ignorant and superstitious could by any means be induced to replace what they had wrongfully appropriated.' Several years later, Owen reiterated his view that, as detectives, conjurors 'occupied a well-defined and useful place in rural morality'.[15] The anonymous biographer of Richard Morris, who was admittedly ambivalent about his friend's dealings in charms and spells, believed Morris's detective abilities to be a great boon to society. He claimed that wherever Morris was known, 'robberies were seldom or never committed, and when done, the goods if inquired after of him, were sure to be restored to the owner'. In consequence, he believed that the 'country conjuror' was 'as useful as the village attorney, or the magistrate of the metropolis', and contemplated whether he was 'not of more service than a county gaol or gallows'.[16]

Most of the enquiries made to cunning-folk about lost or stolen property involved cash and petty items such as clothing, but they were also sometimes asked to locate stolen and strayed animals, and to provide information about missing or absent people. Thus a concerned woman wrote to an Essex cunning-man nicknamed Dummy, asking, 'What was the reesen my sun do not right? – i meen that solger.'[17] A more unusual request was asked of Maria Giles, the 'Newbury Cunning Woman'. In 1864, she was prosecuted after promising a woman she could magically recover the property of her deceased mother.[18] In a similar vein, some cunning-folk, like Sarah Roxborough, also claimed they could 'get bad debts in'. In 1823, she was indicted before the Staffordshire quarter sessions for defrauding a respectable tradesman of £25, by promising she could, by magical means, force his debtors to pay up. Her fee was to be a shilling for each pound secured.[19]

There is considerable evidence to suggest that cunning-folk were, in-deed, effective in having stolen property returned. In fact, a publicly announced threat to visit a cunning-person by a victim of theft was often enough for the fearful thief to return the stolen goods. As the Rev. Atkinson observed, 'the thief must at once feel that detection was in-evitable, and that his best plan would be to restore the plunder, and, if in such a way as to avoid exposure, so much the better.'[20] In Yorkshire it was usual for people to scare thieving boys by saying they would 'fetch wise man tiv him'.[21] In small, rural communities where the petty thief was often likely to be known to the victim, then the latter needed only to drop a hint in the right direction to frighten the suspected thief into returning the stolen items. In December 1843, the Fearon family, on returning from visiting relatives in Aspatria, Cumbria, found that they had been burgled of the sum of £15. Instead of calling in the local constable, Mr Fearon decided to seek the advice of a 'wise woman' of Workington. She 'told him to keep himself easy' since the money had already been returned to his wife. When he returned home, 'he found that the servant girl, frightened by the course he had taken, had given the money to Mrs Fearon pretending that she had found it that morning on a stone by the door'. Sir W. Lawson, hearing of the case, went and questioned the girl, who then confessed. She was immediately dismissed, but no legal action was taken against her. The *Carlisle Journal* decided, however, to make an example of her by publishing her name and in-forming its readership that she was a native of Westnewton.[22]

When the publicly announced threat of a visit to a cunning-person proved ineffective, then the victim of theft might then have to incur further financial loss by actually consulting one. However, cunning-folk's detective abilities were less impressive than the beneficial effect of their reputations. There were, of course, two requests that were addressed to the cunning-person. First, to induce the thief to return the stolen property, and, second, to identify the thief. Both were sometimes demanded, but not always. As we have the seen, in the case of the first type of request the mere knowledge that a visit had been paid to a cunning-person was usually sufficient, and the cunning-person could claim that it had been their magical powers which had forced the thief to return the goods. However, if this aspect of cunning-folk's influence failed, there was little they could do to fulfil their promises to have goods returned, and several cunning-folk subsequently found themselves being prosecuted for false pretences by their clients. Maria Giles was summoned at least twice by disappointed victims of crime. In 1868 she was brought before the Newbury Borough petty sessions for fraudulently claiming she could return the lost watch of Isaac Rivers, a 'respectable looking countryman', living at Hampstead Norris, a village a few miles from Newbury.[23] Over a period of several days in early January, Giles managed to extort a total of 32s 11d from Rivers. After visiting Rivers' home, where she and her partner, William Tranter, had been treated to a meal, she promised she would bring to his house the thief with the watch in his hand. As Rivers stated in court, 'I might have bid at home till now, as she never came back again, and I neither got my watch or money'. Rivers 'gave her the money in the belief that she could get his watch back, yet he told her that if she did not do so he would have her put in prison'. He was as good as his word. She was committed for trial at the assizes, and sentenced to eighteen months' imprisonment with hard labour. Three years later, she was again successfully prosecuted by two women, who had travelled twelve miles to consult her concerning the recovery of some lost property.[24]

Cunning-folk were experts at stringing people along. Because they usually had no idea as to the whereabouts of stolen goods, or had no means to recover them, their policy was to keep deferring judgement, extorting more money each time, in the hope that the client would eventually give up. In the case of William Neale's dealings with the cunning-man John Curtis, of Batcombe, Dorset, in 1848, we can see how this process went on.[25] Neale, who lived at Kingston Russell, some ten miles from Batcombe, lost a sovereign, and was advised by several persons to apply to Curtis. Curtis informed him that the money had been stolen, charged him two shillings and told him to come again in a fortnight. Neale duly consulted Curtis again a fortnight later, only to be told that the money had been changed and therefore, would be more difficult to obtain. Neale paid a further 1s 6d for this information. Curtis then told Neale that, frankly, 'it was like throwing good money after bad, but that if he pleased, he might come again in a month's time, when he must bring another shilling, and he would try to get the sovereign for him'. Curtis presumably wanted to put Neale off, and still keep the money he had already obtained for information concerning the history of the missing sovereign. Unfortunately for him, however, Neale brought a charge against him, and he was sentenced to two months' imprisonment with hard labour. Considering that cunning-folk were prosecuted relatively infrequently for their detective fraud, one can assume that they usually got away with their pretence. It may have been the case that many disappointed clients were too scared of magical reprisals to prosecute.

The identification of thieves was less problematic for cunning-folk, and choices were made in the same way as for the identification of witches. In some cases, a well-informed cunning-person may really have known the identity of the thief. If not, then it was quite easy to pick out someone in the community who already had a bad reputation. Even if they were not actually guilty of the theft, the cunning-person's choice would seem realistic. Cunning-folk occasionally found it necessary to pick on someone who previously had a good reputation. Even if they protested their innocence, the word of the cunning-person was more likely to be believed. Sir John Bowring recounted the fate of one such innocent victim:

> I knew an instance where a body of miners, in consequence of the loss of a jacket belonging to one of them, went to consult a 'wise man,' who pointed out one of their number as the thief, and, though there was not a shadow of evidence against him, they demanded his dismissal, refused to work with him, and made his existence so uncomfortable that he bowed to the storm and left the locality.[26]

A safer and more diplomatic means of identification was to give the client a vague delineation of the thief, and leave it to them to think of a suspect who fitted the description. This was often the only response a cunning-person could give when the client lived some distance away, and the cunning-person had no knowledge of the people in the client's community. In May 1859, for example, a laundress residing in Barton Terrace, Gloucester, consulted a cunning woman at Tewkesbury, a town some ten miles away, concerning some lost garments. She was told: 'The person who stole the articles is dark, but he is neither a man nor a boy, but between the two. When he knows you have consulted me he will bring the things back and hang them on the line.' The goods were not returned, and the laundress subsequently consulted a Gloucester cunning-woman, who also failed to locate either the thief or have the lost garments returned. The laundress finally resorted to the Bible and key.[27]

As with the identification of witches, cunning-folk employed a variety of divinatory techniques to identify thieves. John Curtis ostensibly employed astrology. When Neale visited him, Curtis 'took down a book with pictures and stars in it', and told him that 'the planet looked as if the money had been stolen'. Giles told two of her clients that she ruled the stars, 'and said that if the nights were clear and fine she would be able to recover the goods sooner'. Scrying in a reflective surface was another common method. Giles also practised this. She showed Rivers the identity of the thief in a 'glass resembling those usually attached to birdcages'. Rivers looked into it, 'and saw something in the form of a man's whiskers but no face'. George Lawson, a handloom weaver who lived near Egremont, Cumbria, was unusual in that he used a crystal ball the size of a large orange, and employed his teenage son as a scryer.[28] Written charms were also produced, adjuring spirits to recover stolen goods and to punish thieves.

Those suspected thieves identified by cunning-folk were even occasionally prosecuted on the basis of the latter's evidence. At the Bridport petty sessions, in July 1883, a farmer charged a butcher with stealing two £5 notes. The magistrates dismissed the case, however, after hearing that the farmer based his charge on the word of a cunning-woman he had consulted about the theft.[29] In a similar case heard by the magistrates at Ashburton, Devon, the cunning-woman was actually called to give evidence. Two men had been brought before the petty sessions charged with stealing books from the music loft of the village church. The prosecution was brought by the churchwarden, who stated that he had consulted a cunning-woman, who had successfully identified the thieves. The woman was, therefore, sent for by the magistrates. She declared that she knew they were the guilty ones because she had shuffled the cards and found the initial letters of their names; and, 'sure enough, she repeated, "they be they".' Sir John Bowring was present at the sessions and recalled that 'murmurs of applause filled the room, as if the auditory were the guardians of her reputation'.[30] It is worth noting that a few similar prosecutions also ensued after crime victims had employed the Bible-and-key method of divination. In 1867, for example, a boy was charged with theft at Southampton after his workmate and others had identified him in this way. The bench, not surprisingly, discharged the prisoner.[31]

In general, though, when thieves were identified – falsely or otherwise
– the intent of their victims was not usually to have them prosecuted in
a court of law, but to have their goods returned, and the identity of the
criminal made known publicly. This could be explained in terms of
people's embarrassment at admitting to the magistrates the magical methods they had used to identify the accused thief. Although this may have
been a factor, the lack of prosecutions also seems to reflect on popular
attitudes towards justice. When suspected thieves were identified by
magical means, their victims usually resorted to shaming them in public,
as occurred to the unfortunate miner mentioned earlier. As Alan Macfarlane has hinted, it may also have been the case that theft victims went
to cunning-folk, rather than use more formal and legal means of detection, when friends, relatives or close neighbours were initially suspected.[32]
The petty thief could be shamed, the goods returned, and normal personal
relations maintained without provoking the social disruption which could
ensue from the involvement of law-enforcement agents. However, when
people were wrongly accused of theft, then quite serious disruptions in
social relationships could occur. Considering the likelihood that in many
cases the suspected thief was in fact innocent, such accusations were not
usually well-received by the accused thief. James Gunner, for example,
found himself in court not for theft but for assaulting a couple who had
accused him of the crime. The case was heard before the Guildford
Borough Bench, in August 1864.[33] George and Elizabeth Baker, having
lost some money, consulted a cunning-man, who said that a dark man
had taken it. The 'dark man' corresponded to their suspicions about
Gunner, and, as Elizabeth Baker said, 'If the cap fits you can wear it.'
Gunner, along with a friend, Andrew Gadd, went to the Bakers' house
and asked them why they had accused him. There then ensued some
pushing and shoving, which led to the prosecution.

The significance of the role of cunning-folk in popular crime detection
has undoubtedly been underestimated, and, apart from Clive Emsley's
brief recognition of their importance, studies of crime in the period have
completely ignored their influence.[34] Although other orthodox detection
mechanisms were probably more widely used, they were not necessarily
any more effective, and the reputations of a number of cunning-folk
were largely built upon their apparent success rate. Many cases of petty
theft went unsolved, and, as John Styles has pointed out, the responsibility for investigating them fell firmly on the victim. It was 'a matter of
personal inquiry or search by the victim, often on the basis of well-
established suspicions and restricted to the immediate locality of the

offence'.[35] Faith in policing techniques was not high, and therefore cunning-folk often seem to have been consulted first. They provided a potentially less socially complicated, less time-consuming, and sometimes less expensive means of restoring stolen property.

Another popular aspect of cunning-folk's trade was love divination, and the procuring of love and marriage by magical means. The majority of inquiries on this subject were from young women. It is interesting to note, though, that there is no indication that women were more likely to consult a fellow woman rather than a man about love problems. Among the hundreds of notes written to Dummy were many from young women which began with 'Shall I marry', and 'How many children shall I have?' William Cotton, the 'Cunning Man of Rolvenden', was resorted to by 'hosts of silly girls' to show them in their dreams their future husbands.[36] There were numerous methods of love divination which could be employed without the help of cunning-folk. Such rituals were usually well known, and were widely disseminated through both oral and printed traditions. Fortune-tellers were also able to offer the same service. When it came to procuring love successfully, however, cunning-folk were often consulted. A fairly typical request is revealed in a letter from a young woman of Wellington, Somerset, to the Taunton cunning-man William Brewer: 'would you show me the man that will be my husband, or would you draw out my nativity for me. Sir, their is another young man that will not speak to me. He has walked with me twice and I have drank with him. Could you make him speak to me and be my husband if I wished? I believe you can do any of theise things if you chose.'[37] Despite such general faith in the powers of cunning-folk to procure love, their inability to deliver on their promises to love-lorn young women often led to false expectations and further heartache. Thus another young woman unburdened herself in a letter to Brewer: 'I have rote to tell you that I done has you told me to do every morning, but the young man has passed me just has usual in the street. He have note spoke nor been so far. Could you do anything to make him come and speak to me?' Other clients were not so trusting. In 1854, a Bristol cunning man, Richard Harris, was convicted at the city quarter sessions for stealing different sums of money from two servant women named Boley and Tracey, both in their early twenties. They had consulted him to have their 'destinies ruled'. He told them he could make them a charm which would allow them to have any man they chose for their husbands. They paid the considerable sum of 13s 6d to activate the charm. He then drew a charm in the shape of a heart, and took some paper in which he pretended to wrap the coins. He gave it to them saying they had to keep it in their pockets nine days each, and then in their bosom for three days. When they dared to open the charm, however, they found their money had been converted into lesser change. One of the girls had also purchased some 'charmed toothpowder' from Harris for the same purpose. In his defence, Harris claimed he was merely a 'conjuror' and only did it as a 'sleight of hand trick'.[38]

After dealing with witchcraft, crime detection and marriage guidance, the last main role of cunning-folk was as financial and legal advisors. They were quite often consulted about business ventures, and were asked to predict or magically determine the outcome of various forms of gambling. Henry Harries advertised that he could foretell 'whether fortunate speculations, viz., lottery, dealing in foreign markets, &c.' Richard Morris was 'frequently consulted' upon law suits, games and wagers, and particularly 'upon the event of cock fights'.[39] This last aspect of cunning-folk's trade presumably declined after cockfighting was outlawed during the mid-nineteenth century.[40] The trade in predicting lottery wins must have also declined after the demise of the state lottery in 1826, although, as with cockfighting, illegal lotteries continued to run, and there was also a trade in foreign lottery tickets.[41] Another area of magical speculation, which concerned male clients in particular, was divining the outcome of the militia ballot, and also the magical fixing of the draw. Both John Wrightson and 'Todley Tom', a Shropshire cunning-man, were consulted for such purposes.[42]

It has often been assumed that the most 'superstitious' people in eighteenth- and nineteenth-century society were poor, uneducated, rural labourers. However, one thing which often surprised and dismayed contemporary observers was that not all cunning-folk's customers were found to be illiterate 'bumpkins'. Not only were cunning-folk usually literate artisans, tradesmen and farmers but many of their customers were also from the same class or above. A Yorkshire gentleman, writing about the cunning-man John Wrightson in 1819, observed that 'to this fellow people whose education, it might have been expected, would have raised them above such weakness, flocked.'[43] Many of Mary Cox's clients 'were known to be in good positions'. In 1888, it was commented that Welsh cunning-folk were 'supported by the farmers', and in the mid-nineteenth century the Rev. William Keary, vicar of Nunnington, North Yorkshire, was shocked to find that it was the farmers in his parish rather than their labourers who frequented the local cunning-man's house.[44] Women from leisured society were also not averse to patronising cunning-folk occasionally, usually to have their fortunes told. A Yorkshire clergyman knew of a local cunning-woman who assembled a large collection of silverware and expensive dresses from 'the presentations of wealthy ladies', and it was reported in 1863 that John Collander, the 'White Witch' of Newton Abbot, was consulted by 'certain ladies resident in this town, who, from their position in society, ought to have known better'. He was particularly popular among young ladies from the town's boarding schools.[45] What was even more surprising to some was the extent to which devout church-goers were found to frequent cunning-folk. In the aforementioned Ashburton case, it was the churchwarden who consulted the wise-woman concerning the theft from the music loft. When, in 1849, some £300 was stolen from the Diocesan Registry Office in St Asaph, two of the clerks and one of their wives, all 'devout members' of the Baptist connection, went immediately to see a cunning-woman in the adjacent town of Denbigh. One Welsh observer was surprised to find a 'respectable farmer' he knew, a deacon, consulting a cunning-man from Cheshire about his ailing horses.[46] Another deacon, who lived near Machynlleth, actually practised as a cunning-man during the mid-nineteenth century. On one occasion he was reprimanded at a church meeting for dealing with evil spirits and witchcraft. He denied the charge but confessed that many people consulted him believing he could conjure and exorcise. He said that his attempts at disabusing these people were futile, and so he complied with their requests in order to ease their minds.[47] For many church-goers, though, there was obviously no conflict between their Christian beliefs and their faith in the powers of cunning-folk.

Contrary to general opinion, then, those consulting cunning-folk came from a fairly broad social range. However, it is important to make clear that different social groups went for different purposes. Clients did not necessarily have to accept the whole magical field in which cunning-folk operated in order to consult them – only those aspects which were relevant or acceptable to their own set of beliefs.

Astrologers

As has already been observed, the practice of astrology, or at least the pretence of astrology, contributed to the magical aura that surrounded cunning-folk. There were many other people, however, who practised astrology on an occupational basis without performing some of the other functions of cunning-folk, most notably those concerning witchcraft. The work of Patrick Curry and Ellic Howe has already revealed a great deal of the world of middle-class male astrologers in eighteenth- and nineteenth-century England, particularly those who were known through their almanacs and books.[48] I do not want to plough over the same ground here, although those who read their work will be reunited with a couple of familiar characters. The examination of different source materials, particularly newspaper court reports, and a unique collection of archival material concerning London astrologers, provides a more diverse picture of astrological practice, and also allows a peek behind the façade of astrological respectability to see what really went on in the astrologers' consulting rooms.

Unlike most other methods of divination, astrology is based on pseudo-scientific principles involving quite complex calculations. In the past, to practise judicial astrology and draw up nativities required a disciplined mind and a good knowledge of mathematics. Those who practised astrology on a commercial basis were generally well educated, and, in social terms, ranged from rural craftsmen to middle-class civil engineers. As one folklore collector pointed out from experience, though, there were certainly degrees of astrologers: 'Some were learned and profound, excellent mathematicians and exponents of physical laws; others were superficial, mere charlatans, who learnt a few technical terms with which to astonish the ignorant, and whose knowledge extended no further than to repeat what others had said, or to copy what others did.'[49] For the historian it is difficult to sort out the wheat from the chaff in this respect. We largely have to trust the word of those who knew them. Thus we assume that an early-nineteenth-century astrologer called John Stevens, of Polperro, Cornwall, a shoemaker by trade, was the genuine article because the antiquarian, Dr Jonathan Couch, tells us as much. According to Couch 'he was skilful as well as sincere in the exercise of his science, and in intellect was far above the ordinary conjurer and discoverer of witcheries and thefts.'[50] He possessed a library consisting of ephemerides and a variety of astrological texts, and had the necessary astrological equipment to construct horoscopes properly, including a round shallow box contained three brass plates engraved with the tables and diagrams of planetary motions. Otherwise, the only definite means of ascertaining the probity of an astrologer is by looking at their calculations. Unfortunately, though, very little such documentary evidence survives. The Cornish author A. K. Hamilton Jenkin, was fortunate enough to see the casebook of William Allen, an astrologer who practised in St Ives around the middle of the nineteenth century. It contained diagrams showing the position of the stars most favourable for going out fishing, presumably for the benefit of a local sailor, astrological calculations to reveal thieves, and delineations of the character of various local people. This would seem to be firm evidence of Allen's conscientious application of astrology.[51]

It was undoubtedly the case, however, that many professed astrologers were charlatans in terms of their knowledge of astrology, or, more to the point, their lack of it. It was hardly difficult to set oneself up as an astrologer, particularly in urban areas where people would be unaware of a person's background and credentials. The steps an enterprising individual might take to set him- or herself up as an astrologer were rather accurately portrayed by the nineteenth-century historian, William Connor Sydney:

> To engage a convenient lodging, and to suspend a hatch over the door of it – to darken one chamber and to hang it round with mirrors and awe-inspiring pictures – to deposit where they were most likely to arrest attention ... several skulls, a stuffed animal, a skeleton or two, several musty tomes of Greek, Latin, and Arabic literature to heighten the effect – to place wide open on a table the fourth book of Cornelius Agrippa's 'Occult Philosophy,' for the delectation of visitors, a caduceus, one or two packs of cards, and half-a-dozen gilt shillings on a tray to represent a number of guineas just received by way of fees. ... Surrounded by these outward and visible signs of his profession, the astrologer, arrayed in a rusty or threadbare black academical gown or cloak, sat down to wait for customers, who would be brought in by a touter.[52]

The self-styled 'astronomer of Liverpool', Joseph Railey, who claimed in court that he had only recently taken up the sidereal art, decked out his room in a similar fashion. When the police came to arrest him they found on his desk several old books on astrology, manuscript papers bearing figures and hieroglyphics, a slate, a pack of cards, a large reel, and a tin tube with a two-sided mirror swung in a brass rod at one end of it. He also wore on his chest a circular piece of parchment with a Masonic cross in gold.[53] People would certainly be impressed by the display of such accoutrements, and first impressions were undoubtedly important in building up a clientele from scratch.

While cunning-folk could be found in both town and country, astrologers were mostly urban based. As was observed in 1894, 'It seems strange that the astrologers should live in towns like Bristol, and not on the 'blasted heaths' on the top of Mendip; but such is the fact'.[54] For the ambitious rural astrologer who wanted to make money a removal was advisable. Thus, Philip Wood (d. 1855), son of a respectable clothier of the village of Painswick, Gloucestershire, decided to set up an astrological practice in the nearby town of Stroud. He even put up a large signboard

announcing 'Philip Wood, astrologer' in large letters, with a picture of
the sun and moon on one side and seven stars on the other. He also
distributed handbills in the town and advertised his arrival in the local
papers.[55] After such an advertising blitz Wood was assured of business.

Every city had its professed astrologers of lesser or greater ability and
reputation. Sheffield, for example, was the home of the respected astrologer and herbalist William Joseph Simmonite. He was an erudite and sophisticated astrologer and author, and there is no evidence that he dabbled
in any other occult activities. He taught in various private educational
establishments, and also ran his own Medico-Botanic Dispensary. By the
early 1850s Simmonite seems to have stopped his consultancy work for
some reason, and was passing commissions onto another Sheffield astrologer.[56] Several years later, William's brother, Henry, set up his own astrological practice from the Dispensary, offering his services to the public in
the 1862 edition of his brother's *Meteorologist*. It was not long, however,
before he was in trouble with the police, and from his prosecution in the
same year we gain a rather revealing glimpse at what went on behind the
door of the Dispensary. It would seem that at this point William was only
concerned with running the shop, while Henry carried on his business in
a private room at the back of the premises. Here there was an astrological
library and a variety of instruments, all of which had probably been collected by William. Customers would enter the Dispensary, ostensibly to
buy drugs, herbs and perfumes, and on request would be ushered into
the back room. The police got wind of what was going on at the Dispensary and commissioned two respectably dressed women to consult
Simmonite. The women paid a shilling each, and Simmonite began to
examine his books. After taking counsel from these, he gravely informed
one of the women that her husband had left Sheffield with a 'doxy' or
sweetheart. She asked if he would come back to her. Simmonite consulted his books once more and declared that, although he 'was not like
the police', he thought he could fetch him back, presumably by occult
means. The unfortunate Simmonite obviously failed to interpret the stars
properly, for the woman's husband was waiting faithfully at home at the
time. Henry, whose own astrological credentials seem rather suspect, obviously traded on the name and respected reputation of his brother. The
police confiscated a neatly kept diary containing the names and addresses
of his clients and the nature of their enquiries. The contents of this diary
were of a rather sensitive nature, for some of the most respected names in
Sheffield were found within. In his pocket at the time of arrest was a
letter from a young lady, also of a 'highly respectable position', containing

a number of questions relating to love and marriage. Simmonite was sentenced to one month with hard labour.[57]

Around the same time, another Yorkshire city, Leeds, was graced by the presence of two female astrologers. One was Sarah Owen, who operated from a small haberdashery and advertised that she also cleaned furs in a very superior style. She attracted clients by distributing the following trade card, principally among young women:

> Sarah Owen, Professor of Astrology, 3, Back Cannon-street, Shakspeare-row, Dewsbury-road, Leeds, respectfully announces to the public that she may be consulted daily on all lawful questions relating to life, death, courtship, marriage, sickness, travelling by land or sea, absent friends, entering into business, &c.

In 1853 the mayor of Leeds was informed about her activities and, as was usual in such cases, the police paid a Mrs Megson to visit Owen. According to the police report, Owen's consulting room contained a variety of works on astrology and fortune-telling, including William Simmonite's *Prognosticating Astronomer, or Horary Astrologer*, the *Book of Fate*, the *Dreamer's Oracle*, and a prayer and hymn book. She also had a 'glass of fate', a small mahogany slide-top box, a slate, and 'other indescribable nick-knackeries'. Owen's astrological procedure was described in court by Megson:

> She asked my age, and I told her. She then inquired the day and hour I was born. She made some queer-looking figures upon a slate as I gave my answers, and afterwards referred to the *Prognostic Astronomer*, and then began very busily to make a number of other figures upon the slate, none of which I could understand.
>
> She said "What do you wish to know?" I replied – "I have heard that my husband is dead at Liverpool, and I wish to know whether he is or not." … making some more figures upon the slate, she said she could not tell; but after consulting her book again, and again marking her slate, she replied – "He does not lie dead with you."

This does suggest that Owen was actually drawing up some astrological calculations, or at least making a good pretence of it. Towards the end of the consultation, however, she resorted to the simple, perceptive tricks of the fortune-teller. On learning that Megson lived in the area of Leeds central market, Owen suddenly began to talk about bacon, butter and cheese, and spun a story about how her husband would die, and after three years she would be married to a bacon factor.[58]

Two years later, an elderly woman, 'dressed shabbily-showey', and calling herself 'The Baroness de Schonlenbourg', was charged under the

Vagrancy Act. She, too, distributed trade cards in the streets of Leeds, bearing the words 'Madame Cassandra, astrologer and planet-ruler' on one side, and on the other '114 North-town-end. Ask for the foreign lady.' She was apparently a well-educated woman, and, according to an alternative set of trade cards found upon her, she also gave lessons in French, Italian and the Classics. It would seem that the Baroness was very careful about only distributing her card to young ladies. She was obviously competing for trade with Sarah Owen and a variety of other astrologers, cunning-folk and fortune-tellers who practised in Leeds at the time. To give her an edge in the market, therefore, she took the initiative to write to some of those she had handed cards inviting them for a consultation. Thus she wrote to a Miss Fleischman of the Scarborough Hotel:

> My dear Miss – I met you last in the streets, and delivering to you that card of mine, I was unable to give you an explanation of the meaning. I practice also an art in a country where one must try to earn his bread in any way that agrees with honour. As many ladies come to see me to have my services, I think you will also give me a call on this subject. You are so very amiable a young lady that I suppose that there are also secret wishes in your heart. Please recommend me to your friends when opportunity serves.

Unfortunately Fleischman was not so amiable as to desist from reporting the Baroness to the police. In due course they sent a young lady armed with a marked half-crown. Judging from her consultation with the police agent, the Baroness was not above practising a little love magic. She told the young woman that she would marry an elderly gentleman, and to prevent him from being fickle she should obtain a lock of his hair, enclose it in a dock leaf, then bury the whole, with the injunction that she must 'never say nothing to nobody'.[59]

The evidence suggests that some of these urban astrologers, like the Baroness, possessed the knowledge to deal with requests requiring the aid of magic. The extent to which they were called upon to perform or impart such knowledge probably depended on the nature of the urban setting in which they practised. The main source of income for many cunning-folk in provincial towns derived from dealing with bewitched clients from the outlying villages. In rapidly expanding conurbations like London, Birmingham and Manchester, however, astrologers were unlikely to deal with many witchcraft-related problems by the second half of the nineteenth century. In such places links with rural society became increasingly tenuous. In particular, country folk no longer flooded in on market days bringing along with their produce their problems with bewitched pigs, failed butter, and so forth. The flow of witchcraft-related consultations was reduced accordingly. But there were other forms of magic which might be requested in urban settings. The detection of thieves, for example, was one potential area where magic might be employed. Thief detection could, of course, be carried out by orthodox astrological means. The austere Lincoln astrologer John Worsdale (1766–c.1828), author of several learned books on astrology, gained a local reputation for his astrological detection of thieves.[60] Nevertheless, other less sophisticated practitioners, like Joseph Railey, resorted to written charms instead, which indicates, perhaps, that he lacked the requisite astrological skills. Written charms could also be applied in various other contexts. John Rhodes, a Salford astrologer, produced a charm for one client which commanded that her husband be restored to 'his former situation under the Trent Brewery Company' and that all his enemies would be made to 'crouch in humiliation unto him and acknowledge all the wrongs they have done unto him'.[61] Astrologers might also resort to magic in dealing with affairs of the heart. Henry Simmonite certainly implied that he could compel the errant husbands of his female clients to return to them.

These examples beg the inevitable question: what is the difference between an astrologer who dabbles in magic and a cunning-person who dabbles in astrology? It has to be said that there is no clear-cut boundary. At one end of the scale there were the 'scientific' astrologers like Worsdale and William Simmonite whose erudition was displayed in their published works, and at the other end were cunning-folk like John Curtis who merely made a pretence in order to impress. For many people, particularly in rural areas, little distinction was probably made between the two types of practitioner. It was popularly assumed that those who possessed astrological knowledge were also adepts in other occult fields. Thus Boys Firmin, writing of a Sussex astrologer named Avory, observed that 'the astrologer was a mysterious being to the vulgar. His diagrams, his signs, his terms were all beyond the understanding of the uninitiated; consequently he was regarded as a man of profound learning and wisdom. Everything about him was mystical.'[62] Yet even in this grey area of definition, some distinctions can be made concerning the nature of astrologers' relative practices and the social context in which they operated. First, unlike cunning-folk, astrologers were overwhelmingly urban based. Second, by no means all cunning-folk practised or even pretended to employ astrology. Third, cunning-folk dealt with a much more diverse variety of problems, such as veterinary advice. Fourth, although some astrologers, like cunning-folk, also practised herbalism, they did not operate in the same way. Herbal astrologers only seem to have acted as dispensaries. I have not come across any case of an astrologer making home calls. In contrast, one of the reasons for the popularity of cunning-folk was due to the fact that they frequently visited their patients and were even prepared to stay with them for days and even weeks while treating them.

Astrologers of London

The undoubted centre of astrology was London, and consequently it is the place for which the most comprehensive evidence of astrological practice is found. Two centuries after the astrological reign of Fludd and Lilly, London was still considered the hub of occult learning, and its astrologers the most erudite and effective in the land. It was the home of those awe-inspiring figures, Sibly, Raphael and Zadkiel. Budding astrologers and occultists were drawn to the capital from the provinces to receive instruction. During the late eighteenth century, for example, one John Parkins came to London to learn astrology and magic from Sibly and Francis Barrett before setting up in practice as an astrologer, water-caster and herbalist near Grantham. In 1840 the renowned Welsh cunning-man Henry Harries sought instruction from the Raphael of the time.[63] Others who presumably saw promising career prospects in London stayed for good. Both R. C. Smith (the first Raphael) and his successor, John Palmer, migrated to London from Bristol, while other astrologers such as Richard James Morrison (Zadkiel) and Thomas Oxley also eventually headed for the capital in the 1830s.

Apart from the evidence provided by almanacs, there is unfortunately little information concerning astrological practice in eighteenth-century London. Nevertheless, what evidence there is suggests that astrologers continued to drive a lively trade, even if they were less socially prominent than their seventeenth-century predecessors. The anonymous biographer and friend of the eighteenth-century cunning-man, Richard Morris, expressed not a little provincial contempt for the London astrologers of his day. In a first swipe at the capital's star-gazers, he asserted that Morris 'was not a twelvepenny fortune-teller, like the conjurors of London, who have learnt the knack of scratching a few oblique lines, which they call a figure, and say it is Astrology'. On another page he explained how his 'abilities were superior to the boasted advertisements of the London sidereal artists, whose chief aim was to gain a good living by the credulity of the ignorant'.[64] According to Morris's biographer the principal of these was Mr Creighton, 'a gentleman and a scholar', who lived at the Old Bailey, a

few doors away from Ludgate Hill. Despite being followed by great numbers on account of his predictive and medical skills, Creighton was rather
puzzlingly described as being 'unfortunately very poor'. His predecessor
was one Perkins, an excise officer, 'who was in his way a very clever and
skilful artist, inasmuch that the celebrated Edmund Halley twenty three
years astronomer royal at Greenwich was his good friend, and purchased
his library, after his death'. Creighton was succeeded by 'several of various
fame'; of these, one 'Powel' from Bristol apparently held the greatest sway.
This 'Powel' may, in fact, be the astrologer Joseph Powell, whom we have
already encountered elsewhere. Prior to his court appearance in 1808,
Powell had been convicted on at least three separate occasions. In 1798,
he was charged before the Bow Street magistrate with defrauding Sarah
Cline of 1s 6d by pretending to tell her fortune. At this time he was living
in John Street, Tottenham Court Road.[65] In 1802 he served another prison
sentence for the same offence. His third prosecution, in 1807, was instigated by the Society for the Suppression of Vice.[66] When asked in court
what he had to say in his defence, Powell replied: 'I am exceedingly sorry
for what I have done; I had no manner of ways or means to do for
myself, and my wife and child: we were in the greatest distress; and I did
not know what to do to support existence, until I could get work to earn
a little money.' He was then asked what way of life he was brought up to,
to which he replied, 'Nothing: I was in gentleman's service; I offered to
sweep the street after the dung-cart; but they would not take me, because,
they said, I was not able to stand the work. There is nothing I would not
do for a livelihood.' Powell's woeful tale of incapacity and destitution was
somewhat wide of the truth, since it was asserted on good authority that
he had been practising astrology for at least thirty years. After the experience of at least two previous court appearances Powell was obviously well
versed in the art of courtroom histrionics.

Information concerning two of Powell's contemporaries also derives
from their prosecution. A note written by one Richard Coombs was
found in an ephemeris for 1797 recording his prosecution in that year:

> On the 30 day of January I was dragged away by the Justices men and commit-
> ted to Tothill fields prison, and on the 3rd of February following I was liberated
> in the Court of Kings Bench by Lord Kenyon with these words:– You may go
> home and tell your own fortunes and take care how you tell other peoples
> againe I from That Time Left of astrology and also Calculating nativities.[67]

Six years later, an astrologer named Gray, alias Samuel Best, was brought
before the Union-Hall magistrates at the instance of the Society for the

Suppression of Vice. A member of the Society visited Gray at his residence in Dover Street, St George's Fields, and found his chamber decked out in a manner similar to that described by William Connor Sydney: 'on entering the room he found the Doctor seated at his table surrounded with all the paraphernalia of Astrological impositions; two old Bibles, mutilated charts, hieroglyphical figures, cards on which were written quotations from Scripture, and in the centre the skeleton of a cat with a moveable eye.'[68] Gray, on being asked to tell the Society man's fortune resorted not to astrology, however, but to palmistry, revealing by this method that 'he should be happy in this world and in that to come; to which was added, a rhapsodical address, not proper to be inserted'. When asked to give evidence in court, Gray seemed somewhat demented, rambling on about his friendship with the Angel Gabriel, and was rather unsure as to his past, though he believed he might once have kept a haberdasher's shop at London Wall.

Other evidence of practising astrologers in London shows that, as in the late seventeenth century, female astrologers were able to compete alongside their more prominent male colleagues. In the 1780s, for example, Mrs Williams plied her trade among the ladies who frequented the fashionable spas at Bath and Bristol and also set herself up in London. A couple of decades later another female astrologer, Mrs Corbyn, advertised her services to both sexes. She lived at 8 Charlotte Buildings, Gray's Inn Lane.[69] At some point in the late 1820s or 1830s there were enough female astrologers to consider setting up a short-lived 'Ladies Astrological Society', a card for which survives.

Although it would seem that astrologers were quite numerous in the eighteenth century, we gain little sense from the fragmentary evidence of there having being as strong an astrological fraternity as there had been in the previous century when astrology was still a respected calling. However, from the unique source material found in a scrapbook belonging to a London astrologer named E. Proctor, who practised up until the middle of the nineteenth century, we find a close-knit group of astrologers forming what amounted to a mutual aid society between the years 1820 and 1850.[70] The main members of this select group seem to have been John Denley; Frederick Hockley (1808–1885); R. C. Smith (1795–1832); J. A. Cooke, an 'Astronomer & Sidereal Artist' of 40 Nutford Place, Edgeware Road; Charles Paddon; John Palmer (1807–1837); Thomas Oxley (1789?-1851); and Proctor himself. This was quite a diverse group of astrologers ranging from Smith, an entrepreneurial author and occultist, to the chancer, Paddon, to the sober, technical Oxley, who was a civil engineer by training, author of several detailed astrological works, and sometime lecturer on astronomy and astrology at the Assembly Rooms, 59 Poland Street.[71] What bound them all together was their profound interest in astrology, and their mutual concern about the authorities who threatened their profession. It should be remembered, though, that this fraternity only represented a small percentage of the astrologers operating in London at the time, many of whom we only know of from their advertisements. There was, for example, William Parker of 9 Cambridge Road, who advertised that he was a stationer as well as a lecturer on astrology. Among his contemporaries were S. Phillips, 'Pupil of the late Stiff.', of 6 Webber Street, Westminster Road, and I. Trovell, a 'Professor of Astrology', who could be found at 24 Goswell Terrace, Goswell Road. One Mrs Graham combined astrology with millinery, and by offering free consultations thereby presumably attempted to avoid prosecution for fraudulent practices:

> ASTROLOGY.
>
> Ladies are respectfully informed that a variety of Bonnet Shapes and Stiff Sleeves, are kept on sale at 41, Poland St. Oxford St. N.B. Every Purchaser of the above articles will receive answers to questions on the most important events of life, gratuitously, on Astrological principles by a Pupil of the late RAPHAEL, author of the Prophetic Messenger, &c. Private Door.[72]

The hub of the astrological fraternity identified above seems to have been the antiquarian bookseller John Denley, who had premises first in Gate Street, Lincoln's Inn Fields, then in Catherine Street, and later at 24 Brydges Place, Covent Garden. Denley was the foremost dealer in occult books and manuscripts at the time. The novelist Bulwer-Lytton once described Denley's shop as 'one of his favourite haunts', and Denley made a brief appearance in his occult novel, *Zanoni*. Frederick Hockley, who later became an eminent Freemason, worked for Denley, probably some time in the late 1820s or early 1830s, copying occult manuscripts for Denley to sell on.[73] From the fleeting references he makes to Denley in his later correspondence, Hockley obviously had a deep respect for Denley, and gained much of his occult knowledge from him. In the 1820s Denley also dabbled with publishing. In 1822, he published R. C. Smith's first work, *The Philosophical Merlin*, and three years later he published another of Smith's works, the short-lived astrological periodical *Urania; or, The Astrologer's Chronicle, and Mystical Magazine.*

After arriving in London from Bristol, R. C. Smith had quickly risen to prominence in the astrological world. He worked initially as a clerk in

Upper Thames Street.[74] In 1820 he married Sarah Lucas, and moved to number 5 and later 75 Castle Street East, just off Oxford Street. He soon set up as a professional astrologer, and on his card advertised himself as

R. C. Smith,
Astrologer
Professor of the Sciences
Antient and Modern.
Teacher of Stenography, &c.
From Eleven in the Morning till 8 in the Evening.[75]

After several publishing failures, Smith hit on a winning formula of popular astrological and fortune-telling guides written under the pseudonym of Raphael, the most notable of which was the *Prophetic Messenger*. After the death of Smith, Palmer, who had been previously employed in a chemist's shop in Duke Street, Piccadilly, assumed the name of Raphael and took over the editorship of the *Prophetic Messenger*, initially with the help of P. Moody, a messenger at the House of Lords. According to another astrologer, named Dixon, who had wished to take over Smith's mantle himself, both men were inexperienced and had merely received a few lessons in astrology from Smith shortly before he died. While Palmer took over Smith's business, Charles Paddon, according to a note scribbled in Proctor's scrapbook, subsequently married the widowed Mrs Smith.

The fraternal nature of this circle of astrologers is evident from their response to the arrest of Paddon in January 1836. Paddon was described by a journalist reporting the case as 'a young man of shabby genteel appearance', a description which probably accurately described the social status of not a few of his colleagues. On his advertising card he grandly called himself 'The Astrology of the Nineteenth Century', and pronounced that 'any knowing the time of birth, we are enabled to read in the Heavens, the true Story of our whole lives'. At the time he was residing at 32 Grafton Street East, off Tottenham Court Road. He was brought before the Marylebone magistrates for having obtained half-a-crown under false pretences from Sarah Hamilton, a policeman's wife. A friend of Hamilton had given her Paddon's card, and, being desirous of knowing her future, she paid him a visit:

> the door was opened by a boy, who on being informed of the nature of her business, introduced her with all due solemnity into the first-floor front room, where she beheld the prisoner, who was enveloped in a large dressing-gown, seated in an immense arm-chair, with a number of books, cards, &c., before him, and in the act of making various figures of an extraordinary description,

on a sheet of black-edged paper. On seeing her he bowed lowly his head, and requested her to take a seat ... He next examined her hand, and thrice passing his finger over the various lines, turned his attention to some hieroglyphics on a slate.[76]

When arrested, Paddon exclaimed 'I'm ruined, oh! I'm ruined' and put up some resistance. In reply to the charges made against him, Paddon replied that he had studied the science of astrology for a number of years, had no wish to impose on anyone, and was of the opinion that his calling was as legitimate and fair as that of any person in the realm. Despite this commendable plea, he was committed for six weeks' hard labour as a rogue and vagabond. In response to this arrest of one of the fraternity, Oxley wrote to Frederick Hockley, and no doubt others, informing him that he was raising a subscription for the 'unfortunate affair of Poor Paddon'. Another letter, also addressed to Hockley, but written by J. A. Cooke, must also have been in response to Paddon's arrest. Headed 'Astrologie Philanthropic Meeting' it reads as follows:

Sir, The favor of your attendance is requested at the Cambrian Coffee house Bridges street Covent Garden on Thursday January 28th 1836 at Half Past Eleven in the forenoon.
Yours Respectfully

J A Cooke

Will you be kind enough to desseminate this Notice to the astrologie fraternity who's address you may know. I have been to Proffesor Shepperd, Wheeler, Proctor and Palmer.[77]

Not only did this fraternity act as a support group in financial terms; it also seems that they consulted each other concerning their clients' astrological requests. This is evident from a letter Hockley sent to Proctor on 2 March 1840. At this time Proctor was living at 7 Charles Street, Westminster Road:

Dear Proctor,

Be kind enough to look over the enclosed nativity, you will perceive it is a very singular one for a lady, the query propounded was whether a lodging house would be the most lucrative speculation or if not what other course had better be pursued – do not judge this as a Horary figure ... you will perhaps favor 'Mr Denley' with the results of your judicial investigation with best respects.

Fortunately, Proctor kept a handful of clients' letters written to his fellow astrologers, and these give us some idea of the range of problems they were asked to solve. One hastily scribbled note written on a scrap of paper by one Edward Leviner, who presumably lived close by, requests John Denley to apply his science to thief detection:

> Sir. I shall be obildged if you can tell me where Dison is to be seen he has robbed me of £27.15.0 and has not been seen since Keep it a secret that I have made enquiry of him
>
> I am sir yours –
>
> Edw. E. Leviner

Interestingly, several of the inquirers' letters come from places over a hundred miles away from London, and one wonders how they got to hear of these astrologers far away in the capital. The answer probably lies in the fact that two of them were addressed to 'Raphael', which suggests that they had read advertisements in issues of the *Prophetic Messenger* or one of 'his' other astrological publications. One such letter on a rather ticklish subject, written by Abraham Catterell, with the injunction that the astrologer's response be directed 'under cover' to a Mr George Cross, West Bagborough, near Taunton, reads as follows:

> Sir,
>
> I should feel glad if you would Be so kind as to favour me with a hoary question as quick as possibel / that is to know if ann Dilley is in the family way by me and Wether i shall have to pay to it or not or to know what you think About the matter / The Barrer of this letter will pay the charge of the question pleas to send word on your Letter what your fee is for erecting nativities and legal hoary questions if you pleas to send to me as quick as possibel and I shall send to you again I have sent several letters to you but I supose them were not directed aright but I have found it out by the kindnes of the Barrer
>
> So no more at present from your well wisher
>
> Abraham Catterell

It is not surprising that Catterell had problems directing his letters, for he simply addressed the above to 'Mr Smith The Astrologer London'. One wonders how many similarly addressed letters the Post Office dealt with at the time. The letter was dated 5 September 1840, eight years after the well-known R. C. Smith had died, but it may be that Catterell not knowing of the first Raphael's demise, and having perhaps read some old issue of the *Prophetic Messenger*, decided to consult the deceased London astrologer. Presumably, the above mentioned 'Barrer' finally passed on the letter to Smith's second successor, Raphael III.[78]

On 10 February 1840, a friend of one Matheas Davies, of Pentre Felin, wrote a letter more precisely addressed to:

Mss on Alchemy Raphael Astrologer
Magic N.3 Little Carter-Lane
Doctors Commons
London.

Sir,

Matheas Davies friend of my want for you draw figur his grandmother got 22 houses and he is might[?] hire for the them but he wants to know whether he sall have them or not he put half Crown in the letter and when you will send in answer place to send it to Mr Painter printer Wrexham and he will give half Crown when he shall receive an answer he will pay for the letters Matheas Davies was Born June 27 1812 about nine clock at night.

On the other side of the letter, one Evan Edwards asks for information concerning his birth signs, having been born at half-past-four in the evening on 1 May 1796. Edwards ends his note, saying 'I want to send many more persons figur'. Edwards' desire to have other people's nativities drawn up leads one to speculate that he may have been an enterprising cunning-man who, having little astrological training, commissioned Raphael to draw up his clients' nativities, and then sold them on for a higher price.

Turning to evidence of other London astrologers we find that some of them also dealt with queries concerning lotteries, although, as is evident from the following two cases, this could lead astrologers into rather dubious and unscrupulous areas of practice. One of Joseph Powell's chief sources of income was the sale of 'lucky numbers' which would enhance if not guarantee the chances of winning. Among his correspondence on this matter was a letter from a dejected 'well wisher' dated 12 April 1807:

Sir,

I received your and thank you for you well wishing but I was so very unfortunate in the two last Lotiaries that I never more will have any thing to do with it as I was so much hurt by it and as I am a widdow and cannot afford to loose the little I have to support me I was obligded to debar myself from many things that I wanted through being so very unluckey I write to let you know as I will not trouble you to send any more should I hereafter have anything to do with it I will let you know but at present I cannot get money to spare to try.

Fifty years after Powell's prosecution, Wilhelm Steinthal, a thirty-year-old German, describing himself as a commission agent and astrologer, was brought before the Thames police court charged with obtaining £18 by professing to secure a lottery win. His victim was another German immigrant, Andreas Mag, a baker, who had lived in London for five years.[79] In evidence, Mag, with the aid of an interpreter (Mr Strauss, landlord of the Crown public house, Rupert Street, Whitechapel) recalled

how in the early part of June a German midwife came to him and said
that she knew a man who could tell his fortune and get riches for him:
'I went with her to the prisoner, who said he was a great astrologer, and
laid out a pack of cards and told me that out of those cards there was
much good fortune for me, and that I should have much luck if I played
in the lottery. I consented to stake something in a German lottery, and
he sent to Frankfort for a number.' Obviously not suspicious of a man
who boasted of his astrological skills but who immediately consulted a
pack of cards, Mag was hooked, and Steinthal proceeded to reel him in.
There followed a rather remarkable ritual to ensure the ticket was lucky.
Steinthal demanded of Mag a selection of coinage, ranging from a
sovereign to a half-farthing. Each coin was put into a separate bit of
paper, and the whole of it was wrapped in a large sheet of paper and
deposited in the midwife's bosom. Mag continued: 'I had to say the Lord's
Prayer, and the prisoner sat down on a table and covered his face with
his hands. Then the prisoner put his hand in the midwife's bosom and
took the money out and put it in a box. About every week afterwards,
for three weeks, I had to take the prisoner £2 in different coins, and the
same ceremony was performed on each occasion.' This was not the end
of the matter, for, subsequent to the above proceedings, another round of
rituals took place in Victoria Park at eleven o'clock at night, where a
hole was made in the ground, words were uttered, a sovereign placed in
three handfuls of soil, and the whole placed in Steinthal's pocket. After
several such visits, Mag and Steinthal returned once again to the hole and
placed all the soil and sovereigns back in the hole. They then had to walk
around a large hedge, both with Bibles in hand, repeating the Lord's
Prayer. Not surprisingly, on returning from their circumnavigation of the
hedge, the money had mysteriously vanished. On being sentenced to
three months' imprisonment with hard labour, Steinthal, speaking English
for the first time, replied, 'I have read the act of parliament; I know all
about it.'

The evidence of these prosecutions further confirms that many self-
styled London astrologers actually practised little astrology. Even if the
likes of Gray, Paddon, and Steinthal were able to draw up proper nativities,
they seem to have commonly turned to palmistry, or a pretence of palmistry. One wonders to what extent Paddon for example, gulled those
customers ignorant of astrological principles by merely making a few 'hieroglyphics on a slate', and fobbing of the customer with the usual fortune-teller's patter. One does get the sense that many of these astrologers
worked on two levels, accommodating and to a certain extent cheating

the poor general enquirer who might just as easily have gone to a common fortune-teller to be given the same information, but at the same time also catering to those who knew something of astrological prediction and specifically requested a nativity or horary prediction. In mitigation, the letters found in Proctor's scrap-book do prove that at least the likes of Hockley, Proctor and Denley were conscientious about their astrological work, and, as we can ascertain from the letter from Hockley to Proctor, were truly concerned about the accuracy of their predictions.

I have already touched upon the subject of postal astrology in the context of popular literature, but it is worth returning to it as it was an important development in the mass marketing of astrology during the second half of the nineteenth century. During the eighteenth and early nineteenth centuries, astrologers had used handbills and newspapers to advertise what services they offered and where they could be consulted, but the massive expansion of the local press and the postal system during the nineteenth century enabled astrologers to develop new commercial techniques. From the mid-nineteenth century onwards urban astrologers began to advertise their services all over the country. As long as information on the sex, date and time of birth was provided, astrologers could answer personal questions without ever having to see their clients. Astrologers had long conducted postal business, of course, but face-to-face consultations made up the vast bulk of their trade. By the twentieth century, though, many astrologers seem to have made a living off postal consultations alone. A further development of the postal trade from the 1880s onwards was the offer made by some dubious astrologers to supply photographs of future partners to those enquiring about marriage prospects. This was a blatant fraud. The astrologer merely bought numerous reproductions of a few photographic portraits and sent the same picture to hundreds of different women, who were none the wiser that they were all being presented with the same husband.

The amount of detail postal astrologers provided usually depended on the length of the forecast required. Professor Cattell, for example, of 15 Upper Perry Hill, Bristol, advertised in 1893 that he drew up brief charts for 1s 1d, Seven Years' Events for 2s 6d, and a nativity for 5s.[80] Although it is likely that astrologers like Cattell merely copied out pre-prepared horoscopes, the work involved was still considerable. It was possible to deal with postal enquiries when they arrived in their hundreds, but very difficult to cope with them in their thousands. The next development in the mass marketing of astrology, therefore, would be to find a way around this logistical problem, which was restricting the potential customer base. The first person to seek a solution was William Frederick Allen, better known as Alan Leo.

In 1890, Leo, who was working as a salesman at the time, published *The Astrologer's Magazine* in partnership with another part-time astrologer, F. W. Lacey.[81] To attract custom they offered to provide free horoscopes with brief delineations to subscribers. The idea proved quite successful and over the next four years they sent out more than 4,000 horoscopes. In 1895 Leo took over the running of the magazine and changed its title to *Modern Astrology*. However, the work involved in drawing up so many horoscopes was extremely time-consuming and unrenumerative. Despite employing staff to process all the requests, Leo found himself being swamped with work and shackled with a poor bank balance. In 1900 he hit upon the idea of providing prefabricated horoscopes grouped according to the Sun and Moon signs and the ruling planet relevant to the day of birth. What made this system even more simple was that the time of birth, which many people did not know, was not necessary. I suspect that postal astrologers had been doing something similar for a couple of decades, but Leo took the further step of having the forecasts printed. Leo charged one shilling for these 'Test Horoscopes', and within three years 20,000 mimeographed horoscopes had been despatched, with the offer of a refund if their purchasers were not convinced of their accuracy. Not surprisingly, it was not long before other enterprising astrologers copied the idea of printing standardised horoscopes, and by the mid-1930s the newspapers, too, began to exploit the idea. A consequence of these new commercial developments was that the popular experience of astrology became less and less centred on face-to-face consultations with astrologers or personal contact with them through letters. Astrologers had finally discovered the power of the production line, and, as a consequence, astrological prediction became increasingly anonymous in character.

Fortune-tellers

We have seen that, depending on the nature of the client, and the type of request he or she made, some astrologers resorted to the practices of the common fortune-teller, and on this level there was plenty of competition. Before going further, though, it is necessary to clarify that those defined as fortune-tellers in this discussion were those who professed to predict the future by divinatory means other than astrology; cartomancy, palmistry, reading tea leaves, and crystal-gazing were the most common methods. While male cunning-folk and astrologers outnumbered their female counterparts, the majority of fortune-tellers were women. In terms of their social composition no dominant trends seem to emerge from the sources, though fortune-tellers tended to be of a lower social background than astrologers and cunning-folk, at least up until the latter part of the nineteenth century. The more limited nature of their divinatory practices also meant that their reputations did not depend so much on their actual or supposed erudition. In rural areas fortune-tellers were essentially the inferiors of cunning-folk in terms of esteem and income. Nevertheless, they were still popular, and the practice brought in a supplementary income for many women. By the mid-nineteenth century, though, the majority of fortune-tellers undoubtedly resided in urban areas, and their numbers continued to increase as the urban population expanded. It is with urban fortune-tellers, therefore, that much of this discussion will be concerned.

Despite the relative simplicity of their methods, fortune-tellers were consulted about a fairly wide range of problems. People might ask about legal prospects, for example. In September 1818 the fortune-teller Mary Libden was charged before the Lambeth Street magistrates for obtaining sixpence from Elizabeth Lee, an eighty-year-old brothel-keeper, who consulted her concerning the outcome of a lawsuit she had pending. Lee's complaint arose from the fact that when she visited her in Tower Street, Whitechapel, Libden 'told her a long story about her husband's death, and leaving her with 14 children' instead of informing her about her lawsuit. On being locked up, Libden said she had predicted that some time ago![82] Gambling was another source of enquiries, and by the end of the nineteenth century the content of fortune-tellers' postbags was reflecting the growing popularity of betting on the horses. Thus a letter written in 1900 to the London fortune-teller Zuleika Cavalier asked her to foretell the winner of the Derby, and among the confiscated papers of the London fortune-tellers, the Keiros, were two letters asking them to give the names of horses that would win at Kempton Park and other venues.[83]

The detection of thieves and the tracing of missing goods and people made up a significant portion of fortune-tellers' trade in towns and cities. In urban areas as in rural communities, it would seem that many people continued to place more faith in supernatural means of detection than in the investigative abilities of the police. Thus in the case of a missing baby, heard in a London court in September 1818, the child's mother, Ann Atkinson, of Bermondsey, confessed that on discovering her baby was missing she did not go to the police, but had asked her landlady if she knew of any fortune tellers in the area, 'and both went out to seek one but returned without having done so'.[84] In 1859, Joseph Monk, an old fortune-teller, residing in Tickle Street, London, was prosecuted for pretending to detect stolen property. One Catherine Latham had a dress stolen, and so consulted Monk as to its whereabouts. He told her she would find it at a certain pawnbroker's shop where it had been pledged by a man with light hair. Latham then went to the pawnbroker and demanded her dress, upon which the pawnbroker threatened to call the police unless she did not go about her business.[85] As with cunning-folk, some people were so confident in fortune-tellers' detective abilities that they laid formal charges against the people who had been identified. In 1870, for instance, a young woman went to Henley police station and laid a charge of robbery against another woman. When asked the grounds for her accusation, she confidently reported how she had been to a local fortune-teller, Jane Marshall, who had shown her the thief's face in the cards. In the eyes of the police this information rather invalidated the charge, and instead of arresting the supposed thief they went and picked up Marshall, who was subsequently sentenced to a month's imprisonment with hard labour.[86] It was the fear of attracting such attention, perhaps, which led the mother and accomplice of the Liverpool fortune-teller Margaret Patrick to tell a customer that if her enquiry 'was about stolen goods she could not give her any information'.[87]

Again, in urban as in rural communities serious breakdowns in relations could result from wrongly directed accusations, and in at least one case the involvement of a fortune-teller ended in tragedy for the suspected thief. At the inquest on the body of Mrs Mary Woolley, aged forty-two, the wife of a clerk in the Ordnance Department of the Tower of London, it was heard how she hanged herself after being accused of theft by an Irishwoman who held a menial job in the same department. Having lost some property, the Irishwoman consulted a fortune-teller 'well known in the neighbourhood', who informed her that the thief was to be found in the house in which the deceased resided, in the Circus, Minories. The Irishwoman thenceforth publicly accused the deceased, and even informed the Governor of the Tower of the alleged theft. On returning a verdict of 'Temporary insanity', the coroner called in the Irishwoman and 'severely lectured her on the consequences of her superstition'.[88]

Judging from the prosecution evidence, it would seem that the vast majority of fortune-tellers' clients were young servant women, who simply asked for their fortunes to be told with the hope of hearing some reassuring words as to their future well-being. Usually the fortune-teller foretold good prospects, such as a successful marriage to a handsome husband and a batch of healthy children, though sometimes the servant girls' heads were filled with more fantastic tales. Thus the Bermondsey fortune-teller Tamor Berey made one young woman, named Mary Jones, very happy by predicting the following: 'I was to have a husband who would drive me in his carriage, and that I would have plenty of servants to wait upon me.'[89] Contemporary observers were apt to conclude from these cases that servant women were somehow inherently more gullible than their fellow urban dwellers. As one commentator remarked, 'in London, the credulity is chiefly among servant girls, who give their sixpences to fortune-tellers'.[90] The image of the silly, superstitious servant girl is an unfair one, there being no evidence to suggest that as a group they were any more ignorant or credulous than other sections of urban society. They generated this reputation not only because they were young and female but also because the majority of them came from the country-side, and those coming from rural areas was considered more simplistic and credulous than city dwellers. Ironically, it was this simplicity which actually made them more desirable to London employers, since many better-off householders were prejudiced against employing urban girls as they were thought to be dishonest, cunning and insubordinate.[91]

One of the main reasons for the preponderance of servants in fortune-telling cases is that they made up a significant proportion of the population in urban areas. During the mid- to late nineteenth century, for example, female domestic servants constituted nearly a quarter of the female popu-lation of the West District of London.[92] Another reason was their unmar-ried status and uncertain job prospects, and the fact that many were away from their families for the first time and felt insecure. The wish of most servant girls, like most young women of the period, was to gain some stability and financial security through marriage. Considering that for many the prospect of marriage was the only positive future that could be contemplated, it is not surprising that many servants' sixpences were spent in finding out their marriage prospects. One also wonders to what extent women in service, far more than men, had their aspirations and dreams enhanced by the luxuries of middle- and upper-class life that surrounded them every day. While men were more likely to hit the bottle to blot out the harsh realities of life, servant women dreamed of their employer's lifestyle, and it was these anaesthetic reveries which fortune-tellers so effectively pandered to and encouraged.

Although some people undoubtedly consulted fortune-tellers as a form of amusement, one should not doubt the extent to which many people

seriously believed in the fortune-tellers' patter. Their predictions of forthcoming death could lead to tragic consequences, for example. In 1840 a
Cheltenham fortune-teller told a servant girl that she would die by
hanging. This terrible prediction so terrified her that she went raving
mad and had to be taken to the local lunatic asylum. Three years later, a
gentleman living in Homerton wrote to *The Times* recounting how he
had recently been requested to go and speak to his nursery maid, who
was in a state of violent agitation. It transpired that she had visited a
fortune-teller at Westminster Bridge, who had made the terrible prediction that 'she would either put an end to her existence or die mad in
Bethlehem'. A few days later she disappeared and a letter addressed to her
parents was found in which she stated that 'in order to avoid those predictions, which she was sure would otherwise come to pass, she intended
to wander as far as she could, and then to sit down and die from hunger
and exhaustion, that thus she hoped she might die happily and meet her
parents hereafter in heaven, which she could not hope for if she put an
end to her own existence'. She was found later that day in a state of
'brain fever' and taken to her parents. It was doubted whether she would
ever recover.[93] What we shall never know is whether such tragic predictions were made by fortune-tellers conscientiously interpreting what their
cards or clients' palms revealed, or whether they were motivated by some
form of mischievous or malicious pleasure at scaring vulnerable young
women. Both explanations are viable.

The reinvention of fortune-telling

While rural cunning-folk and fortune-tellers continued to ply their trade
using long-established methods, their urban cousins were more readily
influenced by the new trends in pseudo-science and supernatural belief
which developed and circulated readily in the towns and cities. While
some merely gave themselves an air of respectability by adopting titles
such as 'phrenologist', 'medium', 'clairvoyant', and 'character reader', and
carried on old divinatory practices, others, like the Liverpool fortune-
teller Margaret Patrick, began to innovate new ways of presenting their
prescience. Patrick, who fostered the popular title of 'Margaret the Clair-
voyante', claimed she gained her powers of prescience from a mesmerised
locket which put her into a trance state.[94] One reason for adopting new
practices and identities was to try and elude the laws against fortune-
telling, where palmistry and the like were specifically mentioned. But the
real force for change was the growing sophistication of the fortune-telling

trade in terms of marketing and professionalism, which enabled fortune-tellers to respond to shifting tastes and interests amongst the populace. An initial sign of this trend towards the repackaging of fortune-telling was the adoption of the refined title of 'Madame', which was rather more dignified than the familiar epithet 'Mother' that still accrued around rural female fortune-tellers. Male fortune-tellers also began to assume the title of 'Professor' which astrologers had long employed.

Perhaps a good symbol for this new development was the crystal ball. The present day image of the fortune-teller gazing into her crystal ball is largely a construction of the late nineteenth century. The crystal ball had, of course, been an important occult tool for centuries, but during the mid-nineteenth century it entered a new phase of popularity with influential occultists and spiritualists like Frederick Hockley, Richard Morrison and John George Brown all experimenting with their balls. It is important to stress that such people generally used the crystal as a conduit for angelic or spirit communications. By the late nineteenth century ordinary fortune-tellers, including gypsies, were also adopting the crystal ball in increasing numbers, but their use of it usually differed from the occultists. Rather than acting as a medium for contacting supernatural entities, the crystal ball was merely used as a reflective surface in which images of thieves or future spouses might appear. As one fortune-teller explained to a client, she gazed into the crystal for the purpose 'of concentration' and visions of future events concerning the client would appear.[95] In this sense it was replacing other more commonplace reflective objects or substances such as mirrors and tubs of water, which had also long been employed by cunning-folk. With the renewed popularity and increasing demand for crystal balls, they soon became more widely available and more reasonably priced. During the early 1870s an optician named Slater was producing crystal balls at a trade price of £1 11s 6d, but by the late 1890s prices had dropped significantly, perhaps as a result of advances in manufacturing techniques. In 1897, for example, a Mr Venman advertised that he sold a variety of flint-glass crystal balls, 'the result of 40 years' experimental research', for prices varying from 2s 6d to 5s 6d.[96] By the twentieth century, then, the crystal ball had become an indispensable item, affordable to even the poorest fortune-teller.

The rise of spiritualism during the mid-nineteenth century, and the respect its tenets and practices accrued through the involvement of the middle and upper classes, particularly influenced the way in which some fortune-tellers perceived themselves, and the manner in which they marketed their activities. Some claimed to be 'spiritualists' or 'psychics',

forecasting future events concerning the usual queries about marriage partners and the like by contacting prescient spirits. Almira Brockway, for
example, a 59-year-old 'psychic' residing in Linden Gardens, Kensington,
stated categorically, 'I don't tell fortunes. I simply get into connexion
with the spirits.' Although the police found a crystal ball in her room,
she denied, rather unconvincingly, that she had ever used it. Another
fortune-teller, Kate Ventnor, whose answers to clients' queries were no
different to those of palmists and card-readers, claimed she had a 'sympathetic gift', and 'was not a fortune-teller who deceived servant girls, but
a spiritualist.'[97]

As these cases indicate, the general desire among this new breed of
fortune-teller was to separate themselves from the stigma of 'superstition'
and vulgarity associated with the term 'fortune-telling'. In a sense, they
were attempting to reinvent the trade by putting it on to a more socially
acceptable footing. Thus the exotically attired Zuleika Cavalier, or 'Madame
Zuleika' as she was better known, advertised explicitly that 'her work must
not be confounded with palmistry or fortune-telling'. At her trial in 1900,
it was explained that she was not a fortune-teller, but that she was gifted
so that when she closed her eyes and prayed she saw images of the future.
Her clients had to place a hand on a small cushion, and she would lightly
touch it with her fingers as she received her 'pictures'. Zuleika's presen-
tational skills obviously worked well. Her waiting room in fashionable
Bond Street was not clogged with servants and shop-girls, but frequented
by elegantly dressed West End ladies, a number of whom came to court
to give her moral support. Her account book recorded very healthy profits,
which could not have been achieved by collecting fees from working-class
clients:

1898

Receipts	£694	0	8
Expenditure	£294	8	7
Net profit	£399	12	1

1899

Receipts	£1,369	12	7
Expenditure	£430	10	1
Net profit	£939	2	6

Zuleika's diverse postal correspondence, which was confiscated by the
police, also indicated the well-heeled clientele she attracted. In one letter
a young lady asked her to force a gentleman to propose to her. Another
letter was accompanied by a box of earth with the request that she would

inform the sender whether coal might be found beneath the place the earth came from. A rather moving letter, which provoked unseemly laughter when read out in court, was from an officer in South Africa who wanted to know why in the name of goodness she had not foretold a disaster which had befallen his regiment.[98]

By rebranding themselves, fortune-tellers like Zuleika were able to attract middle- and upper-class clients who would not have deigned to consult someone who was so 'vulgar' as to profess to being a 'fortune-teller' in name and practice. Furthermore, the location of a fortune-teller's premises was obviously an important factor in marketing terms. It was highly unlikely that the well-heeled would travel to working-class Spitalfields to see a fortune-teller. The rents in fashionable Bond Street and the West End may have been considerably higher than the East End, but the cost could easily be offset by the fees which middle and upper clients were willing to pay. Writing in 1911, Mary L. Lewes remarked upon the fashionable Bond Street fortune-tellers, who never looked at a hand for under a guinea.[99]

From the late nineteenth century onwards fortune-telling and fortune-tellers also became increasingly professional in terms of organisation. This was partly driven by the need to co-operate so as to protect themselves more effectively against legal persecution, partly a response to new commercial pressures, and partly because many fortune-tellers were now well-educated, well-off, and aspired towards the middle-class respectability of other professions. One of the first signs of this process was the appearance of dedicated fortune-telling periodicals. First off the presses was the *Palmist's Review* in 1889. It was edited by E. Marsh-Stiles, and ran for a respectable fifteen years. A few years later, in 1892, *The Palmist and Chirological Review* also appeared, edited by K. St Hill, and Charles F. Rideal, who practised palmistry at 4 Park Row, Albert Gate, London. More significant in publishing terms, though, was the appearance in 1894 of the first annually compiled *Directory of Character Readers*. The *Directory* was the idea of an enterprising Blackpool fortune-teller named Ida Ellis. I have been unable to trace the first few editions, but from the *Directory* for 1897 it would seem that her task was proving a moderate success. Ida's aim was compile a comprehensive list of practising 'Character Readers', which was an umbrella term that included palmists, astrologers, graphologists, phrenologists, physiognomists, psychometrists, clairvoyants, trance mediums, hypnotists, and other 'unclassified' types. She confessed in the preface that among those mentioned there were the 'good, bad, and indifferent', and explained that it was impossible for her 'to guarantee the genuineness of every person' listed. The 1897 *Directory* listed a total of 501 practitioners categorised under their place of residence. By 1901 the title had changed slightly to the more all-embracing *Directory of Occult Practitioners*, and was being jointly compiled by Ida Ellis and Joseph Dodson, the astrologising solicitor and Secretary of the Occultists' Defence League. Of course, those mentioned in the *Directory* represented only a small percentage of palmists, astrologers and the like, yet it does provide some idea of their geographical distribution. The *Directory* certainly confirms what is also apparent from prosecutions – that the vast majority of professional fortune-tellers practised in urban areas by the late nineteenth century. London obviously had by far the largest number of entries, followed by the industrial urban towns and cities of northern and midland England such as Bradford, Leeds, Liverpool, Sheffield, Manchester and Birmingham.

Another sign of the growing sophistication and organisation of fortune-telling was the appearance during the late nineteenth and early twentieth century of a variety of small and often short-lived groups such as the Chirological Society in London. Refreshingly, the most influential of these did not develop in the capital or in one of the great industrial cities, but in the flourishing seaside resort of Blackpool. This may seem surprising at first, but the growth of the holiday industry, which burgeoned in response to the development of the railway network, and also better holiday entitlements for the urban middle and working classes, significantly altered the distribution pattern of fortune-tellers.[100] During the eighteenth century, occult practitioners had catered for the well-heeled visitors to the spa resorts. The Derbyshire cunning-man Richard Morris removed to Buxton Wells in the summer of 1747, for example, in order to take advantage of the bustling tourist trade, and the astrologer Mrs Williams advertised during the 1780s that she was 'universally known to all Ladies who frequent the public watering places'.[101] However, the scale of the holiday industry of the second half of the nineteenth century was of a quite different order of magnitude, and therefore, the number of fortune-tellers who gathered at the resorts to exploit the holiday trade was undoubtedly proportionately greater. Resorts like Brighton and Blackpool attracted a considerable middle-class clientele and it was for this social group rather than the working-class excursionists that the new breed of upwardly mobile fortune-tellers principally catered.

By the 1890s, Blackpool was home to numerous occult practitioners. There was the multi-talented Professor and Madame Vane of Freckleton Street; the astrologer and psychometrist W. J. Leeder; Mrs Smith the South Shore palmist; and the palmist and graphologist Professor David Williamson. But the undisputed rulers of the Blackpool scene were Albert, Ida and Frank Ellis.[102] All three were professed phrenologists, physiognomists, graphologists and palmists, and Frank and Ida also practised astrology. They were initially based in Kent Road, Blackpool, but subsequently moved to more conspicuous premises at 81–82 Central Beach, where their name was painted in huge letters on the façade along with the words 'phrenology' and 'palmistry'. Their shop window was plastered with cutouts of hands, and packed with pictures, charts, posters, busts, and other products relating to the trade. No one walking along the promenade could fail to miss it. The Ellises also set up their own publishing house and produced numerous booklets, mostly written by themselves, catering for fortune-tellers and the general public alike. There were titles such as *Signs of Character, Or, How to Read Heads, Faces, Hands, Photos, and Handwriting*; *Catechism of Palmistry*; *Key to Palmistry*; *Hypnotism*; *Law and Occultists*; *Instructions in Crystal Gazing*; and *Indian Card Reading*. The Ellises also cashed in on the vogue for fortune-telling at charity bazaars and garden parties. For charitable events they demanded half the fees received for delineations, and for 'at homes' and garden parties their fee at the turn of the century was the cost of second-class rail travel, plus £2 10s to engage one Ellis, and £4 4s for two. They claimed to have been a great success at bazaars held by, among others, Barnoldswick Conservative Club, Blackburn Free Methodist Church, and Walsden School. During the winter months Albert also conducted visiting lectures, spending five months in London one year lecturing at the Royal Aquarium, Westminster.

The Ellises also developed a postal trade in fortune-telling delineations. Because astrologers only required information on the sex, date and time of birth of their clients, postal astrology had long been a viable practice. Palm-reading by post was, for obvious reasons, rather more problematic. However, by the late nineteenth century photographic reproduction was cheap enough to allow people to send in photographs of their palms to be interpreted. Even cheaper was the use of 'Transferine'. This was a staining substance developed by Albert, which he marketed as 'The New Discovery for obtaining impressions of Hands'. Unlike ink, it washed off easily and was gentle on even 'the most delicate of skin'. It cost only sixpence a bottle, and was given free to those who sent 2s 6d for a reading of their hands.

The family certainly made a comfortable living from all their commercial enterprises, and in one of their printed list of fees Albert proudly inserted two photographic views of his well-appointed house and garden. Over the years they also invested some of their money in real estate, including the Railway Inn near the town station. Due to their prosperity they also gained social influence as well. Albert, in particular, achieved at least local prominence by getting himself elected as a town councillor from 1902 to 1911. They even claimed to be patronised by the Marquis of Queensbury, the actor Edward Terry, the renowned naturalist and spiritualist Alfred Russel Wallace, and W. T. Stead, the enlightened editor of the *Pall Mall Gazette*.

Most significant of all the Ellises' commercial activities was the founding of the first all-embracing, regulatory body for fortune-tellers. Of course, the term 'fortune-telling' was never used. By now it had become a dirty word among the new breed of fashionable diviners. The idea seems to have been the brainchild of Albert, who was also a leading figure in the Universal Phrenological Society. In 1891, however, the ambitious Albert decided to found his own society, the impressively titled British Institute of Mental Science, of which he remained the president until 1904. Ida acted as vice-principal, and Frank as secretary. For the first few years its aims were described as 'purely educational', and membership was 'confined to the pupils of the founder'. They offered postal tuition on phrenology, palmistry and astrology at £1 per course of thirteen lessons. Albert also continued to maintain his links with the Universal Phrenological Society, acting as its chief secretary up until 1899 when it was dissolved, and a number of its members swelled the modest ranks of the British Institute.

The aim of the Institute was to educate, regulate and protect the practitioners of mental sciences, which included those categories of activity that were subsequently listed in the *Directory of Character Readers*. A year's subscription cost six shillings, while life-long membership could be had for £5. This entitled the subscriber to a copy of the Ellises' quarterly publication *Human Nature* (the title was borrowed from a previous monthly publication, produced by the spiritualist James Burns), a membership card, use of the Ellises library and museum, and the use of the Institute's name or initials in advertisements. Later, it was additionally offered that financial assistance might be awarded to some members to help pay legal costs if prosecuted. The Institute also set up a system of grades and awards to regulate the profession. Certificates were granted to members who could give two good references from practitioners willing to verify that they were earnest students of their 'science'. Diplomas were awarded to members who could successfully answer a series of questions, by post or otherwise, set by the Institute's examiners. The highest achievement was to earn a silver or gold medal by passing an examination at the Institute itself. These qualifications allowed members to put the initials A.B.I.M.S. (Cert.), F.B.I.M.S. (Diploma), or F.B.I.M.S. (Medal) after their names.

By 1904 there were enough members to hold the first convention of the British Institute of Mental Science. Not surprisingly it was held at Blackpool, and continued to be held there annually up until 1909 when the venue was changed to the seaside resort of Scarborough, and to Sutton Coldfield in the following year. During this period the presidency switched hands each year, with 'Professor' J. J. Ramsbottom of Dukinfield, Emma Josephine Purdom of Sutton Colefield, Jane Sutcliffe, Bertha Taylor of Morecambe, and Mary Morley of Scarborough, all of whom practised phrenology and palmistry, taking their turn at the top. Membership of the Institute grew only slowly in these years. In 1905 there were 82 members on the register, three years later 125, and by 1911 a respectable 157. It was in this year that the Institute held the last conference for which I have found proceedings. From 17 to 20 March, members, mostly from Northern England, but also from London, gathered at Jenkinson's Cafe, Talbot Square, Blackpool, to hear a variety of lectures and demonstrations. The opening address was given by Mrs Emma Fox, of Lincoln, in which she admitted that the progress of the Institute was 'slow and sure', though it was confidently asserted that 'many of the leading practitioners in the country are taking a lively interest in the movement'. The content of her address also hinted at rivalries and dissension among Institute members, referring at one point to the 'petty professional jealousies' at the commencement of the movement. The tensions obviously refused to go away, for later on she referred to

> those who think more of persons than principles, and these will leave the Institute sooner or later, and the Institute will be the better for their withdrawal. Brother! Listen! What does it really matter whether you disagree with me or any other person? We are only persons, and we have to do with principles, the best of which is Brother hood. If the Institute is to become a power amongst practical Occultists, this must be the central idea.

Some of the weighty papers heard over the ensuing days were 'The Obscure Side of Palmistry' and 'Palmistry in Relation to the Evolution of Human Races' by Ida Ellis; 'A suggested line of uniform study for practical Occultists' by Albert Ellis; 'The Obscure Side of Astrology in its relation to Reincarnation' by Mrs A. Juckes Dixon; 'How to erect and read a Horoscope' by A. H. Postel; and 'The Legal Position of Occultists' by the Institute's solicitor, Roland Robinson.

From this pre-war peak the Institute seems to have dwindled, though further detailed research is required to chart the date and reasons for its eventual demise. The Ellises continued their lucrative trade in Blackpool despite this setback, and from a Mass Observation survey conducted in Blackpool in 1937–38 we gain one last snapshot of the Ellis establishment thirty years after its heyday. The shop on the parade seems to have remained much the same as when photographs of it were taken in the first few years of the century. Seated inside at an office desk was Albert Ellis. He was surrounded by a lot of miscellaneous papers, copies of the *Book of Ellis*, dusty medical and psychology tomes, and a three-foot plaster cast of a man showing the muscle system. It was a scene rather reminiscent of the earlier accounts of the consulting rooms of cunning-folk and astrologers. Ellis, now about seventy-five years old, was neatly dressed and wrapped in a warm rug. He declared that it was his fifty-first year at Blackpool and his forty-seventh on that very spot. When asked whether people were becoming more or less interested in phrenology and palmistry, he replied 'Oh, certainly more so. A few years ago there wasn't much interest, but nowadays people are becoming more and more aware of the psychic forces around them.'[103]

The Ellises attempt to create a national regulatory body may have ultimately failed, but they showed that it was at least feasible in the social climate of the time. Perhaps the fortune-telling trade was just too diverse in terms of both practice and social characteristics ever to be regulated by a popular, unifying body. What the Ellis story does symbolise, though, is the way in which fortune-tellers were able to assess and successfully exploit social change. Urbanisation and the rise of the holiday industry provided the resource base to achieve financial prosperity, while changing educated attitudes towards the supernatural provided the opportunity to lift fortune-telling on to a respectable footing. For the first time, the fortune-tellers not only catered for the middle classes but were themselves able to achieve middle-class social status.

Gypsies

While the occult practitioners discussed so far were established practitioners operating from fixed premises, itinerant gypsy fortune-tellers, who were nearly all women, went looking for custom wherever they encamped. They knocked on doors, accosted people in the streets, mingled with the crowds at fairs and on market days, ostensibly to sell knick-knacks such as clothes pegs or to offer their tinkering services, but with the real aim of plying their far more lucrative trade as fortune-tellers and fortune-makers. There are no reliable statistics for the number of gypsies in Britain during the eighteenth and nineteenth centuries, though it was estimated in 1901 that at the time there were still 20,000 in the country.[104] It is generally assumed that over the period concerned their numbers were in significant decline due to the enclosure of common land, which deprived them of camping sites, and the enforcement of the Vagrancy Act. Writing in 1887, J. Watts De Peyster thought they had 'much diminished of late years' for both these reasons.[105] There is no doubt, though, that up until the early twentieth century gypsies were influential figures in the world of popular magic.

In terms of the nature of their activities, gypsies can be located between fortune-tellers and cunning-folk, yet, as we shall see, they had their own distinctive magical practices as well. To begin with, gypsies were the only category of occult practitioner other than cunning-folk to offer unbewitching services. Thus Ellen Lovell was prosecuted in 1881 after telling Celia Peters, of Dudley, that she was bewitched by a black woman, and that for two shillings she would remove the spell. Lovell gave her a powder, half of which was to be burned at two o'clock, and the rest at midnight using only the left hand. At Northlew, Devon, in 1854 the wife of a farm labourer handed over a total of £22 (£10 of which had been borrowed from a neighbour) to a gypsy to cure her daughter, who actually suffered from consumption but was thought to be bewitched. The gypsy had promised that once the child was cured an angel would appear and return the money.[106] The evidence suggests, though, that gypsies did not really present much of a challenge to cunning-folk's monopoly on unbewitching services. People may have been wary of cunning-folk, but they were even more suspicious of gypsies, who had a strong reputation for casting spells as well as removing them.

By far the most common occult activity practised by gypsies was fortune-telling. They employed a variety of divinatory techniques, some of which differed from the usual practices of sedentary fortune-tellers. During the early nineteenth century, for example, a group of gypsies known as the Natland Potters divined the nature of future husbands by placing a mermaid-shaped piece of catgut flat in the palm of their client's hand. The catgut would move in response to the moisture of the skin, and the part of the body which moved or curled indicated something about the character of the husband to be. Another form of divination consisted of the interpretation of the patterns made by the white of an egg in a glass of water. Julia Lovell was arrested at Bolton in 1909 for this practice.[107] However, Tarot cards, which are now popularly associated with gypsy divination, were never used by British gypsies in the past.[108] There was some debate as to the extent to which gypsies even practised palmistry. The folklorist F. Hindes Groome suggested in 1892 that the popularity of palmistry in England was, in fact, partly due to the influence of gypsies. The gypsy scholar Charles Leland was not convinced though. From his own conversations with over one hundred gypsy fortune-tellers, he concluded that they 'knew next to nothing about palmistry'.[109] The evidence from court reports would suggest that the reality lay somewhere in between. Gypsies certainly made a pretence of palmistry. In 1863, for example, Ellen Brinkley was prosecuted after reading the palm of a young female shop assistant: 'the prisoner laid hold of her hand, opened it, and after looking at the palm, said there was a dark young man and a fair young man in it; and one was named James and the other John, and that the dark young man loved her best.'[110] It is also likely that gypsies made more show of palmistry during the late nineteenth and early twentieth centuries when that form of fortune-telling was particularly in vogue. Nevertheless, it would seem that gypsies traditionally placed more emphasis on physiognomy than palmistry, and even though they might take a client's hand they would often look more at their face than their palm. Thus in 1875 the Birmingham magistrates heard that when Selina Clayton told the fortune of a servant girl she observed that 'there was luck in her eyes'; and Jane Penfold, convicted in 1889, told Mary Aldows, a cook, that 'she had a lucky face'.[111]

Another commonly employed and lucrative practice of gypsy fortune-tellers was their supposed ability to multiply money. Gypsies seem to have had a monopoly on this form of magic. Cunning-folk rarely professed to create wealth, probably because it was an impossible task, which would soon dawn on the customer and undermine the reputation of the cunning-person. However, because gypsies were itinerant they could easily gull people and move on quickly to avoid reprisals. Nevertheless, many were not quick enough, and numerous gypsies were prosecuted for this activity. The gypsies called the manner of their ruse the *hokkano baro*, or 'great trick'. It took various forms but was based on the concept that the client gave the gypsy some money or valuable items, which she then took away with her claiming that she would perform some magical ceremony with them, and so effect the miraculous multiplication of their value. The gypsy, of course, never reappeared and would decamp shortly afterwards with her ill-gotten gains. In 1762, for instance, a man of Crawley, Oxfordshire, gave a gypsy eleven guineas and eighteen pence in return for the promise that two nights later three white doves would place 200 guineas, a watch, a gold ring, and some silver buckles and shirt

buttons under his pillow.[112] At the Oxford assizes in 1859 it was heard
how a gypsy named Phoebe Bunce told a butcher's wife named Prior
that she could conjure up an inheritance she had been cheated out of.
Bunce said she had a magic book and could raise and lay spirits. Prior
gave her half-a-crown to place on the book in order to perform the
necessary spell. The next day Bunce returned and told Prior that she had
been up all night trying to work the spell but needed more costly items
for it to be effective. Prior then gave her all the valuable possessions she
had, which amounted to £10 9s 4d, a gold wedding ring, a silver thim-
ble, a brass ring, five old silver coins, and a shawl. Bunce promised to
return them shortly along with £170, but, rather predictably, she failed
to appear again.[113] One final example should suffice to illustrate the variety
of the *hokkano baro*. In 1846 a gypsy named Mary or Matilda Worden was
prosecuted after fraudulently obtaining money from Mary Pascoe of
Sithney, Cornwall. Worden entered Pascoe's cottage one day and offered
to double any money she possessed. Seduced by the gypsy's proposal,
Pascoe produced £5 and a sovereign. Worden then instructed Pascoe to
get on her knees facing away from her and repeat the Lord's Prayer.
Meanwhile, Worden also performed some sort of ceremony. After this,
Worden gave Pascoe a packet, which she was told not to open until four
days had elapsed, and then she left. Pascoe, however, was too impatient
to see her new fortune and opened the packet only to find it containing
a piece of paper and a halfpenny. She informed the police, and, even
though the gypsy band had decamped swiftly, they caught up with them
at Tregony and arrested Worden. We do not know exactly what Worden
mumbled behind Pascoe's back but perhaps it was a load of 'hokibens'
such as 'Dínelé se gaujé te pátsen te kerélla kóva lóvo', which meant that
non-gipsies were fools to suppose that what they were doing would bring
them wealth.

Farmers, artisans and shopkeepers seem to have been favourite targets
for the fortune-makers, not because they were in any way more gullible
than other social groups, but because they were more likely to have substantial sums of money and valuables ripe for the taking. Even though
the holding of bank accounts was becoming more widespread by the end
of the nineteenth century, many people still preferred to keep their cash
secreted somewhere in the house. Such savings may have been safely
hidden from burglars, but it could easily be charmed out by the persuasive
tongue of the gypsy fortune-maker. In 1890, for example, a farmer handed
over the considerable sum of £105 to a gypsy, who was subsequently
charged at the Huddersfield police court.[114] The success of the trick was

based on the relative realism that to conjure up a large sum of money it was necessary to start with a large sum. It would seem wholly implausible to most people that a gypsy could turn a shilling into £100, since, if that was the case, the gypsies would be rich themselves. Yet turning £10 into £100 or £100 into £1,000 seemed feasible, and was obviously thought to be worth the risk. The mere mention of large amounts of money also acted as a powerful lure. Pretending to double a labourer's shilling was not much of an enticement for either the dupe or the gypsy.

The *hokkano baro* could also be employed in relation to fortune-telling and astrology as well as to fortune-making. The gypsy fortune-teller would often claim that in order to 'rule the planets' properly it was necessary for them to have some of their client's belongings to 'put under the planet', or to give 'a full description of her planet', or so that the 'planets might be invoked', as was explained to various unfortunate dupes.[115] The gypsy would promise to return the goods, of course, but neither was usually seen again, unless it was in court. Unlike cunning-folk, gypsies did not profess to practise judicial astrology, but their outdoor lifestyle, camping under the night skies, gave them a popular reputation for being adepts at natural astrology. They knew the right moment to pick herbs, the most propitious stellar times to conduct both mundane and magical actions, and could foretell the future by merely casting an eye over the position of the planets. It was because of this reputation that non-gypsies were easily duped into handing over goods in order to have their planets 'ruled'.

Contrary to the romantic image of gypsies wandering the bosky byways of the English countryside, they often spent considerable time in towns and cities. Writing in the early nineteenth century, J. Hoyland reckoned in his pioneering work on gypsies that as many as one-third of those he surveyed moved to London during the winter months.[116] Urban areas presented gypsy fortune-tellers with rich pickings, and the ease and way in which they duped their urban clients underlines the extent to which magical beliefs and activities, which have often been considered alien to the city environment, still flourished in the nineteenth century. The *hokkano baro* certainly worked as effectively in urban as rural areas, as we can see from the activities of gypsies in nineteenth-century London.

In August 1818 the following extraordinary story was heard at the Marlborough Street police court. Two years previously, a gypsy named Elizabeth Hay had accosted one Mary Woodward, a servant girl, within a few doors of her master's house in Foley Street, and asked if she would like to have her fortune told. Woodward agreed, and brought her to her master's home where she introduced the young lady of the house to the gypsy. Hay proceeded to tell them that she had discovered that their house had been 'built on fairies' land', and that in a certain spot in the yard there was buried a vast treasure that she, Hay, could reveal, though it would take a few days to prepare the necessary charms. A few days later, Hay returned with two small phials of liquid, one red and the other blue, and all three women went into the yard where Hay explained that both women would have to give her some money, which she would bury in the earth over the spot where the fairy treasure lay. The young lady gave Hay a £10 note, and she wrapped up the money in three sheets of paper and buried the little parcel, muttering some incantation all the while. Hay then instructed the two women that every afternoon for three weeks they were to drop upon the charmed spot three drops out of each of the phials she had brought, and at the end of three weeks a large earthen pot containing gold to the amount of £600 would come out of the earth. Hay returned each day to see how the charm was coming on and to receive little gifts for her efforts. At the end of three weeks the pot failed to appear and so did Hay. Two years later Woodward saw Hay sitting on a step in Marylebone Street, and reported her to the police.[117]

Another popular gypsy trick that was employed in urban areas was, first, to tell the dupe's fortune, then to tell how a good fortune could be ensured by performing a charm whereby some of the dupe's valuables had to be buried in a churchyard. Again, like the story of buried fairy treasure, the performance of charms in churchyards was another element of popular magic which was well known and practised in rural areas. In 1849, for example, Ann Holland, servant to Alexander Bell, Esq., of 58 Upper Norton Street, Portland Place, was plundered of £48 and a quantity of clothes by a hawker of caps, who offered to tell her fortune, and then subsequently to make her fortune by burying some of Holland's valuables in the local church at midnight.[118] In 1858, Jeannette Myers, servant to a gentleman named Collyer residing in Rectory Road, at the back of West Hackney Church, was similarly duped by Ann Williams, a 'swarthy middle-aged woman, with very sinister features'. Williams had knocked on the door and asked if there was any china to mend, and then ventured to ask Myers if she would like to have her fortune told. Williams told Myers that she was not a gypsy but a seventh daughter and that she would tell her destiny for three pence. She informed Myers that she would be a wife and mother in two years, that she would be lucky, receive a sovereign on the 5th of the following month, and get a good situation. While having her fortune told Myers had to squeeze a bottle containing dragon's blood in her hand. After telling her fortune, Williams put one drop of the dragon's blood into the fire and said 'You are not a bad, good-for-nothing girl, or it would blaze.' To ensure that such good things came to pass, Williams said she must have a sovereign's worth of clothes wrapped in paper or rag, which she would then take to the churchyard, where she stated she sat for hours reading every night, and 'throw mould on them and bless them', after which they would be returned. Myers duly handed over a bundle of clothes and Williams left to perform her charm. When Myers looked out of the window, however, she saw Williams turning away from the direction of West Hackney Church. Williams, realising she was being watched, suddenly turned in the right direction and disappeared out of sight, upon which Myers went to Kingsland police station. In court the presiding magistrate asked Myers if she had believed in Williams's power to predict the future, to which Myers replied 'I did, sir; I did believe it.' When asked if she still believed in such things, Myers, after hesitating, answered, 'No, sir.'[119]

In a sense the gypsies were a breath of rural air which periodically drifted into the city, refreshing and reinvigorating old beliefs. They were a cultural link between urban and rural areas, and for many servant girls from the country the gypsies were a familiar if not always welcome sight. This familiarity was something that the gypsy fortune-teller could also play upon to her advantage. Ann Williams ingratiated herself with Jeannette Myers through their shared rural background. Williams, no doubt recognising Myers' country accent, enquired where she came from, and, when Myers told her she was from a place near Poole, Dorset, Williams, presumably lying, replied that she had been married there. As the magistrate remarked on hearing this, 'Aye, of course, and that made you acquainted directly.' 'Yes, sir, it did', replied the young woman.

During the early twentieth century the old, itinerant gypsy lifestyle was further undermined by discriminatory bye-laws and the enforcement of sanitary regulations. As a consequence, the door-knocking gypsies gradually disappeared from both town and country. Nevertheless, fortune-telling remained a profitable activity, and the gypsies were adaptable to their changing circumstances. Rather than wandering the streets looking for custom, they increasingly rented temporary premises in towns and cities. They no longer came to their clients; their clients went to them.[120] The bustling working-class seaside resorts were particularly good hunting grounds for the gypsy fortune-tellers. In fact, so lucrative was the trade in the summer season that some gypsies were actually persuaded to sink permanent roots to practise fortune-telling on a professional basis. In

Yarmouth, for example, they settled along the seafront and in Regent Road. There, in the early twentieth century, could be found Madame Alexander; Madame Lee, 'late of Earl's Court Exhibition'; Madame Nellina; and the crystal-reader Madame Tann. Blackpool was undoubtedly the biggest centre of gypsy fortune-telling. They used to pitch their tents on the South beach along with a host of other fortune-tellers, herbalists, quack-doctors and sideshows. As the holiday industry flourished during the second half of the nineteenth century, attempts were periodically made to remove the gypsies from the beach in order to maintain the social decorum necessary to continue attracting middle-class holiday-makers. In 1908, the gypsy fortune-tellers were ordered to quit following the passing of a bye-law prohibiting the practice. They promised to do so but reneged on it as soon as the holiday season began. The Corporation then passed a resolution requesting the proprietors of land on the South Shore to give their gypsy tenants notice to quit. The landowners were loath to do so as the fortune-tellers were paying between £20 and £25 a season for their plots, but they were pressured into acquiescing in January 1909. The gypsy fortune-tellers packed up slowly while an appeal was made to secure exemption from the ban for some of those born on the sands. In April the police finally moved in and charged Louisa Young, Adelaide Smith, Clara Boswell, and the eighty-year-old Regenda Townsend, who had also been prosecuted back in the 1891 raid. Only the descendants of Sarah Boswell were able to retain their pitch, while the rest either took houses or pitched tents on the outskirts of town.

The seaside gypsy fortune-tellers were certainly looked down upon by the middle-class practitioners, who considered them to be socially inferior and generally ignorant of the 'true' predictive sciences. It is not surprising, therefore, that the *Directory of Occult Practitioners* failed to mention any of Blackpool's sedentary gypsy fortune-tellers. In terms of clientele it would seem that the gypsies catered largely for the working-class holiday-makers, while the likes of the Ellises targeted those of their own social group. The gypsies may have charged less as a result, but the sheer number of clients meant that in 1909 some were earning as much as £10 a day. The two groups were not, therefore, necessarily in direct competition with each other. However, as the middle classes turned their backs on the seaside holiday, and the working classes effectively came to dominate the resorts, the genteel fortune-tellers found themselves eventually having to compete for the same trade as the gypsies. This was not at all to their liking. As Albert Ellis complained in 1937, 'Nowadays we have to cater for the masses instead of the classes.'

Fortune-telling and the First World War

The period of the First World War was a lucrative time for fortune-tellers. Under the title of 'Fortune-telling and the War', an editorial in *The Justice of the Peace* bemoaned that the 'troubled waters created by the war have favoured the operations of those who dangle the dazzling bait of "magic" before the less wary fish of the human shoal.'[121] There was certainly a substantial increase in their numbers. In 1917 it was estimated that just in and around the Edgeware Road in London as many as thirty fortune-tellers had established themselves since the beginning of the war. In one metropolitan division alone the police had calculated that there were at least fifty-three female practitioners.[122] Some advertised quite openly, even to the extent of having signboards placed in the streets with slogans such as 'excellent advice in war-time'.[123] Not surprisingly, as the fortune-tellers multiplied they attracted more police attention. Prior to the First World War there had been intermittent campaigns against fortune-tellers, but the authorities now exhibited increased concern about their effect on public morale. As in any period of wartime, the state became suspicious if not slightly paranoid about any influence that might undermine the jingoistic and misleading propaganda being put out. When thoroughly controlled, fortune-telling could be effectively employed for propaganda purposes, but when uncontrolled, as it obviously was, it was seen as a danger to the state. Most fortune-tellers were well aware of the illegality of their trade, though, and avoided making general predictions about the war effort, and stuck to the fortunes of specific individuals. Nevertheless there were a few who, either out of sincere belief in their powers of foresight, or out of opportunism to make a name for themselves, ventured into divinatory no-man's-land. Some boasted of their foresight with the comfort of hindsight. Thus the gypsy fortune-teller Selina Smith claimed at her trial at Reading in 1918 that she had told the Kaiser's fortune twenty-seven years previously and had accurately predicted the coming war with Germany.[124] However, the precarious position of the fortune-tellers was undermined by those few who made bold and disturbing prophecies about forthcoming disasters. In 1917, for example, Laura Jones was summoned before the Liverpool magistrates for a third time. At a clairvoyant service she had said that she saw in a cloud 'great fighting in Salonika', and that they might expect a terrible British disaster in the coming week that would affect all of those present.[125]

For those relatives and friends with loved ones fighting in the trenches the war was obviously a time of great uncertainty and anxiety, and it is not surprising that many sought some comfort in the reassuring future certainties dealt out by the fortune-tellers. Indeed, it is no coincidence that spiritualism also reached a peak of popularity at the same time.[126] Most of our evidence for this mass resort to fortune-telling during war-time derives from the prosecution of its practitioners. When, for example, Beatrice Smith was tried at the Marylebone police-court for fortune-telling in 1916, a police inspector said that he had seen twenty to thirty women enter the premises, most of whom were relatives of men fighting at the front.[127] A young woman who gave evidence at the trial of the fortune-teller Elizabeth Sixsmith said that she consulted her to enquire about her brother who was at the front. Sixsmith looked into a crystal ball and reassured her that he would not be wounded, and would return on leave before Christmas.[128] Fortune-tellers predicted mostly what wives, sisters and mothers wanted to hear – that their menfolk would be return-ing to them alive. Yet the scale of the slaughter in the trenches was so great that many soldiers would never return home. It was, perhaps, the realisation of this awful truth that led the fortune-teller Marie Charles, otherwise known as Madame Charles, to inform a number of her clients that they would never see their loved ones again. In 1916 she told one lady whose husband had just returned from Egypt, and was about to leave for France, that he 'would never return to her'. She also told a group of women who had sons in the army that 'she did not like to tell it, but one of the young men would not come back'. Charles was probably realistic in her assessment, but, nevertheless, the anguish caused to her clients in this way must have been great. According to the prosecuting lawyer at her trial, 'pretences to foretell were doing much more harm now than in other days and many women had been most grievously distressed.'[129]

Soldiers about to go to the front, particularly those who were returning after leave, must have been burdened with a terrible fear of the un-known, of the knowledge that only sheer luck might prevent them being the next victim of the war. Some soldiers carried charms and amulets for protection, such as mandrake roots, four-leaf clovers, old beads and bones. Holed stones, which had long been used to ward of witchcraft, were also employed.[130] It is not surprising, therefore, that when police raided the premises of fortune-tellers they often found soldiers as well as their female relatives among their clients. Elizabeth Sixsmith, known professionally as 'Madam Betty', told the police in 1916 that she was very busy with soldiers, and at the time Agnes McDonald, alias 'Madame Vox', was arrested, she was engaged in examining the palm of a wounded officer through a magnifying glass. It is obvious from the prosecution evidence that it was not just lowly privates who sought out fortune-tellers. Even high-ranking army staff were drawn to their dens. When, in 1918, Detective Inspector Bedford paid a visit to the house of Marie Charles in Brompton Road, he found her being consulted by a brigadier-general no less. When Bedford presented her with an arrest-warrant, the brigadier-general spoke up for her, saying 'Madame is a friend of mine. I have just dropped in to see her. I am going to the front to-morrow. She had just cut the cards, but I don't know what she was going to tell me. I paid her no money.'[131] The fact that the two undercover detectives who arrested Louise Hutchinson disguised themselves as army lieutenants is also indicative of the large numbers of soldiers passing through the fortune-tellers' doors. She looked at their palms and told them they would be wounded again. She closed the interview by saying that she would obtain charms or medals for the soldiers, and have them blessed before sending them on.[132]

Whether one believes in fortune-telling or not, it is worth asking oneself whether the fortune-tellers were really behaving any worse than the government, who misled the people with their comforting propaganda in the name of the war effort. In fact, apart from those few who predicted death and disaster, fortune-tellers were, for all the calumny heaped upon their heads, actually doing an admirable job for the government in that they were helping to assuage the nation's fears. On a purely individual level they acted as a form of counselling service for both soldiers and their relatives. They were in a sense an alternative clergy, the representatives of omniscience rather than omnipotence, providing supernatural succour for the masses. But such aid did not come for free, and while many fortune-tellers undoubtedly believed in what they practised and predicted, there were many who cynically set themselves up as fortune-tellers when they saw how much money could be made out of the distress and vulnerability of others in wartime.

As has already been discussed in the first chapter of this book, attitudes towards fortune-telling changed noticeably after the First World War. Part of the reason for that change was surely due to the experience of those years. Fortune-telling entered the popular consciousness to an extent that it had never done in peacetime. During the war many people who had probably never been to a fortune-teller before found themselves seeking their advice. Men, in particular, now poured into the parlours of fortune-tellers up and down the country. They had previously made up only a small minority of fortune-tellers' clients, and were more likely to dismiss as rubbish what they had not experienced at first hand. Now thousands of men, not a few of them part of the middle-class establishment, fell back on any form of reassurance which could be found, even if they had previously deemed it 'superstitious'. If a fortune-teller's positive predictions came true, then few of her clients would ever forget it. Going through the minds of many both during and after the war must have been the thought, 'perhaps there is something in it after all'.

For several hundred years, the occult practitioners described in this chapter had thrived in both town and country. Contrary to the received view, it was not just the labouring classes who sought them out, but at various times, and under certain circumstances, representatives of all social groups. Servant girls and society ladies, labourers and prosperous farmers, privates and generals all opened their purses and put their faith in cunning-folk, fortune-tellers and astrologers. In this lay their strength. If it was only the lower classes who supported occult practitioners they would have had less social influence, and might have been more effectively suppressed. However, during the early twentieth century the fortunes of cunning-folk diverged quite dramatically from those of astrologers and fortune-tellers. While the latter continued to thrive, cunning-folk went into terminal decline. Why was it that they were unable to follow the successful path of their occult counterparts?

As has been shown, fortune-tellers and astrologers were able to adapt and diversify when faced with new social trends during the nineteenth century. Cunning-folk proved to be far less flexible. Professionalism became an increasingly essential prerequisite for the survival of any group of service providers, but, because cunning-folk remained largely rural based in a by now urban dominated society, they were consequently little prepared to explore and exploit the new avenues of marketing, commercialisation and organisation that were opening up. Furthermore, unlike fortune-tellers and astrologers, cunning-folk were manipulators as well as interpreters of occult forces. The basis of their existence depended on a way of life very much dictated by the supernatural. However, as people's lives became more financially stable, they were less tempted to achieve security through the magical manipulation of the world around them, and so cunning-folk became increasingly irrelevant in people's lives. As a result, there was an undoubted diminution in the traditional range of business conducted by occult practitioners. People no longer resorted to magic to detect lost or stolen property, for example. The most influential impact on cunning-folk, though, was the dwindling trade in unbewitching. Witchcraft was the glue which connected all their various activities. Divination was used to identify witches, charms were written to keep them away, herbalism was used to cure the bewitched. It was their role as unbewitchers which primarily distinguished them from astrologers, fortune-tellers and herbalists. Therefore, to really understand the decline of cunning-folk during the early twentieth century, it is necessary to consider the reasons for the declining popular belief in witchcraft.

CHAPTER 6

DECLINING BELIEF
IN WITCHCRAFT

It is important to remember that while some aspects of popular magic declined, others continued and even thrived in the fast-changing world of the early twentieth century. Magical beliefs were not all bound up with each other like some monumental cultural artefact. Social, economic and intellectual changes which affected one expression of popular magic did not necessarily have an impact on others. Specific magical practices declined, continued, or even advanced depending on different and often localised social trends. In some parts of western England and Wales, for instance, people continued up until the 1970s to resort to charmers to heal simple ailments like warts. Astrology and fortune-telling are alive and well today, though in a rather narrow and degraded form. Through the power of the mass media, they have gained a social credibility not witnessed since the seventeenth century. Conversely, a raft of long-held magical beliefs and practices concerning well-worship, fairies, theft magic, love magic, and, most important of all, witchcraft, disappeared by the first half of the present century. There is, therefore, no overall unifying explanation for the decline of magic, and, although many magical beliefs were interconnected, it is necessary to recognise the distinctiveness of each belief or practice in order to understand how they were individually affected by social, economic and intellectual pressures. This is why I have restricted myself in this final chapter to considering only the decline of witchcraft.

When scrutinised carefully, many previously held assumptions concerning the declining popular belief in witchcraft and magic prove to have little foundation. Historians and other social commentators, both past and present, who have perpetuated eighteenth- and nineteenth-century assumptions concerning social 'progress' (education as the great moral improver, cities as centres of rationality, the efficacy of authoritarian censure), have, because of those assumptions, not even bothered to look for signs of the continuance of magical beliefs in certain cultural contexts such as urban areas. Once the blinkers of societal progress are removed, and we begin to look more closely at popular mentalities, it becomes apparent that growing educational provision and increasing popular literacy, rather than eradicating the world of magic, may actually have helped sustain and even promote certain magical beliefs and practices. Greater access to medical provision, rather than usurping the role of occult medical practitioners and magical medicine, merely provided greater choice in the medical market place. Attempts by the authorities at suppressing popular magic were only partially successful, and even then, only indirectly as a result of increasing state control over communal policing and the concomitant decline of traditional social-control mechanisms. The attempt at suppressing occult practitioners was patently a failure.

If further confirmation were needed that long-held beliefs concerning witchcraft and magic can coexist with the trappings of modernity, we need only look at the numerous ethnographic studies of the continued manifestation of witchcraft and magic in contemporary Europe.[1] Just across the English channel, in the villages and small towns of Normandy, people continue to complain of *maleficium*, and people still accrue a reputation for witchcraft. In the last decade, I have been informed of several cases in the department of Seine-Maritime where people have lodged official complaints against those accusing them of witchcraft.[2] Unbewitchers still drive a lively trade, and it is not uncommon to find their advertising handbills in one's letter box. This knowledge provokes the important question of why it is that in Normandy, and elsewhere in France, some people are still considered to exercise the power of witchcraft, and accusations of witchcraft still occur, when they had discontinued in England and Wales by mid-century? Unfortunately, this is not the place to enter into a detailed comparative analysis of social change, culture and belief in the two countries, though an important study waits to be done along these lines, but the knowledge that witchcraft still functions in Normandy proves that many of the beliefs discussed in this book can function in modern western society. If we are to understand the decline of witchcraft in England and Wales, therefore, we must divest ourselves of any pre-conceptions regarding the concept of social and intellectual progress.

Measuring declining belief

How can the declining popular belief in witchcraft, or any other magical belief for that matter, be measured? As Charles Phythian-Adams has observed, there 'are no censuses of mental attitudes to help us.'[3] Quantifying an individual's level of belief in the supernatural, whether it be in religious or magical terms, is hard enough, particularly when the strength of his or her belief is likely to fluctuate over time and according to personal circumstances, but measuring a whole nation's thought processes is an impossibility. Although it is not feasible to measure belief itself, it is at least possible to measure the external expressions and physical manifestations of some beliefs.

One way that we can assess the declining belief in witchcraft is by examining the frequency with which people conducted related magical rituals and observances. The horseshoe, for example, was once a very potent charm against witchcraft. To give but one of many instances, Samuel Bamford the radical recalled stopping at a humble pothouse in Redburn, and on his finding a horseshoe nailed inside the weatherboard of the door, the old dame of the house informed him, 'with perfect seriousness, that it was to keep all witches and bewitched persons and things out of the place, and that so long as it remained there nothing under the influence of witchcraft could enter.'[4] This practice certainly declined during the second half of the nineteenth century. Thus John Glyde, writing in 1872, remarked that its presence on cottage doors in Norfolk was 'much less than it was some years ago'.[5] The presence or disappearance of physical artefacts like the horseshoe can also help identify localised trends. In the West End of London, for example, the practice of placing a horseshoe outside the door declined significantly after the 1820s, suggesting that the threat of witchcraft diminished in some large urban settlements at least fifty years before it did in many rural areas.[6] However, there are a couple of reasons why caution is necessary when attempting to use magical practices as a measure of belief. First, it has to be acknowledged that just because a practice or custom falls into disuse this does not necessarily indicate a decline in its associated belief. To give one obvious example, during the early modern period the method of divination by the sieve and shears was a very popular practice, but for unknown reasons it seems largely to have died out by the nineteenth century. What is obvious is that the practice did not disappear due to a declining belief in divination, since related practices such as the Bible and key remained popular until the early twentieth century. Second, the meaning of a magical practice can sometimes alter over time. Thus the tradition of placing a horseshoe above the door did not necessarily decline at a rate concomitant with the declining belief in witchcraft. Although it certainly began to lose its function as a preventative against witchcraft, it was still looked upon as a good-luck charm. Consequently, some people continued to nail horseshoes to doors, or at least refrained from removing them. When, in 1881, a contributor to the *Folklore Record* saw a horseshoe over a building at Southampton railway station he asked a porter its significance, and was told that the workers had put it there for luck. Witchcraft was not mentioned.[7]

In his seminal study of religion and society in nineteenth-century Lincolnshire, James Obelkevitch viewed the latter process as being symptomatic of a general transition whereby magic 'subsided to the level of luck, its impersonal lowest common denominator'.[8] For Obelkevitch luck is a 'residual category' representing the last stage in the long-term decline of magical beliefs during the nineteenth century. I am not sure, though, that this is the best way of interpreting the phenomenon. The concept of luck was a key constituent of popular magic, and many practices and observances were concerned with preventing bad luck and promoting good luck, whether it be through marriage, financial prosperity or good health. Witchcraft was just one aspect of the popular experience of misfortune or bad luck, albeit a very important one. What was happening during the late nineteenth century was that many long-held magical beliefs and practices such as the horseshoe were undergoing a diminution in terms of their scope and potency. The complex structure of magical beliefs was being partially dismantled, revealing the core belief in promoting good luck and preventing bad luck. There was a stripping away of long-held supernatural explanations for misfortune such as witchcraft until it came to the point that people no longer sought explanations for bad luck, although they continued to avert the possibility of it occurring. Thus, although the horseshoe lost its dominant function as an anti-witchcraft measure, it retained its more general purpose as a charm against misfortune. Luck, therefore, was not merely a residual category but was both the beginning and end point of popular magic

Another gauge of declining belief in witchcraft is the frequency of accusations. The problem, of course, is that most accusations went unrecorded and are completely unquantifiable. However, the prosecution cases of those who threatened, intimidated or assaulted supposed witches do provide some indication. I cannot give any significant statistical data, since that would require the extensive systematic surveying of a large selection of local newspapers from around the country. Nevertheless, my own substantial but incomplete survey of newspapers from the county of Somerset, and partial surveys of newspapers from elsewhere in the country, suggests that from a peak in prosecutions during the 1850s and 1860s, there was a significant decline from the late 1880s onwards. By the 1890s, cases concerning witchcraft conflicts in towns had virtually ceased, though a trickle of rural cases continued up until the 1930s.[9] Of course, this decline in recorded accusations does not necessarily indicate declining belief. It is possible, for instance, that, faced with more effective policing, people became increasingly wary about assaulting or threatening suspected witches, and employed alternative means of negating the symptoms of witchcraft. This may, indeed, have contributed partly to the decline of reverse witch-trials during the late nineteenth century. But when other evidence is taken into account, the prosecution data, albeit only impressionistic at the present stage of research, does at least indicate that face-to-face confrontations between witch and victim were occurring less and less. It is worthwhile looking more closely now at three late court cases concerning witchcraft, both as a record of the last of the reverse witch-trials and to see if the circumstances behind them tell us anything further about the decline of witchcraft.

In December 1924, Alfred John Matthews, aged forty-three, a small-holder of Clyst St Lawrence, Devon, appeared at the Cullompton petty sessions for scratching and drawing blood from Ellen Garnsworthy, a middle-aged, married woman of the same village. Matthews had a sow which would not fatten, and suspected it had been ill-wished by Garnsworthy, who lived only two doors away from him. On 21 November, Garnsworthy was on her way to fetch water from the village pump, but as she passed Matthews's door he took the opportunity to scratch her with a pin, saying 'perhaps that will teach you to leave other people's things alone'. Matthews declared in court that Garnsworthy was in possession of 'a crystal – a globe like thing. The police have to protect the public in such a matter, and I do not see why I should not ask them to make a raid on her house in search of such a thing.' One of the magistrates, A. W. Hopkins, then asked if he was alleging witchcraft, to which Matthews replied in the affirmative. When Hopkins remarked that 'such a fallacy died out years ago', Matthews forthrightly asserted, 'Oh, no, it didn't. It hasn't with some of us.' To Matthews's amazement, he was sentenced to a month's imprisonment. Before being taken away he insisted again that the police search Garnsworthy's house.[10]

Matthews was perfectly correct in his assertion that witchcraft had not died out among some people, for two years later George Davies and his brother-in-law, Benjamin Thorpe, of Gospel Oak, Staffordshire, were prosecuted at the Tipton police court for threatening Jessie Haddington, an educated woman, eighty-four years of age, and damaging her property.

Haddington lived with her daughter and granddaughter in three large caravans stationed on a plot of land they had bought for the purpose at Gospel Oak. Not surprisingly their mode of life attracted gossip, but the Haddingtons' were neither gypsies nor travellers. The family were tubercular and had moved from the town to the country in the hope that the fresh air would ease their suffering. They had no mains supply, of course, so they used to fetch water from the property of Davies and Thorpe, and also used their lavatory. This suggests that relations could not have been too bad, until, that is, Davies's wife, Lizzie, fell ill and had to be sent to a mental infirmary. The intrusions of the Haddingtons into the Davies's private space obviously preyed on Lizzie's mind. As her husband stated in court, 'This woman caused her to go mad. She got on her nerves so bad. She was frightened to death because these people came and used our water and lavatory.' Davies and Thorpe claimed that Lizzie had been 'overlooked' by Jessie Haddington, and over two successive nights the two men apparently demanded admission to Jessie's caravan, hammered on her door and threw stones at the windows. One witness to the scene was another neighbour, Mary Jones, who stated that Haddington was 'a funny old woman. She makes you feel peculiar.' When the magistrate asked if Jones was afraid she might put a spell on her, she replied 'Yes; I never have anything to do with her … I don't go close to her, because I've been told she'll put something on you.' The defendants had to pay a fine of 5s 6d, court costs of 8s 6d, and were bound over £10 to keep the peace.[11]

For our final case we must track back a few years to a trial that was rather different in nature to the previous two; for, in this instance, the perceived social pest was not the supposed witch but the person who considered herself bewitched. Just after Christmas in 1917, the magistrates at the Dorchester petty sessions presided over a case of assault between two women of Burleston, a village some five or six miles from the county town. The prosecutrix was Mrs Emily Jane Christopher, who accused her neighbour, Mrs Alice Trevett, wife of Daniel Trevett, a butcher's assistant, of assault. Mrs Christopher claimed that on the morning of the 7th she was about to step out and get a bit of meat for dinner when Mrs Trevett grabbed hold of her, shook her, and demanded that she get herself back inside that instant. In evidence, Mrs Christopher, whose behaviour was slightly eccentric, explained that 'Mrs Trevett says that the first time she catches me out she will beat me into apple dumplings; and I hope that every gentleman here will have a taste, so that they will know whether she makes them tasty or not.' As the questioning proceeded, it emerged that Mrs Christopher had moved to Burleston in the preceding year, apparently after having been popularly ejected from the neighbouring village of Chesilborne. The magistrates heard how she had not been in Burleston long before 'she started about witchcraft, over-looking, and conjuring, and became an extreme nuisance to the neighbourhood'. Mrs Critchell, wife of Frederick Critchell, carter, and next-door neighbour to Mrs Christopher, was called as a witness. She said that Trevett never touched Christopher, and that the latter 'had annoyed the neighbourhood by reports of witchcraft and over-looking'. Mrs Trevett then gave evidence, stating that as soon as Christopher had moved in she 'started to "bombard" her with notions about witchcraft and overlooking. She took every opportunity of telling her about extraordinary happenings.' Trevett said she 'had listened to her notions in order to keep the peace and quietness'. Mrs Christoper claimed, for example, that a woman named Upshall had helped to 'witch' her with the aid of a clergyman. A letter she wrote to the local policeman, Mr Jay, was read out in court, in which she also accused him and his wife of having cast a spell over her. After hearing all the evidence the magistrates decided to dismiss the case, and Christopher was ordered to pay the court costs.[12]

The first observation to be made concerning these cases is that they all occurred in fairly isolated rural settlements. At the time, Clyst St Lawrence and Burleston were small villages situated miles from the nearest town. Although Gospel Oak was less geographically isolated in terms of its proximity to Tipton and the expanding urban sprawl around Dudley, it was very much separated from its urban neighbours in terms of the rural way of life of its inhabitants. Indeed, the defendants in the Gospel Oak case were described by the *Tipton Herald* as a 'handful of nobodies, in a remote and isolated part of the parish'. This would suggest that the last locations where the fear of witchcraft still manifested itself in terms of violent confrontation were in small rural settlements where social relations and the pattern of life had not yet been profoundly affected by new external social and economic forces. However, one does get the impression from these last cases and others that a smaller and smaller pool of people were involved in the formulation of accusations. The actions of witch assaulters were no longer the culmination of a process of communal legitimation. By the early twentieth century, witchcraft had become purely an affair between witch and victim, and not between community and witch. When victims of witchcraft attempted to involve the community, as in the Burleston case, they were not well received. Their attempts to garner sympathy and support with their complaints of bewitchment provoked only irritation and embarrassment among neighbours. In fact, the Burleston case provides a snapshot of a defining period in the history of witchcraft when the bewitched found themselves in the same isolated and despised position as the witch.

Our final means of assessing declining belief in witchcraft is by examining the opinions of those who were part of the cultural world of witches and magic, who believed in witches, and who bore witness to the demise of such people. How did the witch-believers themselves explain the decline of witches within their own lifetime? By the early twentieth century there was an undoubted general popular perception that there were fewer witches than there used to be. Towards the end of the 1890s, for instance, Rosalind Northcote found that people living near Exeter thought that witches 'used formerly to flourish'.[13] When a folklorist from the Sussex–Surrey border asked a young girl about witchcraft in 1898, she was regaled with numerous stories concerning the activities of the local witches, but when the same girl was asked again 'some years later' whether there were still any witches, she replied that 'she thought not, but said her father had seen a woman sitting on the roadside and had said "good evening" to her; she did not answer and father said he thought she must have been a witch.'[14] Similarly, in Flora Thompson's account of an Oxfordshire hamlet in the 1880s, a young girl asks her mother whether there were any witches still, to which her mother answers seriously, 'No. They seem to have all died out. There haven't been any in my time; but when I was your age there were plenty of old people alive who had known or even been ill-wished by one.'[15] Witches became increasingly scarce then. They disappeared from the community, but could still, perhaps, be met with in the guise of an uncanny old woman, encountered on the road at twilight. We are, therefore, faced with the apparent paradox that witches disappeared while people still believed in them. In other words, witchcraft declined without people actually rejecting the reality of witchcraft. Obviously we have to look beyond the notion of a popular conscious rejection of witchcraft, and look instead at why communities ceased to generate witch-figures.

Cultural change and the retiring witch

A few historians have attempted, albeit briefly, to characterise the process of the decaying structure of popular belief in witchcraft. James Obelkevitch has suggested that witchcraft disappeared after 'completing a long-term process of depersonalisation'.[16] He has talked of the formation of 'abstraction witchcraft' and the existence of 'witchcraft without witches'. He illustrates these concepts by using the scenario that when the butter refused to churn this failure came to be explained in terms of witchcraft without a particular witch needing to be identified. The personal figure of the witch became divorced from the idea of witchcraft, and once divorced, the belief in both witches and witchcraft languish. Similarly, John Putnam Demos has posited that the declining belief in witchcraft resulted from a gradual reduction of both 'effect' and 'imagery', with the figure of the witch being 'effectively scaled down'. According to Demos, the nineteenth-century witch was a distinctly eccentric figure that he labels the 'hag-witch': 'she retains power in one sort, and to this extent she may still inspire fear. Yet she is also a fit target for contempt, for mockery, for mischief, at the hands of her peers and neighbours ... When witches had come to seem pathetic, their final demise as cultural referents could not be far off.'[17]

Neither Obelkevitch nor Demos really attempt to explain what led to this supposed belittling and 'depersonalisation' of the witch figure. Both works, while excellent discussions of their respective areas of study, are not, however, primarily concerned with witchcraft in the eighteenth and nineteenth centuries. Obelkevitch's research was based on just one area of the county of Lincolnshire, which, as he recognised himself, limited the range of relevant source material when it came to studying witchcraft beliefs, as did the limited period of time he covered. Demos's work is primarily a study of witchcraft in early modern New England, and while he provides some circumstantial evidence for his theory of decline, he fails to cite one case of a post-1736 prosecution resulting from the belief in witchcraft that might have illustrated the continued popular belief in the existence of the 'death-dealing' witch. Thus both theories are founded on a minimal base of relevant information, and as a result they are deceptive. Both have relied solely on folk legends and anecdotes concerning witches that were recorded by late-eighteenth- and nineteenth-century folklorists, and which often concerned events that happened 'forty or fifty' years before. Such tales of feeble, eccentric old witches who turned themselves into hares had long existed, but they become more prominent in the historical record of the nineteenth century because of their recording by folklorists and antiquarians. As the reverse witch-trials illustrate, the death-dealing powers of the witch had in no way diminished by the nineteenth century, and I would suggest that the same is also true for parts of America. The folklore witch and the death-dealing witch had always coexisted, being bound together in the popular conception of witchcraft.

Although Obelkevitch's theory is attractive, it is not convincing. I have not gained any real sense of the 'depersonalisation' of the witch as part of a process of decline. For those who believed in witchcraft, specific, individual misfortunes were hardly ever blamed on witches in general. Thus when in 1857 a class of schoolboys in Norfolk was asked the meaning of 'a witch', they did not discuss witches as an unspecified group, but instead 'every boy save one answered simultaneously, "There's one at ——, Sir," "There's another at ——," &c. Each boy knew of some poor creature upon whom this *malafama* had settled.'[18] If someone suspected witchcraft, he would immediately have a well-known local witch in mind, or if there was not one, then suspicion would fall on a new suspect, often after having consulted a cunning-person. Of course, there had always been a fear of witches in general, as well as in the particular. Prophylactics like horseshoes, for instance, were hung up to protect the house and its occupants from witches in general, both known and unknown, but when it came to accusations blame was always directed at specific individuals. In the sense that the witch figure disappeared before the belief in witchcraft, there was a *belief* in witchcraft without witches, but not, as Obelkevitch suggests, *acts* of witchcraft without witches. So, what circumstances led to this if it was not directly related to so-called 'progressive' factors, or related to notions of abstraction? I suggest that we must look to the changing structure of community and lifestyle patterns in nineteenth-century rural England and Wales.

In 1898, Richard Blakeborough asked an 'honest Yorkshireman', 'Are things in general really much different now from what they were, say, fifty years ago?' To which he received the laconic reply, 'Nowt's t' saam'. 'Nothing could have been more forcible', remarked Blakeborough, 'the words meant much, and the tone in which they were uttered meant more.'[19] What happened in this period which profoundly affected rural life, and the structure of popular beliefs and practices, was the decline of the self-sufficient, subsistence rural culture, and the formation of a new dependency culture wholly reliant upon external agencies for its economic survival, social organisation and governance. This process was not chronologically or geographically uniform, but in every case the changes which brought about this process began to have a significant impact from the mid-nineteenth century onwards.

Rural villages and small provincial towns in England and Wales have never been timeless, static, unchanging communities. As the landscape itself bares witness, over the centuries whole villages have disappeared, dwindled or flourished in relation to external forces such as plague, enclosure and industrialisation. Few villages from the early modern period onwards remained unaffected by the patterns of seasonal and permanent migration. Nor, as is sometimes portrayed, were most settlements completely isolated from the outside world. Even in the seventeenth century few communities did not receive visits from itinerant gypsies, hawkers, and chapmen. In the eighteenth century, canals and improvements in road building, which made possible the expansion of coach services, had a significant effect on huge numbers of rural towns and villages. One has to be careful, therefore, in referring to communities as self-enclosed, isolated or traditional in the sense that they remained impervious to external forces of change. But in terms of the social structure and the nature of the local economy, little had changed profoundly in rural life for several centuries. According to G. E. Mingay, 'The nineteenth century witnessed the closing phase of a rural society which, through gradually adapting itself to the times, had shown a remarkable degree of stability over a period of some four or five hundred years.'[20] J. Geraint Jenkins has defined this phase of rural society as one in which

> all the commodities required by the community were produced within the region. Each individual realised his ambitions within his own immediate locality, rarely finding it necessary to go outside that locality for the means of life. All the food required by the community could be produced locally; as well as all the products of the farm ... therefore, the rural neighbourhood, 'characterised by an intimacy of association within a territorial space', was an economic as well as a social entity.[21]

Jean Robin's detailed study of the Essex village of Elmdon reinforces this picture of 'intimacy of association'. The small world of Elmdon farm workers encompassed only the villages and hamlets within a radius of five miles. Fifty-four of the agricultural workers in 1861 were married men, and of these, exactly half had chosen wives born within Elmdon parish. All but one of the other twenty-seven wives had been born within five miles of Elmdon.[22] As B. J. Davey observed from his study of Ashwell, Hertfordshire, 'if a man moved, it was only to lead a similar life-style in a neighbouring village, so there was little motive for such a step.'[23]

Up until 1901 the national census reveals that agriculture was still the largest single employer in England. In 1851 there were nearly twice as many people employed in agriculture as in the industrial mills and factories, and nearly three times as many agricultural workers as there were miners.[24] Furthermore, the whole of rural society, and not just farmers, were involved in agricultural production, and in livestock rearing in particular. As Mick Reed has shown, many tradesmen followed some form of agriculture either as a major or subordinate source of income, and Alun Howkins has pointed out that even in larger villages and small towns, farm landholding was widespread, and there were, therefore, many more people who had farming functions than can be calculated from the census returns.[25] Some farm labourers even owned a little land on which they could maintain a cow or two. In 1873, Henry Evershed, referring to the Sussex Weald, commented that anyone 'desirous of seeing a farm labourer with land, should come down here before it is too late'. He described 'the small plot and cow-keeping of old England', which kept the family provided with butter and milk, and a quantity of spare butter for sale.[26] Even the poorest of cottagers were often able to fatten up a pig and keep a few chickens. Thus the whole community, in one way or another, lived according to the vagaries and uncertainties of agricultural production.

Everyday foodstuffs such as milk, cheese, butter and beer were all produced, processed and consumed locally. The community usually purchased straight from the producer, goods often being paid for in kind. Up until mid-century 'there was a sector of the economy in which the cash nexus was only partially operative'.[27] Cash was usually employed only when dealing with larger or distant neighbours, or simply as an accounting device. The milling of corn was usually done locally, and each household made its own bread. Items such as cloth, soap, paper, literature, tea, coffee and sugar could be obtained in person from the nearest town, or purchased through intermediaries such as packmen, pedlars and local carriers. Carriers provided an important social and economic link between villages and the local market towns which provided an outlet for surplus produce, goods and labour.

Although such communities were far from harmonious, there existed a complex web of social relationships which often operated for mutual benefit, and, as Geraint Jenkins has pointed out, 'no farmer could exist as an independent and separate unit'.[28] Co-operation between farmers was crucial. Labour, implements and draught animals were all exchanged, especially among the large class of small farmers. Many such farmers did not own their own bulls, boars or rams, so there was a continual traffic in borrowing for insemination. Gathering the hay harvest, a time-consuming and labour-intensive exercise, usually required the co-operation not only of the majority of farmers in a neighbourhood, but of the whole community. Such communal gatherings of agricultural co-operation were cemented by associated ritual ceremonies and customs. There was, then, a 'community of interest', where everyone 'was caught up in the fortunes of the parish economy'.[29]

Not only were such communities self-sufficient in terms of production and consumption; they were also self-sufficient in terms of control over the infrastructure of their community. As we have seen in an earlier chapter, up until the 1850s most small rural communities very much policed themselves. And in other ways, too, power was located within the community and enacted by its members, rather than by the state and external agencies. Much of the powers of self-government were held by the Vestry, a body which officially included all owners and ratepayers in the parish, and which was presided over by the vicar. It had a wide range of duties in the parish, including the controlling of parish land and property, the maintenance of roads and bridges, the occasional settling of local disputes, and it elected all the main parish officers, such as the overseers of the poor.

It is in these largely independent rural communities that witchcraft accusations continued to be generated. Witchcraft was not exclusive to an agricultural way of life, but rather to the above type of small, self-sufficient community. The social environment of some early modern urban communities was still conducive to the generation of witchcraft accusations, and mining and fishing villages were no less prone to witchcraft accusations than strictly agricultural communities. What they all had in common was an intimacy of association, a local economy where people, to a large extent, had to depend on others within the community, and where there was often a continued reliance on back-yard agriculture. However, from the 1860s onwards the social and economic fabric of this type of society was irrevocably broken up in a multitude of ways. Change was brought about by new technological innovations and new economic competition; by urbanisation and migration; by the extension of national and local government power at the local level; and by the forging of new social relationships and antagonisms.

The rise of mechanised farming machinery, initially horse-drawn and then engine driven, in the last two decades of the nineteenth century wrought massive social and cultural changes in the structure of the rural labour force and in inter-communal relations. The introduction of horse-drawn mowing machines replaced the communal scything gangs, and wheeled rakes and hay-tossers disposed of the need for local casual labour, as did threshing machines and manure spreaders. The machine binder came in for some of the most bitter criticism. In 1898 a Yorkshire man told Blakeborough that 'Eddication an' self-binnders is gahin ti to'n t' wo'lld upsahd doon.'[30]Similarly, David Jenkins has observed that in south-west Wales, 'People who remember the period are perfectly clear that it was the self-binder ... that brought an end to the society than once existed.'[31] This mechanisation of agricultural production and processing meant that communal participation in the agricultural calendar was no longer necessary and this led to an inexorable reduction in the local labouring workforce and a rupture in social relationships. As Gareth W. Williams has explained, 'The transition from social device (the work-group) to mechanical device (the machine) disrupted the connection be-tween farmer and labourer so that looser, more impersonal relations prevailed, and the mutual interest in one another's affairs ebbed.'[32] These changes also hit village craftsmen and women. Tools such as scythes, hay-rakes, and forks were no longer required in the same numbers. Initially the rise of horse-powered machinery was no bad thing for the village blacksmith and saddler, but this was short-lived with the increasing prepon-derance of the engine. Horses used in farming declined in number from 802,044 in 1892 to 132,481 in 1954.[33] Craftsmen and tradesmen were also badly affected by the agricultural depression and urban competition, and it was members of this group which most readily considered migration and emigration.[34] Urban mass production of goods proved disastrous for rural manufacturing, with sawyers, carpenters and blacksmiths all suffering from the production of ready-made doors, window frames, gates and wheels, and village tailors and shoemakers were unable to compete with mass-produced ready-to-wear shoes and clothing. Thus in Cerne Abbas, Dorset, there were fifty-seven tradesmen in 1851 but only eleven by 1901.[35]

The breach in long-established relationships between farmers, cottagers, craftsmen and their families was further exacerbated by general trends in terms of land tenure during the same period, such as the break-up of large estates and the fragmentation of holdings. In the village of Laxton, a once stable turnover of tenant farms ended up between the wars with three or four farms changing hands annually, and it even became difficult to attract new tenants.[36] The declining influence of the squire and estate also had a destabilising effect on rural communities. A job and a cottage for life were no longer assured. The anchor families of small communities were breaking up and dispersing. As the Lincolnshire folklorist Mabel Peacock bemoaned in 1901, 'In almost every village, strangers are now replacing the old families which have lived there or in the surrounding parishes from before the time that manorial records first began.'[37]

The impact of new technological advances and the ever-improving communications network were also responsible for the destruction of the old, barter-run local economy, and the rise of the national and inter-national market economy. The development of freezer ships meant that by 1870 beef was being imported all the way from Argentina, mutton from Australia, and bacon and cheese from Denmark. By 1876 about 21 per cent of food supplies were being imported, whereas forty years before it was only around 5 per cent. Just before the First World War as much as 60 per cent of all British food consumption was imported.[38] By the mid-nineteenth century grocers' shops were appearing in villages where pre-viously no shops had existed or were necessary. Increasing imports of foreign grain and the invention of the process of roller milling in 1875, led to the decline of local milling and the urban domination of a once rural industry. With this decline, flour was no longer available from the source; instead it was marketed and sold in shops, or turned into bread by urban bakeries and then sold out to rural villages. Local brewing also declined as urban breweries began to expand their market, and, as a result, huge numbers of alehouses went out of business.[39] In 1880, Richard Jefferies noted sadly that cottagers were buying almost everything they needed and producing nothing, not even a home-made loaf.[40]

The railway network enabled farmers, once they became familiar with the new market forces, to exploit distant urban markets. In Wensleydale, for example, the coming of the railway in 1877 enabled the sale of milk to Leeds, Newcastle, and as far away as Liverpool. Previously this milk would have been turned into cheese and butter for local distribution.[41] When, in 1851, the branch line from Hitchin to Cambridge was opened it apparently had little direct impact on the daily lives of the inhabitants of Ashwell, in that it was little used as a means of personal transport. Its real significance 'lay in the fact that it was the symptom and the vehicle of economic revolution which was taking place outside'.[42]

The setting up of the Milk Marketing Board in 1933 was to be the final nail in the coffin of the old local economy. The Board offered secure outlets for all milk that could be produced by guaranteeing a buyer and organising the allocation of supplies. As J. V. Beckett found in Laxton, 'whereas the Laxton farmers had kept a handful of milking cows and their wives had made butter for sale at Newark and Twyford markets, from the 1930s they turned their attention instead to the sale of fresh milk.'[43] In South Cardiganshire, J. Jenkins found that with the creation of the Board the production of butter and the number of store cattle declined, sheep and pigs disappeared, and the production of liquid milk became the basis of the economy.[44] The small-scale mixed farming of the nineteenth century gave way to a specialised dairy economy.

All the changes that have been described led to a decreasing reliance on the community as a producer, processor and provider, to the disappearance of the exchange economy and neighbourhood reciprocity, and to the rise of individual self-reliance and the cash economy. The variability of this decline, to which the decline of witch-accusations is related, was considerably dependent on the proximity of communities to urban markets. The old domestic economy certainly continued to survive longer in some areas than in others. M. K. Ashby found, for example, that although by 1914 'monetary profit' was coming to the fore in the village of Bledington, Gloucestershire, home consumption of products was still important on small farms; the mill still ground local grain, and a good deal of bread was made at home; and bacon, milk, eggs, and fowl were still sold to neighbours.[45] It is probably in small rural communities like these that witchcraft accusations persisted during the twentieth century.

For those who continued to live an agricultural way of life, there was undoubtedly an increasing level of security in financial terms, which made individual misfortunes less serious. Keith Thomas, referring to the eighteenth century, has suggested that the growth of the insurance industry generated a new feeling of economic security that affected the way in which misfortune was perceived.[46] However, for the majority of people it was only in the later nineteenth century that the insurance industry became accessible to the majority of people[47] Although "cow clubs" had operated as friendly societies during the late eighteenth century, they wee often short-lived and many collapsed under the strain of cattle epidemics and lack of capital. From the 1830s onwards, though, a diversity of village benefit clubs seems to have flourished. In the village of Ashwell, for example, a Medical Club was set up in 1835 in response to the new Poor Law, and a Clothing Club, a Pig Club and a Coal Club were all formed, and were supported by the Vestry.[48] As well as these small village clubs, larger benefit societies such as the Independent Order of Oddfellows and the Ancient order of Foresters also became popular in rural areas. Such clubs and societies not only fostered a greater feeling of financial security but also, as a Report on Wages and Conditions stated in 1919 (when such clubs were in terminal decline), 'The older societies formed bonds of fellowship, and tended to bring men into social contact, a benefit that village life can ill afford to lose.'[49]

Professional agricultural insurance companies only began to appear in the 1840s with the founding of the Farmers' and Graziers' Cattle Insurance Company, and the Cattle Insurance Company. They offered to insure not only cattle, as their names suggested, but horses, sheep and pigs as well. The limited influence of livestock insurance was apparent, though, from the devastating cattle plague of 1864–66 which caused estimated losses of £5 million. In response, in 1866 an Act of Parliament permitted the transaction of cattle insurance under amenable Friendly Society rules, and this led to an increasing take-up of policies over the next few decades. In terms of personal sickness, insurance cover began to have a significant social impact only from the early twentieth century onwards. The first general accident and sickness insurance policy was available in 1900 and proved popular among the self-employed. The growth of the popular insurance market undoubtedly contributed to a general easing of the severity of misfortune in terms of agricultural production and personal health. This was complemented in the early twentieth century by new social legislation. In 1909 the passing of the Old Age Pension Act assured the labourer a crucial pittance on retirement. Previously, as many as 45 per cent of aged agricultural labourers had been 'condemned' to outdoor relief or the prison-like conditions of the workhouse.[50] In 1911 the National Insurance Act also introduced a low rate of state sickness benefit for wage-earners. Furthermore, the creation of the Central and District Wages Boards led to the fixing of a minimum wage, after which agricultural wages rose.

The social transformations that have just been outlined led to the creation of the following five interrelated circumstances, which effectively hampered the mechanisms that had produced accusations of witchcraft within any given community, and ultimately resulted in the declining belief in witchcraft.

Communal instability

Witchcraft accusations were generated in a social environment where there was a considerable degree of long-term social stability, and where there was an intimacy of association in which one person's affairs were the affairs of the whole community. These were communities where the knowledge of local beliefs and genealogies were perpetuated through the existence of anchor families who had remained in the same village, and sometimes even the same house, for centuries. The oral transmission of local lore from one generation to another made possible the formation of reputations (a process crucial in the creation of witches) through the communally stored accumulation of incidents and events which accrued around every person in the village. Thus the daughter of a suspected witch often accrued the same reputation as her mother, and a person of unblemished reputation could suddenly become a suspect after one suspicious incident recalled other previously inauspicious coincidences held in the collective memory. These bonds of intimacy and association that bound the community together in terms of work and leisure, and unified it with a sense of a shared past and present, gradually fell away with the decline of the barter economy, the advent of mechanisation, and as a result of the rupture this brought about between all levels of rural society. With the exodus of the young and the death of the old, with the break-up of estates, the increasing turnover of tenancies and the influx of newcomers, the stream of inherited oral tradition ran dry. Family histories were no longer remembered, communal dialogue became less intense and less pervasive, and thus the long-term generation of reputations that produced witch figures no longer occurred.

Decline of self-governance and the intrusion of state and local government

Until the mid-nineteenth century rural communities had been allowed, to a great extent, to manage their own affairs, and to police themselves. Although, superficially, the squire, magistrate and clergyman were the embodiment of authority in the community, in reality the most influential power group in the parish was the small farmer/tradesman class. It was members of this rural group who held sway in the Vestry, and who held all the official posts in the community such as that of constable, overseer and churchwarden. Significantly, this same group was often responsible for controlling unofficial justice as well, as is evident from cases of communal action against witches. However, with the inception of new market forces and the rise of mechanisation, this social group's influence began to decline. Many craft products were no longer necessary. Cheap urban imports put many rural tradesmen and craftsmen out of business, and the whole basis of rural industry was undermined. This group had been the backbone of the rural community, not only in economic terms but also in terms of parochial self-government, both official and unofficial. From the 1870s onwards, however, this backbone gave way under external pressures, and the consensus and communal action which that social group galvanised was weakened as a consequence.

Power increasingly slipped from the hands of the community – initially with the passing of the Poor Law Amendment Act, and subsequently with the creation of County Constabularies and the institution of County Councils and Rural District Councils in 1888 and 1894. With the inception of a full-time, uniformed police force and increasing numbers of stipendiary magistrates, the popularly perceived right to mob and swim witches was hindered and suppressed. Such communal actions against witches had been powerful displays of collective belief, which reinforced the utility of making public accusations, attracted sympathy for the victim of witchcraft, and provided a graphic public display of the reality of witchcraft. With the waning power of the old dominant rural class, and in the new atmosphere of rural policing, the generation of a communal consensus concerning the identity and punishment of a suspected witch was no longer so easy to elicit, and an organised authoritative response was less likely. As a result, public accusations against witches became less advisable and increasingly ineffectual. Accusation could still be made without the vociferous sanction of the community as a whole, but there was less likelihood of any direct action being taken by the individual without that unity of expression. In this way the utility of the accusations themselves became increasingly redundant.

Separation from livestock and food production

Livestock represented a living investment of capital and labour: as such, cows, pigs and horses were perceived as vulnerable targets for malevolent attacks. In such terms the death of livestock was often as disastrous as the death of family members. When, for example, Sabine Baring-Gould went to sympathise with an Essex farmer (the owner of a 'minute' farm) over the loss of a cow, he was told: "'Wives,' said he, wiping his nose, "you've only to hold up your hand and whistle, and a score applicants for the sitiwation [sic] will come about you. Wives," he added, again wiping his nose with his fingers, "is wery cheap; but pigs is costly, and cows is plaguy ruinous."'[51] Farmers, of course, continued to maintain their close link with livestock, but, with the decline of the domestic economy, the importation of cheap meat, and the increasing availability of pre-prepared and processed meat sold through burgeoning retail outlets, many of those other members of rural society, such as labourers, cottagers and craftsmen, discontinued the tradition of cow plots and back-yard agriculture. As a result, one of the most vulnerable and economically important members of the family group in rural society was lost, and a common source of witchcraft accusations dried up.

With the separation of farm processing from farm production another avenue of potential witch-inspired misfortune was closed. The churn and the cheese press fell into disuse as many farmers increasingly sold their milk to distant urban markets where factories turned it into cheese and butter which would eventually be sold back to the farmers through retail outlets. The witch could no longer be accused of interfering with the churning of butter and the setting of the cheese, and could no longer sour the alehouse beer or make the bread fail to rise – unless she betook herself to the nearest brewery or bakery. Thus there was a decreasing reliance on the vagaries of food production and food processing, and as a result there was a concomitant reduction in the scope of witchcraft accusations.

Personal security and state welfare

According to Keith Thomas, during the late seventeenth century the tensions and guilt generated by demands on private charity, that had produced allegations of witchcraft, withered away as the Poor Law became a 'more regular system of relief.'[52] The reliance on private charity did not disappear entirely, though, and Thomas confidently claimed that the majority of eighteenth- and nineteenth-century accusations conformed to the 'same old pattern of charity evaded, followed by misfortune incurred'.[53] I have two serious reservations about these assertions. First, although some accusations were made against begging witches, such cases by no means made up a majority, and accusations were, in fact, generated as the result of a multitude of individual circumstances. Second, while I agree to a certain extent that the reduced need for private charity contributed to declining accusations, I would place this process much later than Thomas does, and suggest that it is only one of several factors responsible for the decline.

At no time after the seventeenth century was Poor Law relief so generous that it stopped the necessity for begging and therefore alleviated demands upon private charity. In fact, after 1834, private charity was called upon even more. The recommendations of the Poor Law Amendment Act of 1834 ostensibly cut back on Poor Law provision. No longer was the bulk of relief outdoor relief (doles given in money and in kind) provided on personal application to the overseer. Instead, the Amendment Act stated that no relief should be given to able-bodied people outside the workhouse. If relief were claimed, the applicant had to enter a workhouse, and the conditions of relief inside had to be such that the position of the pauper was worse than that of the meanest labourer outside. This certainly created little incentive to rely on state provision for relief, and many people found a hand-to-mouth begging existence preferable to a place in the workhouse. As a result private charity continued to be widely called upon.

The removal of the burden of individual charity along with growing personal financial security did affect the formulation of witch-accusations, but not quite in the way Thomas conceived it. Accusations of witchcraft were usually made when an inexplicable misfortune or a series of misfortunes threatened economic security. When people lived a subsistence existence, just one such misfortune could result in great economic hardship. For farmers, the growth of the insurance market slowly led to a cushioning of the effects of agricultural misfortune. The growth of popular banking and the rise of the cash economy also generated a greater feeling of security, and misfortunes became less financially ruinous. The old-age pension removed the need for aged cottagers to rely on the community. Flora Thompson recalled their joy in 1909: 'They were suddenly rich. Independent for life! At first when they went to the Post Office to draw it, tears of gratitude would run down the cheeks of some ... and there were flowers from their gardens and apples from their trees for the girl who merely handed them the money.'[54] As general living conditions began to improve slightly during the early twentieth century, as labourers' wages began to rise, and with the formation of an embryonic social security system, the need for personal charity definitely eased, and with it the communal obligations which fed the mumping witch and sustained her vindictive reputation.

Shifting balance of population from rural to urban

By 1911, 78 per cent of the population of England and Wales lived in urban districts. Considering that the modern urban environment does not seem to have been conducive to the formation of witchcraft accusations, the fact that nearly three-quarters of the population were living in large towns and cities must have had a considerable impact on the frequency of accusations, and consequently on the level of belief nationwide. However, urbanisation not only affected the belief in witchcraft due to its effect on urban populations but also in terms of its wider social and economic influence upon rural life. Urban industries and markets played a fundamental role in the breakdown of the old local economy and the decline of rural trades, and as such was partly responsible for the communal instability described above. Urban areas also generated new hopes, aspirations and mores in the younger rural population, which boded ill for the perpetuation of rural tradition. As Seebohm Rowntree remarked, 'doubtless the fascination of the town, when once experienced, disqualifies them for the old life.'[55] Women, in particular, were thought to be drawn to the new possibilities offered by urban living. Thus a contemporary of Seebohm Rowntree explained that 'country women look upon town as a kind of Eden for them ... No more pigs to be fed and tended, no more toil in the garden or on the allotment, hardly any baking to be done.'[56] Under the influence of the urbanite lifestyle, rural life became less introspective, rural customs and leisure pursuits less engrossing, and village matters appeared rather insipid. The rural community's overriding interest in its own affairs, of which tales and instances of local witchcraft were an integral part, was increasingly submerged by external, largely urban, considerations and events.

One would have thought that the decline in witchcraft-accusations was indicative of the declining belief in witchcraft, but this was clearly not the case. People who believed in witches did not know themselves why there were no longer any left. What this suggests is that it was the decline of witchcraft-accusations which resulted in the declining belief in witchcraft, rather than the other way round. This precludes the notion of a reasoned popular denial of witchcraft, a conscious rejection of a long-held framework of supernatural causation, explanation and cultural referents. It cannot be denied that many working-class people, educated, informed and experienced, did consciously reject the existence of witch-craft and magic: we know as much from their autobiographies.[57] For the mass of people, though, witchcraft simply became an irrelevance which no longer played a part in their daily lives and in their interaction with other people. Once out of sight, the witch was very much out of mind.

Witchcraft was functional at a personal level in that it not only accounted for misfortune but allowed for a means of reversing misfortune. If the butter continually refused to churn, then by accusing a witch and then taking some counter-action against that person, there was the pos-sibility that the butter might stop failing. If someone fell ill and doctors could not effect a cure through orthodox diagnosis and treatment, then by subsequently blaming it on witchcraft the patient opened up a new avenue for a possible cure. Once socio-economic circumstances created communities in which accusations were no longer applicable or expedient, then the belief in witchcraft served no purpose. In small communities witch figures were no longer created, not because they were no longer believed in, but because potential witches, in the absence of public accusations, no longer accrued a reputation. People continued to believe in witchcraft for a while after witches had disappeared, but the frame-work of beliefs surrounding witchcraft became redundant. With the decline of the oral tradition and the transmission of stories that may have kept traditional witchcraft beliefs alive, the reality of witchcraft became a dim memory. The popular belief in witchcraft declined largely because witchcraft was not adaptable to the fundamentally different uncertainties and demands of new market forces and modern mass culture. Its demise, therefore, was rooted firmly in the cultural rather than in the intellectual sphere.

CONCLUSION

The experience of misfortune has changed profoundly in our pre-dominantly urban, welfare society. Once the state began to provide more securities in life, such as pensions, unemployment benefits, national insur-ance and subsidies, and with the extension of universal suffrage and basic human rights, not only was the scope and impact of misfortune mitigated, but blame for the experience of misfortune began to be apportioned to the failures of these welfare mechanisms. In our modern social climate, people are far more aware of the national and global factors influencing their lives in political, economic and environmental terms. While financial hardship no longer results from the death of a pig or a cow, for instance, the reduction of European subsidies constitutes a serious case of mis-fortune for farmers. As a result, the bureaucrats in Brussels rather than village witches are now the scapegoats in farming communities. Never-theless, although the actions of the mass of the people are no longer strongly bound by occult forces, they continue to maintain a variety of observances to ward off misfortune. However, such practices are no longer employed against individuals who emanate supernatural malign influence, but against an impersonal, abstract conception of bad luck. Many people also retain a fascination with the professed ability to interpret occult forces. The belief in fortune-telling continues, for instance, because it functions as a means of assuaging personal insecurities about the future. The ex-pression of these insecurities may have changed over the centuries, but the fundamental fear of being hurt, emotionally or financially, will always lead people to seek comfort in the realm of magic.

In other ways, the popular belief in the supernatural has continued by a process of adaptation to changing perceptions of the world. Thus the inexplicable, violent movement of objects, supernatural stone-throwing and bed-rocking, which were once attributed to witchcraft, are now seriously explained in terms of poltergeist activity. Is the former explanation any more 'irrational' than the latter? And although few people still believe in fairies and fairy abduction, many now believe in UFOs, egg-headed aliens, and alien abduction. Stories of such encounters are probably as widely deliberated in modern mass culture as stories of fairies were in the old rural culture. For many people today the experience of the supernatural is no longer circumscribed by the parish boundary but by the expanding universe. We have to question, therefore, the very validity of dichotomies expressing mental progress in relation to the supernatural beliefs of past societies and cultures. In the 1980s and 1990s we have heard how an American president patronised an astrologer, how British jurists consulted a ouija-board to ascertain a defendant's guilt, how a multinational mineral extraction company employed a spoon-bender to find hidden mineral reserves, and of leading quantum theorists and astrophysicists expressing a devout belief in Christianity. We must seriously consider if we really are any more rational than the witch-believers of the past. Instead of thinking of the modern period as an age in which the mass of the population has advanced from a state of supernatural credulity to one of scientific rationality, we must look at it as a period in which expressions of 'irrational' belief have continued by a process of translation. Furthermore, it is not impossible that at some point in the future, profound economic and environmental upheavals will once more create the social and cultural conditions in which once widespread beliefs and practices concerning witchcraft and magic may return. The mumping witch may come knocking once more.

NOTES

Chapter 1

1 See Ian Bostridge, 'Witchcraft Repealed', in Jonathan Barry, Marianne Hester and Gareth Roberts (eds), *Witchcraft in Early Modern Europe* (Cambridge, 1996), pp. 321–9; I. Bostridge, *Witchcraft and its Transformations c. 1650–1750* (Oxford, 1997).

2 Meric Casaubon, *Of Credulity and Incredulity* (London, 1668, 1670); John Wagstaffe, *The Question of Witchcraft Debated* (London, 1669, 1671); Joseph Glanvill, *A Blow at Modern Sadducism* (London, 1668); John Webster, *The Displaying of Supposed Witchcraft* (London, 1677).

3 *The Witch of Endor: or, A Plea for the Divine Administration of the Agency of Good and Evil Spirits. Written some Years ago, at the Request of a Lady; and now Reprinted with a Prefatory Discourse, Humbly Adressed to the Honourable Members of the House of C———s, who brought in their Bill (Jan. 27) for Repealing the Statute of 1 Jac. Cap. 12. concerning* WITCHCRAFT (London, 1736).

4 *Ibid.*, p. iv.

5 *Ibid.*, p. xiviii.

6 *A Discourse on Witchcraft. Occasioned by a* BILL *now depending in* PARLIAMENT, *to repeal the statute made in the first Year of the Reign of King James I* (London, 1736), p. 3.

7 Webster, *The Displaying of Supposed Witchcraft*, p. 68; *A Discourse*, p. 4.

8 *A Discourse*, p. 29.

9 *Ibid.*, p. 47; Wagstaffe, Question of Witchcraft, p. 79.

10 John Locke, *Two Treatises of Government*, ed. Peter Laslett (Cambridge, 1963), p. 347.

11 E. P. Thompson, *Whigs and Hunters: The Origins of the Black Act* (London, 1975), p. 21.

12 J. M. Beattie, 'Crime and the Courts in Surrey 1736–1753', in J. S. Cockburn (ed.), *Crime in England 1550–1800* (London, 1977), p. 179.

13 Brian Easlea, *Witch-hunting, Magic and the New Philosophy* (London, 1980), p. 240.

14 Douglas Hay, 'Property, Authority and the Criminal Law', in Douglas Hay, Peter Linebaugh, John G. Rule, E. P. Thompson and Cal Winslow, *Albion's*

Fatal Tree: Crime and Society in Eighteenth-Century England (London, 1975), pp. 17–63.

15 *Ibid.*, p. 47.

16 John Langbein, 'Albion's Fatal Flaw', *Past and Present* 98 (1983) 96–120.

17 *Ibid.*, p. 105. See also Nicholas Rogers, 'Confronting the Crime Wave: The Debate over Social Reform and Regulation, 1749–1753', in Lee Davison, Tim Hitchcock, Tim Keirn and Robert Shoemaker (eds), *Stilling the Grumbling Hive: The Response to Social and Economic Problems in England, 1689–1750* (Stroud, 1992).

18 William Blackstone, *Commentaries on the Laws of England* (Oxford, [1765] 1775), vol. 4, p. 60.

19 *The Spectator*, 14 July 1711.

20 James Boswell, *Journal of a Tour to the Hebrides* (London, 1875), entry under Monday, 16 August.

21 I. P., 'Progress and Decline of Witchcraft', *Gentleman's Magazine* (1830) 108.

22 Notes and Queries, 3rd S. 6 (1864) 209.

23 Theophilus Evans, *The History of Modern Enthusiasm* (London, 1752), p. 33.

24 Simon Schaffer, 'A Social History of Plausibility: Country, City and Calculation in Augustan Britain', in Adrian Wilson (ed.), *Rethinking Social History: English Society 1570–1920 and its Interpretation* (Manchester, 1993), p. 148.

25 John Richard Green (ed.), *Essays of Joseph Addison* (London, 1924), pp. 18–19.

26 Jonathan Barry, 'Public Infidelity and Private Belief? The Discourse of Spirits in Enlightenment Bristol' (forthcoming).

27 *A Narrative of Some Extraordinary Things that Happened to Mr. Richard Giles's Children at the Lamb, without Lawford's Gate, Bristol: supposed to be the effect of witchcraft. By the late Mr. Henry Durbin, chymist, who was an eye witness of the principal herein related* (Bristol, 1800), pp. 5–6.

28 'An Extraordinary Narrative of a Cabalist', *Gentleman's Magazine* (September 1762), p. 418.

29 *St. James's Evening Post*, 7–10 January 1738.

30 Walter Scott, *Letters on Demonology and Witchcraft* (London, [1830] 1884), p. 221.

31 John Dove, *A Vindication of the Hebrew scriptures; with animadversions on the mark set on Cain, the giantship, wizardry, and witchcraft, mentioned in the Pentateuch and the Prophets* (London, 1771), p. 44.

32 Samuel Norman, *Authentic Anecdotes of George Lukins, the Yatton Doemoniac* (Bristol, 1788), p. 44.

33 *Anti-canidia: or, Superstition Detected and Exposed. In a Confutation of the Vulgar Opinion concerning Witches, Spirits, Demons, Magick, Divination, Omens, Prognostications, Dreams, Augurys, Charms, Amulets, Incantations, Astrology, Oracles, &c.* (London, c. 1762), p. 5.

34 *Ibid.*, p. 4.

35 *Ibid.*, p. 6.

36 *Ibid.*, p. 13.

37 Roy Palmer, *The Folklore of Gloucestershire* (Tiverton, 1994), p. 147; James Sharpe, *Instruments of Darkness: Witchcraft in England 1550–1750* (London, 1996), p. 280.

38 *Sherborne Mercury*, 28 August 1739; D. Rhys Phillips, *The History of the Vale of Neath* (Swansea, 1925), p. 583; Paul Hawkins Fisher, *Notes and Recollections*

of Stroud, Gloucestershire (London, 1871), pp. 22–3.

39 John Bisset, *A Doctrinal testimony against many prevailing evils at this day. A sermon, preached in the New Church of Aberdeen* (Glasgow, 1744).

40 John Wesley, *The Journal of the Rev. John Wesley* (8 vols), ed. N. Curnock (London, 1909–16), entry for 25 May 1768.

41 These accounts were first published in Joseph Priestley, *Original Letters by the Rev. John Wesley and his Friends, Illustrating His Early History, with other curious Papers, Communicated by the late Rev. S. Badcock* (Birmingham, 1791), pp. 118–66.

42 *Arminian Magazine* 7 (1784) 548–50, 606–8, 654–6.

43 *A Discourse on Witchcraft*, p. 25.

44 M. J. Naylor, *The Inanity and Mischief of Vulgar Superstitions. Four Sermons preached at All-Saint's Church, Huntingdon, on the 25th Day of March, in the years 1792, 1793, 1794, 1795* (Cambridge, 1795), p. iii.

45 For further discussion, see Owen Davies, 'Methodism, the Clergy and the Popular Belief in Witchcraft and Magic', *History* 82 (1997) 252–65.

46 J. H. Davies (ed.), *The Life and Opinions of Robert Roberts, a Wandering Scholar, as Told by Himself* (Cardiff, 1923), p. 49.

47 Edward Hamer, 'Parochial Account of Llanidloes', *Montgomeryshire Collections* 10 (1877) 239–40.

48 *Rheolau a Dybenion y Cymdeithasau Neillduol ym mhlith y bobl a elwir y Methodistiaid yng Nghymru* (1801); cited in Gereint H. Jenkins, 'Popular Beliefs in Wales from the Restoration to Methodism', *Bwletin y Bwrdd Gwybodau Celtaidd* 27 (1977) 460.

49 R. Pearce, *Methodism in Portland and A Page of Church History* (London, 1898), pp. 76–7.

50 R. Lyne, *The Sinfulness and Idolatry of Charms, and of all unbidden Christianlike ways of Worshipping God, shewn in two letters Addressed to the Inhabitants of Little Petherick, in the County of Cornwall* (Bodmin, 1817), pp. 36–8.

51 Edward Hamer, 'Parochial Account of Llanidloes', *Montgomeryshire Collections*, 10 (1877) 233.

52 J. E. Vaux, *Church Folklore* (London, 1894); A. Smith, *The Established Church and Popular Religion 1750–1850* (London, 1971), pp. 19–22.

53 Christopher Wordsworth, 'Two Yorkshire Charms or Amulets: Exorcisms and Adjurations', *Yorkshire Archaeological Journal* 17 (1902–03) 386.

54 Sabine Baring-Gould, *The Vicar of Morwenstow. A Life of Robert Stephen Hawker* (London, 1876), pp. 153, 156.

55 *Ibid.*, p. 154; the passage is from Mark vii. 21.

56 J. F. C. Harrison, *The Second Coming: Popular Millenarianism 1780–1850* (London, 1979), p. 118.

57 In a letter to Montague Summers; see Summers, *The Geography of Witchcraft* (London 1927), p. 182.

58 Christina Hole (ed.), *Witchcraft at Toner's Puddle*, pamphlet (1964).

59 For comparison, see Kay S. Wilkins, 'Attitudes to Witchcraft and Demonic Possession in France during the Eighteenth Century', *Journal of European Studies* 3 (1973) 348–62.

60 *St. James's Evening Post*, 7–10 January 1738.

61 *A Narrative of Some Extraordinary Things that Happened to Mr. Richard Giles's Children.*

62 *A Narrative of the Extraordinary Case of Geo. Lukins, of Yatton, Somersetshire …*

Extracted from the Manuscripts of several Persons who attended, to which is prefixed a letter from the Rev. W. R. W. (Bristol, 1788); Joseph Easterbrook, *An Appeal to the Public Respecting George Lukins* (Bristol, 1788); Samuel Norman, *Authentic Anecdotes of George Lukins, The Yatton Doemoniac; with a View of the Controversy, and a Full Refutation of the Imposture* (Bristol, 1788); Samuel Norman, *The Great Apostle Unmasked* (Bristol, 1788).

63 Norman, Authentic Anecdotes, p. 11.

64 *Ibid.*, p. 13.

65 *Ibid.*

66 *A Narrative of the Extraordinary Case of Geo. Lukins*, pp. 10–11.

67 *Ibid.*, p. 17.

68 Norman, *Authentic Anecdotes*, p. 8.

69 Norman, *Authentic Anecdotes*.

70 Copy held in Bath Central Library. The same copy also contains the following handwritten note, dated 15 October 1834: 'Mr Jay told me that in his hearing John Wesley said – "I as much believe that Lukins' case was a real possession as anyone recorded in the four Evangelists".'

71 Norman, *Authentic Anecdotes*, p. 20.

72 For example, Wesley, *Journal*, vol. 2, pp. 298, 301–2; vol. 5, pp. 374–5. More generally, see Clarke Garrett, *Spirit Possession and Popular Religion From the Camisards to the Shakers* (Baltimore and London, 1987), pp. 74–105.

73 Garrett, *Spirit Possession*, pp. 80–3.

74 John Brand, *Observations on the Popular Antiquities of Great Britain* (London, 1910), p. 113.

75 Rev. J. C. Atkinson, *Forty Years in a Moorland Parish* (London, 1891), p. 59.

76 Joan Connell, The Roman Catholic Church in England 1780–1850 (Philadelphia, 1984), p. 152.

77 Rev. E. Peach, *A Circumstantial Account of a Successful Exorcism, Performed at King's Norton, Worcestershire, in the Year 1815; Accompanied by Reflections which that Extraordinary Event Produced in the Mind of the Exorcist* (Birmingham, 1836).

78 A brief biography and a full bibliography of Peach's published work can be found in Joseph Gillow's B*ibliographical Dictionary of the English Catholics* (London, n.d.), Vol. 5.

79 Peach, *A Circumstantial Account*, p. 10.

80 *Ibid.*, pp. 11–12.

81 *Ibid.*, p. 18.

82 Sharpe, *Instruments of Darkness*, p. 195.

83 For the early modern period, see D. P. Walker, *Unclean Spirits: Possession and Exorcism in France and England in the Late Sixteenth and Early Seventeenth Century* (Philadelphia, 1981); Sharpe, *Instruments of Darkness*, pp. 190–211; Keith Thomas, *Religion and the Decline of Magic* (revised edition, London, 1973), pp. 569–88.

84 Western Gazette, 29 November 1872.

85 *The Times*, 24 April 1851.

86 Margaret Courtney, *Cornish Feasts and Folk-lore* (Penzance, 1890), p. 99.

87 See Garrett, *Spirit Possession*, pp. 1–13; John Putmos Demos, *Entertaining Satan: Witchcraft and the Culture of Early New England* (Oxford, 1982), pp. 128–31.

88 See, for example, Judith Devlin, *The Superstitious Mind* (New Haven, 1987),

pp. 120 40; Eloïse Mozzani, *Magie et superstitions de la fin de l'Ancien Régime à la Restauration* (Paris, 1988), pp. 55–7, 137–9, 243–7. For a detailed account of the Morzine case, see Catherine-Laurence Maire, *Les Posedées de Morzine 1857–1873* (Lyons, 1981).

89 The best works on the history of poltergeists are still Andrew Lang, *Cock Lane and Common Sense* (London, 1894); A. Lang 'The Poltergeist, Historically Considered', *Proceedings of the Society for Psychical Research* 17 (1901–02), 305–26; Harry Price, *Poltergeist Over England* (London, 1945).

90 Catherine Crowe, *The Night Side of Nature: Or, Ghosts & Ghost Seers* (London [1848] 1852).

91 Price, *Poltergeist*, p. 2.

92 For the history of English spiritualism, see Ruth Brandon, *The Spiritualists: The Passion for the Occult in the Nineteenth and Twentieth Centuries* (London, 1983); Janet Oppenheim, *The Other World: Spiritualism and Psychical Research in England, 1850–1914* (Cambridge, 1985); Logie Barrow, *Independent Spirits: Spiritualism and English Plebeians 1850–1910* (London, 1986); Alex Owen, *The Darkened Room: Women, Power and Spiritualism in Late Victorian England* (London, 1989). See also Ronald Pearsall, *The Table-Rappers* (London, 1972). For a useful comparison with similar developments in France, see Nicole Edelman, *Voyantes, guérisseuses et visionnaires en France 1785–1914* (Paris, 1995).

93 G. Slade Butler, 'Appearance of Spirits in Sussex', *Sussex Archaeological Collections* 14 (1862) 32. The author obviously means D. D. Home.

94 See Oppenheim, *The Other World*, pp. 159–99; Russel M. Goldfarb, 'Madame Blavatsky', *Journal of Popular Culture* 5 (1971) 32–44.

95 *The Times*, 9 January 1909.

96 Edward Hamer, 'Parochial Account of Llanidloes', *Montgomeryshire Collections* 10 (1877) 233.

97 C. R. Straton, 'Witches' Brooms', *Wiltshire Archaeological Magazine* 29 (1897) 158.

98 Robert Stephen Hawker, *Footprints of Former Men* (London, 1870), p. 165.

99 Elizabeth Lynn Linton, *Witch Stories* (London, [1861] 1883), p. 319.

100 See also Gillson's *A Watchman's appeal, with especial reference to the unexplained wonders of the Age* (Bath, 1853).

101 Gillson, *Table-Talking*, p. 5.

102 *Ibid.*, p. 6.

103 *Ibid.*, p. 19.

104 Edward Gillson, *The Relapsed Demoniac; a warning to England against the return of Popery* (Bath, 1845).

105 Francis Close, *Table-Turning not Diabolical. A tract for the times* (London, 1853); Bishop of Calcutta, *Satanic Agency not connected with Table-Turning: a reply to two publications on the subject* (London, 1853); John Prichard, *A Few Sober Words of Table-talk about Table-Spirits, and the Rev. N. S. Godfrey's incantations* (London, 1853); Anon., *Table-Turning and Table Talking, considered with reference to some pamphlets published by the Rev. N. S. Godfrey and the Rev. E. Gillson. By a Member of the University of Cambridge* (Cheltenham, 1853); Rev. William Connor Magee, *Talking to Tables, a great folly or a great sin; being the substance of a sermon* (Bath, 1853).

106 John Jones, *Spiritualism the Work of Demons* (Liverpool, 1871). See also Charles Cowan, *Thoughts on Satanic Influence; or Modern Spiritualism Considered* (London, 1854); J. B. Clifford, *Modern Witchcraft, or Spiritualism: a Sign of the Times*

(London, 1873); M. J. Williamson, *Modern Diabolism: Commonly Called Modern Spiritualism* (London, 1873); H. A. H., *The Satanic Origins and Character of Spiritualism* (London, 1876); Miles Grant, *Spiritualism unveiled, and shown to be the Work of Demons: an Examination of its Origins, Doctrines and Politics* (London, n.d.).

107 Thomas Brevior, *A Reply to a Sermon By the Rev. John Jones, Entitled 'Spiritualism the Work of Demons'* (London, 1872), p. 1.

108 Henry Parr, *Sermons Preached in the Parish Church of Tunbridge, Kent* (London, 1861), p. 198.

108 Quoted in James Gillingham, *The Errors of Spiritualism. Its Errors, its Unlawfulness, and its Insanity* (Frome, 1922), p. 73. See also Clifford, *Modern Witchcraft, or Spiritualism*.

110 Montague Summers, *The History of Witchcraft and Demonology* (London, 1926), p. 256.

111 The following account is based on detailed and lengthy reports of the case in *The Salisbury and Winchester Journal*, 5 October 1889, and the *Salisbury Times*, 5 October 1889.

112 *The Salisbury and Winchester Journal*, 12 October 1889.

113 *Ibid.*, 16 October 1889.

114 *Somerset County Herald*, 12 January 1895.

115 See P. Vandermeersch, 'The Victory of Psychiatry over Demonology: The Origin of the Nineteenth-Century Myth', *History of Psychiatry* 2 (1991), 351–63; Judith Devlin, *The Superstitious Mind* (New Haven and London, 1987), pp. 215–30.

116 The state of British psychology during the period is well discussed in Roy Porter, *Mind-forg'd Manacles* (London, 1987); Michael Donnelly, *Managing the Mind* (London and New York, 1983); A. Scull (ed.), *Madhouses, Mad-doctors, and Madmen: The Social History of Psychiatry in the Victorian Era* (Philadelphia, 1981).

117 Parr, *Sermons*, p. 199.

118 *Somerset County Herald*, 25 February 1871; *Transactions of the Devonshire Association* [hereafter *TDA*] 26 (1894) 85.

119 *Dean Forest Mercury*, 26 May 1905.

120 *The Times*, 19 August 1867.

121 See Owen Davies, 'Hag-riding in Nineteenth-Century West Country England and Modern Newfoundland: An Examination of an Experience-centred Witchcraft Tradition', *Folk Life* 35 (1997) 36–53.

122 *The Times*, 17 December 1875.

123 *Bideford Weekly Gazette*, 1 June 1886; *TDA* 26 (1894) 84–5.

124 *TDA* 26 (1894) 85.

125 *Western Mail*, 4–5 November 1904; *The Times*, 4 November 1904.

126 See J. S. Neki, B. Joinet, N. Ndosi, G. Kilonzo, J. G. Hauli and G. Duvinage, 'Witchcraft and Psychotherapy', *British Journal of Psychiatry* 149 (1986) 145–55.

127 Mary Kinnear, 'The Correction Court in the Diocese of Carlisle, 1704–1756', *Church History* 59 (1990) 191–206; Jan Albers, 'Seeds of Contention: Society, Politics and the Church of England in Lancashire, 1689–1790', Ph.D. dissertation, Yale University, 1988.

128 Albers, 'Seeds of Contention', p. 267.

129 National Library of Wales, Ms LL/CC/G 279; R. F. Suggett, 'Some Aspects

of Village Life in Eighteenth-Century Glamorgan', B. Litt. dissertation, University of Oxford, 1976, p. 201.

130 Ann Ashley, 'The Spiritual Courts of the Isle of Man, especially in the Seventeenth and Eighteenth Centuries', *English Historical Review* 72 (1957) 31–59.

131 W. Walter Gill, *A Second Manx Scrapbook* (London, 1932), p. 84.

132 Tina Isaacs, 'The Anglican Hierarchy and the Reformation of Manners 1688–1738', *Journal of Ecclesiastical History* 33 (1982) 391–411.

133 Isaac Nicholson, *A Sermon Against Witchcraft, Preached in the Parish Church of Great Paxton, in the County of Huntingdon, July 17, 1808* (London, 1808), p. i. The famous case of witchcraft at Warboys, Huntingdonshire, occurred in 1589. For details, see Anne Reiber DeWindt, 'Witchcraft and Conflicting Visions of the Ideal Village Community', *Journal of British Studies* 34 (1995) 427–63.

134 Nicholson, *Sermon Against Witchcraft*, p. 120.

135 Thomas Hawkins, The Iniquity of Witchcraft, Censured and Exposed (Halifax, 1808), p. vii.

136 *Ibid.*, p. xi.

137 *Ibid.*, p. 27.

138 R. Lyne, *The Sinfulness and Idolatry of Charms, and of all unbidden Christianlike ways of Worshipping God, shewn in two letters Addressed to the Inhabitants of Little Petherick, in the County of Cornwall* (Bodmin, 1817), p. 3.

139 Revd. William Vowles, *The Question of Apparitions and Supernatural Voices considered. A Sermon Occasioned by the Extraordinary circumstances which Immediately followed the Death of Ann Taylor* (Tiverton, 1814), p. 28.

140 *Ibid.*, p. 26.

141 *ANTIPAS: A Solemn Appeal to the Right Reverend The Archbishops and Bishops of the United Churches of England and Ireland; with Reference to Several Bills passed, or passing Through the Imperial Parliament; especially that concerning Witchcraft and Sorcery* (London, 1821), p. 21.

142 *Ibid.*, p. 35.

143 Nicholson, *Sermon Against Witchcraft*, p. iv-v.

144 *Ibid.*, p. ix.

145 Mrs Gutch, *County Folklore: North Riding* (London, 1899), pp. 158–9. This incident was recounted by Keary's daughter.

146 David Vincent, *Literacy and Popular Culture: England 1750–1914* (Cambridge, 1989), p. 173.

147 Lawrence Stone, 'Literacy and Education in England 1640–1900', *Past and Present* 42 (1969) 69–139; Carl Kaestle, '"Between the Scylla of Brutal Ignorance and the Charybdis of a Literary Education": Elite Attitudes towards Mass Schooling in Early Industrial England and America', in Lawrence Stone (ed.), *Schooling and Society* (Baltimore, 1976), pp. 171–91; Harvey J. Graff, *The Legacies of Literacy* (Bloomington and Indianapolis, 1987).

148 Cited in Stone, 'Literacy and Education', 87.

149 Cited in Roy Porter, *English Society in the Eighteenth Century* (London, 1982), p. 181.

150 William Lovett, *Life and Struggles of William Lovett* (London, [1876] 1967), p. 111.

151 Adam Smith, *An Inquiry into the Nature and Cause of the Wealth of Nations* (London, [1776] 1904), vol. 2, pp. 272–3.

152 William Hone (ed.), *The Year Book* (London, 1831), vol. 2, p. 781.

153 *Proceedings of the Dorset Natural History and Antiquarian Field Club* 5 (1884) 15.

154 Richard Johnson, 'Educational Policy and Social Control in Early Victorian England', *Past and Present* 49 (1970) 96—119.

155 Graff, *The Legacies of Literacy*, p. 337.

156 James Augustus St John, *The Education of the People* (London, 1858), p. 30.

157 *Ibid.*, p. 29.

158 *The Standard*, 22 September 1880; *Folklore Record* 3 (1880) 288.

159 *Tipton Herald*, 16 January 1926.

160 Richard Phayre, *A Sermon Preached in the Parish Church of Raynham St. Mary, on the Sinfulness of Astrology* (Norwich, 1849), p. 17.

161 For a general discussion on the Society, see M. J. D. Roberts, 'The Society for the Suppression of Vice and its Early Critics, 1802—1812', *The Historical Journal* 26 (1983) 159—76; E. Bristow, *Vice and Vigilance: Purity Movements in Britain Since 1700* (Dublin, 1977).

162 *Part the First, of an Address to the Public from the Society for the Suppression of Vice, Instituted, in London, 1802* (London, 1803), pp. 44—5.

163 *Ibid.*, p. 90.

164 For a history of the Norwood gypsies, see Eric Otto Winstedt, 'The Norwood Gypsies and their Vocabulary', *Journal of the Gypsy-Lore Society*, NS. 9 (1915—16) 129—52.

165 *Mist's Weekly Journal*, 12 March 1726.

166 *The Times*, 22 August 1797.

167 *London Chronicle*, 13—15 October 1803.

168 *The Trial of Joseph Powell, the Fortune-Teller, At the Sessions-House, Clerkenwell, October 31, 1807; Taken in Short-Hand by Mr. Gurney: with an Appendix and Notes* (London, 1808), p. 25.

169 *Ibid.*, p. 20.

170 *Illustrated London News*, 11 November 1871.

171 *Birmingham Daily Mail*, 30 January 1883.

172 Sabine Baring-Gould, *Devonshire Characters and Strange Events* (London, 1908), p. 83.

173 *The Times*, 17 September 1912.

174 *Hansard*, House of Commons, 5th S. 25, cols 1021—2.

175 *Ibid.*, col. 1629—30.

176 *Hansard*, House of Commons, 5th S. 31, col. 806.

177 *Hansard*, House of Commons, 5th S. 40, col. 323; 5th S. 42, col. 526.

178 *The Justice of the Peace*, 21 April 1917, p. 155.

179 *Ibid.*, 20 January 1917, p. 28.

180 *The Morning Leader*, 1 September 1904; *The Times*, 1 September 1904.

181 *The Treasury of Literature and the Ladies' Treasury*, 1 December 1873, p. 297.

182 Gertrude Kingston, 'Prosecution or Persecution?', *The Fortnightly Review* 105 (1919) 456. Konstam sometimes used the pseudonym Kingston.

183 *The Justice of the Peace*, 30 May 1896, p. 348.

184 E. René, *Hands and How to Read Them: A Popular Guide to Palmistry* (London, [1901] 1920), p. 103.

185 'Fortune Tellers and Society. The Pleasure of Hearing about Ourselves', *The Times*, 21 May 1914.

186 *The Justice of the Peace*, 21 February 1903, p. 94.

187 *Somerset County Herald*, 3 February 1894.

188 *The Times*, 9 September 1904.

189 *The Justice of the Peace*, 21 April 1917, p. 156.

190 See Ellic Howe, *Urania's Children* (London, 1969), pp. 34–47; Patrick, *A Confusion of Prophets* (London, 1992), pp. 61–109.

191 See the *Bath Chronicle*, 25 December 1851.

192 Christopher Cooke, *A Plea for Urania: Being a Popular Sketch of Celestial Philosophy with observations on the impolicy of the Law which is supposed to prohibit the practice of Astral Science in the present Age* (London, 1854), p. xiv. See also his articles, 'Astrology and the Statute Book', *The Biological Review* 1:3 (1858); 'The Legal Position of Astrology', *The Biological Review* 1:4 (1859).

193 Cooke, *A Plea for Urania*, pp. 338–9.

194 *Ibid.*, p. 8.

195 *Ibid.*, p. 28.

196 M. A. (Oxon) [W. Stainton Moses], *The Slade Case: Its Facts and its Lessons. A Record and a Warning* (London, 1877), p. 25.

197 *Ibid.*

198 *Light*, 19 March 1881, p. 87.

199 Reprinted in *The Spiritualist* 11 (1877) 23.

200 *The Justice of the Peace*, 7 April 1877, pp. 214–16.

201 *The Justice of the Peace*, 12 March 1887, pp. 167–8. Further background information on Penny can be found in Curry, *A Confusion of Prophets*, pp. 141, 181.

202 *The Justice of the Peace*, 12 March 1887, pp. 167–8.

203 *The Justice of the Peace*, 8 July 1899, pp. 423–4.

204 L. G. Wickham Legg (ed.), *Dictionary of National Biography 1931–1940* (Oxford, 1949), p. 211.

205 *The Times*, 10 August and 1 September 1904; *The Justice of the Peace*, 26 November 1904.

206 *The Justice of the Peace*, 18 September 1909, pp. 463–4.

207 *The Justice of The Peace*, 18 October 1919, p. 460.

208 *The Times*, 20 April 1921.

209 D. Aikenhead Stroud, 'Fortune-telling and Mens Rea', *The Law Quarterly Review* 37 (1921) 489; *The Justice of The Peace*, 30 April 1921, p. 191.

210 *Ibid.*

211 *Strand*, December 1920, pp. 463–8. Doyle also published a book on the subject, *The Coming of the Fairies* (London, 1922). See Joe Cooper, *The Case of the Cottingley Fairies* (London, 1990).

212 *Justice of the Peace and Local Government Review*, 23 June 1928, p. 417.

213 *Ibid.*, 418.

214 Kingston, 'Prosecution or Persecution?', p. 456.

215 *The Justice of the Peace*, 30 May 1896, p. 348.

216 *The Brierley Hill Advertiser*, 24 March 1894.

217 *The Justice of the Peace*, 18 October 1919.

218 *Hansard*, House of Commons, 5th S. 245, cols 1320–4.

219 *Hansard*, House of Commons, 5th S. 247, cols 571–2.

220 *Justice of the Peace*, 5 November 1927, p. 826; *The Times*, 6 January 1939.

221 *Standing Committee A*, 4 March 1948, cols 1332–3.

222 *Hansard*, House of Commons, 5th S. 481, col. 1499.

223 *Ibid.*, col. 1493.

224 *Ibid.*, col. 1478.

225 *Ibid.*, col. 1479.

226 *Ibid.*, cols 1490–1.

227 *Ibid.*, col. 1498.

228 *The Times*, 13 December 1950.

229 *Hansard*, House of Lords, 5th S. 171, cols 718–29.

230 Peter Burke, *Popular Culture in Early Modern Europe* (New York, 1978).

231 *Stamford Mercury*, 13 November 1789; cited in Robert Malcolmson, *Popular Recreations in English Society 1700–1850* (Cambridge, 1973), p. 135.

Chapter 2

1 Mrs Bray, *Traditions, Legends, Superstitions and Sketches of Devonshire* (London, 1888), vol. 2, p. 170; *Transactions of the Devonshire Association* 7 (1875) 261; *Daily Chronicle*, 15 February 1879; D. Leslie Davies, 'The Black Arts in Wrexham', *Denbighshire Historical Transactions* 19 (1970) 232.

2 J. S. Cockburn (ed.), *Calendar of Assize Records: Surrey Indictments, Elizabeth I* (London, 1980).

3 Alan Macfarlane, *Witchcraft in Tudor and Stuart England* (London, 1971), p. 201.

4 Greater London Record Office, Acc. 890, pp. 296–7.

5 Alan Macfarlane, 'Witchcraft in Tudor and Stuart Essex', in J. S. Cockburn (ed.), *Crime in England 1550–1800* (London, 1977), p. 75.

6 *Surrey Archaeological Collections* 12 (1895) 129.

7 Norma Landau, *The Justices of the Peace 1679–1760* (Los Angeles and London, 1984), p. 207.

8 C. L'Estrange Ewen, *Witchcraft and Demonianism* (London, 1933), p. 302. See also James Sharpe, *Instruments of Darkness: Witchcraft in England 1550–1750* (London, 1996), p. 155.

9 Percentages extrapolated from numbers in C. L'Estrange Ewen, *Witch Hunting and Witch Trials* (London, 1929).

10 Landau, *The Justices of the Peace*, p. 21.

11 Peter Virgin, *The Church in an Age of Negligence: Ecclesiastical Structure and Problems of Church Reform 1700–1840* (Cambridge, 1989), p. 115.

12 See T. C. Curtis, 'Quarter Sessions Appearances and their Background: A Seventeenth-Century Regional Study', in Cockburn (ed.), *Crime in England*, p. 148.

13 *A Full and True Account of the Apprehending and Taking of Mrs. Sarah Moordike* (London, 1701).

14 The case provoked a flurry of pamphlets. See Phyllis J. Guskin, 'The Context of Witchcraft: The Case of Jane Wenham (1712)', *Eighteenth Century Studies* 15 (1981) 48–71.

15 See Virgin, *The Church in an Age of Negligence*, for discussion of clergyman justices.

16 W. Gilbert, 'Witchcraft in Essex', *Transactions of the Essex Archaeological Society*, NS. 6 (1911) 211–18.

17 *Historical Society of West Wales Transactions* 9 (1920–23) 127; J. H. Matthews (ed.), *Cardiff Records* (Cardiff, 1898–1911), vol. 3, pp. 202–3.

18 *Witches Apprehended, Examined and Executed, for notable villanies by them committed*

both by Land and Water. With a Strange and most true trial how to know whether a woman be a Witch or not (London, 1613).

19 Keith Thomas, *Religion and the Decline of Magic* (revised edition, London, 1973), p. 658.

20 In the East Slavic world the swimming of suspected witches was practised as far back as the twelfth century. See Russell Zguta, 'The Ordeal by Water (Swimming of Witches) in the East Slavic World', *Slavic Review* 36 (1977) 220–31.

21 Reginald Scot, *The Discoverie of Witchcraft* (London, 1584); William Perkins, *A Discourse of the Damned Art of Witchcraft* (Cambridge, 1608), p. 206. Perkins' work was printed after his death in 1602.

22 James I, *Daemonologie, in forme of a Dialogue, Divided into three Bookes* (Edinburgh, 1597), p. 80.

23 Stuart Clark, 'King James's *Daemonologie*: Witchcraft and Kingship', in Sydney Anglo (ed.), *The Damned Art* (London, 1977), p. 156.

24 Margaret Kerr, Richard Forsyth and Michael Plyley, 'Cold Water and Hot Iron: Trial by Ordeal in England', *Journal of Interdisciplinary History* 22 (1992) 579.

25 John Cotta, *Triall of Witch-craft* (London, 1616), p. 104.

26 Clive Holmes, 'Popular Culture? Witches, Magistrates, and Divines in Early Modern England', in Steven Kaplan (ed.), *Understanding Popular Culture* (Berlin, 1984), p. 105.

27 David Underdown, 'The Taming of the Scold: The Enforcement of Patriarchal Authority in Early Modern England', in Anthony Fletcher and John Stevenson (eds), *Order and Disorder in Early Modern England* (Cambridge, 1985); pp. 116–37; Martin Ingram, '"Scolding women and cucked or washed": A Crisis in Gender Relations in Early Modern England?', in Jenny Kermode and Garthine Walker (eds), *Women, Crime and the Courts in Early Modern England* (London, 1994), pp. 48–80; J. W. Spargo, *Juridicial Folklore in England Illustrated by the Cucking Stool* (Durham NC, 1944).

28 For the detailed instructions given to Enger see *Witches Apprehended* (London, 1613); Ewen, *Witchcraft and Demonianism*, p. 205.

29 Ewen, *Witchcraft and Demonianism*, pp. 207–8. At the same assizes it was heard how another suspected witch, Alice Abbott, 'being for trial cast into the water with her hands and feet bound could not sink to bottom by any means'; *ibid.*, p. 211.

30 *The Examination, Confession, Triall, and Execution of Joane Williford, Joan Cariden and Jane Hott* (London, 1645).

31 John Stearne, *A Confirmation and Discovery of Witchcraft* (London, 1648), p. 18. Hopkins believed that the Devil actually advised witches 'to be swome'; Matthew Hopkins, *The Discovery of Witches* (London, 1647), p. 56.

32 *Gentleman's Magazine*, NS. 33 (1856) 39; Gilbert, 'Witchcraft in Essex'; Landau, *The Justices of the Peace*, p. 91.

33 John Cotta, *A Short Discoverie of the Unobserved Dangers* (London, 1612), p. 54.

34 Thomas Ady, *A Candle in the Dark* (London, 1656), p. 100.

35 Hopkins, *Discovery*, pp. 5–6; Stearne, *Confirmation*, p. 18.

36 Francis Hutchinson, *An Historical Essay Concerning Witchcraft* (London, 1718), pp. 139–40.

37 *A Full and Impartial Account of the Discovery of Sorcery and Witchcraft, Practis'd by Jane Wenham of Walkerne in Hertfordshire* (London, 1712).

38 Ewen, *Witchcraft and Demonianism*, p. 390.

39 *Daily Journal*, 15 January 1731; *Gentleman's Magazine* 1 (1731) 29.

40 *Northamptonshire Notes and Queries* 2 (1888) 19; J. W. Wickwar, *Witchcraft and the Black Art* (London, 1925), pp. 292–3.

41 Thomas Skyrme, *History of the Justices of the Peace* (Chichester, 1991), vol. 2, pp. 92–3.

42 Martin Ingram, 'Ridings, Rough Music and Mocking Rhymes in Early Modern England', in Barry Reay (ed.), *Popular Culture in Seventeenth Century England* (London, 1985), p. 189.

43 Joseph Juxon, *A Sermon Upon Witchcraft. Occasion'd by a late illegal attempt to discover witches by swimming. Preach'd at Twyford, in the county of Leicestershire, July 11, 1736, by Joseph Juxon. Vicar of Twyford and Hungarton* (London, 1736). In the same year Philip Stubs also preached a sermon entitled *The witchcraft of the scriptures: a sermon preach'd on a special occasion* (London, 1736).

44 *A Sermon Upon Witchcraft*, pp. 19–20.

45 *Ibid.*, pp. 26–7.

46 *Ibid.*, p. 19.

47 Wallace Notestein, *A History of Witchcraft in England* (New York, [1911] 1965), p. 315.

48 Hutchinson, *An Historical Essay*, p. 139.

49 Juxon, *A Sermon Upon Witchcraft*, p. 25.

50 Cited in Charles James Billson, *Folk-Lore of Leicestershire and Rutland* (London, 1895), pp. 51–2. See also John H. Pruet, 'A Late Stuart Leicestershire Parson: The Reverend Humphrey Michel', *Transactions of the Leicestershire Archaeological and Historical Society* 54 (1978–79) 26–38.

51 Walter Scott, *Letters on Demonology and Witchcraft* (London, [1830] 1884), pp. 219–20; W. Page (ed.), *Victoria History of the County of Bedfordshire*, (London, 1920) vol. 2, p. 149; William Connor Sydney, *England and the English in the Eighteenth Century: Chapters in the Social History of the Times* (2nd edn, Edinburgh, 1891), vol. 1, pp. 283–4. Although the above sources present the facts of the case accurately, they all date it wrongly. The correct date has been established in George L. Kittredge, *Witchcraft in Old and New England* (Cambridge MA, 1929), p. 541, n.56.

52 *The East Anglian* 1 (1864) 48.

53 *The Tryal of Thomas Colley ... For the cruel and inhuman Murder of Ruth Osborne, Wife of John Osborne of Tring, in Hertfordshire* (London, 1751); *The Remarkable Confession, and Last Dying Words of Thomas Colley ... Together with Copies of Original Letters which Colley sent to his Wife and Friends during his lying under Condemnation* (London, 1751). Most witchcraft historians have relied on the account of events given in the *Gentleman's Magazine*, which contains a number of inaccuracies. See W. B. Carnochan's revisionist account, 'Witch-hunting and Belief in 1751: The Case of Thomas Colley and Ruth Osborne', *Journal of Social History* 4 (1971) 389–403.

54 *Leicester and Nottingham Journal*, 6 July 1776; Billson, *Folklore of Leicestershire and Rutland*, pp. 50–1.

55 *Annual Register* 3 (1760) 113, 120.

56 *Public Advertiser*, 1 January 1761; Sydney, *England and the English*, p. 286.

57 From a newspaper cutting dated May 1751 cited in Page (ed.), *Victoria History of Bedfordshire*, vol. 3, p. 402.

58 *The Salisbury and Winchester Journal*, 15 March 1773; Edward Bradby, *Seend:*

A Wiltshire Village Past and Present (Gloucester, 1981); Bob Bushway, "'Tacit, Unsuspected, but Still Implicit Faith": Alternative Belief in Nineteenth-Century Rural England', in Tim Harris (ed.), *Popular Culture in England, c. 1500–1850* (London, 1995), p. 204.

59   Kittredge, *Witchcraft*, p. 540; Eric Maple, *The Dark World of Witches* (London, 1962), p. 123.

60   *Northamptonshire Notes and Queries* 11 (1888) 20; W. Gardiner, *Music and Friends* (London, 1838), vol. 1, pp. 406–8.

61   *The Times*, 19 July 1825.

62   *The Times*, 27 April 1857.

63   Elizabeth Lynn Linton, *Witch Stories* (London, [1861] 1883), p. 320; C. R. Stratton, 'Witches' Brooms', *Wiltshire Archaeological & Natural History Magazine* 29 (1897) 158.

64   Robert Malcolmson, *Life and Labour in England: 1700–1780* (London, 1981), p. 90.

65   *The Chelmsford Chronicle*, 9 July 1880. The defendants were each bound over in their own recognisance for £5 to keep the peace for six months, and to pay costs amounting to 11s 6d.

66   For example, Robert Filmer, *An Advertisement to the Jurymen of England Touching Witches* (London, 1653).

67   *The Times*, 7 April 1857.

68   Holmes, 'Popular Culture?', p. 105.

69   *Leicester and Nottingham Journal*, 6 July 1776.

70   *The Times*, 24 September 1863. Both Smith and Stammers were convicted at the Chelmsford assizes, and sentenced to six months' hard labour.

71   Christina Hole, *Witchcraft in England* (London, 1977), p. 175.

72   *The Times*, 7 April 1857.

73   H. Colley March, 'Dorset Folklore Collected in 1897', *Folklore* 10 (1899) 487.

74   Sabine Baring-Gould, *A Life of Robert Stephen Hawker* (London, 1876), pp. 157–8.

75   Cecil Torr, *Small Talk at Wreyland* (Oxford, [1918] 1979), p. 26.

76   W. H. Howse, *Radnorshire* (Hereford, 1949), p. 196.

77   *The Spectator*, 17 February 1894.

78   *Somerset County Herald*, 9 May 1863.

79   *The Times*, 7 April 1857.

80   *The Times*, 27 April 1857.

81   *The Times*, 19 July 1825.

82   John Glyde, *The Norfolk Garland* (London, 1872), p. 51.

83   John Symonds Udal, *Dorsetshire Folk-Lore* (Hertford, 1922), pp. 208–9; 'Scraps of English Folklore, xvi. Herefordshire', *Folklore* 39 (1928) 390.

84   *Somerset County Herald*, 13 March 1852.

85   Glyde, *The Norfolk Garland*, p. 51.

86   Eveline Camilla Gurdon, *County Folk-Lore: Suffolk* (Ipswich, 1893), p. 185. Taken from a newspaper of 1792. Seven years earlier, a woman of Mear's Ashby, Northamptonshire, also volunteered herself to be swum. She was thrown into a pond, sank instantly, and was pulled out to cries of 'No witch! No witch!'; *Gentleman's Magazine* 55 (1785) 658.

87   L. Salmon, 'Folklore in the Kennet Valley', *Folklore* 13 (1902) 427; Boys Firmin, *An Illustrated Guide to Crowborough* (Brighton and London, [1890] 1905), p. 158.

88 *The Times*, 7 April 1857.

89 *Pulman's Weekly News*, 14 June 1892.

90 *The Times*, 17 December 1875. Leviticus xx. 27 states: 'A man also or woman that hath a familiar spirit, or that is a wizard, shall surely be put to death.'

91 Glyde, *The Norfolk Garland*, p. 53.

92 Alfred Russel Wallace, *My Life: a record of events and opinions* (London, 1905), vol. 1, p. 217.

93 E. P. Thompson, *Customs in Common* (London, 1991); E. P. Thompson, 'Rough Music Reconsidered', *Folklore* 103 (1992) 3–26; Paul Robinson, 'Royal Justice and Folk Justice: Conflict Arising Over a Skimmington in Potterne in 1857', *Wiltshire Archaeological and Natural History Magazine* 83 (1990) 147–54; Rosemary A. N. Jones, 'Popular Culture, Policing, and the Disappearance of the *Ceffyl Pren* in Cardigan c. 1837–1850', *Ceredigion* 11 (1988–9) 19–39; Ingram, 'Ridings, Rough Music and Mocking Rhymes in Early Modern England'; A. James Hammerton, 'The Targets of "Rough Music": Respectability and Domestic Violence in Victorian England', *Gender & History* 3 (1991) 23–44.

94 Thompson, *Customs in Common*, p. 530.

95 Thompson, 'Rough Music Reconsidered', p. 15.

96 Jones, 'Popular Culture, Policing', p. 25.

97 *The Times*, 13 April 1857.

98 *The Times*, 10 April 1827.

99 *Remarkable Confession, and Last Dying Words of Thomas Colley*, p. 7.

100 Thompson, *Customs in Common*, p. 490.

101 Sharpe, *Crime in Early Modern England*, p. 90.

102 *The Times*, 24 September 1863.

103 James Obelkevitch, *Religion and Rural Society: South Lindsey, 1825–75* (Oxford, 1976), p. 300.

104 *The Times*, 10 April 1827.

105 See, for example, Thompson, 'Rough Music Reconsidered', p. 15.

106 See Eric Hobsbawm and George Rudé, *Captain Swing* (London, 1973), pp. 206–8.

107 Mick Reed, 'The Peasant of Nineteenth-Century England: A Neglected Class?', *History Workshop Journal* 18 (1984) 67.

108 Keith Wrightson, 'Two Concepts of Order: Justices, Constables and Jurymen in Seventeenth-century England', in John Brewer and John Styles (eds), *An Ungovernable People* (London, 1980), pp. 21–47; also J. A. Sharpe, 'Crime and Delinquency in an Essex Parish 1600–1640', in Cockburn (ed.), *Crime in England*, p. 95.

109 Cited in Robert Storch, 'Policing Rural Southern England before the Police: Opinion and Practice, 1830–1856', in Douglas Hay and Francis Snyder (eds), *Policing and Prosecution in Britain 1750–1850* (Oxford, 1989), p. 224.

110 Storch, 'Policing Rural Southern England', p. 224.

111 J. G. Rule, 'Social Crime in the Rural South in the Eighteenth and Early Nineteenth Centuries', *Southern History* 1 (1979) 135–53.

112 Joan Kent, 'The English Village Constable, 1580–1642: The Nature and Dilemmas of the Office', *Journal of British Studies* 20 (1981), 30; J. Kent, '"Folk Justice" and Royal Justice in Early Seventeenth-Century England: A "Charivari" in the Midlands', *Midland History* 8 (1983) 70–85.

113 Isaac Nicholson, *A Sermon Against Witchcraft* (London, 1808), pp. i–ix.

114 *The Times*, 19 July 1825; extracted from the *Suffolk Chronicle*.

115 *The Times*, 10 April 1827.

116 Cited in Storch, 'Policing Rural Southern England', pp. 238–9.

117 Robert Storch, 'The Policeman as Domestic Missionary: Urban Discipline and Popular Culture in Northern England, 1850–1880', *Journal of Social History* 9 (1976) 481–504; Jones, 'Popular Culture, Policing'; David Philips, *Crime and Authority in Victorian England* (London, 1977), pp. 84–5.

118 *The Times*, 23 September 1858; reprinted from the *Essex Standard*.

119 Carolyn A. Conley, *The Unwritten Law: Criminal Justice in Victorian Kent* (Oxford, 1991), p. 32.

120 *Devizes and Wiltshire Gazette*, 12 March 1857; see Paul Robinson, 'Royal Justice and Folk Justice: Conflict Arising over a Skimmington in Potterne in 1857', *Wiltshire Archaeological and Natural History Magazine* 83 (1990) 147–54.

121 *Pulman's Weekly News*, 24 August 1858.

122 Jones, 'Popular Culture, Policing'; Storch, 'The Policeman as Domestic Missionary'; Philips, *Crime and Authority*.

123 Storch, 'The Policeman as Domestic Missionary', p. 492.

124 *The Times*, 10 August 1853; extracted from the *Sunderland Herald*.

125 For some Wiltshire examples, see Robinson, 'Royal Justice and Folk Justice', pp. 151–2.

126 Conley, *The Unwritten Law*, pp. 23–4, p. 41.

127 See E. P. Thompson, *The Making of the English Working Class* (London, 1963); E. P. Thompson, 'The Moral Economy of the English Crowd in the Eighteenth Century', *Past and Present*, 50 (1971) 76–136; George Rudé, *The Crowd in History* (New York, 1964).

128 Mrs Gutch and Mabel Peacock, *County Folklore: Folk-Lore Concerning Lincolnshire* (London, 1908), p. 74.

Chapter 3

1 Alfred Wallis, 'A Sketch of the Early History of the Printing Press in Derbyshire', *Derbyshire Archaeological Society* 3 (1881) 138.

2 James Guest, 'A Free Press, and How it Became Free', in W. Hutton (ed.), *The History of Birmingham* (Birmingham, 1861); cited in Maureen Perkins, *Visions of the Future: Almanacs, Time, and Cultural Change* (Oxford, 1996), p. 68.

3 Wallis, 'A Sketch', 138.

4 See Roger Chartier, *The Cultural Uses of Print in Early Modern France* (Princeton, 1987).

5 *The British Dictionary* (London, 1933).

6 Charles Godfrey Leland, *Gypsy Sorcery and Fortune Telling*, (New York, [1891] 1962), p. xxxiii.

7 R. S. Schofield, 'Dimensions of Illiteracy in England 1750–1850', in H. Graff (ed.), *Literacy and Social Development in the West* (Cambridge, 1981); David Vincent, *Literacy and Popular Culture: England 1750–1914* (Cambridge, 1989); Lawrence Stone, 'Literacy and Education in England, 1640–1900', *Past and Present* 42 (1969) 69–139.

8 Flora Thompson, *Lark Rise to Candleford* (London, [1945] 1948), p. 74.

9 Barry Reay, 'The Context and Meaning of Popular Literacy: Some Evidence

from Nineteenth-Century Rural England', *Past and Present* 131 (1991) 118.

10 See David Vincent, 'The Decline of the Oral Tradition in Popular Culture', in Robert Storch, *Popular Culture and Custom in Nineteenth-Century England* (London, 1982), pp. 20–48.

11 Vincent, *Literacy and Popular Culture*, p. 176.

12 See Owen Davies, 'Healing Charms in Use in England and Wales 1700–1950', *Folklore* 107 (1996) 19–33.

13 See Leslie Shepard, *The Broadside Ballad* (London, 1962); also the foreword by Michael Hughes to Charles Hindley's *Curiosities of Street Literature* (New York, [1871] 1970).

14 *The Trial of Joseph Powell, the Fortune-Teller, At the Sessions-House, Clerkenwell, October 31, 1807; Taken in short-hand By Mr. Gurney* (London, 1808).

15 *Liverpool Courier*, 28 October 1857.

16 See H. Delehaye, 'Note sur la Légende de la Lettre du Christ tombée du ciel', *Académie Royale de Belgique. Bulletin de la Classe des Lettres* (Brussels, 1899) 171–213; Ellen Ettlinger, 'British Amulets in London Museums', *Folklore* 50 (1939) 170–2; Judith Devlin, *The Superstitious Mind*, (New Haven, 1987), pp. 140–3.

17 See Davies, 'Healing Charms in Use in England and Wales'.

18 C. A. Parker, 'A Seventeenth Century Charm', *Transactions of the Cumbrian and Westmorland Antiquarian and Archaeological Society* 12 (1911) 82–5.

19 Mrs Gutch and Mabel Peacock, *Folk-Lore Concerning Lincolnshire* (London, 1908), pp. 126–7.

20 E. M. Leather, *The Folk-Lore of Herefordshire* (London, 1912), p. 113.

21 Edward Jesse, *Scenes and Tales of Country Life* (London, 1844), p. 42; *Notes and Queries*, 2nd S. 17 (1856) 331; L. Salmon, 'Folklore in the Kennet Valley', *Folklore* 13 (1902) 424; E. M. Leather, *Folk-Lore of Herefordshire* (London, 1912) p. 112; Charlotte Latham, 'Some West Sussex Superstitions Lingering in 1868', *Folk-Lore Record* 1 (1878) 24.

22 *Notes and Queries*, 5th S. 1 (1874) 325.

23 *A Copy of a Letter written by our Blessed Lord and Saviour* (London, *c.* 1720).

24 William Henderson, *Folklore of the Northern Counties* (2nd edn, London, 1879), p. 194.

25 Valenze, 'Prophecy and Popular Literature', p. 91.

26 *West Lancashire Magazine* 2:1 (n.d.).

27 Victor Neuberg, *Chapbooks: A Bibliography of References to English and American Chapbook Literature of the Eighteenth and Nineteenth Centuries* (London, 1964), pp. 15–30.

28 See Robert Collison, *The Story of Street Literature* (London, 1973); Robert Hays Cunningham, *Amusing Prose Chap-Books Chiefly of Last Century* (London, 1889); John Ashton, *Chap-books of the Eighteenth Century* (London, 1882); Victor Neuberg, *Chapbooks: a bibliography of references to English and American chapbook literature of the eighteenth and nineteenth centuries* (London, 1964); Frances M. Thomson, *Newcastle Chapbooks* (Newcastle, 1969); Emanuel Green, 'On Some Somerset Chap-Books', *Somerset Archaeological and Natural History Society Proceedings* 24 (1878) 50–66; C. Ferguson, 'On the Collection of Chap-Books in the Bibliotheca Jacksoniana', *Transactions of the Cumberland and Westmorland Antiquarian and Archaeological Society* 14 (1897) 1–90; P. J. Cropper, *The Nottinghamshire Printed Chap-Books* (Nottingham, 1892). For excellent discussions of seventeenth-century material, see Margaret Spufford, *Small Books*

and *Pleasant Histories* (Cambridge, 1981); Tessa Watt, *Cheap Print and Popular Piety, 1550–1640* (Cambridge, 1991).

29 Ferguson, 'Chap-Books in the Bibliotheca Jacksoniania', p. 1.

30 See for example, *The Golden Dreamer; or, Dreams Realised, Containing the Interpretation of a Great Variety of Dreams* (Glasgow, *c.* 1850); also *Napoleon Bonaparte's Book of Fate* (Glasgow, *c.* 1850).

31 *The High-German Fortune-Teller. Laying down True Rules and Directions by which Both Men and Women May Knoe their Good and Bad Fortune … Written by the High German Artist* (London, *c.* 1750). It was printed again in Newcastle (*c.* 1780), London (*c.* 1785), Birmingham (*c.* 1810), London (*c.* 1815), and London (*c.* 1825).

32 See Otho T. Beall, Jr., 'Aristotle's Master Piece in America: A Landmark in the Folklore of Medicine', *William and Mary Quarterly*, 3rd S., 20 (1963) 207–22; Janet Blackman, 'Popular Theories of Generation: The Evolution of Aristotle's Works, The Study of an Anachronism', in John Woodward and David Richards (eds), *Health Care and Popular Medicine in Nineteenth Century England* (London, 1977), pp. 56–88; Angus McLaren, *Reproductive Rituals* (London, 1984); Roy Porter, '"The Secrets of Generation Display'd": Aristotle's Master-piece in Eighteenth-Century England', in Robert Purks Maccubbin (ed.), *'Tis Nature's Fault: Unauthorized Sexuality during the Enlightenment* (Cambridge, 1987).

33 See *The New Book of Knowledge: showing the Effects of the Planets, and other Astronomical Constellations; with the Strange Events that befall Men, Women and Children, born under them* (London, 1758).

34 Printed in London, probably around 1750, and reprinted again *c.* 1790.

35 Charles Godfrey Leland, *Gypsy Sorcery and Fortune Telling*, p. xxxiii.

36 Charles Mackay, *Extraordinary Popular Delusions and the Madness of Crowds* (London, 1852), p. 295.

37 John Harland and T. T. Wilkinson, *Lancashire Folk-Lore* (London, 1882), p. 145; Mrs Gutch (ed.), *County Folklore: East Riding of Yorkshire* (London, 1912), p. 73.

38 In the nineteenth century, Mother Bunch's name was also used to merchandise another chapbook, *Mother Bunch's Golden Fortune-Teller*, printed first in Newcastle around 1840, and again in Newcastle and Glasgow around 1880.

39 Eric Partridge, *A Dictionary of Historical Slang* (London, 1961).

40 See George L. Gomme, *Mother Bunch's Closet Newly Broke open, and the History of Mother Bunch of the West* (London, 1885).

41 For example, *The Universal Fortune Teller: or; Mrs Bridget's – commonly called the Norwood Gipsey – Golden Treasury explained* (London, *c.* 1790); *The New Norwood Gipsy; or Art of Fortune Telling* (London, 1840); *The Norwood Gipsy Fortune Teller* (Glasgow, *c.* 1835).

42 Another fortune-telling chapbook similarly found and printed for the enlightenment of society was *The Dreamer's Oracle; or Future Revealer, found in the ark of a late celebrated wizard* (Newcastle, *c.* 1850).

43 Eric Otto Winstedt, 'The Norwood Gypsies and their Vocabulary', *Journal of the Gypsy Lore Society*, NS., 9 (1915–16) 134.

44 Jonathan Caredig Davies, *Folk-Lore of West and Mid-Wales* (Aberystwyth, 1911), p. 10.

45 Eveline Camilla Gurdon, *County Folklore: Suffolk* (Ipswich, 1893), p. 99.

46 See *Napoleon Bonaparte's Book of Fate* (Glasgow, *c.* 1850), p. 23; *The Dreamers Oracle* (Derby, 1838); John Glyde, *Norfolk Garland* (London, 1872), pp. 9–10; Gurdon, *County Folklore: Suffolk*, p. 97; E. M. Leather, *The Folk-Lore of Herefordshire* (London, 1912), pp. 61–2; Violet Mason, 'Scraps of English Folklore. XIX. Oxfordshire', *Folklore* 40 (1929) 382.

47 See also the *High German Fortune-Teller*.

48 *The New Infallible Fortune Teller; or, a Just Interpretation of Dreams and Moles. To which is added, Rules to foretell the Weather, Drawn up from the strict observance of nearly half a century* (Edinburgh, 1818).

49 One of the few discussions concerning dream-books is Susan Gallagher 'Jack Blunt and His Dream Book', *American Literature* 58 (1986) 614–19.

50 Edward Lyndoe, *Everybody's Book of Fate and Fortune* (London, 1935), p. 294.

51 Herman Melville, *Redburn* (New York, [1849] 1971), pp. 90–1.

52 *Shrewsbury Chronicle*, 6 September 1884.

53 T. Sharper Knowlson, *The Origins of Popular Superstitions* (London, n.d.), pp. 123–4.

54 Other than the chapbooks already cited, see *The Old Egyptian Fortune-Teller's Last Legacy* (London, *c.* 1820); *New Fortune Book, or Conjurer's guide; the only real Fortune-Teller* (Glasgow, *c.*1850); *The Fortunate Gypsy; or, the Young Lady Turn'd Fortune-Teller* (London, *c.* 1820); *The New Fortune Book for Bachelors, Husbands, Widowers, Wives, Maids, and Widows* (Coventry, *c.* 1810); *Partridge and Flamsted's New and Well-Experienced Fortune Book* (London, *c.* 1750, and numerous later editions).

55 See, for example, *Mother Bunch's Golden Fortune Teller* (Glasgow, *c.* 1880); *The Spaewife; or Universal Fortune-Teller* (Glasgow, *c.* 1850); *The Norwood Gypsey Wheel of Fortune* (London, *c.* 1873).

56 Mackay, *Extraordinary Popular Delusions*, p. 291.

57 *Anti-Canidia: or, Superstition Detected and Exposed* (London, *c.* 1762), p. 42; *The Fortune Teller's Conjuring Cap* (Banbury, *c.* 1815), p. 2.

58 Denys Forrest, *Tea for the British* (London, 1973); Arthur Reade, *Tea and Tea Drinking* (London, 1884).

59 Davies, *Folk-Lore of West and Mid-Wales*, pp. 14–15.

60 *Somerset County Herald*, 24 July 1869.

61 Davies, *Folk-Lore of West and Mid-Wales*, p. 15.

62 *Ashton-under-Lyne Reporter*, 17 January 1857; *Foklore Society News* 16 (1992) 12–13; *Somerset County Herald*, 27 March 1880.

63 For further discussion on prophecy and popular literature in the period, see Deborah M. Valenze, 'Prophecy and Popular Literature in Eighteenth-Century England', *Journal of Ecclesiastical History* 29 (1978) 75–92. For the Wandering Jew, see Galit Hasan-Rokem and Alan Dundes (eds), *The Wandering Jew: Essays in the Interpretation of a Christian Legend* (Bloomington, 1986); Gaël Milin, *Le cordonnier de Jérusalem: la Véritable histoire du Juif errant* (Rennes, 1997).

64 J. F. C. Harrison, *The Second Coming* (London, 1979), pp. 53–4.

65 See W. E. A. A[xon] (ed.), *Nixon's Cheshire Prophecies ... with an introductory essay on popular prophecies* (London, 1878).

66 See William H. Harrison, *Mother Shipton Investigated. The Result of critical examination in the British Museum Library, of the literature pertaining to the York-shire sybil* (London, 1881); Anon. (ed.), *Mother Shipton: A collection of the earliest editions of her prophecies* (Manchester, 1881).

67 *The Prophecies of Mother Shipton in the Raigne of King Henry the Eighth* (London, 1641).

68 R. Head, *The Life and Death of Mother Shipton* (London, 1667); *The Strange and Wonderful History of Mother Shipton* (London, 1686).

69 *Mother Shipton's Legacy, or a favourite fortune book* (York, 1797); *The Dreamers Oracle* (Derby, 1838); *Mother Shipton's Universal Dreamer* (London, *c.* 1840); *Mother Shipton's Fortune-telling book* (London, *c.* 1860); *The Gypsy's Oracle; by the celebrated Mother Shipton* (London, *c.* 1860); *Mother Shipton's Wheel of Fortune* (London, 1861).

70 John Clare, 'Autobiographical Fragments', in E. Robinson (ed.), *John Clare's Autobiographical Writings* (Oxford, 1983), p. 2.

71 Mackay, *Extraordinary Popular Delusions*, p. 268.

72 See *Mother Shipton: A collection of the earliest editions*, pp. vii–xi.

73 *Somerset County Herald*, 8 November 1890.

74 *The Life, Prophecies and Death of the famous Mother Shipton* (London, 1862).

75 *The End of the World! and other remarkable Prophecies, by Mother Shipton* (London, 1872); *"The End of the World" in 1881–2, according to Mother Shipton, the Great Pyramid of Ghizeh, and other ancient prophecies relating to Russia and Turkey* (London, 1880).

76 *Notes and Queries*, 4th S. 11 (1873) 355.

77 *Somerset County Herald*, 26 November 1881.

78 There is a useful discussion on the folklore surrounding historical figures in Hilda Ellis Davidson, *Patterns of Folklore* (Ipswich, 1978), pp. 1–20.

79 For example, *The Life and Prophecies of Ursula Sontheil, better known as Mother Shipton* (Leeds, 1918).

80 Keith Thomas, *Religion and the Decline of Magic* (revised edition, London, 1973), p. 405.

81 See Elic Howe, *Urania's Children* (London, 1967), ch. 11 and ch. 14; C. W. C. Oman, 'Presidential Address', *Transactions of the Royal Historical Society*, 4th S. 1 (1918) 25; David Robb, *Nostradamus on Napoleon, Hitler and the Present Crisis* (London, 1941).

82 Samuel Bamford, *Early Days* (London, 1893), p. 87.

83 This account is based on *The History of the Lancashire Witches. Also a Treatise of Witches in general* (London, *c.* 1785). Other editions vary little in content.

84 Diane Purkiss, *The Witch in History* (London, 1996), pp. 233–5; Montague Summers, *The History of Witchcraft* (London, 1927), p. 309.

85 *The History of the Lancashire Witches*, pp. 21–2.

86 Cecil James Sharp, *The Idiom of the People*, edited with an introduction by James Reeves (New York, 1965), pp. 25–6.

87 R. S. Thomson, 'The Development of the Broadside Ballad Trade and its Influence on the Transmission of English Folk-songs', Ph.D. dissertation, Cambridge University, 1974.

88 Francis Hutchinson, *Historical Essay Concerning Witchcraft* (London, 1718), p. xiv.

89 See, for example, *History of Dr John Faustus. Shewing how he sold himself to the devil, to have power for 24 years to do whatever he pleased* (London, *c.* 1800).

90 See *A dreadful warning piece to atheists, deists and prodigals … A most dismal account of a young gentleman … who became a prey to the devil* (London, *c.* 1750); *Earthly piety, or, an example for young children. Shewing how one Mr. Johnson's child of Barnet, was tempted by the devil to forsake God* (London, *c.* 1775); *A timely warning to all rash and disobedient children, being a strange and wonderful*

*relation of Thomas Williams, a young gentleman in the parish of Bridgewater, that
sold himself to the devil for 12 years* (London, *c.* 1780).

91 See, for example, J. C. Jeaffreson (ed.), *Middlesex County Records*, vol. 3 (London, 1886–92), pp. 88–9.

92 T. Quiller Couch, *The History of Polperro* (Penzance, 1871), pp. 144–5.

93 *Ibid.*, p. 144.

94 *The Times*, 19 July 1856.

95 See Louis James, *Fiction for the Working Man, 1830–1850* (Oxford, 1963); Michael Anglo, *Penny Dreadfuls and Other Victorian Horrors* (London, 1977); John Springhall, '"A Life Story for the People"? Edwin J. Brett and the London "Low-Life" Penny Dreadfuls of the 1860s', *Victorian Studies* 33 (1990) 223–47.

96 Excelsior Library No. 3 (London, 1889).

97 Frederick Elworthy, *The Evil Eye* (London, 1895), p. 235.

98 Almanacs have been treated to several excellent studies. See Bernard Capp, *Astrology and the Popular Press: English Almanacs 1500–1800* (London, 1979); Patrick Curry, *Prophecy and Power: Astrology in Early Modern England* (Cambridge, 1989); Patrick Curry, *A Confusion of Prophets: Victorian and Edwardian Astrology* (London, 1992); Maureen Perkins, *Visions of the Future: Almanacs, Time, and Cultural Change* (Oxford, 1996).

99 Cited in Capp, *Astrology and the Popular Press*, p. 264.

100 For a fairly late example of the zodiac man, see *Rider's British Merlin: For the Year of Our Lord God 1780* (London, 1780), B3.

101 Robert Forby, *The Vocabulary of East Anglia*, vol. 2 (London, 1830), p. 404.

102 Charles Knight, *Passages of a Working Life During Half a Century*, vol. 1 (London, 1864–65), p. 151.

103 *The Times*, 9 January 1909.

104 *Salisbury and Winchester Journal*, 12 October 1889.

105 Lucy Baxter, *The Life of William Barnes* (London, 1887), p. 125.

106 John Udal, *Dorsetshire Folk-Lore* (Hertford, 1922), p. 262.

107 See, for example, C. Swainson, *A Handbook of Weather Folk-Lore* (London, 1873); John Harland and T. T. Wilkinson, *Lancashire Legends* (Manchester, 1873), pp. 231–4; Gurdon, *County Folklore: Suffolk*, pp. 160–6; Davies, *Folk-Lore of West and Mid-Wales*, pp. 219–22; T. F. Thiselton Dyer, *English Folk Lore* (London, 1878), pp. 247–63; K. G. Spencer, 'Wild Birds in Lancashire Folk-Lore', *Journal of the Lancashire Dialect Society* 15 (1966) 2–15; Glyde, *Norfolk Garland*, pp. 151–8;.

108 M. C. F. Morris, *Yorkshire Reminiscences* (Oxford, 1922), p. 327.

109 Forby, *The Vocabulary of East Anglia*, p. 404.

110 T. T. Wilkinson, 'On the Popular Customs and Superstitions of Lancashire', *Transactions of the Historical Society of Lancashire and Cheshire* 11 (1859) 162.

111 Margaret Eyre, 'Folk Lore of the Wye Valley', *Folklore* 16 (1905) 170; *Pulman's Weekly News*, 14 June 1892.

112 *The Welshman*, 27 December 1895.

113 See also George Beaumont, *Fixed Stars: or, An Analyzation and Refutation of Astrology* (Norwich, 1803).

114 See Perkins, *Visions of the Future*, ch. 2.

115 *The Fortune Teller's Conjuring Cap*, p. 2.

116 *Ibid.*, pp. 5–6.

117 *Tawney Rachel; or the Fortune Teller: with some Account of Dreams, Omens, &*

Conjurors (London, *c.* 1810).

118 M. G. Jones, *Hannah More* (Cambridge, 1952); Susan Pedersen, 'Hannah More Meets Simple Simon: Tracts, Chapbooks, and Popular Culture in Late Eighteenth-Century England', *Journal of British Studies* 25 (1986) 84–113.

119 *Tawney Rachel*, pp. 15–16.

120 Pedersen, 'Hannah More', p. 110.

121 Natalie Zemon Davis, *Society and Culture in Early Modern France* (Cambridge, 1987), p. 225.

122 W. Sparrow Simpson, 'On a Seventeenth Century Roll containinng Prayers and Magical Signs', *Journal of the British Archaeological Association* 40 (1884) 297.

123 For the history of newspapers in the period, see R. M. Wiles, *Freshest Advices: Early Provincial Newspapers in England* (Ohio, 1965); G. A. Cranfield, *The Development of the Provincial Newspaper, 1700–1760* (Oxford, 1962); G. Boyce, J. Curran and P. Wingate (eds), *Newspaper History* (London, 1978); Michael Harris and Alan Lee (eds), *The Press in English Society from the Seventeenth to Nineteenth Centuries* (London, 1986).

124 For further discussion, see Owen Davies, 'Newspapers and the Popular Belief in Witchcraft and Magic in the Modern Period', *Journal of British Studies* 37 (1998) 139–66.

125 *Somerset County Herald*, 26 May 1866.

126 Reprinted in Christopher Cooke, *A Plea for Urania* (London, 1854), p. 339.

127 *Western Morning News*, 3 March 1932.

128 *Somerset County Herald*, 22 April 1893.

129 *Somerset County Herald*, 27 March 1880. I suspect for various reasons that Major was an alias of the pseudo-prophet and fortune-teller, John Hartwell.

130 Lady Rosalind Northcote, 'Devonshire Folklore, Collected Among the People Near Exeter Within the Last Five or Six Years', *Folklore* 11 (1900) 216.

131 Peter Burke, *Popular Culture in Early Modern Europe* (London, 1978), p. 253.

132 D. R. Woolf, 'The "Common Voice": History, Folklore and Oral Tradition in Early Modern England', *Past and Present* 120 (1988) 48.

133 Mabel Peacock, 'Folklore of Lincolnshire', *Folklore* 12 (1901) 180.

134 Eugen Weber, 'Fairies and Hard Facts: The Reality of Folktales', *Journal of the History of Ideas* 42 (1981) 112.

135 Gustav Jahoda, 'Witchcraft, Magic and Literacy', *New Society* 16 (1963) 15–17.

136 *The Times*, 27 April 1857.

Chapter 4

1 Due to lack of space I have been unable to refer to all the works consulted.

2 For a comparison with the Dutch archives, see Ton Dekker, 'Witches and Sorcerers in Twentieth Century Legends', in Marijke Gijswijt-Hofstra and Willem Frijhoff (eds), *Witchcraft in the Netherlands from the Fourteenth to the Twentieth Century* (Rotterdam, 1991), pp. 183–96.

3 Discussions on the reliability of oral testimony can be found in Jan Vansina, *Oral Tradition: A Study in Historical Method* (London, 1965); Gillian Bennett, *Traditions of Belief* (London, 1987); George Ewart Evans, *Where Beards Wag All* (London, 1970).

4 L. H. Hayward, 'Shropshire Folklore of Yesterday and To-Day', *Folklore* 49 (1938) 223.

5 *The Times*, 7 April 1857.

6 See, for example, Edward Goddard, 'Witchcraft in Wiltshire', *Wiltshire Archaeological and Natural History Magazine* 29 (1897) 165; Ethel Rudkin, *Lincolnshire Folklore* (Gainsborough, 1936), p. 85; Robert Hunt, *Popular Romances of the West of England* (second edition, London, [1865] 1881), pp. 338–9; Isaac Nicholson, *A Sermon Against Witchcraft* (London, 1808), p. iii.

7 Rev. M. C. F. Morris, *Yorkshire Folk-Talk* (London, 1892), p. 241.

8 *Transactions of the Devonshire Association* [hereafter *TDA*] 39 (1907) 103; *Sussex Notes and Queries* 4 (1933).

9 Rev. Canon Eddrup, 'Notes on some Wiltshire Superstitions', *Wiltshire Archaeological and Natural History Magazine* 22 (1885) 334.

10 *The Times*, 16 September 1930.

11 *Notes and Queries*, 4 May (1850) 429.

12 Hunt, *Popular Romances*, p. 318.

13 Hermann Lea, 'Dorset Superstitious Still!', *The Dorset Year Book* (1914–15), pp. 25–6.

14 Anon., 'Anecdotes of English Rural Life. By an English Clergyman', *Chambers's Journal*, 25 September 1880, p. 617.

15 Edward Hamer, 'Parochial Account of Llanidloes', *Montgomeryshire Collections* 10 (1877) 240.

16 Morris, *Yorkshire Folk-Talk*, p. 241.

17 L. Salmon, 'Folklore in the Kennet Valley', *Folklore* 13 (1902) 427; *TDA* 93 (1961) 113; J. Ceredig Davies, *Folk-Lore of West and Mid-Wales* (Aberystwyth, 1911), p. 231.

18 William Howells, *Cambrian Superstitions* (Tiptree, 1831), p. 90.

19 Eric Parker, *Surrey* (London, 1947), p. 219.

20 Eric Maple, 'The Witches of Canewdon', *Folklore* 71 (1960) 241–50; E. Maple, 'Witchcraft and Magic in the Rochford Hundred', *Folklore* 76 (1965) 213–24; Edward M. Wilson, 'Folk Traditions in Westmorland', *Journal of the Folklore Institute* 2 (1965) 291–2; John Smith, 'Some West-Country Traditions Relating to Conjuring and Witchcraft', *Journal of the Lancashire Dialect Society* 25 (1976) 26–7; Robin Gwyndaf, 'The Past in the Present: Folk Beliefs in Welsh Oral Tradition', *Fabula* 35 (1994) 226–60.

21 Smith, 'Some West-Country Traditions', p. 27.

22 Hermann Lea, 'Wessex Witches, Witchery, and Witchcraft', *The Nineteenth Century* 19–20 (1903) 1024; Angelina Parker, 'Oxfordshire Village Folklore (1840–1900)', *Folklore* 24 (1913) 83.

23 *The Spectator*, 14 April 1894, p. 503.

24 Rudkin, *Lincolnshire Folklore*, pp. 71, 88; *TDA* 66 (1934) 80; Paul Karkeek, 'A Budget of Witch Stories', *TDA* 14 (1882) 394.

25 H. E. Malden, 'Witchcraft in Surrey', *Surrey Archaeological Society* 35 (1923) 119–20; Northcote, 'Devonshire Folklore', p. 215.

26 *The Times*, 7 April 1857; *The Spectator*, 14 April 1894, p. 503.

27 Karkeek, 'A Budget of Witch Stories', p. 388.

28 Percy Manning, 'Stray Notes on Oxfordshire Folklore', *Folklore* 13 (1902) 290–1.

29 Margaret Eyre, 'Folk Lore of the Wye Valley', *Folklore* 16 (1905) 171; *Notes and Queries*, 3rd S. 2 (1862) 325.

30 Charlotte Burne, *Shropshire Folk-Lore* (London, 1883), p. 148.

31 H. E. Malden, 'Witchcraft in Surrey', 119.

32 *The Diary of Benjamin Newton* (Cambridge, 1933), p. 75. See also *Westmorland Gazette*, 22 June 1839.

33 *Witchcraft Detected & Prevented* (Peterhead, 1824), p. 104.

34 Elias Owen, 'Folklore, superstitions, or what-not, in Montgomeryshire and elsewhere', *Montgomeryshire Collections* 15 (1882) 134.

35 Hermann Lea, 'Some Dorset Superstitions', in Thomas Perkins and Herbert Pentin (eds), *Memorials of Old Dorset* (London, 1907), p. 301.

36 *TDA* 39 (1907) 104; L. Salmon, 'Folklore in the Kennet Valley', *Folklore* 13 (1902) 427; Davies, *Folk-Lore of West and Mid-Wales*, p. 231; James Sharpe, *Instruments of Darkness: Witchcraft in England 1550–1750* (London, 1996), pp. 151–2.

37 James Obelkevitch, *Religion and Rural Society: South Lindsey, 1825–75* (Oxford, 1976), p. 276.

38 Elias Owen, *Welsh Folk-Lore* (Aberystwyth, 1896), p. 144.

39 Angelina Parker, 'Oxfordshire Village Folklore (1840–1900)', *Folklore* 24 (1913) 84.

40 *The Times*, 7 April 1857.

41 Thomas Quiller Couch, 'The Folklore of a Cornish Village: Witchcraft, Etc.', *Notes and Queries* 11 (1855) 497.

42 Lea, 'Some Dorset Superstitions', p. 295.

43 Karkeek, 'Budget of Witch Stories', p. 394.

44 Rosalind Northcote, 'Devonshire folklore collected among the People near Exeter Within the last five or six years', *Folklore* 11 (1900) 215.

45 *Notes and Queries*, 3rd S. 2 (1862) 325. See also Eyre, 'Folklore of the Wye Valley', p. 170.

46 A. R. Milton, 'The Wicked Old Woman', *Sussex County Magazine* 17 (1943) 48.

47 *Ibid.*, p. 49; *Sussex Notes and Queries* 4 (1933) 182.

48 *The Times*, 3 September 1915; *The Times*, 16 September 1930. Niggets were described as 'creepy-crawly things', and one witch fed them on bits of chopped-up grass.

49 Sharpe, *Instruments of Darkness*, p. 137.

50 *The Times*, 27 April 1857.

51 Hermione Jennings, 'A Cambridgeshire Witch', *Folklore* 16 (1905) 187–90. See also Rudkin, *Lincolnshire Folklore*, p. 87.

52 John Glyde, *The Norfolk Garland* (London, 1872), p. 55. For other accounts of succession, see Enid Porter, *Cambridgeshire Customs and Folklore* (London, 1969), p. 161; Maple, 'The Witches of Canewdon', pp. 246–7.

53 Catherine E. Parsons, 'Notes on Cambridgeshire Witchcraft', *Proceedings of the Cambridgeshire Antiquarian Society* 19 (1915) 44.

54 *The Times*, 7 April 1857.

55 Nicholson, *A Sermon Against Witchcraft*, pp. iii–iv.

56 Boys Firmin, *An Illustrated Guide to Crowborough* (Brighton and London, [1890] 1905), pp. 159, 164.

57 S. E. Robinson, 'Tom Reed: A Man and His Lore', *Sussex County Magazine* 9 (1935) 59.

58 Rudkin, *Lincolnshire Folklore*, p. 88.

59 Brian C. Luxton, 'William Jenkin, the Wizard of Cadoxton-juxta-Barry',

Morgannwg 24 (1980) 43.

60 *The Times*, 10 April 1827.

61 *The Times*, 7 April 1857.

62 Elijah Cope, 'Some Local Fairies', in Rev. W. Beresford (ed.), *Memorials of Old Staffordshire* (London, 1909), p. 93; E. S. Hartland, *The Science of Fairy Tales, an Inquiry into Fairy Mythology* (London, 1891), p. 348;

63 Henry More, *Antidote against Atheism* (London, 1655), p. 232.

64 See L. V. Grinsell, *The Ancient Burial Mounds of England* (second edition; London, 1953), pp. 70–85; L. V. Grinsell, 'Witchcraft at Some Prehistoric Sites', in V. Newell (ed.) *The Witch Figure* (London, 1973).

65 Ronald Hutton, *The Triumph of the Moon: A History of Modern Pagan Witchcraft* (Oxford, 1999), ch. 6.

66 J. S. Udal, *Dorsetshire Folk-Lore* (Hertford, 1922), p. 212.

67 Parsons, 'Notes on Cambridgeshire Witchcraft', 39; Rudkin, *Lincolnshire Folklore*, pp. 72–3.

68 W. Y. Evans-Wentz, *The Fairy Faith in Celtic Countries* (Oxford, 1911), p. 144; H. S. Toms, 'Witches and Hares', *Sussex County Magazine* 9 (1935) 194; Fletcher Moss, *Folk-Lore, Old Customs and Tales of my Neighbours* (Manchester, 1898), p. 207.

69 H. Colley March, 'Dorset Folklore Collected in 1897', *Folklore* 10 (1899) 487. See also Burne, *Shropshire*, p. 157; E. J. Begg, 'Cases of Witchcraft in Dorsetshire', *Folklore* 52 (1941) 71.

70 W. Ll. Davies, 'The Conjuror in Montgomeryshire', *Montgomeryshire Collections* 45–46 (1937–40) 169; Cope, 'Some Local Fairies', p. 93.

71 Richard Bovet, *Pandaemonium* (East Ardsley, [1684] 1975), p. 124.

72 J. Raine (ed.), *Depositions from the Castle of York* (Durham, 1861), pp. 93, 125; C. L'Estrange Ewen, *Witchcraft and Demonianism* (London, 1933), p. 374; *Somerset and Dorset Notes and Queries* 28 (1968) 142–6.

73 Owen, *Welsh Folk-Lore*, p. 219; Charles Mackay, *Memoirs of Extraordinary Popular Delusions* (London, [1841] n.d.), p. 559; Richard Blakeborough, *Yorkshire Wit, Character, Folklore and Customs* (London, 1898), p. 168.

74 Lea, 'Wessex Witches', p. 1024; Lea, 'Some Dorset Superstitions', pp. 298–9.

75 A. K. Hamilton Jenkin, *Cornwall and the Cornish. The Story, Religion, and Folklore of the Western Land* (London, 1933), p. 250; Hayward, 'Shropshire Folklore', p. 242; Evans-Wentz, *Fairy Faith*, p. 160; Sidney Oldall Addy, *Household Tales and Traditional Remains* (London, 1895), p. xii.

76 Keith Thomas, *Religion and the Decline of Magic* (revised edition, London, 1973), p. 529.

77 Ian Bostridge, *Witchcraft and its Transformations c. 1650–c. 1750* (Oxford, 1997), pp. 166–70.

78 *The Times*, 19 September 1930; Ruth Tongue, *Somerset Folklore* (London, 1965), p. 67; *The Times*, 16 September 1930. See also Burne, *Shropshire Folklore*, pp. 156–7.

79 E. M. Leather, *The Folk-Lore of Herefordshire* (London, 1912), p. 53.

80 Percy Manning (ed.), 'Stray Notes on Oxfordshire Folklore', *Folklore* 13 (1902) 291; Jennings, 'A Cambridgeshire Witch'; Parsons, 'Notes on Cambridgeshire Witchcraft', p. 39; Porter, *Cambridgeshire Customs and Folklore*, p. 172; Maple, 'Witches of Canewdon', p. 243; Leather, *The Folk-Lore of Herefordshire*, p. 53.

81 March, 'Dorset Folklore', p. 111; Owen Davies, 'Hag-riding in Nineteenth-century West Country England and Modern Newfoundland', *Folk Life* 35 (1997) 41.

82 *The Times*, 7 April 1857.

83 Lea, 'Wessex Witches', p. 1024

84 Mabel Peacock, 'Folklore of Lincolnshire', *Folklore* 12 (1901) 172; Rev. T. A. Davies, 'Folklore of Gwent', *Folklore* 48 (1937) 51; E. W. Swanton and P. Woods, *Bygone Haslemere* (London, 1914), p. 285; Eyre, 'Folk-Lore of the Wye Valley', p. 171.

85 William Brockie, *Legends and Superstitions of Durham* (Sunderland, 1886), pp. 6–8; *The Taunton Courier*, 20 September 1837.

86 J. C. Atkinson, *Forty Years in a Moorland Parish* (London, 1891), pp. 87–90; Blakeborough, *Yorkshire Wit*, p. 190.

87 Owen, *Welsh Folk-Lore*, pp. 345–6

88 Brockie, *Legends*, p. 31; Begg, 'Cases of Witchcraft', p. 70; Mary M. Banks, 'Witch Lore from the Borders of Sussex and Surrey. (1895–1898)', *Folklore* 52 (1941) 75.

89 Peacock, 'Folklore of Lincolnshire', p. 172. See also Davies, 'The Conjuror in Montgomeryshire', p. 169.

90 *Sussex Notes and Queries* 4 (1933) 182; Firmin, *An Illustrated Guide to Crowborough*, p. 161.

91 Malden, 'Witchcraft in Surrey', 119–20

92 Banks, 'Witch Lore', p. 74–5.

93 Thomas, *Religion and the Decline of Magic*, p. 529.

94 See, for example, Ewen, *Witchcraft and Demonianism*, pp. 153, 325, 359, 366–7, 374, 377, 449.

95 See *A Most Wicked worke of a Wretched Witch (the like whereof none can record these manie yeares in England)* (London, 1593); George Gifford, *A Dialogue Concerning Witches and Witchcraftes* (London, 1593; facsimile reprint for the Shakespeare Association, 1931), A4; Edward Fairfax, *Daemonologia: A Discourse on Witchcraft as it was acted in the family of Mr. Edward Fairfax, of Fuyston, in the county of York, in the year 1621* (Harrogate, 1882), p. 95.

96 Fairfax, *Daemonologia*, p. 97.

97 Robin Briggs, *Witches and Neighbours* (London, 1996), p. 88.

98 Jean-Claude Marquis, *Loups, sorciers, criminels … une histoire du fait divers au XIXè siècle en Seine-Inférieure* (Luneray, 1993), pp. 38–53; Amélie Bosquet, *La Normandie Romanesque et Merveilleuse* (Paris and Rouen, 1845), pp. 223–43.

99 Oliver Rackham, *The History of Countryside* (London, 1986), pp. 34–5.

100 Norman Cohn, *Europe's Inner Demons* (London, 1975), pp. 206–25; Briggs, *Witches and Neighbours*, p. 381;

101 Gustav Henningsen, 'Witch Persecutions after the Era of the Witch Trials: A Contribution to Danish Ethnohistory', *ARV. Scandinavian Yearbook of Folklore* 44 (1988) 103. First published in Danish in *Folk og Kultur* (1977).

102 Adrian Pollock, 'Social and Economic Characteristics of Witchcraft Accusations in Sixteenth- and Seventeenth-Century Kent,' *Archaeologia Cantiana* 95 (1979) 39; Malcolm Gaskill, 'Witchcraft in Early Modern Kent: Stereotypes and the Background to Accusations', in Jonathan Barry, Marianne Hester and Gareth Roberts (eds), *Witchcraft in Early Modern Europe* (Cambridge, 1996), p. 264, n. 22; Alan Macfarlane, *Witchcraft in Tudor and Stuart England* (London, 1970), p. 160; Sharpe, *Instruments of Darkness*, p. 108.

103 Newspaper clipping, *c.* 1840, in scrapbook in Harry Price Library; *The Rock*, 25 April 1879; *Folklore Record* 2 (1879) 207–9.

104 *Somerset County Herald*, 21 February 1846.

105 Charlotte Latham, 'Some West Sussex Superstitions Lingering in 1868', *Folklore Record* 1 (1878) 23; *Somerset County Herald*, 22 July 1865; Nicholson, *A Sermon Against Witchcraft*, p. v.

106 Thomas, *Religion and the Decline of Magic*, p. 696.

107 *Somerset County Herald,* 7 July 1888; *Somerset County Herald*, 2 February 1861. A similar scenario is probably behind the case, in 1900, of a couple who stated that their ill-cared-for children had been overlooked by a gypsy. The prosecution was brought by the National Society for the Prevention of Cruelty to Children. See *Notes and Queries*, 9th S. 5 (1900) 285. These cases are not part of the sample survey.

108 *Whitby Gazette*, 12 June 1858; cited in David Clark, *Between Pulpit and Pew: Folk Religion in a North Yorkshire Fishing Village* (Cambridge, 1982), p. 148.

109 Willem de Blécourt, *Termen van toverij* (Nijmegen, 1990); Christine D. Worobec, 'Witchcraft Beliefs and Practices in Prerevolutionary Russian and Ukrainian Villages', *The Russian Review* 54 (1995) 165–87.

110 *Somerset County Herald*, 16 October 1852.

111 Nicholson, *Sermon Against Witchcraft*, pp. i–ii.

112 See, for example, Ewen, *Witchcraft and Demonianism*, pp. 374–7, 381, 390.

113 *Gentleman's Magazine* 32 (1762) 596.

114 *The worlds wonder being a most strange and wonderful relation of one Richard Hathaway* (London, 1701); *The Tryal of Richard Hathaway upon an Information for being a Cheat and Impostor* (London, 1702);.

115 *The Times*, 3 May 1870; *The Times*, 19 August 1867.

116 Glyde, *The Norfolk Garland*; Owen, *Welsh Folk-Lore*; Davies, *Folk-Lore of West and Mid-Wales*; Tongue, *Somerset Folklore*; Rudkin, *Lincolnshire Folklore*; Hunt, *Popular Romances*.

117 *The Times*, 3 December 1867.

118 *Langport Herald*, 15 June 1895; *Daily Chronicle*, 8 June 1895.

119 *Gentleman's Magazine* 39 (1769) 506.

120 *The Standard*, 7 March 1890; *Folklore* 2 (1891) 248.

121 *Somerset County Herald*, 16 October 1852; *The Times*, 3 May 1870.

122 Davies, 'Hag-riding', p. 46; *The Times*, 3 December 1867.

123 Elworthy, *Evil Eye*, p. 11; Leather, *Folk-Lore of Herefordshire*, p. 58; Eyre, 'Folk-Lore of the Wye Valley', p. 170.

124 Edward Lovett, *Folk-Lore and Legend of the Surrey Hills and of the Sussex Downs and Forests* (Caterham, 1928), p. 7.

125 *Somerset County Herald*, 15 May 1858; Jennings, 'A Cambridgeshire Witch', 190; *The Times*, 7 April 1857.

126 Leather, *Folk-Lore*, p. 58; Frederick Thomas Elworthy, *The Evil Eye* (London, 1911), p. 11.

127 Charles Kightly, *Country Voices: Life and Lore in English Farm and Village* (London, 1984), p. 73.

128 Flora Thompson, *Lark Rise to Candleford* (Oxford, 1948), p. 252.

129 B. Seebohm Rowntree and May Kendall, *How the Labourer Lives* (London, 1913), p. 235.

130 Michael Winstanley, 'Voices from the Past: Rural Kent at the Close of an Era', in G. E. Mingay (ed.), *The Vanishing Countryman* (London, 1989), p. 90.

131 H. D. Gordon, *The History of Harting* (London, 1877), p. 217.

132 *The Times*, 7 April 1857.

133 March, 'Dorset Folklore', p. 108.

134 *Lindsey and Lincolnshire Star*, 1 October, 1904.

135 Mary L. Lewes, *Stranger than Fiction* (London, 1911), p. 181. See also Owen, *Welsh Folk-Lore*, p. 228.

136 *Bye-gones* 6 (1883) 221.

137 *Warrington Examiner*, supplement, 16 September 1876.

138 John Harland and T. T. Wilkinson, *Lancashire Legends* (London, 1873), p. 235; *Somerset County Herald*, 19 February 1859.

139 *TDA* 24 (1892) 53; *Sunday Times*, 13 April 1890; Christina Hole, *Witchcraft in England* (London, 1977) p. 178.

140 *Somerset County Herald*, 20 February 1847.

141 Lyndal Roper, *Oedipus and the Devil* (London, 1994), ch. 9; Diane Purkiss, *The Witch in History* (London, 1996), ch. 4.

142 *Somerset County Herald*, 24 July 1869.

143 Joseph Hammond, *A Cornish Parish: Being an Account of St. Austell* (London, 1897), p. 367.

144 Barbara Freire-Marreco, 'Surrey', *Folklore* 20 (1909) 490–1; Milton, 'The Wicked Old Woman', p. 48.

145 *Somerset County Herald*, 30 July 1859.

146 André Julliard, 'Dans l'Ain, des leveurs de sorts', in Françoise Loux (ed.), *Panseurs de douleurs* (Paris, 1992), pp. 99–107.

147 See David Underdown, *Revel, Riot and Rebellion: Popular Politics and Culture in England 1603–1660* (Oxford, 1985); D. Underdown, 'Regional Cultures? Local Variations in Popular Culture During the Early Modern Period', in Tim Harris (ed.), *Popular Culture in England, c. 1500–1850* (London, 1995), pp. 28–48.

148 Briggs, *Witches and Neighbours*, p. 271.

149 *The Times*, 27 October 1866.

150 Henry Swainson Cowper, *Hawkshead* (London, 1899), pp. 308–9.

151 Cited in Trevor Rowley, *Villages in the Landscape* (Gloucester, [1978] 1987), p. 151.

152 Davies, *Folk-Lore of West and Mid-Wales*, p. 236.

153 De Blécourt, *Termen van toverij*.

154 Robert Rowland, '"Fantasticall and Devilishe Persons": European Witch-Beliefs in Comparative Perspective', in Bength Ankarloo and Gustav Henningsen (eds), *Early Modern European Witchcraft: Centres and Peripheries* (Oxford, 1990), p. 169.

155 See, for example, Willem de Blécourt, 'On the Continuation of Witchcraft', in Barry, Hester and Roberts (eds), *Witchcraft in Early Modern Europe*, pp. 335–52; de Blécourt, *Termen van toverij*; Gijswijt-Hofstra and Frijhoff (eds), *Witchcraft in the Netherlands*; Bernard Traimond, *Le pouvoir de la maladie. Magie et politique dans les Landes de Gascogne, 1750–1826* (Bordeaux, 1988); Marie-Sylvie Dupont-Bouchat, 'Le diable apprivoisée. La sorcellerie revisitée: magie et sorcellerie au XIXè siècle', in Robert Muchembled (ed.), *Magie et sorcellerie en Europe du Moyen âge à nos jours* (Paris, 1994), pp. 235–66; Judith Devlin, *The Superstitious Mind* (New Haven and London, 1987); Inge Schöck, 'Das Ende der Hexenprozesse – das Ende des Hexengalubens?', in Sönke Lorenz and Dieter R. Bauer (eds), *Hexenverfolgung. Beiträge zur Forschung* (Würzburg, 1995).

Chapter 5

1 See also Owen Davies, 'Cunning-Folk in England and Wales during the Eighteenth and Nineteenth Centuries', *Rural History* 8 (1997) 91–107; O. Davies, 'Cunning-Folk in the Medical Market-Place during the Nineteenth Century', *Medical History* (1999, forthcoming); Ronald Hutton, *The Triumph of the Moon: A History of Modern Pagan Witchcraft* (Oxford, 1999).

2 *Eastern Daily Press*, 18 December 1968.

3 Arthur Norway, *Highways and Byways in Devon and Cornwall* (London, 1911), p. 45.

4 *Somerset County Herald*, 3 February 1894.

5 Robert Hunt, *Popular Romances of the West of England*, (London, [1865] 1923), pp. 316–17; W. Y. Evans-Wentz, *The Fairy Faith in Celtic Countries* (Oxford, 1911), p. 174; A. K. Hamilton Jenkin, *Cornwall and the Cornish* (London, 1933), pp. 269–71.

6 Thomas De Quincey, *Leaders in Literature with a Notice of Traditional Errors Affecting Them* (Edinburgh, 1882), pp. 271–83. Mochyn Nant, who was also held up to ridicule by the Welsh bard Jonathan Hughes, died around 1856, and was buried at Ruabon; *Bye-Gones*, 29 August, 1888, pp. 177–8.

7 *The Genuine Life and Confession of Richard Walton, a reputed Conjuror* (London, [1733] 1744).

8 *Western Daily Mercury*, 28 January 1875; *The Times*, 13 April 1857.

9 Eric Maple, 'Cunning Murrell', *Folklore* 71 (1960) 38; J. H. Bell, 'Some Fragments of Local Medical History', *Bradford Antiquary* 1 (1888) 90; William Connor Sydney, *The Early Days of the Nineteenth Century in England 1800–1820* (London, 1898), vol. 2, p. 73.

10 Paul Karkeek, 'Recent Cases of Supposed Witchcraft in Devonshire', *Transactions of the Devonshire Association* [hereafter *TDA*] 7 (1875) 261–2.

11 *Somerset County Herald*, supplement, 2 January 1869; *The Times*, 23 September 1858.

12 *The Times*, 13 January 1877.

13 *Somerset County Herald*, 16 April 1864.

14 *The Times*, 13 June 1842; Hunt, *Popular Romances*, p. 411.

15 Elias Owen, 'Folk-Lore, Superstitions, or What-Not, in Montgomeryshire and Elsewhere', *Montgomeryshire Collections* 16 (1883) 152; E. Owen, *Welsh Folk-Lore* (Aberystwyth, 1896), p. 217,

16 Anon., *The Life and Mysterious Transactions of Richard Morris, Esq.* (London, 1799), pp. 19, 4, 39.

17 *The Times*, 24 September 1863.

18 *The Justice of the Peace*, 26 November 1864, p. 756.

19 *The Times*, 22 October 1823.

20 J. C. Atkinson, *Forty Years in a Moorland Parish* (London, [1891] 1923), p. 123.

21 John Nicholson, *Folk Lore of East Yorkshire* (Driffield, 1890), p. 91.

22 *Carlisle Journal*; reprinted in *The Times*, 26 December 1843.

23 *The Times*, 13 February 1868.

24 *Illustrated London News*, 11 November 1871.

25 *Somerset County Herald*, 6 May 1848.

26 *TDA* 2 (1867–8) 74.

27 *Somerset County Herald*, 21 May 1859; reprinted from the *Gloucester Journal*.

28 William Dickinson, *Cumbriana* (Whitehaven, 1875), pp. 106–9.

29 *The Times*, 19 July 1883.

30 *TDA* 2 (1867–68) 73–4.

31 *The Times*, 24 January 1867.

32 Alan Macfarlane, *Witchcraft in Tudor and Stuart England* (London, 1970), p. 122.

33 *Surrey Advertiser*, 3 September 1864.

34 Clive Emsley, *Crime and Society in England, 1750–1900* (London, 1987), p. 82.

35 John Styles, 'Print and Policing: Crime Advertising in Eighteenth-Century Provincial England', in D. Hay and F. Snyder (eds), *Policing and Prosecution in Britain, 1750–1850* (Oxford, 1989), p. 55. See also Richard Williams, 'Securing Justice in Eighteenth-Century England: The Example of Berkshire', *Southern History* 18 (1996) 43–60.

36 *The Times*, 24 September 1863; *The Times*, 24 April 1851.

37 *Taunton Courier*, 31 December 1890.

38 *The Times*, 6 January 1854.

39 *Cymru Fu*, 10 March 1888, p. 118; Anon., *The Life and Mysterious Transactions*, pp. 44–5.

40 J. H. Porter, 'Cockfighting in the Eighteenth and Nineteenth Centuries: from Popularity to Suppression', *TDA* 118 (1986) 63–71.

41 John Aston, *A History of English Lotteries* (London, 1893).

42 Atkinson, *Forty Years*, p. 111; Charlotte Burne, *Shropshire Folk-Lore* (London, 1883), p. 170. In France cunning-folk were often prosecuted for this activity; Eloïse Mozzani, *Magie et superstitions de la fin de l'ancien régime à la restauration* (Paris, 1988), p. 135; Judith Devlin, The *Superstitious Mind* (New Haven, 1987), p. 172.

43 Atkinson, *Forty Years*, p. 111.

44 *Western Morning News*, 17 July 1893; Llywarch Hen, 'Welsh Astrologers, Sorcerers, &c', *Bye-Gones*, 22 August 1888, p. 177; Mrs Gutch, *County Folk-lore: North Riding* (London, 1899), pp. 158–9.

45 'Anecdotes of English Rural Life. By an English Clergyman', *Chambers's Journal*, 25 September 1880, p. 618; *Somerset County Herald*, 27 June 1863.

46 *Somerset County Herald*, 7 July 1849; reprinted from the *Swansea Herald*; *Bye-Gones*, 20 November 1889, p. 259.

47 Griff Evans, 'Exorcism in Wales', *Folklore* 3 (1892) 275–6.

48 Patrick Curry, *A Confusion of Prophets* (London, 1992); Ellic Howe, *Urania's Children* (London, 1967).

49 Boys Firmin, *An Illustrated Guide to Crowborough* (Brighton and London, [1890] 1905), p. 168.

50 Thomas Quiller Couch, *The History of Polperro* (Penzance, 1871) pp. 125–6.

51 Jenkin, *Cornwall and the Cornish*, p. 242.

52 William Connor Sydney, *England and the English in the Eighteenth Century: Chapters in the Social History of the Times* (2nd edn, Edinburgh, 1891), p. 265.

53 *The Liverpool Courier*, 28 October 1857.

54 *The Spectator*, 17 February 1894, p. 231.

55 Paul Hawkins Fisher, *Notes and Recollections of Stroud, Gloucestershire* (London, 1871), p. 24.

56 See Howe, *Urania's Children*, pp. 48–9.

57 *Somerset County Herald*, 5 July 1862.

58 *Somerset County Herald*, 12 March 1853.

59 *Somerset County Herald*, 20 October 1855.

60 See Patrick Curry, *Prophecy and Power* (London, 1989), pp. 132–4; James Obelkevitch, *Religion and Rural Society: South Lindsey, 1825–75* (Oxford, 1976), pp. 288–290.

61 From a Manchester newspaper of 1865; cited in Charles Hardwick, *Traditions, Superstitions, and Folklore* (London, 1872), p. 120.

62 Firmin, *Illustrated Guide to Crowborough*, p. 168.

63 See Francis X. King, *The Flying Sorcerer* (Oxford, 1992), pp. 39–50; Davies, 'Cunning-Folk in England and Wales', pp. 95–6.

64 Anon., *The Life and Mysterious Transactions of Richard Morris*, pp. 9, 24.

65 *The Times*, 3 August 1798.

66 *The Trial of Joseph Powell, the Fortune-Teller* (London, 1808).

67 John Denley found the note and gave it to Proctor.

68 *The Times*, 7 March 1803.

69 *Morning Post*, 12 January 1788; Sydney, *England and the English in the Eighteenth Century*, p. 271; Howe, *Urania's Children*, p. 23n.

70 The scrapbook is now in the Harry Price Library.

71 Handbill in Proctor's scrapbook dated 1834.

72 Cards for these astrologers can be found in Proctor's scrapbook.

73 What little information there is on Hockley's career can be found in John Hamill, *The Rosicrucian Seer* (Wellingborough, 1986). Hamill seems to have been unaware of Proctor's scrapbook.

74 For further details of Smith's career, see Curry, *A Confusion of Prophets*, pp. 46–60.

75 His card can be found in Proctor's scrapbook.

76 *Morning Advertiser*, 21 January 1836.

77 Cooke presumably meant Brydges Place in Covent Garden, where Denley ran his bookshop.

78 There has been some confusion as to the identity of Raphael in the years between Palmer's death in 1837 and the turn of Edwin Medhurst around 1846. For several reasons I believe that Hockley was Raphael in these years. See Owen Davies, 'The Decline in the Popular Belief in Witchcraft and Magic', Ph.D. dissertation, University of Lancaster, 1995, pp. 326–7.

79 *The Times*, 23–24 September 1858.

80 *Somerset County Herald*, 25 March 1893.

81 For details of Leo's career, see Howe, *Urania's Children* pp. 57–65; Curry, *A Confusion of Prophets*, ch. 5.

82 *Westmorland Gazette*, 19 September 1818.

83 *The Times*, 1 September 1904; *Daily Mail*, 7 April 1900. For the rise of the popular gambling industry, see Mark Clapson, *A Bit of a Flutter: Popular Gambling in England, c. 1823–1961* (Manchester, 1992).

84 *Westmorland Gazette*, 12 September 1818.

85 *Somerset County Herald*, 17 September 1859.

86 *The Times*, 2 December 1870.

87 *Somerset County Herald*, 30 July 1864.

88 *Somerset County Herald*, 7 November 1846.

89 *Westmorland Gazette*, 26 May 1832.

90 *All The Year Round*, 6 November 1869, p. 541.

91 Pamela Horn, *The Rise and Fall of the Victorian Servant* (London, 1975), p. 28.

92 Gareth Stedman Jones, *Outcast London* (Oxford, 1971), p. 138.

93 *Bath Chronicle*, 17 December 1840; *The Times*, 27 December 1843.

94 *Somerset County Herald*, 30 July 1864

95 *The Justice of the Peace*, 24 February 1917.

96 Ida Ellis (ed.), *Directory of Character Readers* (Blackpool, 1897), p. 43.

97 *The Times*, 12 December 1916; *The Times*, 22 October 1915.

98 *Daily Mail*, 7 April 1900.

99 M. L. Lewes, *Stranger Than Fiction* (London, 1911), p. 180.

100 For the growth of seaside resorts in general, see John Walton, *The English Seaside Resort: A Social History, 1750–1914* (Leicester, 1983); James Walvin, *Beside the Sea: A Social History of the Popular Seaside Holiday* (London, 1978); Gareth Shaw and Allan Williams (eds), *The Rise and Fall of British Coastal Resorts* (London, 1997).

101 Anon., *The Life and Mysterious Transactions of Richard Morris*, p. 13; *Morning Post*, 12 January 1788.

102 The following account of the Ellises has been constructed from their fee lists, book lists, registers, yearbooks, directories and convention proceedings, housed in the British Library and Blackpool Central Library. I would like to thank John Walton for locating the material in Blackpool Central Library, and also for providing further background information on Albert Ellis.

103 Gary Cross (ed.), *Worktowners at Blackpool: Mass-Observation and Popular Leisure in the 1930s* (London, 1990), p. 118.

104 Norman N. Dodds, *Gypsies, Didikois and other Travellers* (London, 1966), p. 17.

105 J. Watts De Peyster, *Gypsies: Some Curious Investigations* (Edinburgh, 1887), p. 56.

106 *Leeds Mercury*, 23 April 1881; *TDA* 8 (1876) 782.

107 *Lonsdale Magazine* 3 (1821) 64–6; *Journal of the Gypsy Lore Society*, NS. 5 (1911–12) 121.

108 Brian Vesey-Fitzgerald, *Gypsies of Britain* (London, 1951), p. 129.

109 F. Hindes Groome, 'The Influence of the Gypsies on the Superstitions of the English Folk', in Joseph Jacobs and Alfred Nutt (eds), *The International Folk-Lore Congress 1891: Papers and Transactions* (London, 1892), p. 308.

110 *Somerset County Herald*, 10 October 1863.

111 *The Times*, 11 September 1875; *Manchester Courier*, 13 July 1889.

112 *Oxford Journal*, 9 October 1762.

113 *Somerset County Herald*, 5 December 1846; *Oxford Journal*, 19 February and 12 March 1859.

114 *Manchester Examiner*, 3 April 1890.

115 *Gypsy and Folk-Lore Gazette* 1 (1912) 87; *Manchester Courier*, 13 July 1889; *The Times*, 11 September 1875.

116 J. Hoyland, *An Historical Survey of the Customs, Habits, and Present State of the Gypsies* (London, 1816).

117 *Westmorland Gazette*, 22 August 1818.

118 *Somerset County Herald*, 31 March 1849.

119 *Somerset County Herald*, 2 October 1858.

120 *Journal of the Gypsy Lore Society*, 3rd S. 13 (1934) 129–30.

121 *The Justice of the Peace*, 20 January 1917, p. 28.

122 *The Times*, 19 February 1917.

123 *The Times*, 30 December 1916.

124 *The Times*, 11 March 1918.

125 *The Times*, 24 May 1917.

126 See J. M. Winter, *Sites of Memory, Sites of Mourning: The Great War in European*

Cultural History (Cambridge, 1995).

127 *The Times*, 23 December 1916.

128 *The Times*, 18 November 1916.

129 *The Times*, 9 December 1916.

130 See Ellen Ettlinger, 'British Amulets in London Museums', *Folklore* 50 (1939), 148–75; Edward Lovett, *Magic in London* (Croydon, 1925); 'Superstitions in War-time', *Lancet*, 27 May 1916, p. 1108.

131 *The Times*, 18 November 1916; *The Times*, 19 March 1918.

132 *The Times*, 28 December 1917.

Chapter 6

1 See, for example, Hans Sebald, *Witchcraft: Heritage of a Heresy* (New York, 1978); Jeanne Favret-Saada, *Deadly Words: Witchcraft in the Bocage* (Cambridge and Paris, 1980; first published in French 1977); Favret-Saada and Joseé Contreras, *Corps pour corps* (Paris, 1981); an important collection of essays in *Cahiers du LASA* (Laboratoire de sociologie-anthropologie de l'Université de Caen, 1985); Dominique Camus, *Pouvoirs sorciers* (London, 1988); Jean-Louis Boncoeur, *Le village aux sortilèges* (Paris, 1979); Patrick Gaboriau, *La pensée ensorcelée: la sorcellerie actuelle en Anjou et en Vendée* (Paris, 1987); Ioana Andreesco-Miereanu, 'Espace et temps de la magie dans un village Roumain actuel', *Cahiers Internationaux de Sociologie* 72 (1982) 251–66; Aldona Christina Schiffman, 'The Witch and the Crime: The Persecution of Witches in Twentieth-century Poland', *ARV. Scandinavian Yearbook of Folklore* 43 (1988) 147–65; Vassos Argyrou, 'Under a Spell: The Strategic Use of Magic in Greek Cypriot Society', *American Ethnologist* 20 (1993) 256–71; Carmelo Lison Tolosana, *Sorcellerie, Structure Sociale et Symbolisme en Galice* (Paris, 1994; first published in Spanish 1978).

2 Personal communications.

3 Charles Phythian-Adams, 'Rural culture', in G. E. Mingay (ed.), *The Vanishing Countryman* (London, 1989), p. 84.

4 Samuel Bamford, *Passages in the Life of a Radical* (London, [1844] 1984), p. 292.

5 John Glyde, *The Norfolk Garland* (London, 1872), p. 50.

6 Owen Davies, 'Urbanization and the Decline of Witchcraft: An Examination of London', *Journal of Social History* 30 (1997) 611.

7 *Folklore Record* 4 (1881) 189.

8 James Obelkevitch, *Religion and Rural Society: South Lindsey, 1825–75* (Oxford, 1976), p. 311.

9 The last isolated prosecution actually occurred in 1947, when an army pensioner named Gordon Sutton, of East Dereham, was prosecuted for assaulting his neighbour, an elderly lady called Mrs Spinks, whom he accused of bewitching him. *News Chronicle*, 6 January 1947; Christina Hole, *Witchcraft in England* (London, 1977), p. 178.

10 *Somerset County Herald*, 13 December 1924.

11 *The Tipton Herald*, 16 January 1926.

12 *Dorset County Chronicle*, 3 January 1918.

13 Rosalind Northcote, 'Folklore Collected Among the People near Exeter Within the Last Five or Six Years', *Folklore* 11 (1900) 216.

14 Mary M. Banks, 'Witch Lore from the Borders of Sussex and Surrey (1895–1898)', *Folklore* 52 (1941) 75.

15 Flora Thompson, *Lark Rise to Candleford* (Oxford, [1945] 1948), p. 252.

16 Obelkevitch, *Religion and Rural Society*, pp. 283–7.

17 John Putnam Demos, *Entertaining Satan* (Oxford, 1982), p. 392.

18 *The Times*, 27 April 1857.

19 Richard Blakeborough, *Yorkshire Wit, Character, Folklore and Customs* (London, 1898), p. 1.

20 G. E. Mingay, *Rural Life in Victorian England* (London, 1977), p. 184.

21 J. Geraint Jenkins, 'Technological Improvement and Social Change in South Cardiganshire', *The Agricultural History Review* 13 (1965) 96.

22 Jean Robin, *Elmdon: Continuity and Change in a North-West Essex Village 1861–1964* (Cambridge, 1980), p. 77.

23 B. J. Davey, *Ashwell 1830–1914: The Decline of a Village Community* (Leicester, 1980), p. 22.

24 Alun Howkins, *Reshaping Rural England: A Social History 1850–1925* (London, 1991), p. 8.

25 Mick Reed, 'The Peasantry of Nineteenth-Century England: A Neglected Class', *History Workshop Journal* 18 (1984) 56; Howkins, *Reshaping Rural England*, p. 39.

26 Henry Evershed, 'Farm Labourers and Cow Plots', *The Fortnightly Review* 14 (1873), 79–81; quoted in Reed, 'The Peasantry of Nineteenth-Century England', 57.

27 Read, 'The Peasantry of Nineteenth-Century England', p. 62.

28 Jenkins, 'Technological Improvement and Social Change', p. 96.

29 Davey, *Ashwell*, p. 22.

30 Blakeborough, *Yorkshire, Wit, Character*, p. 1.

31 David Jenkins, *The Agricultural Community in South-West Wales at the Turn of the Twentieth Century* (Cardiff, 1971), p. 258.

32 Gareth W. Williams, 'The Disenchantment of the World: Innovation, Crisis and Change in Cardiganshire c. 1880–1910', *Ceredigion* 9 (1983) 312.

33 C. W. Chalkin, 'The Decline of the Country Craftsman and Tradesman', in G. E. Mingay (ed.), *The Vanishing Countryman* (London, 1989), p. 2.

34 Davey, *Ashwell*, pp. 55–6.

35 Trevor Rowley, *Villages in the Landscape* (Gloucester, [1978] 1987), p. 151.

36 J. V. Beckett, *A History of Laxton* (Oxford, 1989), p. 298.

37 Mabel Peacock, 'Folklore of Lincolnshire', *Folklore* 12 (1901) 180.

38 B. A. Holderness, 'The Victorian Farmer', in Mingay, *Vanishing Countryman*, p. 24.

39 Beckett, *A History of Laxton*, pp. 208–9.

40 Cited in Mingay, *Rural Life in Victorian England* , p. 177.

41 Philip S. Bagwell, 'The Decline of Rural Isolation', in G. E. Mingay (ed.), *The Victorian Countryside* (London, 1981), p. 37.

42 Davey, *Ashwell*, p. 37.

43 Beckett, *A History of Laxton*, p. 296.

44 Jenkins, 'Technological Improvement and Social Change', p. 100.

45 M. K. Ashby, *The Changing English Village* (Kineton, 1974), p. 385.

46 Keith Thomas, *Religion and the Decline of Magic* (revised edition, London, 1973), pp. 779–82.

47 See W. A. Dinsdale, *History of Accident Insurance in Great Britain* (Brentford,

1954); H. A. L. Cockerell and Edwin Green, *The British Insurance Business 1547–1970* (London, 1976); Oliver Westall, *The Provincial Insurance Company 1903–1938* (Manchester, 1992).

48 Davey, *Ashwell*, p. 31.

49 E. W. Martin (ed.), *Country Life in England* (London, 1967), pp. 194–5.

50 E. N. Bennett, *Problems of Village Life* (London, n.d.), p. 90.

51 Sabine Baring-Gould, *Further Reminiscences 1864–1894* (London, 1925), p. 48.

52 Thomas, *Religion and the Decline of Magic*, p. 695.

53 *Ibid.*, p. 696.

54 Thompson, *Lark Rise*, p. 89.

55 Seebohm Rowntree and May Kendall, *How the Labourer Lives* (London, 1913), p. 325.

56 Quoted in Mingay, *Rural Life in Victorian England*, p. 188.

57 See David Vincent, *Literacy and Popular Culture in England 1750–1914* (Cambridge, 1989).

INDEX